POLITICS OF PIETY

POLITICS OF PIETY

THE ISLAMIC REVIVAL AND THE FEMINIST SUBJECT

With a new preface by the author

Saba Mahmood

PRINCETON UNIVERSITY PRESS • PRINCETON AND OXFORD

Published by Princeton University Press, 41 William Street,
Princeton, New Jersey 08540

In the United Kingdom: Princeton University Press,
6 Oxford Street, Woodstock, Oxfordshire OX20 1TW

press.princeton.edu

First printing, 2005
Paperback reissue, with a new preface, 2012
ISBN: 978-0-691-14980-6

The Library of Congress has cataloged the first edition of this book as follows

Mahmood, Saba, 1962–
Politics of piety : the Islamic revival and the feminist subject / Saba Mahmood.
p. cm.
Based on the author's thesis (Stanford University, 1998).
Includes bibliographical references and index.
ISBN 0-691-08694-X (cl : alk. paper) – ISBN 0-691-08695-8 (pb : alk. paper)
1. Feminism—Islamic countries. 2. Muslim women—Egypt—Cairo—Religious life—Case studies. 3. Islamic renewal—Egypt—Cairo—Case studies. 4. Feminism—Religious aspects—Islam. 5. Women in Islam. 6. Gender identity—Islamic countries. I. Title: Islamic revival and the feminist subject. II. Title.

HQ1785.M34 2005
305.48′697′096216—dc22 2004044289

British Library Cataloging-in-Publication Data is available

This book has been composed in Goudy

Printed on acid-free paper. ∞

Printed in the United States of America

10 9 8 7 6 5 4 3 2

Dedicated to my father and other spirits who
have watched over me. . . .

CONTENTS

Preface to the 2012 Edition ix

Preface xxi

Acknowledgments xxv

Note on Transcription xxix

CHAPTER 1
The Subject of Freedom 1

CHAPTER 2
Topography of the Piety Movement 40

CHAPTER 3
Pedagogies of Persuasion 79

CHAPTER 4
Positive Ethics and Ritual Conventions 118

CHAPTER 5
Agency, Gender, and Embodiment 153

Epilogue 189

Glossary of Commonly Used Arabic Terms 201

References 205

Index 225

PREFACE TO THE 2012 EDITION

As I write this preface to the second edition of *Politics of Piety*, Egypt is experiencing one of its most momentous developments since the anticolonial struggles of the early twentieth century. In a stunning display of power and perseverance, Egyptian protesters from all walks of life ousted the twenty-year-old brutal dictatorship of Hosni Mubarak on February 11, 2011. Their demands were succinct and clear: the restoration of full civil and political rights under a democratic system committed to the establishment of some measure of economic justice. The fact that this revolutionary mobilization cut across divisions of political and religious affiliations, class, and gender made this a watershed moment in the history of the postcolonial Middle East. It remains to be seen whether the ruling classes of Egypt will yield to the substantive demands of the movement or whether the inertia of the system will prove intractable. Whatever the outcome may be, this grassroots movement against a notoriously corrupt police state has certainly transformed the political consciousness of ordinary Egyptians and their sense of collective agency. As I write these lines, demonstrations have spread across the Middle East, inspired by the overthrow of the Mubarak regime, echoing similar demands. The question looms large as to what the future will hold for the inhabitants of the region.

Part of the aim of this new preface is to reflect on how the arguments of *Politics of Piety* are situated in relation to these developments. How should we place the politics of the da'wa—or piety—movement in the vast coalition that brought down the Mubarak regime? How do the arguments of the book speak to the latest turn of events in Egypt? In this preface I also address broader issues related to the reception of the book. These include: (1) the relationship between agency and politics; (2) my insistence on inserting questions of embodiment and ethics into the analysis of politics; and (3) the wider implications of my argument about da'wa/Islamic piety for theoretical debates about modern religiosity. In what follows, I take up these three issues before turning to the demands posed by the present turn of events in Egypt.

My remarks will necessarily be inadequate to those who seek a "response" to their engagements with *Politics of Piety*. No author can claim to be entirely sovereign over her text. Ultimately, the arguments of this book have taken on a life of their own; they animate conversations and debates that are well beyond the aim and scope of the book itself but have now become a part of the life and reception of *Politics of Piety*. The remarks below are therefore written in the spirit of contributing to the engagements the text has engendered rather than asserting the sovereignty of the author over it.

Agency, Politics, Hermeneutics

Since its publication, *Politics of Piety* has elicited both the praise and the ire of feminists: some have hailed the book for restoring agency to religiously devout Muslim women hitherto denounced for their patriarchal proclivities. Others have condemned the book for precisely the same reason: insomuch as the book is read as an exposé of the "agency" of the women who constitute the piety movement, it is charged with leveling critical differences between women who are upholders of patriarchal norms (dangerous, supine, submissive) and those who fight these norms in the name of liberty and freedom (heroic subjects of history). Both these readings ignore the fact that I was not interested in delivering judgments on what counts as a feminist versus an antifeminist practice, to distinguish a subversive act from a nonsubversive one. While acts of resistance to relations of domination constitute one modality of action, they certainly do not exhaust the field of human action. Rather, the aim of this book is to develop an analytical language for thinking about modalities of agency that exceed liberatory projects (feminist, leftist, or liberal). *Politics of Piety*, however, goes beyond describing these modalities of agency to focus on two related analytical and political problems that are far more central to its architecture: (a) the kinds of capacities—embodied, rational, technical—these various modalities of agency require; and (b) the conceptions of the body, personhood, and politics these capacities presuppose, enable, and construct.

My exposition of the elaborate program of self-cultivation practiced by the women's piety movement has sometimes been characterized as a "hermeneutical exercise" that abnegates or sidesteps questions of politics. This characterization has puzzled me, since much of the book is a reflection upon the kinds of political projects presupposed and enabled by the piety movement and those it challenges or remains indifferent toward. As I argue in this book, while the piety movement undoubtedly seems at times inimical and at times indifferent to feminism (understood as a project for establishing the conditions for gender equality), the pietists' main concern lies elsewhere: namely, the cultivation of submission to what its members interpret to be God's will. Despite the self-avowedly apolitical stance of the pietists, their practices have a profoundly transformative affect in the social and political fields. They have transformed the very ground on which nationalist, statist, and other kinds of secular-liberal projects can be envisioned and practiced. To ignore the transformative potential of the piety movement is to fail to understand its power and force in Egyptian society.

Politics of Piety is not a hermeneutical exercise in another important sense: its primary preoccupation has less to do with the meaning of practices than with the work they perform in the making of subjects, in creating life worlds, attachments, and embodied capacities. For example, while interpretations of the veil abound in Egypt, two main views prevail among its practitioners and its critics: one understands the veil to be a divine command; the other regards it as a symbolic marker, no different from other signifiers (religious and nonreligious) that represent a Muslim woman's identity. In *Politics of Piety* I endorse neither interpretation, since it is not the veracity of these claims that interests me. Instead, I analyze both understandings of the veil as speech acts that perform very different kinds of work in the making of a religious subject.[1] I argue in this book that to understand a bodily practice (such as veiling) as a symbolic act presumes a different relationship between the subject's exteriority and interiority from that entailed by an understanding in which a bodily act is both an expression of, and a means to, the realization of the subject.

My point is not to dismiss semiotic processes (as some critics have charged), but to inquire into practices whose assumptions about semiosis do not map onto the model of signs that stand for meaning or identity. My arguments here are informed by the work of philosophers such as Ludwig Wittgenstein, Charles Sanders Peirce, and J. L. Austin, who, in their different ways, have made us think of semiotic practices in registers other than those of meaning, communication, and symbolic signification. More recently, as Talal Asad, William Connolly, Charles Hirschkind, and Webb Keane remind us in distinctly different ways, many dimensions of practice—both linguistic and nonlinguistic—cannot be grasped in terms of a theory of representation alone.

In my more recent work, I have developed this point further by thinking critically about two different understandings of the Quran among Muslims: one

[1] Following Judith Butler, I understand a speech act to include not only oral or textual enunciations but also bodily acts. See Butler 1993.

that treats it as the literal word of God and another that claims that the Quran is a symbolic text whose meaning is historically determined.[2] Once again, I am less interested in championing the veracity of one claim over another. I analyze both these claims as two distinct kinds of performative speech acts that enable very different conceptions of power, truth, interpretive schema, critical norms, and the reading/reciting subject. In some ways, the question of agency in *Politics of Piety* is less central to my overall argument than is an explication of the constructive work different conceptual understandings of a practice accomplish in the making of subjects and the creation of distinct social and political imaginaries. It is unfortunate that this dimension of *Politics of Piety* has been least engaged in the commentaries the book has elicited. Instead, most of the attention has focused on who is or is not deemed "an agent."

Ethics, Politics, and Criticism

I am sometimes chided for failing to denounce the participants of the piety movement for blindly following an orthodox interpretation of the Islamic tradition and associated patriarchal values. Despite my exegesis of their elaborate program of corporeal discipline, reasoned reflection, commentary, and pedagogy, some readers of this book assume that the pietist subjects are unreflexively conformist and self-abnegating. Such a judgment fails to recognize what is at stake in my analysis of the practices of the piety movement: to lay bare a parochial and narrow conception of autonomized agency that refuses to grant legitimacy to any other form of subjectivity or criticality. Part of the task of *Politics of Piety* is to provide a thick account of disciplines of subjectivity pursued by the pietists, which profoundly challenge the very assumptions on the basis of which they are judged as passive, obsequious, and uncritical.

My point is not that the program of ethical self-cultivation pursued by the piety movement is "good" or conducive to establishing relations of gender equality, or that it should be adopted by progressives, liberals, feminists, and others. I argue instead that the disciplines of subjectivity pursued by the pietists profoundly parochialize conceptions of the subject, autonomous reason, and objectivity, through which the pietists are understood to be lacking in faculties of criticism and reason. If academic knowledge production aims to be something more than an exercise in denunciation and judgment, it must surely think beyond its own naturalized conceptions in order to grasp what other notions of criticism, evaluation, and reasoned deliberation operate in the world. This in turn requires opening up a comparative (and dare I say critical?) study of differ-

[2] Saba Mahmood, "Secularism, Hermeneutics, and Empire," *Public Culture* 86:2 (2006), 323–47.

ent forms of subjectivity and concomitant disciplines of ethical self-formation. A worthy project in this vein would be the analysis of practices of self-cultivation through which a commitment to the truth of the sovereign subject and autonomized agency is produced and sustained.[3] Not all the practices, I suspect, will be as reasoned as they are assumed to be.

My argument in *Politics of Piety* suggests that political projects are not only the result of coalitional organizing, ideological mobilization, and critical deliberation. They are predicated upon affective, ethical, and sensible capacities that are often ignored as consequential to the analysis of politics. Departing from one's accustomed political stance and adopting a new one requires more than an ideational, judgmental, or conceptual shift. It necessitates a whole series of affective and sensible reorientations, some of which are undertaken systematically and others of which are acquired through social and cultural exposure and imbibing. Social movements sometimes try to thematize and stage such practices of ethical self-transformation. Various examples come to mind, including gay pride marches; collective actions staged by the civil rights movement to performatively create a different space for the exercise of civil and political equality; and the establishment of public soup kitchens in the 1960s to perform/establish a distinct ethics of care. Practices may also be undertaken on a smaller scale wherein people teach themselves to inhabit a different kind of a body, sensibility, aesthetics, or argumentative form. *Politics of Piety* is a thematic exploration of the ethical practices and affective attachments that undergird distinct political projects. As such, this book does not offer a sociology of the piety movement, but forces us instead to link what are often presumed to be two distinct domains of human life in liberal political theory: politics and ethics, each supposedly sequestered in the public and private domains.

Religion and Religious Subjectivity

Is the model of religiosity and religious formation I discuss in this book applicable only to Islam and the da'wa movement, or does it extend to other religious traditions as well? The dominant understanding of religion against which I am working in this book is one that regards religion as a set of beliefs expressed in a set of propositions to which an individual gives assent. While this privatized and individualized concept of religion has a Protestant genealogy, it has come to command a normative force in modernity and is often upheld as the measure against which the adequacy of other religious traditions is measured and judged.

[3] I have written more on this topic in *Is Critique Secular? Blasphemy, Injury, and Free Speech*, ed. Talal Asad, Wendy Brown, Judith Butler, and Saba Mahmood (Berkeley: University of California Press, 2009).

This secularized conception of religiosity commands particular weight in the development of non-Protestant religious traditions—particularly non-Western traditions—in the modern period and has largely transformed them from within. This has to do not so much with the "superior" conception of religiosity that Protestantism embodies but with the inequality of power relations that characterizes the relationship between Western Christendom and its Others, the West and the non-West—an inequality that sets up the history of Protestant Christianity as the entelechy that all other religious traditions must emulate in order to become truly modern.[4]

For a scholar of contemporary Islam, reading the scholarship on early modern Judaism evokes many parallels, key among them the argument that Jewish law and its concern with "orthopraxy" made Judaism incommensurable with modernity. In these arguments, Jewish law (like present day shari'a) was regarded as indexical of not only a lesser and unenlightened form of religiosity but also the social and political backwardness of the community, rendering it incapable of inhabiting the norms of a modern polity (similar to how Muslims are portrayed these days). It is not the legitimacy of this judgment that interests me, but rather the various movements of reform that such parameters and judgments have unleashed in response within these traditions modeled on the Protestant Reformation.[5] Importantly, this push toward reform has invariably been met with resistance of various kinds, often described pejoratively as traditionalist or fundamentalist.[6] Such a depreciatory account does little to analyze what was/is at stake in the resistance mobilized against secularized notions of religiosity, and the alternative concepts of religion, the subject, ethics, and morality that these movements propagate.

Politics of Piety is an attempt to understand a contemporary movement within Islam—the da'wa movement—that is articulated against many of the concepts, sensibilities, practices, and forms of life associated with a secular-liberal understanding of religion (as a privatized and individualized system of belief). The shari'a enjoys a pride of place in the pietists' practices—shari'a understood not as a state-centered juridical discourse but as a discourse of ethical and moral cultivation (not dissimilar to Halakha, or traditional Jewish law, in Judaism). It would be a mistake, however, to understand this movement in oppositional terms

[4] For a discussion of this point, see my essay "Can Secularism Be Other-wise?" in *Varieties of Secularism in a Secular Age*, ed. Michael Warner, Jonathan VanAntwerpen, and Craig Calhoun (Cambridge, MA: Harvard University Press, 2010).

[5] For an influential account of this in Judaism, see Jonathan Hess, *Germans, Jews and the Claims of Modernity* (New Haven, CT: Yale University Press, 2002). For a general account of how the emergence of the universal category of religion is indebted to the history of Protestantism, see Talal Asad 1993.

[6] For a powerful critique of such a reductionist account, see Jay M. Harris, "'Fundamentalism': Objections from a Modern Jewish Historian," in *Fundamentalism and Gender*, ed. John Stratton Hawley (Oxford: Oxford University Press, 1994), 137–74.

alone, since secularism and secularity provide the structuring conditions for the articulation of the da'wa/piety movement. As such, despite its avowed antagonism toward secularism, the da'wa/piety movement presupposes many key secular concepts (about time, history, causality, and so on), making the movement far more hybrid in character than its practitioners would acknowledge.

That said, the da'wa movement also challenges many aspects of secular religiosity, key among them the conceptual relationship posited between embodied practice and the believing subject. Simply put, the Protestant conception of religiosity presupposes a distinction between a privatized interiority that is the proper locus of belief and a public exteriority that is an expression of this belief. In this view, while rituals and bodily practices might represent belief, they are not essential to its acquisition or expression. Much of the energy of modern religious reformers has been spent trying to establish and stabilize the distinction between the "true" nature of belief in divinity (abstract, universal, a-contextual) and the fickle world of religious signs whose meanings are *this*-worldly and only contingently (not necessarily) related to the abstractions they signify.[7] As I have discussed elsewhere, part of the aim of many contemporary Muslim reformers writing under the rubric of "liberal Islam" is to establish this distinction by grounding it in the resources and scriptures of Islam.[8]

In contrast to such an understanding of religion, the pious subjects of this book posit a very different relationship between outward bodily acts (including rituals, liturgies, and worship) and inward belief (state of the soul). Not only are the two inseparable in their conception, but, more importantly, belief is the product of outward practices, rituals, and acts of worship rather than simply an expression of them. Why is this difference consequential? Because far from being an ideational or intellectual stance, it affects the way people live and order their lives; their sense of self and personhood; their understanding of authority and its proper relationship to individual desires and capacities; and distinct conceptions of human flourishing. As I suggested earlier, this topography of the self has profound consequences for how politics is imagined and lived. As a result, battles between orthodox and reformist interpretations of religion (in a variety of traditions) often enfold contrastive conceptions of the subject and politics—the importance of which is often overlooked by students of religion and politics alike.

My analysis of religious formation among the pietists has resonances with similar kinds of practices found in a number of traditions, key among them Christianity and Judaism. My recourse to an Aristotelian framework to analyze

[7] It is this conception that makes the project of comparative religion possible, in that the phenomenal forms of religion (rituals, scriptures, liturgies, acts of worship) come to be understood as the cultural and temporal representations of the abstract and atemporal truth of the divine.

[8] Mahmood 2006.

the pedagogy of ethical cultivation among the women of the da'wa movement has important resonances in Christianity that I discuss in chapter 4. I found the Aristotelian tradition to be relevant not only because of its rearticulation in contemporary Islam, but also because the behavioral pedagogy it offers presents a very different account of subject formation from the one presumed in theoretical debates in the academy on this topic. By reversing the direction between outward bodily acts and subjective interiority (the former enact the latter rather than represent or express the latter), the Aristotelian model raises interesting questions about bodily capacities and routine daily acts that make particular kinds of subjects and sociopolitical imaginaries possible.[9]

Since I wrote *Politics of Piety*, I have received notes from a range of academics and nonacademics who have found my discussion of the Aristotelian conception of *habitus* useful for thinking about a range of practices that fall outside the purview of the traditions I mention above. For example, a long-time practitioner of martial arts wrote that the arguments of *Politics of Piety* resonated with his experience of teaching and practicing tae kwon do. People are attracted to martial arts, he noted, for a variety of reasons: some want to get stronger, others pursue it to learn self-defense, and yet others might want to enact a Bruce Lee fantasy. Over time, however, some come to realize that there are goods internal to the martial arts tradition that are beyond any such ends—ends that can, after all, be achieved through other means (such as working out in a gym). Such a realization, he suggests, often changes one's relationship to the practice, which becomes something more than a means to goals that are contingently related to the practice but not central to its conceptual architecture. For such people, performative bodily behavior becomes a means for realizing virtues that are internal to the practice of martial arts itself.

I quote my martial arts correspondent here in part because he captures a dimension of my argument that was not entirely apparent to me when I wrote *Politics of Piety* and has since expanded my thinking. It has also helped me articulate a response to those readers who have read this book as a culturalist argument and assume it to be about "Muslim women" or Islamic religiosity as such. This is a mistake for two primary reasons. One, there are just as many Muslims (women and men) who embrace the conception of religiosity I emphasize in this text as there are Muslims who strongly disagree with it. Two, the conception of religiosity that the pietists embrace is extant in many religious traditions, often eliciting the same kinds of dismissals that the women's da'wa movement encounters. These dismissals, I suggest, should be analyzed as diagnostic of the normative place assigned to religion in a secular imaginary. While the ethnographic mate-

[9] My work, as my readers know well, is inspired by the scholarship of Talal Asad, who first opened this question to intellectual reflection in the *Genealogies of Religion*, and has since taken it up in regard to secular formations as well (Asad 2003).

rial presented in this book is about the da'wa movement in Egypt, my analysis of this movement raises issues that cut across the divide between the West and the non-West, the Muslim and the non-Muslim world.

The Egyptian Uprising and Politics of Piety

The fact that the Egyptian uprising in 2011 did not have pronounced Islamic overtones or Islamist leadership has led a number of scholars to hastily pronounce the dawning of a new "post-Islamist era" where the Islamic politics that dominated the Middle East over the last two decades have become irrelevant. Not only does this rush to judgment need to be rethought, but the very meaning of the terms "Islamic/Islamist politics" should be unpacked. While there is no doubt that the preeminent Islamist political party, the Muslim Brotherhood, like other Egyptian political parties, did not play a key organizing role in the demonstrations, it would be wrong to conclude that Egyptians with strong Islamic proclivities were not an integral part of the mobilization. In fact, all reports indicate that these demonstrations were significant precisely because they did not rely on old networks of mobilization, instead drawing support from all sectors of Egyptian society, cutting across secularist, leftist, liberal, and Islamist lines. The demands of the protesters did not have a religious dimension and centered around three points: the restoration of political and civil rights, the establishment of a just democratic system, and the reinstatement of some semblance of a social welfare state.

The fact that the uprising took this shape did not surprise many of us who have been following Egyptian politics over the past decade. In contrast to the mid-1990s, by 2008—when I returned to Cairo to do field research—the old entrenched divisions between the secularists and Islamists had softened. The newly emergent opposition press published writers from both sides of the divide and reported on various atrocities the regime committed regardless of the victims' political and religious affiliations.[10] Faced with the increasing decline in public services, rising poverty, and the impudent and ubiquitous brutality of the security police, most Egyptians had come to feel that their common enemy was the corrupt and nepotistic government rather than the factions between them. Young Egyptians, fed up with the inertia of the geriatric leadership of opposition parties (including the Muslim Brotherhood), turned to issue-based activ-

[10] In the mid-1990s, there was only one prominent opposition newspaper, *al-Sh'ab*, published from an Islamist point of view. It was shut down by the Mubarak government in the late 1990s. In contrast, in 2008 there were at least three independent newspapers (*al-Dustour*, *al-Masry al-Youm*, and *al-Badeel*), two of which have prominent Islamic intellectuals contributing regular columns along with secular writers.

ism, working across divisions that their elders could not overcome. Social networking technologies and the Internet (blogs, Facebook, Twitter) were one avenue for this new activism, but there were others, key among them labor union politics that cut across lines of difference to create a common political project.[11] A small indication of this transformation was the suggestion made by a prominent young blogger from the Muslim Brotherhood in 2008 that instead of the slogan "Islam is the solution," extant in the 1990s, the Brothers should adopt "Egypt for Egyptians," which spoke far better to the aspirations of most people. This was indeed the slogan that emanated from the protesters across Egypt in 2011.[12]

So what does this mean for the da'wa movement? Not only is it alive and vibrant, but many of those involved in it participated in the protests and did not find their demands for political and civic freedoms to be incongruent with their commitment to Islamic forms of piety. Furthermore, I would argue that it is precisely because their commitment to piety was not premised on a state-centered conception of social change that they could embrace the movement for the ouster of the Mubarak regime without considering it a modification of their religious stance. The members of the piety movement were as affected as other Egyptians by the corruption and brutality of the Mubarak regime and the impoverishment of daily life it had engendered. In fact, the Mubarak government had been especially brutal in the 1990s toward Egyptians—particularly men—who displayed overt signs of religiosity, viewing them as potential members of Islamic militant organizations. It is no surprise, therefore, that pietists joined their fellow citizens to demand the government's ouster.

The judgment that this is a "post-Islamist" era is complicated for another reason. The term "Islamist" often enfolds within itself the assumption that those who ascribe to Islamic forms of sociability (such as the ones propagated by the da'wa movement) are opposed to democratic political and economic formations.[13] The fact that Egyptian Muslims who exhibited signs of this sociability were an integral part of the democratic protests of 2011 casts doubt on the easy line of causality drawn between abidance by conservative social mores and the danger posed to democratic projects. Do orthodox religious sensibilities, includ-

[11] For my comments on the Egyptian uprising, see "Architects of the Egyptian Revolution," http://www.thenation.com/article/158581/architects-egyptian-revolution.

[12] Charles Hirschkind, "The Road to Tahrir," http://blogs.ssrc.org/tif/2011/02/09/the-road-to-tahrir/.

[13] Post-Mubarak Egypt has witnessed the emergence of groups who label themselves "Salafi." They are known to have launched attacks on Sufi shrines, Coptic churches, and women not wearing the hijab. The sociological basis of these self-described Salafi groups is unclear, and they are rumored to be part of the "anti-revolutionary" trend in Egypt. While the Salafis share the emphasis on sartorial markers of piety with the da'wa movement, there is no necessary relationship between them. Many in the da'wa movement have condemned the attacks on the Sufi shrines and the churches.

ing those that challenge secular norms of sociability, actually threaten the entire edifice of a liberal democratic system? If so, how? Or does the threat that democracy currently faces in countries like Egypt stem far more from geopolitical and neo-liberal formations than from orthodox Islamic social mores? As the recent events in Egypt show, the answers to these questions are far more open-ended than has been assumed so far.

Notably, Egypt is quite different from Saudi Arabia, Iran, or Pakistan—three countries where Islamic social mores have proliferated over the last several decades, and where the goals of political, civil, and economic equality remain stubbornly elusive. In each of these three cases, while the authoritarian regimes have opportunistically used the "morality" card to retain a tight hold over power, it would be hard to conclude that orthodox Islamic social mores constitute the greatest threat to the establishment of substantive democracy in these countries. There are other far more important factors that make such a project difficult—such as the Saudi monarchy and its geopolitical and economic coalition with the United States; the authoritarian clerical regime in Iran that draws sustenance from its oppositional stance against the Saudi-American geopolitical alliance; or the military junta in Pakistan that has made a Faustian bargain with the U.S. government and the Taliban alike to maintain its suffocating grip on power. Egypt's democratic aspirations are subject to similar and parallel geopolitical forces; while the da'wa/piety movement is an important player in the national landscape, it has hardly been the key impediment to the development of projects for social and political equality.

The hasty judgment that the revolutionary uprising in Egypt heralds a "post-Islamist" era also fails to take into account the transformations the da'wa movement has wrought in Egyptian society—the sensibilities it has created, the lifestyles it has made extant, the gender norms it has established—all of which are not going to dissolve or become irrelevant overnight. Whatever the sociopolitical struggles and projects that lie ahead, it is clear that they would emerge from a sociality that has been deeply marked by the activities of the piety/da'wa movement. It seems to me that the issues *Politics of Piety* raised are even more relevant now, but I suspect that the courage and ingenuity of the Egyptian people will have a lot more to teach us than this book could anticipate. I look forward to this challenge.

March 14, 2011
Berkeley, California

PREFACE

Even though this book is about Islamist politics in Egypt, its genesis owes to a set of puzzles I inherited from my involvement in progressive left politics in Pakistan, the country of my birth. By the time my generation of Pakistanis came to political consciousness during the 1970s and 1980s, the high moment of postcolonial nationalism had passed and there was considerable disillusionment with what the now "not-so-new" nation could provide for its citizens. There was, however, still a sense among the feminist left in Pakistan that some form of critical Marxism, combined with a judicious stance toward issues of gender inequality, could provide a means of thinking through our predicament and organizing our pragmatic efforts at changing the situation in which we lived. In this we were perhaps not so different from our counterparts in countries like Algeria, Egypt, and Tunisia, where the postcolonial condition had generated a similar sense of disappointment but also a continued sense of nourishment, borne out of the promises that the twin ideologies of critical Marxism and feminism held out for us.

This sense of stability and purpose was slowly eroded for a number of us in Pakistan for reasons that are too complex to fully recount here, but two developments in particular stand out. One was the solidification of the military dictatorship of Zia ul-Haq (1977–1988), who, while using Islam to buttress his brutal hold on power, turned Pakistan into a frontline state for the United States's proxy war against the Soviet occupation of Afghanistan. The military and monetary advantage that this alignment bestowed on Zia ul-Haq's regime made any effective organized opposition to it infeasible. Furthermore, Zia ul-Haq's top-down policy of "Islamizing" Pakistani society through the use of the media, the educational system, and, more important, the judiciary (which included the promulgation of a number of discriminatory laws against women), cemented in the minds of progressive feminists like myself that our very survival depended upon an unflinching stance against the Islamization of Pakistani society. If there was any shred of doubt in our minds that Islamic forms of patriarchy were responsible for our problems, this doubt was firmly removed given the immediate targets of our day-to-day struggles: feminist politics came to require a resolute and uncompromising secular stance.

A second development that I recall being crucial to our sense of being embattled emerged more slowly over time: it started with the eruption of the Iranian revolution in 1979, an event that confounded our expectations of the role Islam could play in a situation of revolutionary change and, at the same time, seemed to extinguish the fragile hope that secular leftist politics represented in the region. While the Iranian revolution was a product of the intense repression carried out by the Shah's regime, it coincided with a gradual but inexorable movement within many Muslim societies toward a reemphasis on Islamic doctrines and forms of sociability. Most surprising for feminists of my generation was the fact that this movement was not limited to the marginalized or the dispossessed, but found active and wide support among the middle classes who increasingly conjoined a critique of their emulation of Western habits and lifestyles with a renewed concern for living in accord with Islamic social mores. We in the Pakistani left frequently dismissed this upsurge of religiosity as superficial, on the grounds that it did not translate into success at the polls for Pakistani Islamic political parties. (A coalition of Islamic political parties did, however, win a significant majority in the National Assembly for the first time in Pakistani history in 2002).

Progressive leftists like myself explained this turn of the "masses" to Islamic forms of sociability in a number of ways: sometimes we attributed it to the lack of education and enlightened thinking among the vast majority of the population, sometimes to the conservative form of Saudi Islam that immigrant laborers returning from the Arabian Gulf states had brought back into Pakistan, and sometimes to the mimetic effects that Zia ul-Haq's repressive regime had inevitably engendered in the populace. And then there was always the explanation that the unholy alliance between Western capital (particularly American) and oil-rich monarchies of the Gulf (notably Saudi Arabia, Kuwait, and the United Arab Emirates) had actively aided and abetted a conservative form of Islam around the Muslim world so as to defeat those progressive movements that might have opposed such alliances.

While none of these explanations is entirely without merit, over the last twenty years or so, I have increasingly come to find them inadequate. Part of this dissatisfaction stems from a recognition that the social and political constellations mobilized by Islamic revival movements vary dramatically and have often taken forms quite distinct from what has been happening in Pakistan from the period of Zia ul-Haq's rule to the present. In a number of Middle Eastern countries, for example, Islamic political parties have been instrumental in giving voice to popular demands for democratization of the political arena, for an end to single-party rule, and for a more critical stance toward U. S. hegemony in the region. Moreover, Islamic welfare organizations around the Muslim world have increasingly stepped in to fill the vaccum left by postcolonial states as these states, under neoliberal economic pressures, have withdrawn from providing social services to their citizens.

The reason progressive leftists like myself have such difficulty recognizing these aspects of Islamic revival movements, I think, owes in part to our profound dis-ease with the appearance of religion outside of the private space of individualized belief. For those with well-honed secular-liberal and progressive sensibilities, the slightest eruption of religion into the public domain is frequently experienced as a dangerous affront, one that threatens to subject us to a normative morality dictated by mullahs and priests. This fear is accompanied by a deep self-assurance about the truth of the progressive-secular imaginary, one that assumes that the life forms it offers are the best way out for these unenlightened souls, mired as they are in the spectral hopes that gods and prophets hold out to them. Within our secular epistemology, we tend to translate religious truth as force, a play of power that can be traced back to the machinations of economic and geopolitical interests.

I am certainly glossing over a number of different complications for the sake of brevity here, but what I want to communicate is the profound sense of dissatisfaction I have come to feel about my ability, as well as the ability of those I have shared a long trajectory of political struggle with, to understand how it is that the language of Islam has come to apprehend the aspirations of so many people around the Muslim world. I have come to question our conviction, however well-intentioned, that other forms of human flourishing and life worlds are necessarily inferior to the solutions we have devised under the banner of "secular-left" politics—as if there is a singularity of vision that unites us under this banner, or as if the politics we so proudly claim has not itself produced some spectacular human disasters. This self-questioning does not mean that I have stopped struggling or fighting against the injustices—whether they pertain to issues of gender, ethnicity, class, or sexuality—that currently compound my social existence. What it does mean is that I have come to believe that a certain amount of self-scrutiny and skepticism is essential regarding the certainty of my own political commitments, when trying to understand the lives of others who do not necessarily share these commitments.

This is not an exercise in generosity but is born out of the sense I have that we can no longer arrogantly assume that secular forms of life and secularism's progressive formulations necessarily exhaust ways of living meaningfully and richly in this world. This realization has led me to parochialize my own political certitude as I write analytically about what animates parts of the Islamist movement, and has compelled me to refuse to take my political stance as the necessary lens through which the labor of analysis should proceed. In short, it has compelled me to leave open the possibility that my analysis may come to complicate the vision of human flourishing that I hold most dear, and which has provided the bedrock of my personal existence.

The fact that this book focuses on the Islamist movement in Egypt, a place distant from the land of my birth and my formative struggles, is one indication of the kinds of intellectual and political dislocations I felt were necessary in order for me to think through these conundrums, puzzles, and challenges. The fact that Egypt does not face an immediate situation of civil warfare in which Islamists are central players, as is the case in Pakistan and Algeria, made Egypt a more conducive place to undertake the labor of thought—a labor that cannot thrive under a pace of events that constantly demands political closure and strategic action. I do not think I could ever have been able to see what I was made to see during the course of my fieldwork in Egypt had I remained within the familiar grounds of Pakistan. I hope that my attempts at thinking through this postcolonial predicament within the Muslim world will find some resonances with my readers.

ACKNOWLEDGMENTS

I have incurred innumerable debts in the writing of this book that I would like to acknowledge here, however inadequately. I feel a profound sense of gratitude toward my mentors and teachers, without whom I would never have quite learned what it means to stay with a problem, to dwell on its multiple complexities, to push against one's own inadequacies of comprehension, and moreover, to savor the slow process of discovery. Foremost among these are Talal Asad and Jane Collier, both of whom, through their exemplary scholarship and patient interlocutions, have made the undertaking of this project both a tremendous challenge and a tremendous pleasure. Those who are familiar with Talal Asad's work will recognize the influence of his thought permeating practically every page of this book: there is no greater gift that a scholar can bestow and no adequate words that can express one's gratitude for such a gift. If I am successful in re-creating even a modicum of the acumen and courage that Talal's work represents, I will be happy. Jane Collier has extended to me both her intellect and her labor through practically every phase of this project—from its initial conception to its present form. This is a debt that I can never hope to repay except perhaps by extending to my own students the same generosity Jane has offered to me. Sylvia Yanagisako will herself recognize how her provocations about bodily practice and gender have born fruit, perhaps in directions that neither she nor I could have predicted. Whether in her office or at her kitchen table, those moments of exchange marked the conception of many of the ideas animating this book. To Ira Lapidus I am indebted for guiding me through a panoramic view of the history of Islam, where my own predilections would have sequestered me to the Middle East. He has also inspired me to live more richly and expansively, despite the pressures of academic life, through his own exemplary practice.

My colleagues at the University of Chicago sustained me through the rewriting of various drafts of this book through their friendship, collegiality, and intellectual engagements. I would like to thank Nadia Abu El-Haj, Catherine Brekus, Dipesh Chakrabarty, Jim Chandler, Jennifer Cole, Jean and John Comaroff, Wendy Doniger, Bruce Lincoln, Martin Rieserbrodt, Richard Rosengarten, and Lisa Wedeen. I would particularly like to thank Lauren Berlant and Elizabeth Povinelli for inviting me to participate in the Late Liberalism Project, which proved to be one of the more stimulating contexts in which to collectively mull over the multiplicity of forms that the discourse of liberalism has taken in the last century. Though I only overlapped with Amy Hollywood at Chicago for a short time, she has nevertheless become, I believe, a lifelong interlocutor who will always push me to think more thickly about the vexing topic of gender and religion. Her reading of various chapters of this book was invaluable in working through the knotty subject of feminist theory.

Then there are colleagues and friends who are dispersed across the academy but whose engagements with the arguments in this book at various stages of their gestation have pushed me to be attentive to a number of issues that would have otherwise escaped my attention. In this regard, I would like to thank Lila Abu-Lughod, Janice Boddy, John Bowen, Steve Caton, William Connolly, Bill Hanks, Stefan Helmreich, Enseng Ho, Suad Joseph, Webb Keane, Michael Lambek, Bill Maurer, Paul Rabinow, Peter van der Veer, and Michael Watts. I would like to thank Brinkley Messick for his close reading of the manuscript and his insistence that I show the contemporaneity of this movement, an insistence without which chapters 2 and 3 would never have been written in their current form. I am not sure how adequately these chapters address his concerns, but I am grateful for what Brinkley's comments made me see about the modern character of Islamic practices. To Judith Butler I am indebted for reading through the manuscript and pointing me in directions that I would not have necessarily followed had it not been for her interventions. The thought and labor she put into her comments has restored my faith that interdisciplinary dialogue is not only possible in the academy but is also the most gratifying aspect of this business. While this text does not address all the issues Judith raised, I hope that we have initiated a conversation that will continue in the years to come. I am grateful to Donald Moore for his erudite peregrinations through the pages of this text, which have proved to be a source of insight and inspiration. It is rare that one has the opportunity to passionately discuss the connections between Cairo pietists and Zimbabwean peasant struggles, but Donald's gifted imagination has always made this pleasure a reality. To Michael Warner I owe the pleasure of a series of conversations around the theme of secularism that have proven to be crucial to my thinking. And to Iftikhar Dadi I owe a special debt for his artful counsel.

In Egypt, where I conducted my fieldwork, I have a debt that I can never repay to the women I worked with, the participants in the mosque movement, whose generosity and insights animate the words and phrases in this book. Without their patience and eloquence, it would not have been possible for me to write about many of the issues addressed here. Then there are colleagues and friends who made life in Cairo not only livable but pleasurable, taking the sting out of the difficulties that inevitably characterize fieldwork. In this regard, I would like to thank Kamran Asdar Ali for introducing me to Cairo on my first visit; to Asef Bayat, Linda Herrera, Abdel Wahab el-Messiri, and May al-Ibrashy for their generous hospitality during my two years in Cairo; to Clarissa Bencomo and Jamal Abdul Aziz for challenging conversations about Egyptian politics; to Michael Gasper for making the streets of Cairo seem a plausible place to discuss the vagaries of academia; to Samira Haj for her invaluable camaraderie and friendship; to Saif al-Hamdan for his searing and witty questioning of my interest in Islamist politics; and finally, to Ted Swedenburg for the fabulous dinners and animated discussions his home always provided for interlopers like myself. My thanks also to Akhil Gupta and Purnima Mankekar for providing me a home base in the United States during my field work when such a center seemed to escape me.

This book rests on research conducted with generous support from the Social Science Research Council, the Wenner-Gren Foundation for Anthropological Research, and the National Science Foundation. During the writing phase of this book, I was fortunate to be supported by a Chancellor's Postdoctoral Fellowship at the University of California at Berkeley and a Harvard Academy Fellowship at Harvard University. This book also benefited from a semester's leave at the University of Leiden, the International Institute for the Study of Islam in the Modern World, in the Netherlands.

I am indebted to Mary Murrell at Princeton University Press and my copy editor Krista Faries for their impeccable assistance with the completion of this book. I am also grateful for the suggestions and comments made by the anonymous reviewers for Princeton University Press. I do not know how I could have finished this undertaking without the assiduous research assistance of Noah Salomon, to whom I extend my heartfelt thanks. I am also grateful to Catherine Adcock, Fatma Naib, Scott Richard, Alicia Turner, and Warda Yousef for their help in procuring the research materials for this book.

Finally, I would like to thank certain friends and family members whose care, affection, and support have borne me through the many impasses I have encountered in undertaking this journey—of which this book is only a small part. The sustenance and nourishment William Glover's longstanding friendship has provided me cannot be measured in words or deeds—none of the critical decisions I have taken in the last twenty years, especially the decision to change careers midstream, could have been possible without his support, advice, and unquestioning confidence in my ability to succeed. I would like to extend my thanks also to George Collier, Dawn Hansen, Nadeem Khalid, Khalid Mah-

NOTE ON TRANSCRIPTION

In general, I have used a modified version of the system outlined in the *International Journal of Middle Eastern Studies (IJMES)* for transcribing words and phrases in Modern Standard Arabic. For words and phrases that appear in Egyptian Colloquial Arabic, particularly in ethnographic quotes, I have followed a combination of sources, key among them *A Dictionary of Egyptian Arabic* composed by El-Said Badawi and Martin Hinds. In order to make the transcription of Modern Standard Arabic words and Egyptian Colloquial Arabic words as consistent as possible, while still conveying the flavor of Egyptian colloquial speech, I have adapted the Badawi and Hinds system to that of *IJMES*. In case of proper names, honorific titles, and Arabic terms that are found in an unabridged English dictionary, I have omitted the use of diacritical marks. I have deferred to transcriptions that have been used in standard bibliographic reference texts, and to the styles that have been chosen by authors for their own names when these have appeared in English-language publications. English-language titles that incorporate Arabic words retain the original style of transcription.

POLITICS OF PIETY

1

The Subject of Freedom

Over the last two decades, a key question has occupied many feminist theorists: how should issues of historical and cultural specificity inform both the analytics and the politics of any feminist project? While this question has led to serious attempts at integrating issues of sexual, racial, class, and national difference within feminist theory, questions regarding religious difference have remained relatively unexplored. The vexing relationship between feminism and religion is perhaps most manifest in discussions of Islam. This is due in part to the historically contentious relationship that Islamic societies have had with what has come to be called "the West," but also due to the challenges that contemporary Islamist movements pose to secular-liberal politics of which feminism has been an integral (if critical) part. The suspicion with which many feminists tended to view Islamist movements only intensified in the aftermath of the September 11, 2001, attacks launched against the United States, and the immense groundswell of anti-Islamic sentiment that has followed since. If supporters of the Islamist movement were disliked before for their social conservatism and their rejection of liberal values (key among them "women's freedom"), their now almost taken-for-granted association with terrorism has served to further reaffirm their status as agents of a dangerous irrationality.

Women's participation in, and support for, the Islamist movement provokes strong responses from feminists across a broad range of the political spectrum. One of the most common reactions is the supposition that women Islamist supporters are pawns in a grand patriarchal plan, who, if freed from their bondage, would naturally express their instinctual abhorrence for the traditional Islamic mores used to enchain them. Even those analysts who are skeptical of the false-consciousness thesis underpinning this approach nonetheless continue to frame the issue in terms of a fundamental contradiction: why would such a large number of women across the Muslim world actively support a movement that seems inimical to their "own interests and agendas," especially at a historical moment when these women appear to have more emancipatory possibilities available to them?[1] Despite important differences between these two reactions, both share the assumption that there is something intrinsic to women that *should* predispose them to oppose the practices, values, and injunctions that the Islamist movement embodies. Yet, one may ask, is such an assumption valid? What is the history by which we have come to assume its truth? What kind of a political imagination would lead one to think in this manner? More importantly, if we discard such an assumption, what other analytical tools might be available to ask a different set of questions about women's participation in the Islamist movement?

In this book I will explore some of the conceptual challenges that women's involvement in the Islamist movement poses to feminist theory in particular, and to secular-liberal thought in general, through an ethnographic account of an urban women's mosque movement that is part of the larger Islamic Revival in Cairo, Egypt. For two years (1995–97) I conducted fieldwork with a movement in which women from a variety of socioeconomic backgrounds provided lessons to one another that focused on the teaching and studying of Islamic scriptures, social practices, and forms of bodily comportment considered germane to the cultivation of the ideal virtuous self.[2] The burgeoning of this movement marks the first time in Egyptian history that such a large number of women have held public meetings in mosques to teach one another Islamic doctrine, thereby altering the historically male-centered character of mosques as well as Islamic pedagogy. At the same time, women's religious participation within such public arenas of Islamic pedagogy is critically structured by, and serves to uphold, a discursive tradition that regards subordination to a tran-

[1] This dilemma seems to be further compounded by the fact that women's participation in the Islamist movement in a number of countries (such as Iran, Egypt, Indonesia, and Malaysia) is not limited to the poor (that is, those who are often considered to have a "natural affinity" for religion). Instead the movement also enjoys wide support among women from the upper- and middle-income strata.

[2] In addition to attending religious lessons at a number of mosques catering to women of various socioeconomic backgrounds, I undertook participant observation among the teachers and attendees of mosque lessons, in the context of their daily lives. This was supplemented by a year-long study with a shaikh from the Islamic University of al-Azhar on issues of Islamic jurisprudence and religious practice.

scendent will (and thus, in many instances, to male authority) as its coveted goal.[3]

The women's mosque movement is part of the larger Islamic Revival or Islamic Awakening (al-Ṣaḥwa al-Islāmiyya) that has swept the Muslim world, including Egypt, since at least the 1970s. "Islamic Revival" is a term that refers not only to the activities of state-oriented political groups but more broadly to a religious ethos or sensibility that has developed within contemporary Muslim societies. This sensibility has a palpable public presence in Egypt, manifest in the vast proliferation of neighborhood mosques and other institutions of Islamic learning and social welfare, in a dramatic increase in attendance at mosques by both women and men, and in marked displays of religious sociability. Examples of the latter include the adoption of the veil (*ḥijāb*), a brisk consumption and production of religious media and literature, and a growing circle of intellectuals who write and comment upon contemporary affairs in the popular press from a self-described Islamic point of view. Neighborhood mosques have come to serve as the organizational center for many of these activities, from the dissemination of religious knowledge and instruction, to the provision of a range of medical and welfare services to poor Egyptians.[4] This Islamization of the sociocultural landscape of Egyptian society is in large part the work of the piety movement, of which the women's movement is an integral part, and whose activities are organized under the umbrella term *daʿwa* (a term whose historical development I trace in chapter 2).[5]

The women's mosque movement, as part of the Islamic Revival, emerged twenty-five or thirty years ago when women started to organize weekly religious lessons—first at their homes and then within mosques—to read the Quran, the *ḥadīth* (the authoritative record of the Prophet's exemplary speech and actions), and associated exegetical and edificatory literature. By the time I began my fieldwork in 1995, this movement had become so popular that

[3] This is in contrast, for example, to a movement among women in the Islamic republic of Iran that has had as its goal the reinterpretation of sacred texts to derive a more equitable model of relations between Muslim women and men; see Afshar 1998; Mir-Hosseini 1999; Najmabadi 1991, 1998.

[4] According to available sources, the total number of mosques in Egypt grew from roughly 28,000 reported in 1975 to 50,000 in 1985 (Zeghal 1996, 174); by 1995 there were 120,000 mosques in Egypt (al-Ahram Center for Political and Strategic Studies 1996, 65). Of the 50,000 mosques tabulated in the year 1985, only 7,000 were established by the government (Gaffney 1991, 47).

[5] There are three important strands that comprise the Islamic Revival: state-oriented political groups and parties, militant Islamists (whose presence has declined during the 1990s), and a network of socioreligious nonprofit organizations that provide charitable services to the poor and perform the work of proselytization. In this book, I will use the terms "the daʿwa movement" and "the piety movement" interchangeably to refer to this network of socioreligious organizations of which the mosque movement is an important subset.

there were hardly any neighborhoods in this city of eleven million inhabitants that did not offer some form of religious lessons for women.[6] According to participants, the mosque movement had emerged in response to the perception that religious knowledge, as a means of organizing daily conduct, had become increasingly marginalized under modern structures of secular governance. The movement's participants usually describe the impact of this trend on Egyptian society as "secularization" (*ʿalmana* or *ʿalmāniyya*) or "westernization" (*tagharrub*), a historical process which they argue has reduced Islamic knowledge (both as a mode of conduct and a set of principles) to an abstract system of beliefs that has no direct bearing on the practicalities of daily living. In response, the women's mosque movement seeks to educate ordinary Muslims in those virtues, ethical capacities, and forms of reasoning that participants perceive to have become either unavailable or irrelevant to the lives of ordinary Muslims. Practically, this means instructing Muslims not only in the proper performance of religious duties and acts of worship but, more importantly, in how to organize their daily conduct in accord with principles of Islamic piety and virtuous behavior.

Despite its focus on issues of piety, it would be wrong to characterize the women's mosque movement as an abandonment of politics. On the contrary, the form of piety the movement seeks to realize is predicated upon, and transformative of, many aspects of social life.[7] While I will discuss in chapters 2 and 4 the different ways in which the activism of the mosque movement challenges our normative liberal conceptions of politics, here I want to point out the scope of the transformation that the women's mosque movement and the larger piety (daʿwa) movement have effected within Egyptian society. This includes changes in styles of dress and speech, standards regarding what is deemed proper entertainment for adults and children, patterns of financial and household management, the provision of care for the poor, and the terms by which public debate is conducted. Indeed, as the Egyptian government has come to recognize the impact that the mosque movement in particular, and the piety movement in general, have had on the sociocultural ethos of Egyptian public and political life, it has increasingly subjected these movements to state regulation and scrutiny (see chapter 2).

The pious subjects of the mosque movement occupy an uncomfortable place in feminist scholarship because they pursue practices and ideals em-

[6] The attendance at these gatherings ranged from ten to five hundred women, depending on the popularity of the teacher.

[7] Unlike some other religious traditions (such as English Puritanism) wherein "piety" refers primarily to inward spiritual states, the mosque participants' use of the Arabic term *taqwa* (which may be translated as "piety") suggests both an inward orientation or disposition and a manner of practical conduct. See my discussion of the term *taqwa* in chapter 4.

bedded within a tradition that has historically accorded women a subordinate status. Movements such as these have come to be associated with terms such as fundamentalism, the subjugation of women, social conservatism, reactionary atavism, cultural backwardness, and so on—associations that, in the aftermath of September 11, are often treated as "facts" that do not require further analysis. While it would be a worthy task to dissect the reductionism that such associations enact on an enormously complex phenomenon, this is not my purpose in this book. Nor is it my aim to recover a "redeemable element" within the Islamist movement by recuperating its latent liberatory potentials so as to make the movement more palatable to liberal sensibilities. Instead, in this book I seek to analyze the conceptions of self, moral agency, and politics that undergird the practices of this nonliberal movement, in order to come to an understanding of the historical projects that animate it.[8]

My goal, however, is not just to provide an ethnographic account of the Islamic Revival. It is also to make this material speak back to the normative liberal assumptions about human nature against which such a movement is held accountable—such as the belief that all human beings have an innate desire for freedom, that we all somehow seek to assert our autonomy when allowed to do so, that human agency primarily consists of acts that challenge social norms and not those that uphold them, and so on. Thus, my ethnographic tracings will sustain a running argument with and against key analytical concepts in liberal thought, as these concepts have come to inform various strains of feminist theory through which movements such as the one I am interested in are analyzed. As will be evident, many of the concepts I discuss under the register of feminist theory in fact enjoy common currency across a wide range of disciplines, in part because liberal assumptions about what constitutes human nature and agency have become integral to our humanist intellectual traditions.

AGENCY AND RESISTANCE

As I suggested at the outset, women's active support for socioreligious movements that sustain principles of female subordination poses a dilemma for feminist analysts. On the one hand, women are seen to assert their presence in previously male-defined spheres while, on the other hand, the very idioms

[8] For studies that capture the complex character of Islamist movements, and the wide variety of activities that are often lumped under the fundamentalist label, see Abedi and Fischer 1990; Bowen 1993; Esposito 1992; Hefner 2000; Hirschkind 2001a, 2001b, 2004; Peletz 2002; Salvatore 1997; Starrett 1998.

they use to enter these arenas are grounded in discourses that have historically secured their subordination to male authority. In other words, women's subordination to feminine virtues, such as shyness, modesty, and humility, appears to be the necessary condition for their enhanced public role in religious and political life. While it would not have been unusual in the 1960s to account for women's participation in such movements in terms of false consciousness or the internalization of patriarchal norms through socialization, there has been an increasing discomfort with explanations of this kind. Drawing on work in the humanities and the social sciences since the 1970s that has focused on the operations of human agency within structures of subordination, feminists have sought to understand how women resist the dominant male order by subverting the hegemonic meanings of cultural practices and redeploying them for their "own interests and agendas." A central question explored within this scholarship has been: how do women contribute to reproducing their own domination, and how do they resist or subvert it? Scholars working within this framework have thus tended to analyze religious traditions in terms of the conceptual and practical resources they offer to women, and the possibilities for redirecting and recoding these resources in accord with women's "own interests and agendas"—a recoding that stands as the site of women's agency.[9]

When the focus on locating women's agency first emerged, it played a crucial role in complicating and expanding debates about gender in non-Western societies beyond the simplistic registers of submission and patriarchy. In particular, the focus on women's agency provided a crucial corrective to scholarship on the Middle East that for decades had portrayed Arab and Muslim women as passive and submissive beings shackled by structures of male authority.[10] Feminist scholarship performed the worthy task of restoring the absent voice of women to analyses of Middle Eastern societies, portraying women as active agents whose lives are far richer and more complex than past narratives had suggested (Abu-Lughod 1986; Altorki 1986; Atiya 1982; S. Davis 1983; Dwyer 1978; Early 1993; Fernea 1985; Wikan 1991). This emphasis on women's agency within gender studies paralleled, to a certain extent, discussions of the peasantry in New Left scholarship, a body of work that also sought to restore a humanist agency (often expressed metonymically as a "voice") to the peasant in the historiography of agrarian societies—a project articulated against classical Marxist formulations that had assigned the peasantry a non-place in the making of modern history (Hobsbawm 1980; James

[9] Examples from the Muslim context include Boddy 1989; Hale 1987; Hegland 1998; MacLeod 1991; Torab 1996. For a similar argument made in the context of Christian evangelical movements, see Brusco 1995; Stacey 1991.

[10] For a review of this scholarship on the Middle East, see Abu-Lughod 1990a.

Scott 1985). The Subaltern Studies Project is the most recent example of this scholarship (see, for example, Guha and Spivak 1988).[11]

The ongoing importance of feminist scholarship on women's agency cannot be emphasized enough, especially when one remembers that Western popular media continues to portray Muslim women as incomparably bound by the unbreakable chains of religious and patriarchal oppression. This acknowledgment notwithstanding, it is critical to examine the assumptions and elisions that attend this focus on agency, especially the ways in which these assumptions constitute a barrier to the exploration of movements such as the one I am dealing with here. In what follows, I will explore how the notion of human agency most often invoked by feminist scholars—one that locates agency in the political and moral autonomy of the subject—has been brought to bear upon the study of women involved in patriarchal religious traditions such as Islam. Later, in the second half of this chapter, I will suggest alternative ways of thinking about agency, especially as it relates to embodied capacities and means of subject formation.

Janice Boddy's work is an eloquent and intelligent example of the anthropological turn to an analysis of subaltern gendered agency. Boddy conducted fieldwork in a village in an Arabic-speaking region of northern Sudan on a women's *zār* cult—a widely practiced healing cult that uses Islamic idioms and spirit mediums and whose membership is largely female (1989). Through a rich ethnography of women's cultic practices, Boddy proposes that in a society where the "official ideology" of Islam is dominated and controlled by men, the zār practice might be understood as a space of subordinate discourse—as "a medium for the cultivation of women's consciousness" (1989, 345). She argues that zār possession serves as "a kind of counter-hegemonic process . . . : *a feminine response to hegemonic praxis*, and the privileging of men that this ideologically entails, which ultimately escapes neither its categories nor its constraints" (1989, 7; emphasis added). She concludes by asserting that the women she studied "use perhaps unconsciously, perhaps strategically, what we in the West might prefer to consider *instruments of their oppression* as means to assert their value both collectively, through the ceremonies they organize and stage, and individually, in the context of their marriages, so insisting on their dynamic complementarity with men. *This in itself is a means of resisting and setting limits to domination. . . .*" (1989, 345; emphasis added).

The ethnographic richness of this study notwithstanding, what is most relevant for the purposes of my argument is the degree to which the female agent in Boddy's work seems to stand in for a sometimes repressed, sometimes active

[11] It is not surprising, therefore, that in addition to seeking to restore agency to the peasantry, Ranajit Guha, one of the founders of the Subaltern Studies Project, also called for historians to treat women as agents, rather than instruments, of various movements (Guha 1996, 12).

feminist consciousness, articulated against the hegemonic male cultural norms of Arab Muslim societies.[12] As Boddy's study reveals, even in instances when an explicit *feminist* agency is difficult to locate, there is a tendency among scholars to look for expressions and moments of resistance that may suggest a challenge to male domination. When women's actions seem to reinscribe what appear to be "instruments of their own oppression," the social analyst can point to moments of disruption of, and articulation of points of opposition to, male authority—moments that are located either in the interstices of a woman's consciousness (often read as a nascent feminist consciousness), or in the objective effects of women's actions, however unintended these may be. Agency, in this form of analysis, is understood as the capacity to realize one's own interests against the weight of custom, tradition, transcendental will, or other obstacles (whether individual or collective). Thus the humanist desire for autonomy and self-expression constitutes the substrate, the slumbering ember that can spark to flame in the form of an act of resistance when conditions permit.

Lila Abu-Lughod, one of the leading figures among those scholars who helped reshape the study of gender in the Middle East, has criticized some of the assumptions informing feminist scholarship, including those found in her own previous work (Abu-Lughod 1990b, 1993). In one of her earlier works, Abu-Lughod had analyzed women's poetry among the Bedouin tribe of Awlād ʿAli as a socially legitimate, semipublic practice that was an expression of women's resistance and protest against the strict norms of male domination in which Bedouin women live (Abu-Lughod 1986). Later, in a reflective essay on this work, Abu-Lughod asks the provocative question: how might we recognize instances of women's resistance without "misattributing to them forms of consciousness or politics that are not part of their experience—something like a feminist consciousness or feminist politics?" (Abu-Lughod 1990b, 47). In exploring this question, Abu-Lughod criticizes herself and others for being too preoccupied with "explaining resistance and finding resisters" at the expense of understanding the workings of power (1990b, 43). She argues:

> In some of my earlier work, as in that of others, there is perhaps a tendency to *romanticize resistance*, to read all forms of resistance as signs of ineffectiveness of systems of power and of *the resilience and creativity of the human spirit in its refusal to be dominated*. By reading resistance in this way, we collapse distinctions between forms of resistance and foreclose certain questions about the workings of power. (1990b, 42; emphasis added)

[12] For a somewhat different approach to women's zar practices in the Sudan, which, nonetheless, utilizes a similar notion of agency, see Hale 1986, 1987.

As a corrective, Abu-Lughod recommends that resistance be used as a "diagnostic of power" (1990b, 42), to locate the shifts in social relations of power that influence the resisters as well as those who dominate. To illustrate her point, Abu-Lughod gives the example of young Bedouin women who wear sexy lingerie to challenge parental authority and dominant social mores. She suggests that instead of simply reading such acts as moments of opposition to, and escape from, dominant relations of power, they should also be understood as reinscribing alternative forms of power that are rooted in practices of capitalist consumerism and urban bourgeois values and aesthetics (1990b, 50).

Abu-Lughod concludes her provocative essay with the following observation:

> My argument . . . has been that we should learn to read in various local and everyday resistances the existence of a range of specific strategies and structures of power. Attention to *the forms of resistance in particular societies* can help us become critical of partial or reductionist theories of power. The problem has been that those of us who have sensed that there is something admirable about resistance have tended to look to it for hopeful confirmations of the failure—or partial failure—of systems of oppression. Yet it seems to me that *we respect everyday resistance* not just by arguing for the dignity or heroism of the resisters but by letting their practices teach us about complex interworkings of historically changing structures of power. (1990b, 53; emphasis added)

While Abu-Lughod's attention to understanding resistance as a diagnostic of differential forms of power marks an important analytical step that allows us to move beyond the simple binary of resistance/subordination, she nevertheless implies that the task of identifying an act as one of "resistance" is a fairly unproblematic enterprise. She revises her earlier analysis by suggesting that in order to describe the specific forms that acts of resistance take, they need to be located within fields of power rather than outside of them. Thus, even though Abu-Lughod starts her essay by questioning the ascription of a "feminist consciousness" to those for whom this is not a meaningful category (1990b, 47), this does not lead her to challenge the use of the term "resistance" to describe a whole range of human actions, including those which may be socially, ethically, or politically indifferent to the goal of opposing hegemonic norms. I believe it is critical that we ask whether it is even possible to identify a universal category of acts—such as those of resistance—outside of the ethical and political conditions within which such acts acquire their particular meaning. Equally important is the question that follows: does the category of resistance impose a teleology of progressive politics on the analytics of power—a teleology that makes it hard for us to see and understand forms of being and action that are not necessarily encapsulated by the narrative of subversion and reinscription of norms?

What perceptive studies such as these by Boddy and Abu-Lughod fail to problematize is the universality of the desire—central for liberal and progressive thought, and presupposed by the concept of resistance it authorizes—to be free from relations of subordination and, for women, from structures of male domination. This positing of women's agency as consubstantial with resistance to relations of domination, and the concomitant naturalization of freedom as a social ideal, are not simply analytical oversights on the part of feminist authors. Rather, I would argue that their assumptions reflect a deeper tension within feminism attributable to its dual character as both an *analytical* and a *politically prescriptive* project.[13] Despite the many strands and differences within feminism, what accords the feminist tradition an analytical and political coherence is the premise that where society is structured to serve male interests, the result will be either neglect, or direct suppression, of women's concerns.[14] Feminism, therefore, offers both a *diagnosis* of women's status across cultures and a *prescription* for changing the situation of women who are understood to be marginalized, subordinated, or oppressed (see Strathern 1988, 26–28). Thus the articulation of conditions of relative freedom that enable women both to formulate and to enact self-determined goals and interests remains the object of feminist politics and theorizing. Freedom is normative to feminism, as it is to liberalism, and critical scrutiny is applied to those who want to limit women's freedom rather than those who want to extend it.[15]

feminism and freedom

In order to explore in greater depth the notion of freedom that informs feminist scholarship, I find it useful to think about a key distinction that liberal theorists often make between negative and positive freedom (Berlin 1969; Green 1986; Simhony 1993; Taylor 1985c). Negative freedom refers to the

[13] As a number of feminist scholars have noted, these two dimensions of the feminist project often stand in a productive tension against each other. See W. Brown 2001; Butler 1999; Mohanty 1991; Rosaldo 1983; Strathern 1987, 1988.

[14] Despite the differences within feminism, this is a premise that is shared across various feminist political positions—including radical, socialist, liberal, and psychoanalytic—and that marks the domain of feminist discourse. Even in the case of Marxist and socialist feminists who argue that women's subordination is determined by social relations of economic production, there is at least an acknowledgment of the inherent tension between women's interests and those of the larger society dominated and shaped by men (see Hartsock 1983; MacKinnon 1989). For an anthropological argument about the universal character of gender inequality, see Collier and Yanagisako 1989.

[15] John Stuart Mill, a figure central to liberal and feminist thought, argues: "the burden of proof is supposed to be with those who are against liberty; who contend for any restriction or prohibition. . . . The *a priori* presumption is in favour of freedom. . . ." (Mill 1991, 472).

absence of external obstacles to self-guided choice and action, whether imposed by the state, corporations, or private individuals.[16] Positive freedom, on the other hand, is understood as the capacity to realize an autonomous will, one generally fashioned in accord with the dictates of "universal reason" or "self-interest," and hence unencumbered by the weight of custom, transcendental will, and tradition. In short, positive freedom may be best described as the capacity for self-mastery and self-government, and negative freedom as the absence of restraints of various kinds on one's ability to act as one wants. It is important to note that the idea of self-realization itself is not an invention of the liberal tradition but has existed historically in a variety of forms, such as the Platonic notion of self-mastery over one's passions, or the more religious notion of realizing oneself through self-transformation, present in Buddhism and a variety of mystical traditions, including Islam and Christianity. Liberalism's unique contribution is to link the notion of self-realization with individual autonomy, wherein the process of realizing oneself is equated with the ability to realize the desires of one's "true will" (Gray 1991).[17]

Although there continues to be considerable debate about these entwined notions of negative and positive freedom,[18] I want to emphasize the concept of individual autonomy that is central to both, and the concomitant elements of coercion and consent that are critical to this topography of freedom. In order for an individual to be free, her actions *must* be the consequence of her "own will" rather than of custom, tradition, or social coercion. To the degree that autonomy in this tradition of liberal political theory is a *procedural* principle, and not an ontological or substantive feature of the subject, it delimits the necessary condition for the enactment of the ethics of freedom. Thus, even illiberal actions can arguably be tolerated if it is determined that they are undertaken by a freely consenting individual who is acting of her own accord. Political theorist John Christman, for example, considers the interesting situation wherein a slave *chooses* to continue being a slave even when external obstacles and constraints are removed (Christman 1991). In order for such a

[16] Within classical political philosophy, this notion (identified with the thought of Bentham and Hobbes) finds its most common application in debates about the proper role of state intervention within the private lives of individuals. This is also the ground on which feminists have debated proposals for antipornographic legislation (see, for example, Bartky 1990; MacKinnon 1993; Rubin 1984; Samois Collective 1987).

[17] The slippery character of the human will formed in accord with reason and self-interest is itself a point of much discussion among a range of liberal thinkers such as Hobbes, Spinoza, Hegel, and Rousseau (Heller, Sosna, and Wellberry 1986; Taylor 1989). In late-liberal Western societies, the disciplines of psychoanalysis and psychology have played a crucial role in determining what the "true inner self" really is, and what its concomitant needs and desires should be (see, for example, Hacking 1995; Rose 1998).

[18] See Hunt 1991; MacCallum 1967; Simhony 1993; West 1993.

person to be considered free, Christman argues, an account is required of the process by which the person acquired her desire for slavery. Christman asserts that as long as these desires and values are "generated in accordance with the *procedural* conditions of autonomous preference formation that are constitutive of freedom, then no matter what the 'content' of those desires, the actions which they stimulate will be (positively) free" (1991, 359).[19] In other words, it is not the substance of a desire but its "origin that matters in judgments about autonomy" (Christman 1991, 359). Freedom, in this formulation, consists in the ability to autonomously "choose" one's desires no matter how illiberal they may be.[20]

The concepts of positive and negative freedom, with the attendant requirement of procedural autonomy, provide the ground on which much of the feminist debate unfolds. For example, the positive conception of freedom seems to predominate in projects of feminist historiography (sometimes referred to as "her-story") that seek to capture historically and culturally specific instances of women's self-directed action, unencumbered by patriarchal norms or the will of others.[21] The negative conception of freedom seems to prevail in studies of gender that explore those spaces in women's lives that are independent of men's influence, and possibly coercive presence, treating such spaces as pregnant with possibilities for women's fulfillment or self-realization. Many feminist historians and anthropologists of the Arab Muslim world have thus sought to delimit those conditions and situations in which women seem to autonomously articulate "their own" discourse (such as that of poetry, weaving, cult possession, and the like), at times conferring a potentially liberatory meaning to practices of sex segregation that had traditionally been under-

[19] This "procedural" or "content-neutral" account of autonomy is most influentially advocated by contemporary theorists like Rawls, Habermas, and Dworkin (their differences notwithstanding). It contrasts with a "substantive" account of autonomy in which a person's actions are not only required to be the result of her own choice, but also must, in their *content*, abide by predetermined standards and values that define the ideal of autonomy. In the latter version, a person who willingly chooses to become a slave would not be considered free. It should be noted, however, that the substantive account is only a more robust and stronger version of the procedural account of autonomy. On this and related issues, see Friedman 2003, especially pages 19–29.

[20] This long-standing liberal principle has generated a number of paradoxes in history. For example, the British tolerated acts of *sati* (widow burning) in colonial India, despite their official opposition to the practice, in those cases where the officials could determine that the widow was not coerced but went "willingly to the pyre" (for an excellent discussion of this debate, see Mani 1998). Similarly, some critics of sadomasochism in the United States argue that the practice may be tolerated on the condition that it is undertaken by consenting adults who have a "choice" in the matter, and is not the result of "coercion."

[21] For an illuminating discussion of the historiographical project of "her-story," see Joan Scott 1988, 15–27.

stood as making women marginal to the public arena of conventional politics (Ahmed 1982; Boddy 1989; Wikan 1991).

My intention here is not to question the profound transformation that the liberal discourse of freedom and individual autonomy has enabled in women's lives around the world, but rather to draw attention to the ways in which these liberal presuppositions have become naturalized in the scholarship on gender. It is quite clear that both positive and negative notions of freedom have been used productively to expand the horizon of what constitutes the domain of legitimate feminist practice and debate. For example, in the 1970s, in response to the call by white middle-class feminists to dismantle the institution of the nuclear family, which they believed to be a key source of women's oppression, Native- and African American feminists argued that freedom, for them, consisted in being able to form families, since the long history of slavery, genocide, and racism had operated precisely by breaking up their communities and social networks (see, for example, Brant 1984; Collins 1991; A. Davis 1983; Lorde 1984).[22] Such arguments successfully expanded feminist understandings of "self-realization/self-fulfillment" by making considerations of class, race, and ethnicity central, thereby forcing feminists to rethink the concept of individual autonomy in light of other issues.

Since then a number of feminist theorists have launched trenchant critiques of the liberal notion of autonomy from a variety of perspectives.[23] While earlier critics had drawn attention to the masculinist assumptions underpinning the ideal of autonomy (Chodorow 1978; Gilligan 1982), later scholars faulted this ideal for its emphasis on the atomistic, individualized, and bounded characteristics of the self at the expense of its relational qualities formed through social interactions within forms of human community (Benhabib 1992; Young 1990). Consequently, there have been various attempts to redefine autonomy so as to capture the emotional, embodied, and socially embedded character of people, particularly of women (Friedman 1997, 2003; Joseph 1999; Nedelsky 1989). A more radical strain of poststructuralist theory has situated its critique of autonomy within a larger challenge posed to the *illusory* character of the rationalist, self-authorizing, transcendental subject presupposed by Enlightenment thought in general, and the liberal tradition in particular. Rational thought, these critics argue, secures its universal scope and authority by performing a necessary exclusion of all that is bodily, femi-

[22] Similarly "A Black Feminist Statement" by the Combahee River Collective rejected the appeal for lesbian separatism made by white feminists on the grounds that the history of racial oppression required black women to make alliances with male members of their communities in order to continue fighting against institutionalized racism (Hull, Bell-Scott, and Smith 1982).

[23] For an interesting discussion of the contradictions generated by the privileged position accorded to the concept of autonomy in feminist theory, see Adams and Minson 1978.

nine, emotional, nonrational, and intersubjective (Butler 1999; Gatens 1996; Grosz 1994). This exclusion cannot be substantively or conceptually recuperated, however, through recourse to an unproblematic feminine experience, body, or imaginary (*pace* Beauvoir and Irigaray), but must be thought through the very terms of the discourse of metaphysical transcendence that enacts these exclusions.[24]

In what follows, I would like to push further in the direction opened by these poststructuralist debates. In particular, my argument for uncoupling the notion of self-realization from that of the autonomous will is indebted to poststructuralist critiques of the transcendental subject, voluntarism, and repressive models of power. Yet, as will become clear, my analysis also departs from these frameworks insomuch as I question the overwhelming tendency within poststructuralist feminist scholarship to conceptualize agency in terms of subversion or resignification of social norms, to locate agency within those operations that resist the dominating and subjectivating modes of power. In other words, I will argue that the normative political subject of poststructuralist feminist theory often remains a liberatory one, whose agency is conceptualized on the binary model of subordination and subversion. In doing so, this scholarship elides dimensions of human action whose ethical and political status does not map onto the logic of repression and resistance. In order to grasp these modes of action indebted to other reasons and histories, I will suggest that it is crucial to detach the notion of agency from the goals of progressive politics.

It is quite clear that the idea of freedom and liberty as *the* political ideal is relatively new in modern history. Many societies, including Western ones, have flourished with aspirations other than this. Nor, for that matter, does the narrative of individual and collective liberty exhaust the desires with which people live in liberal societies. If we recognize that the desire for freedom from, or subversion of, norms is not an innate desire that motivates all beings at all times, but is also profoundly mediated by cultural and historical conditions, then the question arises: how do we analyze operations of power that construct different kinds of bodies, knowledges, and subjectivities whose trajectories do not follow the entelechy of liberatory politics?

Put simply, my point is this: if the ability to effect change in the world and in oneself is historically and culturally specific (both in terms of what constitutes "change" and the means by which it is effected), then the meaning and sense of agency cannot be fixed in advance, but must emerge through an analysis of the particular concepts that enable specific modes of being, respon-

[24] For an excellent discussion of this point in the scholarship on feminist ethics, see Colebrook 1997.

sibility, and effectivity. Viewed in this way, what may appear to be a case of deplorable passivity and docility from a progressivist point of view, may actually be a form of agency—but one that can be understood only from within the discourses and structures of subordination that create the conditions of its enactment. In this sense, agentival capacity is entailed not only in those acts that resist norms but also in the multiple ways in which one *inhabits* norms.

It may be argued in response that this kind of challenge to the natural status accorded to the desire for freedom in analyses of gender runs the risk of Orientalizing Arab and Muslim women all over again—repeating the errors of pre-1970s Orientalist scholarship that defined Middle Eastern women as passive submissive Others, bereft of the enlightened consciousness of their "Western sisters," and hence doomed to lives of servile submission to men. I would contend, however, that to examine the discursive and practical conditions within which women come to cultivate various forms of desire and capacities of ethical action is a radically different project than an Orientalizing one that locates the desire for submission in an innate ahistorical cultural essence. Indeed, if we accept the notion that all forms of desire are discursively organized (as much of recent feminist scholarship has argued), then it is important to interrogate the practical and conceptual conditions under which different forms of desire emerge, including desire for submission to recognized authority. We cannot treat as natural and imitable only those desires that ensure the emergence of feminist politics.

Consider, for example, the women from the mosque movement with whom I worked. The task of realizing piety placed these women in conflict with several structures of authority. Some of these structures were grounded in instituted standards of Islamic orthodoxy, and others in norms of liberal discourse; some were grounded in the authority of parents and male kin, and others in state institutions. Yet the *rationale* behind these conflicts was not predicated upon, and therefore cannot be understood only by reference to, arguments for gender equality or resistance to male authority. Nor can these women's practices be read as a reinscription of traditional roles, since the women's mosque movement has significantly reconfigured the gendered practice of Islamic pedagogy and the social institution of mosques (see chapters 3 and 5). One could, of course, argue in response that, the intent of these women notwithstanding, the actual effects of their practices may be analyzed in terms of their role in reinforcing or undermining structures of male domination. While conceding that such an analysis is feasible and has been useful at times, I would nevertheless argue that it remains encumbered by the binary terms of resistance and subordination, and ignores projects, discourses, and desires that are not captured by these terms (such as those pursued by the women I worked with).

Studies on the resurgent popularity of the veil in urban Egypt since the

1970s provide excellent examples of these issues. The proliferation of such studies (El Guindi 1981; Hoffman-Ladd 1987; MacLeod 1991; Radwan 1982; Zuhur 1992) reflects scholars' surprise that, contrary to their expectations, so many "modern Egyptian women" have returned to wearing the veil. Some of these studies offer functionalist explanations, citing a variety of reasons why women take on the veil voluntarily (for example, the veil makes it easy for women to avoid sexual harassment on public transportation, lowers the cost of attire for working women, and so on). Other studies identify the veil as a symbol of resistance to the commodification of women's bodies in the media, and more generally to the hegemony of Western values. While these studies have made important contributions, it is surprising that their authors have paid so little attention to Islamic virtues of female modesty or piety, especially given that many of the women who have taken up the veil frame their decision precisely in these terms.[25] Instead, analysts often explain the motivations of veiled women in terms of standard models of sociological causality (such as social protest, economic necessity, anomie, or utilitarian strategy), while terms like morality, divinity, and virtue are accorded the status of the phantom imaginings of the hegemonized.[26] I do not, of course, mean to suggest that we should restrict our analyses to folk categories. Rather, I want to argue for a critical vigilance against the elisions any process of translation entails, especially when the language of social science claims for itself a transparent universalism while portraying the language used by "ordinary people" as a poor approximation of their reality.[27]

My argument should be familiar to anthropologists who have long acknowledged that the terms people use to organize their lives are not simply a gloss for universally shared assumptions about the world and one's place in it, but are actually constitutive of different forms of personhood, knowledge, and experience.[28] For this reason I have found it necessary, in the chapters that follow, to

[25] See, in contrast, Lila Abu-Lughod's interesting discussion of the veil as a critical aspect of the concept of modesty (*ḥasham*) among Egyptian Bedouins (1986, 159–67).

[26] For example, in a survey conducted among veiled university students in Cairo, a majority of the interviewees cited piety as their primary motivation for taking up the veil. In commenting on the results of this survey, the sociologist Sherifa Zuhur argues that "rather than the newfound piety" her informants claimed, the real motivations for veiling inhered in the socioeconomic incentives and benefits that accrue to veiled women in Egyptian society (Zuhur 1992, 83).

[27] For a thoughtful discussion of the problems entailed in the translation of supernatural and metaphysical concepts into the language of secular time and history, see Chakrabarty 2000; Rancière 1994.

[28] For an excellent exploration of the use of language in the cultural construction of personhood, see Caton 1990; Keane 1997; Rosaldo 1982. Also see Marilyn Strathern's critique of Western conceptions of "society and culture" that feminist deconstructivist approaches assume in analyzing gender relations in non-Western societies (1992b).

attend carefully to the specific logic of the discourse of piety: a logic that inheres not in the intentionality of the actors, but in the relationships that are articulated between words, concepts, and practices that constitute a particular discursive tradition.[29] I would insist, however, that an appeal to understanding the coherence of a discursive tradition is neither to justify that tradition, nor to argue for some irreducible essentialism or cultural relativism. It is, instead, to take a necessary step toward explaining the force that a discourse commands.

POSTSTRUCTURALIST FEMINIST THEORY AND AGENCY

In order to elaborate my theoretical approach, let me begin by examining the arguments of Judith Butler, who remains, for many, the preeminent theorist of poststructuralist feminist thought, and whose arguments have been central to my own work. Central to Butler's analysis are two insights drawn from Michel Foucault, both quite well known by now. Power, according to Foucault, cannot be understood solely on the model of domination as something possessed and deployed by individuals or sovereign agents over others, with a singular intentionality, structure, or location that presides over its rationality and execution. Rather, power is to be understood as a strategic relation of force that permeates life and is productive of new forms of desires, objects, relations, and discourses (Foucault 1978, 1980). Secondly, the subject, argues Foucault, does not precede power relations, in the form of an individuated consciousness, but is produced through these relations, which form the necessary conditions of its possibility. Central to his formulation is what Foucault calls the paradox of *subjectivation*: the very processes and conditions that secure a subject's subordination are also the means by which she becomes a self-conscious identity and agent (Butler 1993, 1997c; Foucault 1980, 1983). Stated otherwise, one may argue that the set of capacities inhering in a subject—that is, the abilities that define her modes of agency—are not the residue of an undominated self that existed prior to the operations of power but are themselves the products of those operations.[30] Such an understanding of power and subject formation

[29] The concept "discursive tradition" is from T. Asad 1986. See my discussion of the relevance of this concept to my overall argument in chapter 3.

[30] An important aspect of Foucault's analytics of power is his focus on what he called its "techniques," the various mechanisms and strategies through which power comes to be exercised at its point of application on subjects and objects. Butler differs from Foucault in this respect in that her work is not so much an exploration of techniques of power as of issues of performativity, interpellation, and psychic organization of power. Over time, Butler has articulated her differences with Foucault in various places; see, for example, Butler 1993, 248 n. 19; 1997c, 83–105; 1999, 119–41; and Butler and Connolly 2000.

encourages us to conceptualize agency not simply as a synonym for resistance to relations of domination, but as a capacity for action that specific relations of *subordination* create and enable.

Drawing on Foucault's insights, Butler asks a key question: "[I]f power works not merely to dominate or oppress existing subjects, but also forms subjects, what is this formation?" (Butler 1997c, 18). By questioning the prediscursive status of the concept of subject, and inquiring instead into the relations of power that produce it, Butler breaks with those feminist analysts who have formulated the issue of personhood in terms of the relative autonomy of the individual from the social. Thus the issue for Butler is not how the social enacts the individual (as it was for generations of feminists), but what are the discursive conditions that sustain the entire metaphysical edifice of contemporary individuality.

Butler's signal contribution to feminist theory lies in her challenge to the sex/gender dichotomy that has served as the ground on which much of feminist debate, at least since the 1940s, has proceeded. For Butler, the problem with the sex/gender distinction lies in the assumption that there is a prerepresentational matter or sexed body that grounds the cultural inscription of gender. Butler argues not only that there is no prerepresentational sex (or material body) that is not already constituted by the system of gender representation, but also that gender discourse is *itself* constitutive of materialities it refers to (and is in this sense not purely representational).[31] Butler says, "To claim that discourse is formative is not to claim that it originates, causes, or exhaustively composes that which it concedes; rather, it is to claim that there is no reference to a pure body which is not at the same time a further formation of that body. In this sense, the linguistic capacity to refer to sexed bodies is not denied, but the very meaning of 'referentiality' is altered. In philosophical terms, the constative claim is always to some degree performative" (Butler 1993, 10–11).

What, then, is the process through which the materiality of the sexed and gendered subject is enacted? To answer this, Butler turns not so much to the analysis of institutions and technologies of subject formation, as Foucault did, but to the analysis of language as a system of signification through which sub-

[31] Feminist philosophers Elizabeth Grosz and Moira Gatens, influenced by the work of Gilles Deleuze, make a similar critique of the problematic distinction between materiality and representation underpinning the sex/gender dichotomy (Gatens 1996; Grosz 1994). While they are similar to Butler in their rejection of any simple appeal to a prerepresentational body, or a feminine ontology, as the foundation for articulating feminist politics, they differ from Butler in that they accord the body a force that can affect systems of representation on terms that are other than those of the system itself. For an interesting discussion of the differences between these theorists, see Colebrook 2000a.

jects are produced and interpolated. In particular, Butler builds upon Derrida's reinterpretation of J. L. Austin's notion of the performative as "that reiterative power of discourse to produce the phenomena that it regulates and constrains" (Butler 1993, 2).[32] For Butler, the subject in her sexed and gendered materiality is constituted performatively through a reiterated enactment of heterosexual norms, which retroactively produce, on the one hand, "the appearance of gender as an abiding interior depth" (1997b, 14), and on the other hand, the putative facticity of sexual difference which serves to further consolidate the heterosexual imperative. In contrast to a long tradition of feminist scholarship that treated norms as an external social imposition that constrain the individual, Butler forces us to rethink this external-internal opposition by arguing that social norms are the necessary ground through which the subject is realized and comes to enact her agency.

Butler combines the Foucauldian analysis of the subject with psychoanalytic theory, in particular adopting Lacanian notions of "foreclosure" and "abjection" to emphasize certain exclusionary operations that she thinks are necessary to subject formation. She argues that the subject is produced simultaneously through a necessary repudiation of identities, forms of subjectivities, and discursive logics, what she calls "a constitutive outside to the subject" (Butler 1993, 3), which marks the realm of all that is unspeakable, unsignifiable, and unintelligible from the purview of the subject, but remains, nonetheless, necessary to the subject's self-understanding and formulation.[33] This foreclosure is performatively and reiteratively enacted, in the sense that "the subject who speaks within the sphere of the speakable implicitly reinvokes the foreclosure on which it depends and, thus, depends on it again" (1997a, 139–40).

Given Butler's theory of the subject, it is not surprising that her analysis of performativity also informs her conceptualization of agency; indeed, as she says, "the iterability of performativity *is* a theory of agency" (1999, xxiv; emphasis added). To the degree that the stability of social norms is a function of their repeated enactment, agency for Butler is grounded in the essential openness of each iteration and the possibility that it may fail or be reappropriated or resignified for purposes other than the consolidation of norms. Since all social formations are reproduced through a reenactment of norms, this makes these formations vulnerable because each restatement/reenactment can fail. Thus the condition of possibility of each social formation is also "the possibil-

[32] Whereas for Austin the performative derives its force from the conventions that govern a speech act, for Derrida this force must be understood in terms of the iterable character of all signs (see Derrida 1988). For an interesting critique of Derrida's reading of Austin, see Cavell 1995.

[33] For Butler's discussion of how Foucauldian conceptions of power and the subject may be productively combined with the work of Freud and Lacan, see 1997c, 83–105.

ity of its undoing" (Butler 1997b, 14). She explains this point succinctly in regard to sex/gender:

> As a sedimented effect of a reiterative or ritual practice, sex acquires its naturalized effect, and, yet, it is also by virtue of this reiteration that gaps and fissures are opened up as the constitutive instabilities in such constructions, as that which escapes or exceeds the norm. . . . This instability is the *de*constituting possibility in the very process of repetition, the power that undoes the very effects by which "sex" is stabilized, the possibility to put the consolidation of the norms of "sex" into a potentially productive crisis. (1993, 10)[34]

It is important to note that there are several points on which Butler departs from the notions of agency and resistance that I criticized earlier. To begin with, Butler questions what she calls an "emancipatory model of agency," one that presumes that all humans qua humans are "endowed with a will, a freedom, and an intentionality" whose workings are "thwarted by relations of power that are considered external to the subject" (Benhabib et al. 1995, 136). In its place, Butler locates the possibility of agency within structures of power (rather than outside of it) and, more importantly, suggests that the reiterative structure of norms serves not only to *consolidate* a particular regime of discourse/power but also provides the means for its *destabilization*.[35] In other words, there is no possibility of "undoing" social norms that is independent of the "doing" of norms; agency resides, therefore, within this productive reiterability. Butler also resists the impetus to tether the meaning of agency to a predefined teleology of emancipatory politics. As a result, the logic of subversion and resignification cannot be predetermined in Butler's framework because acts of resignification/subversion are, she argues, contingent and fragile, appearing in unpredictable places and behaving in ways that confound our expectations.[36]

I find Butler's critique of humanist conceptions of agency and subject very compelling, and, indeed, my arguments in this book are manifestly informed by it. I have, however, found it productive to argue with certain tensions that

[34] Butler's analysis of the production of sexed/gendered subjects is built upon a general theory of subject formation, one she makes more explicit in her later writings. See Butler 1997a, 1997c, and Butler, Laclau, and Žižek 2000.

[35] Echoing Foucault, Butler argues, "The paradox of subjectivation (*assujetissement*) is precisely that the subject who would resist such norms is itself enabled, if not produced, by such norms. Although this constitutive constraint does not foreclose the possibility of agency, it does locate agency as a reiterative or rearticulatory practice, immanent to power, and not a relation of external opposition to power" (1993, 15).

[36] See Butler's treatment of this topic in "Gender Is Burning" in Butler 1993, and in Butler 2001.

characterize Butler's work in order to expand her analytics to a somewhat different, if related, set of problematics. One key tension in Bulter's work owes to the fact that while she emphasizes the ineluctable relationship between the consolidation and destabilization of norms, her discussion of agency tends to focus on those operations of power that resignify and subvert norms. Thus even though Butler insists time and again that all acts of subversion are a product of the terms of violence that they seek to oppose, her analysis of agency often privileges those moments that "open possibilities for resignifying the terms of violation against their violating aims" (1993, 122), or that provide an occasion "for a radical rearticulation" of the dominant symbolic horizon (1993, 23).[37] In other words, the concept of agency in Butler's work is developed primarily in contexts where norms are thrown into question or are subject to resignification.[38]

Clearly Butler's elaboration of the notion of agency should be understood in the specific context of the political interventions in which her work is inserted. The theoretical practice Butler has developed over the last fifteen years is deeply informed by a concern for the violence that heterosexual normativity enacts and the way in which it delimits the possibilities of livable human existence. Her theorization of agency therefore must be understood in its performative dimension: as a political praxis aimed at unsettling dominant discourses of gender and sexuality. As a textual practice situated within the space of the academy, the context of Butler's intervention is not limited to the legal, philosophical, or popular discourses she analyzes but is also constituted by the reception her work has garnered within feminist scholarship. Butler has had to defend herself against the charge, leveled against her by a range of feminists, that her work has the effect of undermining any agenda of progressive political and social reform by deconstructing the very conceptions of subject and power that enable it (see, for example, Bordo 1993, and the exchange in Benhabib et al. 1995). To counter these claims, Butler has continually positioned her work in relation to the project of articulating a radical democratic

[37] For example, in discussing the question of agency, Butler writes, "an account of iterability of the subject . . . shows how agency may well consist in opposing and transforming the social terms by which it is spawned" (Butler 1997c, 29). Note the equivalence drawn here between agency and the ability of performatives to oppose normative structures. Such oft-repeated statements stand in tension with her own cautionary phrases, in this case within the same text, when she admonishes the reader that agency should not be conceptualized as "always and only opposed to power" (Butler 1997c, 17).

[38] Amy Hollywood, in her reading of Butler, suggests that Butler inherits her valorization of resignification—the propensity of utterances and speech acts to break from their prior significations—from Derrida. But whereas Derrida, Hollywood argues, remains ethically and politically neutral toward this characteristic of language and signs, Butler often reads resignification as politically positive (Hollywood 2002, 107 n. 57).

politics,[39] and in doing so has emphasized counter-hegemonic modalities of agency.[40] An important consequence of these aspects of Butler's work (and its reception) is that her analysis of the power of norms remains grounded in an agonistic framework, one in which norms suppress and/or are subverted, are reiterated and/or resignified—so that one gets little sense of the work norms perform beyond this register of suppression and subversion within the constitution of the subject.

Norms are not only consolidated and/or subverted, I would suggest, but performed, inhabited, and experienced in a variety of ways. This is a point on which I think Butler would not disagree; indeed, in her writings she often reverts to the trope of the "psyche" and the language of psychoanalysis to capture the density of ties through which the individual is attached to the subjectivating power of norms (see, for example, Butler 1997c). Butler's exploration of this density often remains, however, subservient on the one hand to her overall interest in tracking the possibilities of resistance to the regulating power of normativity,[41] and on the other hand to her model of performativity, which is primarily conceptualized in terms of a dualistic structure of consolidation/resignification, doing/undoing, of norms.

the subject of norms

I would like to push the question of norms further in a direction that I think allows us to deepen the analysis of subject formation and also address the

[39] For Butler's most recent engagement with this project, see Butler, Laclau, and Žižek 2000. It is clear from this text that while Butler is uncomfortable, more so than her interlocutors, with a universalist theory of radical change, she remains interested in theorizing about conditions conducive to creating the possibility of radical democratic politics.

[40] Consider, for example, the following statement by Butler in which she immediately qualifies her objection to a subject-centered theory of agency with the reassurance that her objections do not foreclose the possibility of resistance to subjection: "If . . . subjectivation is bound up with subjection . . . then it will not do to invoke a notion of the subject as the ground of agency, since the subject is itself produced through operations of power that delimit in advance what the aims and expanse of agency will be. It does not follow from this insight, however, that we are all always already trapped, and that there is no point of resistance to regulation or to the form of subjection that regulation takes" (Butler, Laclau, and Žižek 2000, 151).

[41] Butler argues, for example, that Foucault's notion of subjectivation can be productively supplemented with certain reformulations of psychoanalytic theory. For Butler, the force of this supplementation seems to reside, notably, in its ability to address the "problem of locating or accounting for resistance: Where does resistance to or in disciplinary subject formation take place? Does [Foucault's] reduction of the psychoanalytically rich notion of the psyche to that of the imprisoning soul [in *Discipline and Punish*] eliminate the possibility of resistance to normalization and to subject formation, a resistance that emerges precisely from the incommensurability between psyche and subject?" (Butler 1997c, 87).

problem of reading agency primarily in terms of resistance to the regularizing impetus of structures of normativity. In particular, I would like to expand Butler's insight that norms are not simply a social imposition on the subject but constitute the very substance of her intimate, valorized interiority. But in doing so, I want to move away from an agonistic and dualistic framework—one in which norms are conceptualized on the model of doing and undoing, consolidation and subversion—and instead think about the variety of ways in which norms are lived and inhabited, aspired to, reached for, and consummated. As I will argue below, this in turn requires that we explore the relationship between the immanent form a normative act takes, the model of subjectivity it presupposes (specific articulations of volition, emotion, reason, and bodily expression), and the kinds of authority upon which such an act relies. Let me elaborate by discussing the problems a dualistic conception of norms poses when analyzing the practices of the mosque movement.

Consider, for example, the Islamic virtue of female modesty (*al-iḥtishām*, *al-ḥayā'*) that many Egyptian Muslims uphold and value (discussed in chapter 5). Despite a consensus about its importance, there is considerable debate about how this virtue should be lived, and particularly about whether its realization requires the donning of the veil. A majority of the participants in the mosque movement (and the larger piety movement of which the mosque movement is an integral part) argue that the veil is a necessary component of the virtue of modesty because the veil both expresses "true modesty" and is the means through which modesty is acquired. They draw, therefore, an ineluctable relationship between the norm (modesty) and the bodily form it takes (the veil) such that the veiled body becomes the necessary means through which the virtue of modesty is both created *and* expressed. In contrast to this understanding is a position (associated with prominent secularist writers) that argues that the virtue of modesty is no different than any other human attribute—such as moderation or humility: it is a facet of character but does not commit one to any particular expressive repertoire such as donning the veil. Notably, these authors oppose the veil but not the virtue of modesty, which they continue to regard as appropriate to feminine conduct. The veil, in their view, has been invested with an importance that is unwarranted when it comes to judgments about female modesty (see chapter 5).

The debate about the veil is only one part of a much larger discussion in Egyptian society wherein political differences between Islamists and secularists, and even among Islamists of various persuasions, are expressed through arguments about ritual performative behavior. While I will return to this discussion in chapter 4, what I want to point out here is that the most interesting features of this debate lie not so much in whether the norm of modesty is subverted or enacted, but in the radically different ways in which the norm is supposed to be lived and inhabited. Notably, each view posits a very different conceptualization of the relationship between embodied behavior and the virtue or norm of modesty: for the pietists, bodily behavior is at the core of the proper realization of the norm, and for their opponents, it is a contingent and unnecessary element in modesty's enactment.

Some of the questions that follow from this observation are: How do we analyze the work that the body performs in these different conceptualizations of the norm? Is performative behavior differently understood in each of these views and, if so, how? How is the self differently tied to the authority the norm commands in these two imaginaries? Furthermore, what sorts of ethical and political subjects are presupposed by these two imaginaries, and what forms of ethico-political life do they enable or foreclose? These questions cannot be answered as long as we remain within the binary logic of the doing and undoing of norms. They require, instead, that we explode the category of norms into its constituent elements—to examine the immanent form that norms take, and to inquire into the attachments their particular morphology generates within the topography of the self. My reason for urging this move has to do with my interest in understanding how different modalities of moral-ethical action contribute to the construction of particular kinds of subjects, subjects whose political anatomy cannot be grasped without applying critical scrutiny to the precise form their embodied actions take.

This manner of analyzing contemporary debates about Islamic virtues or norms also has consequences for how we might understand the political effects that the piety movement has generated within Egyptian society. Scholars of Islamist movements have often argued that the resurgence of Islamic forms of sociability (such as veiling, increased interest in the correct performance of Islamic rituals, and the proliferation of Islamic charities) within a range of Muslim societies is best understood as an expression of *resistance* against Western politico-cultural domination as well as a form of social protest against the failed modernizing project of postcolonial Muslim regimes (Burgat and Dowell 1997; Esposito 1992; Göle 1996; Roy 1994). In this view, the project of restoring orthodox Islamic virtues crucially depends upon an oppositional stance toward what may be loosely defined as a modernist secular-liberal ethos—an ethos whose agents are often understood to be postcolonial Muslim regimes in cahoots with dominant Western powers.

While this interpretation is not entirely wrong and captures an important aspect of Islamist movements, it nonetheless reduces their complexity to the trope of *resistance* without adequate regard for key questions such as: What specifically do the Islamist movements oppose about Western hegemony, postcoloniality, or a secular-liberal ethos? Toward what end? And, more importantly, what forms of life do these movements enable that are not so easily captured in terms of a relationship of negation to the existing hegemonic order? Furthermore, as I will show in chapter 2, the relationship between Islamism and liberal secularity is one of proximity and coimbrication rather than of simple opposition or, for that matter, accommodation; it therefore needs to be analyzed in terms of the historically shifting, ambiguous, and unpredictable encounters that this proximity has generated. This relationship is best tracked, I want to suggest further, through attention to the specificity of terms that have attended debates about Islamic virtues (or orthodox Islamic norms) in modern history. As I hope to show in the chapters that follow, these debates are ineluctably tied to emergent forms of subjectivity that secular processes have contingently provoked in their wake. In order to set the stage for such an exploration, let me first spell out what I mean when I insist that we attend to the immanent forms Islamic virtues take within contemporary debates about Islamization and what are the analytical stakes in pursuing such an approach.

MANIFEST NORMS AND ETHICAL FORMATION

Cultural critic Jeffery Minson has argued persuasively that one way in which the legacy of humanist ethics, particularly in its Kantian formulation, has continued to be important to post-Enlightenment thought is in the relative lack of attention given to the morphology of moral actions, that is, to their precise shape and form (Minson 1993). Minson argues that this legacy is traceable at least as far back as Kant, for whom morality proper was primarily a rational matter that entailed the exercise of the faculty of reason, shorn of the specific context (of social virtues, habit, character formation, and so on) in which the act unfolded. The Kantian legacy, I would add, becomes particularly important in light of the tradition of Aristotelian ethics it displaces—a tradition in which morality was both realized through, and manifest in, outward behavioral forms.[42] Against this tradition, Kant argued that a moral act could be moral only to the extent that it was not a result of habituated virtue but a product of the critical faculty of reason. The latter requires that one act morally *in spite of* one's inclinations, habits, and disposition.[43] Kant's telescop-

[42] The relative decline of the importance accorded to religious rituals in post-Reformation Christianity constitutes another trajectory of this same development. See T. Asad 1993.

[43] Kant is explicit in his objection to morality that is a result of habituated virtues, acquired through the long process of character formation: "When the firm resolve to comply with one's duty has become a habit, it is called *virtue* also in a legal sense, in its *empirical character* (*virtus phaenomenon*). Virtue here has the abiding maxim of *lawful* actions. . . . Virtue, in this sense, is accordingly acquired *little by little*, and to some it means a long habituation (in the observance of the

ing of moral action down to the movements of the will stands in contrast to the value ascribed to the particular form a moral act took in the Aristotelian worldview.[44] The question of motivation, deliberation, and choice in the Aristotelian tradition was important too, of course, but only from the standpoint of actual practices.

One consequence of this Kantian conception of ethics is the relative lack of attention paid to the manifest form ethical practices take, and a general demotion of conduct, social demeanor, and etiquettes in our analyses of moral systems. As Minson points out, even scholars like Bourdieu, whose work focuses on practices of dress, physical bearing, and styles of comportment—things that Bourdieu calls "the practical mnemonics" of a culture—consider these practices interesting only insofar as a rational evaluation reveals them to be the signs and symbols of a much deeper and more fundamental reality of social structures and cultural logics (Minson 1993, 31). I agree with Minson: when Bourdieu considers the variety of practices that characterize a particular social group (such as their styles of eating, socializing, and entertainment), he is primarily concerned with how these practices embody and symbolize the *doxa* and ethos of the group such that the ideologies the members inhabit come to be congealed in their social or class *habitus* (see, for example, Bourdieu 1977, 1990). One may argue, however, that the significance of an embodied practice is not exhausted by its ability to function as an index of social and class status or a group's ideological habitus.[45] The specificity of a bodily

law), in virtue of which a human being, through gradual reformation of conduct and consolidation of his maxims, passes from a propensity to vice to its opposite. But not the slightest *change of heart* is necessary for this; only a change of mores. . . . However, that a human being should become not merely *legally* good, but *morally* good (pleasing to God) i.e. virtuous according to the intelligible character [of virtue] (*virtus noumenon*) and thus in need of no other incentive to recognize a duty except the representation of duty itself—that, so long as the foundation of the maxims of the human being remains impure, cannot be effected through gradual *reform* but must rather be effected through a *revolution* in the disposition of the human being. . . . And so a 'new man' can come about only through a kind of rebirth, as it were a new creation . . . and a change of heart" (Kant 1998, 67–68).

[44] This does not mean that for Kant morality was purely an individual matter, guided by personal preference; rather, an act was moral only insofar as it was made in accord with a universally valid form of rationality. As Charles Taylor points out, Kant's moral law combines two features: everyone is obligated to act in accord with reason, and "it is an essential feature of reason that it be valid for everyone, for all rational creatures alike. That is the basis of the first form of Kant's categorical imperative: that I should act only according to a maxim which I could at the same time will as a universal law. For if I am right to will something, then everyone is right to will it, and it must thus be something that could be willed for everybody" (Taylor 1985b, 323).

[45] In *Excitable Speech* (1997a), Butler praises Bourdieu's work on *habitus* for its sensitivity to how an individual's social and cultural location comes to be embodied in her disposition. She criticizes him, however, for failing to attend to the potential of the body to resist this system of

practice is also interesting for the kind of relationship it presupposes to the act it constitutes wherein an analysis of the particular form that the body takes might transform our conceptual understanding of the act itself. Furthermore, bodily behavior does not simply stand in a relationship of meaning to self and society, but it also endows the self with certain kinds of capacities that provide the substance from which the world is acted upon.

positive ethics

There is another tradition of ethics, Aristotelian in inspiration, that provides a means of redressing some of the problems discussed above. Michel Foucault's later work draws upon this tradition to formulate what Claire Colebrook aptly calls a "positive conception of ethics" that extends the domain of ethics "beyond notions of norms, justification, legitimation, and meaning to include the consideration of the practices, selves, bodies, and desires that determine (and are codetermined by) ethics" (Colebrook 1998, 50). Foucault's conception of positive ethics is Aristotelian in that it conceives of ethics not as an Idea, or as a set of regulatory norms, but as a set of practical activities that are germane to a certain way of life.[46] Ethics in this conception is embedded in a set of specific practices (what Aristotle called "practices of virtue"). It is only from the standpoint of the dispositions formed through these practices that the Kantian question of moral deliberation can be posed. In this view, you ask not what a particular ethical theory means, but what it does.[47] In contrast to other contemporary writings on "virtue ethics," Foucault's use of Aristotelian ethics is not geared toward asserting its universal validity, or recuperating its various elements for solving contemporary moral problems—such as reclaiming the idea of *telos* or a collective notion of the good life (see, for example, MacIntyre

signification and to pose a challenge to its logic. From the standpoint of my argument here, it is interesting to note that while Butler wants to emphasize how the body becomes a site of resistance to social inscription, and Bourdieu stresses the constraining aspects of embodied social power, both analyze the body through the binary logic of subversion and/or consolidation of social norms. What is elided here are the different modalities through which the body comes to inhabit or live the regulative power of norms, modalities that cannot be captured within the dualistic logic of resistance and constraint.

[46] This should not be taken to mean that Foucault's conception of ethics is anti-Kantian in any simple sense. For an insightful discussion of Kant's influence on Foucault's later work on ethics, in particular the conjoining of ethics and freedom, see the chapter entitled "Self Improvement" in Hacking 2002.

[47] Colebrook argues that Foucault's account of ancient ethics is "a positive ethics in which actions are evaluated according to what they do rather than what they mean, 'each having its specific character or shape'" (1998, 43).

1984; Taylor 1995).[48] Instead, for Foucault, this tradition allows us to think of ethics as always local and particular, pertaining to a specific set of procedures, techniques, and discourses through which highly specific ethical-moral subjects come to be formed.[49] In what follows, I will pursue the direction opened up by this approach—not only because I find it analytically rich but also because, as I will explain in chapter 4, aspects of the Aristotelian tradition have been influential in shaping the pietistic practices of Islam.

Foucault distinguished ethical practices from "morals," reserving the latter to refer to sets of norms, rules, values, and injunctions. "Ethics," on the other hand, refers to those practices, techniques, and discourses through which a subject transforms herself in order to achieve a particular state of being, happiness, or truth (Foucault 1990, 1997a, 1997b, 1997c; Martin, Gutman, and Hutton 1988; see also Davidson 1994, Faubion 2001, and Rabinow 1997).[50] For Foucault, ethics is a modality of power that "permits individuals to effect by their own means or with the help of others, a certain number of operations on their own bodies and souls, thoughts, conduct, and way of being" (Foucault 1997b, 225) in order to transform themselves into the willing subjects of a particular moral discourse. Despite his attention to the individual's effort at constituting herself, the subject of Foucault's analysis is not a voluntaristic, autonomous subject who fashions herself in a protean manner. Rather, the subject is formed within the limits of a historically specific set of formative practices and moral injunctions that are delimited in advance—what Foucault characterizes as "modes of subjectivation." Foucault thus treats subjectivity not as a private space of self-cultivation, but as an effect of a modality of power operationalized through a set of moral codes that summon a subject to constitute herself in accord with its precepts. "Moral subjectivation," in turn, refers to the models available "for setting up and developing relationships with the self, for self-reflection, self-knowledge, self-examination, for the decipherment of the self by oneself, for the transformations that one seeks to accomplish with oneself as object" (Foucault 1990, 29).

For Foucault, the relationship between moral codes and modes of subjectivation is not overdetermined, however, in the sense that the subject simply complies with moral codes (or resists them). Rather, Foucault's framework as-

[48] The neo-Aristotelian tradition of "virtue ethics" generally argues for the reinstatement of the priority of virtue as the central ethical concept over the concept of "the good" or "the right" in contemporary moral thought. On virtue ethics, see Anscombe 1981; Foot 1978; Lovibond 2002.

[49] For a contrasting reading that combines Foucault's work on ethics with the scholarship on virtue ethics, see Lovibond 2002.

[50] Although Foucault draws a distinction between "code-oriented" and "ethics-oriented" moralities, he does not consider them incommensurable. For example, he argues that Christianity has had both moralities functioning side by side, even if, during different periods, the relative emphasis on each has varied (Foucault 1990, 30).

sumes that there are many different ways of forming a relationship with a moral code, each of which establishes a particular relationship between capacities of the self (will, reason, desire, action, and so on) and a particular norm. The precise embodied form that obedience to a moral code takes is not a contingent but a *necessary* element of ethical analysis in that it is a means to describing the specific constitution of the ethical subject. In other words, it is only through an analysis of the specific shape and character of ethical practices that one can apprehend the kind of ethical subject that is formed. These practices are technical practices for Foucault and include corporeal and body techniques, spiritual exercises, and ways of conducting oneself—all of which are "positive" in the sense that they are manifest in, and immanent to, everyday life. Notably, the importance of these practices does not reside in the meanings they signify to their practitioners, but in the *work they do* in constituting the individual; similarly, the body is not a medium of signification but the substance and the necessary tool through which the embodied subject is formed.

I find Foucault's analysis of ethical formation particularly helpful for conceptualizing agency beyond the confines of the binary model of enacting and subverting norms. Specifically, he draws our attention to the contribution of external forms to the development of human ethical capacities, to specific modes of human agency. Instead of limiting agency to those acts that disrupt existing power relations, Foucault's work encourages us to think of agency: (a) in terms of the capacities and skills required to undertake particular kinds of moral actions; and (b) as ineluctably bound up with the historically and culturally specific disciplines through which a subject is formed. The paradox of subjectivation is central to Foucault's formulation in that the capacity for action is enabled and created by specific relations of subordination. To clarify this paradox, we might consider the example of a virtuoso pianist who submits herself to the often painful regime of disciplinary practice, as well as to the hierarchical structures of apprenticeship, in order to acquire the ability—the requisite agency—to play the instrument with mastery. Importantly, her agency is predicated upon her ability to be taught, a condition classically referred to as "docility." Although we have come to associate docility with the abandonment of agency, the term literally implies the malleability required of someone in order for her to be instructed in a particular skill or knowledge—a meaning that carries less a sense of passivity than one of struggle, effort, exertion, and achievement.[51]

[51] One of the meanings listed for docility in the *Oxford English Dictionary* is: "the quality of teachableness, readiness and willingness to receive instruction, aptness to be taught, amenability to training" (OED 1999).

modes of subjectivation and the mosque movement

The approach I am suggesting can be further elaborated by reference to the four elements Foucault posits as central to the study of ethics. This fourfold scheme, however, cannot be taken as a blueprint for the study of ethics; rather, the utility of Foucault's analytical framework lies in the fact that it raises a series of questions about the relationship between moral codes and ethical conduct, questions that are answerable only through an examination of specific practices through which historically located moral norms are lived. The first component, which Foucault calls the "substance of ethics," refers to those aspects of the self that pertain to the domain of ethical judgment and practice. The substance of ethics in medieval Christianity, for example, was flesh and desire, whereas the part of oneself most subject to analysis and labor in the modern period is feelings (Foucault 1997b, 263). The second aspect of ethics, which Foucault calls the "mode of subjectivation," refers to how people are incited or called upon to recognize their moral obligations—for example, whether through divine law, rational rule, or cosmological order. As Nikolas Rose has pointed out, this aspect of ethics draws our attention to the *kind of authority* through which a subject comes to recognize the truth about herself, and the relationship she establishes between herself and those who are deemed to hold the truth (Rose 1998, 27). The third aspect of ethics pertains to the operations one performs on oneself in order to become an ethical subject—a process analyzed under the label "techniques of the self." Finally, the fourth component of ethics is *telos*: the mode of being one seeks to achieve within a historically specific authoritative model.

Foucault's analysis of ethics is useful for understanding key aspects of the women's mosque movement I worked with, and of the piety movement in general. The practices of these movements presuppose the existence of a divine plan for human life—embodied in the Quran, the exegetical literature, and the moral codes derived therefrom—that each individual is responsible for following. Participants in the mosque movement are summoned to recognize their moral obligations through invocations of divine texts and edificatory literature. This form of morality, however, is not strictly juridical. There are no centralized authorities that enforce the moral code and penalize infractions. Rather, the mosque movement has a strong individualizing impetus that requires each person to adopt a set of ascetic practices for shaping moral conduct.[52] Each individual must interpret the moral codes, in accord with tradi-

[52] Chapter 2 describes the ways in which this individualizing trend has been accelerated in the twentieth century.

tional guidelines, in order to discover how she, as an individual, may best realize the divine plan for her life.

In comparison with other currents within the Islamic Revival, the mosque movement is unique in the extraordinary degree of pedagogical emphasis it places on outward markers of religiosity—ritual practices, styles of comporting oneself, dress, and so on. The participants in the mosque movement regard these practices as the necessary and ineluctable means for realizing the form of religiosity they are cultivating. For the mosque participants, it is the various movements of the body that comprise the material substance of the ethical domain. There exists an elaborate system of techniques by which the body's actions and capacities can be examined and worked upon, both individually and collectively. The mosque lessons are one important space where training in this kind of ascetic practice is acquired. As I will explore later, women learn to analyze the movements of the body and soul in order to establish coordination between inner states (intentions, movements of desire and thought, etc.) and outer conduct (gestures, actions, speech, etc.). Indeed, this distinction between inner and outer aspects of the self provides a central axis around which the panoply of ascetic practices is organized. As we will see in chapter 4, this principle of coordination has implications for how we might analyze the conceptual relationship the body articulates with the self and with others, and by extension, the self's variable relationships to structures of authority and power.

The teleological model that the mosque participants seek to realize in their lives is predicated on the exemplary conduct of the Prophet and his Companions. It would be easy to dismiss this ideal as a nostalgic desire to emulate a bygone past, a past whose demands can never be met within the exigencies of the present. Yet to do so would be to miss the significance of such a telos for practical ethical conduct. Among mosque participants, individual efforts toward self-realization are aimed not so much at discovering one's "true" desires and feelings, or at establishing a personal relationship with God, but at honing one's rational and emotional capacities so as to approximate the exemplary model of the pious self (see chapter 4). The women I worked with did not regard trying to emulate authorized models of behavior as an external social imposition that constrained individual freedom. Rather, they treated socially authorized forms of performance as the potentialities—the ground if you will—through which the self is realized. As a result, one of the questions this book raises is: How do we conceive of individual freedom in a context where the distinction between the subject's own desires and socially prescribed performances cannot be easily presumed, and where submission to certain forms of (external) authority is a condition for achieving the subject's potentiality? In other words, how does one make the question of politics integral to the analysis of the architecture of the self?

ETHICS AND POLITICS

Two objections may be raised to my proposal that we think about agency in terms of ethical formation, particularly in its Foucauldian formulation. One, it may be argued that despite my objections to a humanist understanding of the sovereign subject, I have in fact smuggled back in a subject-centered theory of agency by locating agency within the efforts of the self; and two, it may be argued that I have sidestepped the crucial question of politics and social transformation that the formulation of agency-as-resistance was primarily oriented to address. The first objection is, I believe, based on some common misunderstandings about what it means to say that the subject is an effect of power. It is often presumed that to speak about ethical self-formation necessarily requires a self-conscious agent who constitutes herself in a quasi-Promethean manner, enacting her will and hence asserting "her own agency" against structural forces. This presumption is incorrect on a number of scores. Even though I focus on the practices of the mosque participants, this does not mean that their activities and the operations they perform on themselves are products of their independent wills; rather, my argument is that these activities are the products of authoritative discursive traditions whose logic and power far exceeds the consciousness of the subjects they enable. The kind of agency I am exploring here does not belong to the women themselves, but is a product of the historically contingent discursive traditions in which they are located. The women are summoned to recognize themselves in terms of the virtues and codes of these traditions, and they come to measure themselves against the ideals furbished by these traditions; in this important sense, the individual is contingently made possible by the discursive logic of the ethical traditions she enacts. Self-reflexivity is not a universal human attribute here but, as Foucault suggested, a particular kind of relation to oneself whose form fundamentally depends on the practices of subjectivation through which the individual is produced.

Let me now turn to the second objection: that my emphasis on agency as ethical self-formation abandons the realm of politics. This objection in some ways reflects an old distinction within liberal political theory that regards issues of morality and ethics as private, and issues pertaining to politics as necessarily public. This distinction is problematic for a variety of reasons, not the least of which is the existence of a robust disagreement within the liberal tradition itself about the proper role ethics and virtues should, and do, play in the creation of liberal polities (see Pocock 1985; Skinner 1998). This compartmentalization of the ethical and the political is made all the more difficult to sustain if we take into account an insight that has become quite commonplace in the academy today, namely that all forms of politics require and assume a particular kind of a subject that is produced through a range of disciplinary practices that are at the core of the regulative apparatus of any modern political arrangement.

While the validity of this insight is commonly conceded, the line of questioning is seldom reversed: How does a particular conception of the self require and presuppose different kinds of political commitments? Or to put it another way, what sort of subject is assumed to be normative within a particular political imaginary? Stating the question in this manner does not assume that the political ensues from the personal, precisely because, as I have argued above, the self is socially and discursively produced, an effect of operations of power rather than the progenitor of these operations. As such, an inquiry into the constitution of the self does not take the personal preferences and proclivities of the individual to be the object of study, but instead analyzes the historically contingent arrangements of power through which the normative subject is produced. I have found this framework particularly powerful insomuch as it helps denaturalize the normative subject of liberal feminist theory thereby making it possible to approach the lives of the mosque participants in ways not determined by the truths this body of scholarship asserts as universal.

Foucault's formulation of ethics suggests a means of inquiring into various techniques of subject formation, particularly within those traditions that place an emphasis on individualized (rather than juridical) modes of subjectivation. Political theorist William Connolly interprets Foucault's work on the arts of the self as an implicit acknowledgment of the crucial ways in which political engagement is not simply an abstract mode of deliberation but issues forth from "visceral modes of appraisal" (1999). Connolly challenges the regnant rationalist account of politics, arguing that political judgments do not simply entail the evaluation of moral principles but issue forth from intersubjective modes of being and acting that, while not always representable and enunciable, are nonetheless efficacious in regards to social and political behavior (Connolly 1999, 27–46).[53] Indeed, once we recognize that political formations presuppose not only distinct modes of reasoning, but also depend

[53] Connolly draws upon the work of a number of philosophers in making this argument. He writes: "Thinking itself for Deleuze (and Epicurus, Spinoza, Bergson, Freud, and Nietzsche too) operates on more than one level; it moves on the level of the virtual (which is real in its effectivity but not actual in its availability) and that of the actual (which is available to representation, but not self-sufficient). Infrasensible intensities of proto-thinking, for instance, provide a reservoir from which *surprise* sometimes unsettles fixed explanations, new *pressures* periodically swell up to disrupt existing practices of rationality, and new *drives to identity* occasionally surge up to modify the register of justice and legitimacy upon which established identities are placed" (1999, 40).

upon affective modes of assessment, then an analysis of ethical practices of self-formation takes on a new, distinctly political, relevance. Nikolas Rose, who has explored the connection between Foucault's arts of the self and practices of governmentality in late-liberal Western societies, argues that analytical attention to ethico-politics "allows the possibility of opening up the education of forms of life and self-conduct to the difficult and interminable business of debate and contestation" (1999, 192). This is a point that resonates with a longstanding feminist insight that any political transformation necessarily entails working on those embodied registers of life that are often cordoned off from the realm of "pure politics."

ethics and agency

How does this intertwining of the ethical and the political impact my critique of regnant notions of agency within liberal-progressive accounts? First of all, as I hope I have made clear, I am not interested in offering *a* theory of agency, but rather I insist that the meaning of agency must be explored within the grammar of concepts within which it resides. My argument in brief is that we should keep the meaning of agency open and allow it to emerge from "within semantic and institutional networks that define and make possible particular ways of relating to people, things, and oneself" (T. Asad 2003, 78). This is why I have maintained that the concept of agency should be delinked from the goals of progressive politics, a tethering that has often led to the incarceration of the notion of agency within the trope of resistance against oppressive and dominating operations of power. This does not mean that agency never manifests itself in this manner; indeed it sometimes does. But the questions that follow from this relatively simple observation are complicated and may be productively explored, I would suggest, through the nexus of ethics and politics.

Consider, for example, the fact that the practices of the mosque participants often pose a challenge to hegemonic norms of secular-liberal sociability as well as aspects of secular-liberal governance (see chapters 2 and 4). These challenges, however, have impacted conditions of secularity in a manner that has far exceeded both the intentionality of the pietists and the expectations of their most severe retractors. For example, as chapter 4 will show, the pietists' interpretation of Islamic rituals and observances has proved to be enormously unsettling to the state-oriented Islamists as much as their secular critics because of the implicit challenge this interpretation poses to key assumptions about the role ascribed to the body within the nationalist imaginary. As a result, the supposedly apolitical practices of the mosque movement have been met, on the one hand, with the disciplinary mechanisms of the state and, on the other hand, with a robust critique of this form of religiosity from secular-liberal Muslims and Islamist political parties who share a certain nationalist-identitarian worldview. One might say that the political agency of the mosque movement (the "resistance" it poses to secularization) is a contingent and unanticipated consequence of the effects its ethical practices have produced in the social field.

What I want to emphasize here are two interrelated points: first, that it is impossible to understand the political agency of the movement without a proper grasp of its ethical agency; and second, that to read the activities of the mosque movement primarily in terms of the resistance it has posed to the logic of secular-liberal governance and its concomitant modes of sociability ignores an entire dimension of politics that remains poorly understood and undertheorized within the literature on politics and agency.

Note that the activities of the mosque movement, like the rest of the piety movement, seldom engage those institutions and practices that are commonly associated with the realm of politics, such as participating in the electoral process, making claims on the state, using the judicial system to expand the place of religion in public life, and so on.[54] As a result it is easy to ignore the political character of this movement and for its activities to fall off the "political radar" of the analyst. Indeed, it is quite common for scholars to consider movements of this kind—movements that focus on issues of moral reform—apolitical in character (see, for example, Beinin and Stork 1997; Göle 1996; Metcalf 1993, 1994; Roy 1994). This characterization is a gross political and analytical mistake, however, because the transformative power of movements such as these is immense and, in many cases, exceeds that of conventional political groups. The political efficacy of these movements is, I would suggest, a function of the work they perform in the ethical realm—those strategies of cultivation through which embodied attachments to historically specific forms of truth come to be forged. Their political project, therefore, can only be understood through an exploration of their ethical practices. This requires that we rethink not only our conventional understanding of what constitutes the political but also what is the substance of ethics. Part of the analytical labor of this book is directed at addressing this challenge.

[54] This does not mean, of course, that the piety or women's mosque movement does not depend upon structures of modern governance for its organization. As my arguments in chapter 2 will make clear, modern political developments provide the necessary conditions for the emergence and flourishing of the piety movement in Egypt. What I am pointing out here is simply that the piety movement does not seek to transform the state or its policies but aims at reforming the social and cultural field.

ethics and critique

A feminist concerned with relations of gender inequality might ask: How are we to think about the possibility of subverting and challenging those patriarchal norms that the mosque movement upholds? By untethering the concept of agency from that of progressive politics for the purpose of analytical clarity, have we abandoned any means of judging and critiquing which practices subordinate women and which ones allocate them some form of gender parity? Have I lost sight of the politically prescriptive project of feminism in pushing at the limits of its analytical envelope? The response to these questions cannot be given simply in a few phrases or paragraphs, but will, I hope, emerge within the course of this book. Here I only want to suggest some preliminary ways of thinking about these questions.

To begin with, the question of how the hierarchical system of gender relations that the mosque movement upholds should be *practically* transformed is, on the one hand, impossible to answer and, on the other hand, not ours to ask. If there is one lesson we have learned from the machinations of colonial feminism and the politics of "global sisterhood," it is that any social and political transformation is always a function of local, contingent, and emplaced struggles whose blueprint cannot be worked out or predicted in advance (Abu-Lughod 2002; Ahmed 1982; Lazreg 1994; Spivak 1987). And when such an agenda of reform is imposed from above or outside, it is typically a violent imposition whose results are likely to be far worse than anything it seeks to displace (see, for example, Collier 1997; Mani 1998; Massell 1974). As for how might we *theoretically* conceptualize resistance given the model of subjectivation undergirding the practices of the mosque movement, I will offer some thoughts in chapter 5 when I analyze the interrelationship between performativity, embodiment, and agency. Here, let it suffice to say that I think the issue of resistance to modes of domination cannot be asked outside of the embodied forms of attachment that a particular mode of subjectivation makes possible.

As to the question of whether my framework calls for the suspension of critique in regard to the patriarchal character of the mosque movement, my response is that I urge no such stance. But what I do urge is an expansion of a normative understanding of critique, one that is quite prevalent among many progressives and feminists (among whom I have often included myself). Criticism, in this view, is about successfully demolishing your opponent's position and exposing the implausibility of her argument and its logical inconsistencies. This, I would submit, is a very limited and weak understanding of the notion of critique. Critique, I believe, is most powerful when it leaves open the possibility that we might also be remade in the process of engaging another's worldview, that we might come to learn things that we did not already know before we undertook the engagement. This requires that we occasionally turn the critical gaze upon ourselves, to leave open the possibility that we may be remade through an encounter with the other.

It is in light of this expanded notion of critique that, during the course of my fieldwork, I was forced to question the repugnance[55] that often swelled up inside me against the practices of the mosque movement, especially those that seemed to circumscribe women's subordinate status within Egyptian society. This is a sentiment that I share with many secular progressives and liberals who feel a deep sense of discomfort when confronted with socially conservative movements of the kind I describe here—a sentiment that is continually brought home to me both in the sympathy I receive from audiences who marvel at my ability to withstand the asceticism of my informants' lives and in the anger my argumentative framework ignites for its failure to condemn my informants as "fundamentalists."[56]

My strategy in dealing with this repugnance has been to avoid the denunciatory mode that characterizes many accounts of the Islamist movement popular in the academy today. I find such a mode unhelpful in the task of understanding what makes these practices powerful and meaningful to the people who practice them. But more importantly, I have been fascinated and compelled by the repugnance the mosque movement provokes in feminist-progressive scholars like myself and by our inability to move beyond this visceral reaction. We might remind ourselves that the mosque movement (like the larger piety movement of which it is a part) is neither a fascist nor a militant movement, nor does it seek to gain control of the state and make Egypt a theocracy. As such, it is quite different from other politico-religious movements like the Hindutva movement in India, the Gush Emunim in Israel, the Jamāʿt al-Islāmi in Pakistan, or the international group al-Qāʿida. Yet the depth of discomfort the pietistic character of this movement evokes among liberals, radicals, and progressives alike is extraordinary.

I believe that one needs to unpack all that remains congealed under the admission that it is the "social conservatism" of movements like the piety move-

[55] This is a term I take from Elizabeth Povinelli's provocative discussion of how the discourse of multiculturalism is critically limited by what liberalism constructs as culturally "repugnant practices" (Povinelli 2002).

[56] Susan Harding observed over a decade ago that despite the increase in the study of "culturally marginal" groups within a range of academic disciplines, there is a marked absence of studies that focus on groups considered the "cultural and political Others" from the perspective of progressive-liberal scholars—such as the Protestant fundamentalist Harding writes about in the United States (Harding 1991). These "culturally repugnant" groups continue to be understood in oppositional terms—as antimodern, fundamentalist, backward, irrational, and so on—without any regard for how conditions of secular modernity have been crucial both to their production and their reception (see Harding 2000).

ment that makes liberals and progressives uncomfortable, and to examine the constitutive elements and sensibilities that comprise this discomfort. This task takes on a particular urgency since the events of September 11, 2001, wherein a rather heterogeneous collection of images and descriptions associated with "Islamic social conservatism" (key among them, women's subordinate status in Muslim societies) are made to stand in for all that liberals and leftists are supposed to find threatening to their entire edifice of beliefs, values, and political system (see Hirschkind and Mahmood 2002). In many ways, this book is an exploration of, to evoke Connolly again, the "visceral modes of appraisal" that produce such a reaction among many fellow liberal-left intellectuals and feminists, as much as it is an exploration of the sensibilities that animate such movements. The aim of this book, therefore, is more than ethnographic: its goal is to parochialize those assumptions—about the constitutive relationship between action and embodiment, resistance and agency, self and authority—that inform our judgments about nonliberal movements such as the women's mosque movement.

It is in the course of this encounter between the texture of my own repugnance and the textures of the lives of the women I worked with that the political and the ethical have converged for me again in a personal sense. In the course of conducting fieldwork and writing this book, I have come to recognize that a politically responsible scholarship entails not simply being faithful to the desires and aspirations of "my informants" and urging my audience to "understand and respect" the diversity of desires that characterizes our world today (cf. Mahmood 2001a). Nor is it enough to reveal the assumptions of my own or my fellow scholars' biases and (in)tolerances. As someone who has come to believe, along with a number of other feminists, that the political project of feminism is not predetermined but needs to be continually negotiated within specific contexts, the questions I have come to ask myself again and again are: What do we mean when we as feminists say that gender equality is the central principle of our analysis and politics? How does my enmeshment within the thick texture of my informants' lives affect my openness to this question? Are we willing to countenance the sometimes violent task of remaking sensibilities, life worlds, and attachments so that women of the kind I worked with may be taught to value the principle of "freedom"? Furthermore, does a commitment to the ideal of equality in our own lives endow us with the capacity to know that this ideal captures what is or should be fulfilling for everyone else? If it does not, as is surely the case, then I think we need to rethink, with far more humility than we are accustomed to, what feminist politics really means. (Here I want to be clear that my comments are not directed at "Western feminists" alone, but also include "Third World" feminists and all those who are located somewhere within this polarized terrain, since these questions implicate all of us given the liberatory impetus of the feminist tradition.)

The fact that I pose these questions does not mean I am advocating that we abandon our critical stance toward what we consider to be unjust practices in the situated context of our own lives, or that we uncritically embrace and promote the pious lifestyles of the women I worked with. To do so would be only to mirror the teleological certainty that characterizes some of the versions of progressive liberalism that I criticized earlier. Rather, my suggestion is that we leave open the possibility that our political and analytical certainties might be transformed in the process of exploring nonliberal movements of the kind I studied, that the lives of the women with whom I worked might have something to teach us beyond what we can learn from the circumscribed social-scientific exercise of "understanding and translation." In this sense, one can say that the tension between the prescriptive and analytical aspects of the feminist project can be left productively open—that it should not be prematurely foreclosed for the sake of "political clarity." As political theorist Wendy Brown reminds us, to "argue for a separation between intellectual and political life is not to detach the two. The point is to cultivate . . . an appreciation of the productive, even agonistic, interlocution made possible between intellectual life and political life when they maintain a dynamic distance and tension" (2001, 43).

If there is a normative political position that underlies this book, it is to urge that we—my readers and myself—embark upon an inquiry in which we do not assume that the political positions we uphold will necessarily be vindicated, or provide the ground for our theoretical analysis, but instead hold open the possibility that we may come to ask of politics a whole series of questions that seemed settled when we first embarked upon the inquiry.

2

Topography of the Piety Movement

Once a week, in the quiet heat of late afternoon, one can see a stream of women—either singly or in small groups—making their way up a narrow staircase tucked away on one side of the large Umar mosque complex.[1] The mosque is an imposing structure located at one of the busiest intersections of a bustling upper-middle-income neighborhood of Cairo, Muhandiseen. Competing for attention with the relatively somber presence of the mosque is a long avenue of glittering shop fronts, American fast-food restaurants, and large hand-painted billboards advertising the latest Egyptian films and plays. The Umar mosque offers a relief from the opulent and consumerist aura of this thoroughfare, not only in its architectural sobriety, but also in the welfare services it provides to a range of poor and lower-income Egyptians. The women making their way discreetly to the top floor of the mosque are here to attend a religious lesson (*dars*; plural: *durūs*) delivered weekly by a woman preacher/religious teacher (*dāʿiya*; plural: *dāʿiyāt*) by the name of Hajja Faiza.[2]

[1] All the names of the mosques, the preachers, and attendees have been changed to preserve confidentiality.

[2] The term *hajja* (rendered as *ḥājja* in Modern Standard Arabic and as *ḥāgga* in Egyptian colloquial Arabic) literally means "a woman who has performed the pilgrimage to Mecca (the *ḥajj*)," but it is also used in Egyptian colloquial Arabic to respectfully address an older woman. While not all the *dāʿiyāt* had performed the ḥajj, and some were quite young, they were all referred to as *ḥāgga* as a sign of respect. Throughout this book, Arabic honorific terms (such as *hajja*, *sayyid*, and *shaikh*), as with the proper names they precede, are neither italicized nor have diacritical marks. See my earlier note on transcription.

Hajja Faiza gives lessons in two other mosques, as well as in one of the private elite clubs of Cairo. She is well known in mosque circles, both for her scholarly erudition and for her dedication to providing lessons to women since the inception of the mosque movement approximately twenty-five years ago. Each week between fifty and one hundred women sit for two hours in an air-conditioned room listening to Hajja Faiza provide exegetical commentary in colloquial Arabic on selected passages from both the Quran and the *ḥadīth* (the authoritative record of the Prophet's exemplary speech and actions).[3] The attendees listen attentively in pin-drop silence, seated in rows of brown wooden chairs, as Hajja Faiza speaks in gentle and persistent tones from behind a desk on a raised platform.

Some of the attendees are housewives, others are students, and a large number are working women who stop on their way home from work to attend the weekly lessons. While the majority of women are between the ages of thirty and forty, there are attendees as young as twenty and as old as sixty. Some of these women drive to the mosque in private cars, others arrive on Cairo's overcrowded public transportation, and still others come in taxis. The women's attire is striking in its variety. Many come dressed in finely tailored ankle-length skirts and tucked-in blouses, with printed chiffon scarves wrapped tightly around their heads, conveying an air of modest sophistication. Others, including Hajja Faiza, wear well-tailored, dark-colored long coats (*balṭu*) with heavy thick scarves covering their hair and neck. Still others wear the *khimār* (plural: *akhmira*), a form of veil that covers the head and extends over the torso (similar to the cape worn by Catholic nuns), and that is very popular among mosque attendees. There are even bareheaded women dressed in jeans and short tops, with styled hair and face makeup, who attend Hajja Faiza's lessons—a sight almost impossible to find in other mosques. And yet, while a wide variety of attire is represented, it is rare to see a woman wearing the *niqāb*—a more conservative form of the veil that covers the head, face, and torso—at the Umar mosque; the absence of women wearing the niqāb is an indicator of the kind of audience that Hajja Faiza's lessons attract.[4]

In contrast to the Umar mosque is the Ayesha mosque, located in one of the largest and poorest neighborhoods on the outskirts of Cairo. Tucked between teetering cinder block residential buildings, in a narrow and darkened alleyway, the Ayesha mosque is surrounded by the sounds of roosters crowing,

[3] Note that *ḥadīth* when written with a definite article refers to the entire collection of the Prophet's actions and speech (*the* ḥadīth), of which six collections are considered to be the most authoritative. "A ḥadīth" refers to an individual account of the Prophet's actions and speech. See Robson 1999b.

[4] See chapter 3 on the spectrum of positions that the mosque participants take on the veil, and the doctrinal reasoning behind it.

children screaming, and vendors hawking their wares—offering a sharp contrast to the sobriety and order of the Umar complex. The Ayesha mosque is associated with the largest Islamic nonprofit organization in Egypt, al-Jamʿiyya al-Sharʿiyya, and provides extensive welfare services to the neighborhood's residents. Religious lessons are offered twice a week by two women dāʿiyāt, and once a week by the male *imam* (prayer leader) of the mosque. In contrast to the reserved decorum of the Umar mosque, an informal and unceremonious atmosphere characterizes the Ayesha mosque. For example, women attendees often interrupt the teacher to ask questions or to put forward alternative opinions they have heard elsewhere. There is constant banter back and forth between the dāʿiya and her audience. The dāʿiyāt here, as in the other mosques, also speak in Egyptian colloquial Arabic, but their speech is marked by street colloquialisms that are characteristic of their and their audience's working-class (*shaʿbi*) backgrounds.[5] Unlike the air-conditioned seclusion of the Umar mosque, the atmosphere of the Ayesha mosque is saturated with the sounds, smells, and textures of the neighborhood in which the mosque is located.

While the age spectrum of women attendees at the Ayesha mosque is similar to that found at the Umar mosque, their educational backgrounds are more limited: the majority have no more than a high school education, and a large number are illiterate. Women attendees sit on the thinly carpeted concrete floor, most of them dressed in crumpled ankle-length gowns (*galālīb*; singular: *gallābiyya*) and veils that cover their heads and torsos (akhmira). In contrast to the Umar mosque, where women wearing the full face and body veil (niqāb) are almost never present, here a full one-third of the attendees come so attired. A majority wear the customary printed headscarves, and others dress in what has come to be called the *baladi* dress, worn by the rural poor, comprised of a loose black gown and a thin black headscarf tightly wrapped around the head.

If the Umar and Ayesha mosques stand at two extremes of the Cairene socioeconomic spectrum, the Nafisa mosque, located in a prominent suburb of Cairo, represents a middle ground. This suburb is home to a large number of public and state employees, as well as to Egyptians who have returned from the Gulf States after working there during the oil boom years of the 1970s and 1980s.[6] The Nafisa mosque is reputed to be the first Cairene mosque to have

[5] Since both the Quran and the ḥadīth are written in a form of classical Arabic that is quite different from Modern Standard and colloquial Arabic, part of the dāʿiyāt's task is to render these texts into colloquial Egyptian Arabic that their audiences can easily follow.

[6] Some scholars have suggested that the ascendant social conservatism of Egyptian society is partly a result of the "Gulfi" form of Islam (sometimes called "petrodollar Islam") brought back by Egyptians who lost their jobs when the Gulf economies took a downturn in the 1970s and 1980s

started offering lessons to women, around 1980, and it currently commands the largest female audience of any mosque in Cairo. About five hundred women attend the weekly lesson; a majority of them are housewives, although a fair number are students from one of the largest Cairene universities, located nearby. The lessons are delivered by a group of three dāʿiyāt, all of whom were, at the time of my fieldwork, in the process of obtaining formal training in preaching skills from state-run institutes of *daʿwa* (a key term in the Islamic Revival that I explore below). Unlike the women in the other two mosques, all three dāʿiyāt, as well as most attendees (approximately 75 percent) wear the full face and body veil (niqāb). Women who wear the niqāb understand their practice to accord with a strict interpretation of Islamic edicts on female modesty, and often see themselves as more virtuous than women who wear the khimār (the veil that covers the head and torso) or the hijāb (headscarf). The sense of rigorous piety at the mosque embodied in the predominance of the niqāb is further accentuated by the fire-and-brimstone style in which the lessons are delivered, one that stands in sharp contrast to the gentle tones of Hajja Faiza at the Umar mosque and the more casual manner of the dāʿiyāt at the Ayesha mosque.[7]

This brief overview of three of the six mosques where I conducted my fieldwork illustrates the broad-based character of the women's mosque movement, evident in the variety of ages and socioeconomic backgrounds represented among the audience as well as in the range of rhetorical styles, modes of argumentation, and forms of sociability employed by the teachers. Despite differences among the mosque groups, though, the participants all shared a concern for what they described as the increasing secularization of Egyptian society, an important consequence of which is the erosion of a religious sensibility they considered crucial to the preservation of "the spirit of Islam" (*rūḥ al-islām*). In what follows, I will examine what the mosque participants meant when they talked about "secularization," what aspects of social behavior they considered most consequential to this process, and finally, what form of religiosity they sought to restore through their activities. I will situate my discussion within the context of the various currents that comprise the current Islamic Revival, and the relationship of these currents to the history of Egyptian religious activism in the last century. My aim in this chapter is not only to provide a brief sketch of the historical developments against which the contemporary

(Beinin and Stork 1997; Moensch 1988). For the most part, this view is based on an association drawn between the rate of returning workers and the rise of the Islamist movement in Egypt, but I do not know of any sociological or ethnographic study that has tracked or verified this claim.

[7] For a detailed analysis of the rhetorical styles employed by the dāʿiyāt at the three mosques, see chapter 3.

mosque movement has emerged, but also to critically engage with existing themes in the scholarship on Islamic modernism regarding such movements.

AIMS OF THE MOSQUE MOVEMENT

According to participants, the women's mosque movement emerged in response to the perception that religious knowledge, as a means for organizing daily life, had become increasingly marginalized under modern structures of secular governance. Many of the mosque participants criticized what they considered to be an increasingly prevalent form of religiosity in Egypt, one that accords Islam the status of an abstract system of beliefs that has no direct bearing on how one lives, on what one actually does in the course of a day. This trend, usually referred to by the movement's participants as "secularization" (*ʿalmana* or *ʿalmāniyya*) or "westernization" (*tagharrub*), is understood to have reduced Islamic knowledge (both as a mode of conduct and as a set of principles) to the status of "custom and folklore" (*ʿāda wa fulklūr*). While a handful of mosque participants used the terms "secularization" and "westernization" to refer to specific events in recent Egyptian history,[8] most employed the terms more loosely to describe a transformative force beyond their control that was corrosive of the sensibilities and habits of a certain kind of religious life.

Hajja Samira from the Nafisa mosque was one of the dāʿiyāt who spoke passionately and clearly about the kind of religious sensibility that the mosque participants felt was under threat. This is what she had to say during one of her lessons:

> Look around in our society and ask yourselves: who do we emulate? We emulate the Westerners [*gharbiyyin*], the secularists [*ʿalmāniyyin*], and the Christians: we smoke like they do, we eat like they do, our books and media are full of pictures that are obscene [*faḥḥāsh*]. When you enter the homes of Muslims, you are surprised: you can't tell whether it is the house of a Christian or a Muslim. We are Muslims in name, but our acts are not those of Muslims. Our sight, dress, drink, and food should also be for God and out of love for Him [*iḥna muslimīn wi lākin afʿālna mish ka muslimīn: il-ʿēn, wil-libs, wil-shurb, wil-akl lāzim yikun lillah wi fi ḥubb allāh*]. They will tell you that this way of life [the one she is recommending] is

[8] For example, some of the women I worked with used the terms "secularization" and "westernization" to refer to the adoption of the policy of *infitāḥ* (economic liberalization) by President Anwar Sadat in the 1970s, which they said marked a radical transformation in Egyptian social mores and lifestyles. The dāʿiya Hajja Nur, for instance, argued that with increased displays of wealth on the streets, rising inflation, and an influx of imported consumer goods and Western media, she found Egyptians becoming more ambitious, competitive, and selfish, with less regard for their family, friends, and the larger community—a shift she characterized as "secular."

uncivilized [*ghair mutaḥaḍḍir*]: don't listen to them because you know that real civilization [*ḥaḍāra*] for we Muslims is closeness to God.

These remarks may be interpreted as abiding by a discourse of cultural identity, one through which contemporary Egyptian Muslims seek to assert their religious distinctiveness, as expressed in styles of consumption, dress, and communication. I would like to propose an alternative reading, however, that draws upon a set of debates taking place in mosque circles that express concerns quite distinct from those of national or cultural identity. In this alternative reading, Hajja Samira's comments can be understood as critiquing a prevalent form of religiosity that treats Islam as a system of abstract values that is to be cherished but that, nonetheless, remains inessential to the practical organization of day-to-day life. In Hajja Samira's eyes, this is demonstrated by the fact that one cannot tell Muslims apart from either Christians or nonbelievers, since the way Muslims organize their daily affairs gives little indication of their religious commitments. The dāʿiyāt and the mosque attendees want to ameliorate this situation through the cultivation of those bodily aptitudes, virtues, habits, and desires that serve to ground Islamic principles within the practices of everyday living. The mosque lessons provide a training in the requisite strategies and skills to enable such a manner of conduct, and the lives of the most devoted participants are organized around gradually learning and perfecting these skills. As the end of the quote above suggests, Hajja Samira's position is articulated against those Egyptians who consider such quotidian attention to religious practice to be passé, or uncivilized (ghair mutaḥaḍḍir), a judgment Hajja Samira challenges through her appropriation of the term *ḥaḍāra* (a term that carries the same Western-centric biases as the English term "civilized") to describe Islamically devout behavior.

Hajja Samira's concern about the way popular religiosity has been transformed by the process of secularization was shared across mosque groups, despite their disparate class and social backgrounds. Consider, for example, a similar sentiment expressed by Hajja Faiza, from the upper-middle-class Umar mosque, in an interview with me:

Currently, religion seems to have become separated from the texts or scriptures [*nuṣūṣ*], especially in issues of *muʿāmalāt* [commercial and social transactions]. The challenge that we face as Muslims right now is how to understand and follow the example of the Prophet, how to act in accord with the Quran and the ḥadīth in our daily lives [*biyiʿmil bil-ḥadīth wil-qur'ān izzāy*]. All of us [Muslims] know the basics of religion [*al-dīn*], such as praying, fasting, and other acts of worship [*ʿibādāt*]. But the difficult question that confronts us today as Muslims is how to make our daily lives congruent with our religion while at the same time moving with the world [*muḥarrikīn maʿa id-dinya*], especially given that the present period

> is one of great change and transformation. For me, proselytization [*daʿwa*] means doing it from within ordinary acts and practicalities [*ʿamaliyyāt*], and translating worship [*ʿibāda*] into everyday practices so that these are always directed toward God [*fahm il-ʿibāda kullu yittagih ilallah*].

Note that the challenge Hajja Faiza regards as central to her work does not have to do with educating Muslims in the basic performance of religious duties (such as praying five times a day, fasting, and the like); as she says, most of the people she works with perform these duties regularly. She is concerned instead with those Muslims who, despite performing their religious duties, have lost the capacity to render *all* aspects of their lives—of which worship is simply one, albeit an important, part—into a means of realizing God's will. Hajja Faiza's emphasis on practice, therefore, addresses the problem of how to make moral precepts, doctrinal principles, and acts of worship relevant to the organization of everyday life. Her engagement with sacred texts is aimed at deducing a set of practical rules of conduct to guide others in resolving the mundane issues of daily life.

Like the other dāʿiyāt, Hajja Faiza recognizes that there are numerous aspects of contemporary life that are ruled *not* by the dictates of sacred texts (the Quran and the Sunna),[9] but by laws whose rationale is independent from, and at times inimical to, the demands of pious living. The distinction Hajja Faiza makes between acts of worship (ʿibādāt) and those actions pertaining to social transactions (muʿāmalāt)[10] has been part of the Islamic juridical tradition since at least the tenth century. In the modern period, although *sharīʿa* procedures (those moral discourses and legal procedures sometimes glossed as "Islamic law") were unevenly applied in Egypt, most acts in the category of muʿāmalāt came to be regulated by civil law, giving the distinction between worship and social transactions a new valence and institutional force. As was the case with most non-Western nations, Egypt adopted a European legal code (the French code) in the mid-nineteenth century, thereby restricting the application of Islamic law to matters pertaining to family law and pious endowments (Hill 1987).[11] For most of the dāʿiyāt, however, reinstatement of

[9] The Sunna describes the practices of the Prophet and his Companions. In Islamic jurisprudence, the Sunna is considered to be the second most important source for the derivation of Islamic laws after the Quran. For debates among Muslim reformers on this issue, see D. Brown 1999.

[10] The term *muʿāmalāt* may best be translated as "sections of the sharīʿa concerned with transactions, including bilateral contracts and unilateral dispositions" (Messick 1996, 313).

[11] Personal status law (or family law), a legal category that emerged with the adoption of the European legal code, has become a key site of struggle over the identity of the Muslim community in a variety of national contexts. For contentious debates about changes in Muslim family law in India, where Muslims are a significant minority, see Hasan 1994; for similar debates in Egypt, where Muslims are the majority, see Skovgaard-Petersen 1997.

the sharīʿa remains marginal to the realization of the movement's goals, and few lessons address the issue. Even though women like Hajja Faiza do not advocate the abolition or transformation of civil law as do some other Islamists,[12] this does not mean that the mosque movement endorses a privatized notion of religion that assumes a separation between worldly and religious affairs.[13] Indeed, the form of piety women like Hajja Faiza advocate brings religious obligations and rituals (ʿibādāt) to bear upon worldly issues in new ways, thereby according the old Islamic adage "all of life is worship" (*al-ḥayāh kullaha ʿibāda*) a new valence.

Secularism has often been understood in two primary ways: as the separation of religion from issues of the state, and as the increasing differentiation of society into discrete spheres (economic, legal, educational, familial, and so on) of which religion is one part (Berger 1973; Casanova 1994; Durkheim 1965; D. Martin 1978). Since participants in the mosque movement do not argue for the promulgation of the sharīʿa, they do not constitute a challenge to the former aspect of secularism as do some of the more militant and state-oriented Islamist activists.[14] The mosque movement's solution to the problem of Egypt becoming increasingly secularized does not directly confront the political order, even though the social transformations it seeks to bring about necessarily involve changing sociopolitical institutions and ethos. The piety activists seek to imbue each of the various spheres of contemporary life with a regulative sensibility that takes its cue from the Islamic theological corpus rather than from modern secular ethics. In this sense, the mosque movement's goal is to introduce a common set of shared norms or standards by which one

[12] For example, during the question-and-answer period, mothers often raised the issue of sexual intercourse outside the institution of marriage (*zinā'*), particularly premarital sex—an act that is considered to be a cardinal sin in Islam. In response, the dāʿiyāt acknowledged that the classical Islamic punishment for such an act (most commonly, a hundred lashes for each participant) was no longer possible and applicable in Egypt. Instead, it was required of parents that they inculcate a sense of modesty and knowledge of proper conduct in youth so as to prevent them from contemplating such an act. Thus the focus of the mosque lessons was precisely on those manners of thought, movements, and practices that needed to be policed in order to forestall the possibility of zinā', not on the punishment that the act required.

[13] I use the term "worldly" intentionally—instead of the term *muʿāmalāt* (social transactions)—to avoid the juridical connotations of the latter. By "worldly" acts I mean those behaviors that pertain to matters in life that are distinct from acts of worship.

[14] The debate about the promulgation of the sharīʿa peaked in Egypt after the passage of the new family law in 1985. In the mid- to late 1980s, distinct lines were drawn between the supporters of the sharīʿa and those opposed to it, the latter being a loose alliance of intellectuals and journalists who came to be called "the secularists" (*ʿalmāniyyin*). This debate cooled off substantially in the 1990s, and by the time I conducted my fieldwork (1995–97) the focus of the Islamist movement was more on preaching, welfare, and syndicalist activities. For a general discussion of this debate and the reasons for its decline, see Skovgaard-Petersen 1997, 205–208.

is to judge one's own conduct, whether in the context of employment, education, domestic life, or other social activities. The mosque participants' activities, therefore, pose more of a challenge to the second aspect of secularism, namely, the process by which religion is relegated to its own differentiated sphere, its influence curtailed to those aspects of modern life that are deemed either "private" or "moral."

For example, in the last three decades, supporters of the Islamist movement have established a number of "Islamic schools" in order to counter the secular character of modern Egyptian education.[15] Their efforts have been directed not so much at creating a new curriculum (which continues to be determined by the Egyptian government) as at introducing practices that create an Islamic awareness (*al-waʿi al-islāmi*) within existing institutions (see Herrera 2003). This includes emphasizing the study of religious materials that are already part of the curriculum, creating space and time for prayer during school hours, hiring religiously observant teachers, and so on. Insofar as this strategy makes Islamic ethics central to the process of acquiring different kinds of knowledges and skills, it infuses the current educational institutions with a sensibility that is potentially transformative.[16]

the folklorization of worship

An important aspect of the mosque movement's critique of the secularization of Egyptian society focuses upon how the understanding and performance of acts of worship (ʿibādāt) have been transformed in the modern period. Movement participants argue that ritual acts of worship in the popular imagination have increasingly acquired the status of customs or conventions, a kind of "Muslim folklore" undertaken as a form of entertainment or as a means to display a religio-cultural identity. According to them, this has led to the decline of an alternative understanding of worship, one in which rituals are performed as a means to the training and realization of piety in the entirety of one's life. Part of the aim of the mosque movement is to restore this understanding of worship by teaching women the requisite skills involved in its practice.

[15] Beginning in the colonial period, public education came to focus increasingly on secular subjects (such as geography, mathematics, and biology), replacing classical religious topics and supplanting methods of traditional schooling with the disciplinary practices of modern education (see T. Mitchell 1991, 63–127; Starrett 1998, 23–153). The teaching of Islam, however, was not eradicated from the curriculum but continued as one subject among others in public and private schools in Egypt.

[16] It was this transformative character of Islamic education that incited the Egyptian government to implement a number of measures aimed at the regulation of these schools (see Herrera 2003, 171–80). The Turkish state has reacted in a similar fashion, prohibiting students from entering Islamic schools before the age of fifteen (*New York Times* 1998).

Consider for example how Fatma, an active member of the mosque movement, articulated this widely shared view. Fatma was in her late twenties when I met her and, after the death of her father, was one of three breadwinners in a family of ten. Despite the long hours she worked, Fatma found time to attend mosque lessons regularly. She strongly believed that her involvement in the mosque movement had taught her what piety really entailed. In an interview with me, Fatma voiced her concerns about the folklorization of Islam:

> The state and society want to reduce Islam to folklore, as if Islam is just a collection of ceremonies and customs, such as hanging lanterns from doorways or baking cookies during Ramadan, or eating meat on *al-ʿīd al-kabīr* [feast that celebrates the end of Ramadan].[17] Mere ceremonies [*mujarrad al-manāsik*] without any bearing on the rest of life.

Noting the look of puzzlement on my face, Fatma asked, "Have you spent the month of Ramadan in Cairo?" I nodded yes. Fatma continued:

> So you know what happens during Ramadan in Cairo.[18] You must have heard the popular saying in colloquial Arabic that the first third of Ramadan is cookies, the second third is expenses [on food and clothing], and the last third is [visitation of] relatives.[19] Where is worship in this saying [*qaul*]? You find special programs that the state television puts on every evening, showing all kinds of things that are prohibited [*ḥarām*] in Islam. The entire society seems to be focused on preparing food all day long and festivities in the evenings, all of which are contrary [*bititnāqiḍ*] to the real meaning and spirit of Ramadan. If it were not for the mosque lessons [durūs] I began to attend two years ago, I would also have continued to think, like others, that Ramadan was about abstaining from food during the day, and in the evenings eating a lot and going out to the market or al-

[17] Ramadan is the ninth month of the Muslim calendar during which Muslims are required to fast, abstaining from food and drink from sunrise to sunset.

[18] While Ramadan is observed in all parts of the Muslim world, Egypt's celebration of it is distinctive for the festivities that start at sundown and continue well into the early hours of the morning during the entire month. Working hours are limited, and most Egyptian families celebrate by cooking special foods and spending evenings outdoors. Television and the entertainment industry put on special shows, and markets are full of consumer items (prepared foods, household goods, etc.). It is to these aspects of Egyptian Ramadan that Fatma refers.

[19] In contrast to this popular saying was one that I had come to hear in the mosques, but which few Egyptians outside the mosque circles seemed to know: "The first third of Ramadan is kindness of God [*raḥmat allāh*], the second third is His forgiveness [*maghfiratihi*], and the last third is refuge from hell's fire [*ʿitq al-nār*]." This saying is indicative of the special status accorded to Ramadan in Islamic doctrine in that increased frequency of worship during the month is supposed to lead to greater rewards from God.

> Hussein [the area around the tomb of Hussein where Egyptians gather in large numbers in the late evening during Ramadan].

When I questioned Fatma further about what she meant by "the real meaning and spirit of Ramadan," she explained to me that this entailed a range of behaviors that a Muslim must undertake when fasting, behaviors that conveyed the fuller meaning of the fast, such as abstaining from anger and lying, avoiding looking at things that stir one's appetite (sexual or culinary), and being extra diligent in one's prayers. It was not that baking cookies or decorating one's house during Ramadan was wrong, she said: in fact, celebrating Ramadan is considered a "good deed" (*al-ʿamal al-ṣāliḥ*) because it follows the example of the Prophet and his Companions. What gets lost in these popular festivities, she argued, is the understanding that the act of fasting is a necessary means to a virtuous life (what she called "the realization of piety"—*taḥqīq al-taqwa*). "Fasting is not simply abstaining from food," she explained to me, "but it is a condition through which a Muslim comes to train herself in the virtues [*faḍā'il*] of patience [*ṣabr*], trust in God [*tawakkul*], asceticism from worldly pleasures [*zuhd*], etc." In Fatma's view, therefore, an act of fasting that does not enable one to acquire these virtues transforms fasting from a religious act to a folkloric custom.

Fatma's concerns were echoed widely in mosque circles. Hajja Nur was a dāʿiya who had taught at the Nafisa mosque for several years but now gave lessons at another mosque to a small number of women. In her characteristically lucid style of argument, she reiterated Fatma's critique of the way Islamic obligations are currently practiced in Egypt, using a different example:

> It is the project of the government and the secularists [ʿalmāniyīn] to transform religion [al-dīn] into conventions or customs [*ʿāda*]. People may not even know that they are doing this, but in fact what they do in actual behavior [*taṣarrufātuhum al-ḥaqīqiyya*] is to turn religion into no more than a folkloric custom! An example of this is the use of the veil [ḥijāb][20] as a custom [ʿāda] rather than as a religious duty [*farḍ*]. When you [here she addressed me directly] as a foreigner look at Egyptian society right now and see all these women wearing the ḥijāb you must remember that a lot of them wear it as a custom, rather than a religious duty that also entails other responsibilities. These people are in fact no different than those who argue *against* the ḥijāb and who say that the ḥijāb is [an expression of] culture [and therefore a matter of personal choice], rather than a religious command. So what we have to do is to educate Muslim women that it is not enough to wear the veil, but that the veil must also lead us to behave in a

[20] Note that even though the term *ḥijāb* refers to the headscarf (which is distinct from other forms of the veil such as the khimār or the niqāb), it is also used as a general term for the veil in Egyptian colloquial and Modern Standard Arabic.

truly modest manner in our daily lives, a challenge that far exceeds the simple act of donning the veil.

Undergirding Fatma's and Hajja Nur's critique is a conception of religiosity that discriminates between a religious practice that is part of the larger project of realizing Islamic virtues in the entirety of one's life, and a practice that is Islamic in form and style but does not necessarily serve as a means to the training and realization of a pious self. Fatma and Hajja Nur are critical of the process by which practices that are supposed to be part of a larger program for shaping ethical capacities lose this function and become little more than markers of identity: such as when people fast because they have learned that this is simply what Muslims do. In summary, Fatma and Hajja Nur's remarks imply a critique of those forms of Islamic practice whose raison d'être is to signal an identity or tradition and which are, therefore, shorn of their ability to contribute to the formation of an ethical disposition.

Notably, Hajja Nur's statement above suggests that the attitude of those women who wear the veil out of habit is not dissimilar from those who regard the veil as a local custom (similar to regional styles of clothing, eating habits, and so on). In making this observation, she is referring to a widely known argument put forward by Egyptian intellectuals that veiling is not so much a divine injunction as it is a continuation of regional customs, practiced by women in Arabia at the advent of Islam, that has mistakenly become enshrined as a religious edict.[21] Hajja Nur faults both of these attitudes (the one that regards veiling to be a regional custom, and the other that unthinkingly reproduces the tradition of veiling) for ignoring how the practice of veiling is an integral part of an entire manner of existence through which one learns to cultivate the virtue of modesty in all aspects of one's life. In making her argument, she uses a key distinction, often invoked by the mosque participants, between customary and religious acts, a distinction that women like Hajja Nur think is elided when religion is understood as yet another kind of cultural practice.

Hajja Nur's remarks about the veil can be usefully compared to the views of a key Islamist public figure, Adil Hussein, who served as the general secretary of the Islamist Labor Party (Ḥizb al-ᶜAmal) until his death a few years ago. The following is an excerpt from an interview with him in a documentary on the Islamic Revival (produced by the American Public Broadcasting System, PBS), where he explains why he thinks the veil is important:

> In this period of [Islamic] Revival and renewed pride in ourselves and our past, why should we not take pride in the symbols that distinguish us from others [like

[21] See, for example, Harb 1984, 172–98; Muhammed 1996. For a comparable point of view, also see Leila Ahmed's discussion of the origins of the veil (1992, 11–63).

> the veil]? So we say that the first condition is that clothing should be modest. But why can't we add a second condition that we would like this dress to be a continuation of what we have created in this region, like the Indian sari? . . . Why can't we have our own dress which expresses decency, a requirement of Islam, as well as the special beauty that would be the mark of our society which has excelled in the arts and civilization? (York 1992)

While Adil Hussein, like the dāʿiyāt, recognizes that the veil is an expression of the principle of female modesty, there are clear differences between their two views. Hussein regards the veil as a symbol of, among other things, an Islamic identity, culture, and civilization—not unlike the sari worn by South Asian women. For people like Adil Hussein, the increased popularity of the veil is a sign of the vitality of the Islamic Revival (al-Ṣaḥwa al-Islāmiyya), which in turn is interpreted as the Muslim world's awakening to its true identity and cultural heritage. While women like Hajja Nur and Fatma do not entirely disagree with this view, they do, in contrast, regard the phenomenon of veiling as an *insufficient*, though necessary, part of making the society more religiously devout. As Hajja Nur's remarks reveal, the critical issue for her is whether the proliferation of what *appear* to be Islamic practices (in form and style) *actually* enable the cultivation of Islamic virtues in the entirety of a Muslim's life.

The remarks of Adil Hussein and Hajja Nur about the veil register a difference that indexes a key line of fracture between the piety movement (of which the mosque movement is an integral part) and Islamist political organizations. Islamist political figures and publications often criticize mosque participants for promoting a form of religiosity that is devoid of any sociopolitical consequences, especially for the task of restructuring the state. Heba Saad Eddin[22] was a prominent member of the Labor Party, along with Adil Hussein, when I conducted my fieldwork. In the PBS documentary from which I quote above, Saad Eddin is asked how she, as a prominent Islamist activist who is veiled herself, views the popular resurgence of the veil in Egypt. She responds skeptically by saying:

> In many cases religion is used as a kind of escape where the focus of the individual is to pray and read the Quran. But if we mean by [the Islamic] Revival more involvement in social change, I believe then that the [resurgence of the] veil should be understood as religiosity [*al-tadayyun*], but not Revival. It does not necessarily reflect a bigger participation in social life for the sake of social change toward Islam. (York 1992)

[22] Heba Saad Eddin also goes by the name Heba Raouf Ezzat. She has published under both names.

Saad Eddin's position on the veil accords with her larger criticism of the activities that mosques have increasingly undertaken in recent years in Egypt. In one of her weekly columns, "Ṣaut al-Nisā'" ("Women's Voice"), which she used to write for the Labor Party newspaper *al-Shaʿb*,[23] Saad Eddin criticizes Egyptian mosques for having become a space primarily for the performance of prayers and Islamic rituals, rather than a platform for the call to "truth, justice, and freedom," that is, a place where people come to learn "how to analyze their social situation and how to struggle to defend their freedom" (Saad Eddin 1997).[24] In other words, for Islamists like Saad Eddin and Hussein, religious rituals should be aimed toward the larger goal of creating a certain kind of polity, and the mosque movement fails precisely to make this linkage, keeping matters of worship and piety incarcerated within what for them is a privatized world of worship.

the "objectification" of religion?

A number of scholars of the modern Muslim world have noted that, as a result of widespread literacy and mass media, ordinary Muslims have become increasingly familiar with doctrinal concepts and forms of religious reasoning that had previously been the domain of religious scholars alone (Eickelman and Piscatori 1996; Skovgaard-Petersen 1997; Zeghal 1996). In making this observation, these scholars echo an argument made most forcefully by Wilfred Cantwell Smith when he proposed that "religion" in the modern period has come to be understood as a self-enclosed system whose proper practice often entails, even on the part of lay practitioners, some form of familiarity with the doctrinal assumptions and theological reasoning involved in religious rites and rituals (1962). This observation has prompted some scholars of the Middle East to conclude that the proliferation of religious knowledge among ordinary Muslims has resulted in an "objectification of the religious imagination," in that practices that were observed somewhat unreflectively in the premodern period are now the focus of conscious deliberation and debate (Eickelman 1992; Eickelman and Piscatori 1996; Salvatore 1998). Contemporary Muslims' reflections upon the religious character of ritual practices are, therefore, seen as evidence of a "modern objectified religiosity."[25]

[23] Heba Saad Eddin was a regular contributor to *al-Shaʿb* until she ended her affiliation with the Labor Party in 2000. She currently writes for the Islamist website www.islamonline.net.

[24] The Egyptian government banned *al-Shaʿb* in May 2000 for jeopardizing state security interests by publicly criticizing state policies and officials.

[25] For Eickelman and Piscatori (1996), objectification involves three processes: first, "discourse and debate about Muslim tradition involves people on a mass scale" (39); second, there is a tendency to see religious belief and practice "as a system to be distinguished from nonreligious ones"

At first glance it would seem that the debate about the veil is an illustration of this objectifying attitude toward religion, especially in the profusion of discourse on a practice that many would have performed unreflectively in the past.[26] Indeed, Hajja Nur's remarks seem particularly relevant to the observations made by these scholars: she assigns conscious deliberation a privileged role within the performance of religious duties, especially when she criticizes those who adopt the veil unreflectively (out of habit or custom) for failing to apprehend its true *religious* significance. While I generally agree with these scholars that modern conditions of increased literacy, urban mobility, and mass media have undoubtedly made ordinary Muslims more familiar with doctrinal reasoning than was previously the case, I would like to question the claim that this set of changes is best analyzed in terms of a universal tendency toward the "objectification of the religious imagination." There are several reasons for my disagreement.

To begin with, one must note that any kind of skilled practice requires a certain amount of reflection and deliberation on the specific mental and bodily exercises necessary for its acquisition. Insomuch as the capacity to perform a task well requires one to be able to stand back and judge the correctness and virtuosity of one's performance, a certain amount of self-reflection is internal to such labor. For example, in order for a child to learn to pray, the parent must make her conscious of her gestures, glances, and thoughts. When the child undertakes the act hurriedly, or forgets to perform it, her parents may present her with various kinds of explanations for why praying is important, what it signifies, and how it is different from the child's other activities. Such a pedagogical process depends upon inducing self-reflection in the child about her movements and thoughts—and their relationship to an object called God—all of which require some form of reflection about the nature of the practice. In other words, conscious deliberation is part and parcel of any pedagogical process, and contemporary discussions about it cannot be understood simply as a shift from the unconscious enactment of tradition to a critical reflection upon tradition, as the aforementioned authors suggest.

---

(42); and third, a reconfiguration of the "symbolic production of Muslim politics" occurs as a result of the first two processes (43). What is lacking in these authors' writings is an analysis of how the three processes are articulated to produce the effect of objectification.

[26] In regard to the veil, the issue seems to be even more complicated given its embattled history during the colonial period. As Leila Ahmed points out in her seminal study of the discourse on the veil in the colonial and early nationalist periods in Egypt, the practice of veiling acquired a new valence for Egyptians as the British made it a key signifier of "Muslim backwardness" and the Egyptian elite mobilized for its banishment (1992, 127–68). One might argue that the fact that the veil was assigned such a key place in the colonial discourse better explains its salience within contemporary Egyptian politics than does a general theory of the objectification of devotional practices.

At the same time, it should also be acknowledged that practices of self-reflection have varied historically, depending upon shifts in notions of the self and pedagogical conditions of mass publicity and literacy. What is needed to understand changes in notions of reflexivity is an inquiry into the creation of historically specific forms of subjectivity that require, and in some sense make possible, particular modes of self-reflection (see pp. 146–48). Furthermore, in order to grasp what is historically unique about modern forms of reflection in relation to Islamic practices, it is necessary to explore both the discursive conditions under which *specific* kinds of deliberations become possible, and the practical task that an act of reflection is meant to accomplish. For example, it is worth recalling that the distinction Hajja Nur draws between customs/habits and religious obligations has been made by theologians at least as far back as the thirteenth century, and is not just a modern invention.[27] What has changed between a classical invocation and a contemporary one are the *practical* conditions under which the distinction between customary and religious acts is made, the new modes of reflection under which this distinction is taught and learned, and the relations of social hierarchy and institutional power that attend each historical context. Theological and doctrinal issues that were once the provenance of male religious scholars are now debated by ordinary women in the context of mosque lessons modeled to some extent on protocols of public address and modern education (rather than on the traditional Islamic schools, *kuttāb*),[28] where they openly discuss how to render even the most intimate details of their lives in accord with standards of Islamic piety. Similarly, working women and students now bring questions of virtuous practice to bear upon new problems, such as how to conduct oneself modestly on public transportation, and in schools and offices where pious protocols of sex segregation are not observed (for an analysis of these issues, see chapters 3 and 5). We must pay attention to this level of micropractices in order to understand what is unique about the contemporary focus on Islamic arguments and practices, rather than assuming that they are

[27] For example, the preeminent theologian al-Nawawi (d. 1248) wrote, "It is intention [*al-niyya*] that distinguishes between custom [ʿāda] and worship [ʿibāda] or distinguishes between levels of [different acts of] worship. First example, sitting in a mosque for [the purpose of] relaxation constitutes a custom, and when undertaken for *iʿtikāf* [a period of residence in a mosque dedicated to worship marked by minimal interaction with people], it is considered an act of worship, and it is intention that makes it so. And so with bathing: bathing when undertaken for cleanliness is custom, and it is intention that makes it an act of worship" (1990, 18). All translations from Arabic are mine, unless otherwise noted.

[28] *Kuttāb* were traditional Islamic schools, usually associated with the mosque, which came to be slowly replaced by the modern system of schools, colleges, and universities from the late nineteenth century onward in Egypt. For a general discussion of the transformations in the disciplinary practices of education in modern Egypt, see T. Mitchell 1991; Starrett 1998.

instances of a universal modern process wherein previously habitual actions become objects of conscious reflection.[29]

Moreover, one must also learn to distinguish how particular reflections upon a religious practice are geared toward different kinds of ends. In the cases of Adil Hussein, Heba Saad Eddin, and Hajja Nur, even though all three support the adoption of the veil, their remarks are situated within very different visions of a virtuous society. For Adil Hussein, the veil stands in a relation of significance to the expression of one's cultural and nationalist heritage, whereas for women like Fatma and Hajja Nur it is understood to be part of an entire process through which a pious individual is produced. In the eyes of someone like Hajja Nur, one may argue, the meaning of the veil is not exhausted by its significance as a sign (of a civilization, culture, or identity), but encompasses an entire way of being and acting that is learned through the practice of veiling. Similarly, the goals that Heba Saad Eddin wants the practice of veiling to achieve ("truth, justice, and freedom") stand in contrast to those sought by Hajja Nur and Fatma, and even to some extent those of Adil Hussein, with whom she shared a political project. Thus, each of these views needs to be analyzed in terms of the larger goals toward which it is teleologically oriented, the different *practical* contexts in which each type of reflection is located, and the consequences each particular form of understanding has for how one lives practically, both in relationship to oneself and to others.[30]

The practices of the women's mosque movement have not emerged as a result of an abstract tendency toward objectification, but are provoked by a specific problem, namely, the concern for learning to organize one's daily life according to Islamic standards of virtuous conduct in a world increasingly ordered by a logic of secular rationality that is inimical to the sustenance of these virtues. As I observed earlier, the women I worked with argue that they have had to create new structures of learning—in the form of mosque lessons—to inculcate values that were previously part of a social and familial ethos in Egypt, but which are no longer available in those arenas. The devel-

[29] The modern history of Islamic sermons may be used to demonstrate the same point. As Charles Hirschkind notes, the practice of the Friday sermon (*khuṭba*), a key communal event in Muslim societies since the time of Muhammed, only started to receive elaborate doctrinal attention in the last century with the development of a national public sphere and the concomitant rise in the importance of the practice of public speech making (2004). This should not therefore lead us to conclude that khuṭba required little or no self-reflection on the part of the preachers and listeners prior to the modern period. Rather, what this draws our attention to is the particular mode of reflection entailed in the delivery and audition of khuṭba in the modern period, one uniquely tied to the formation of a mass-mediatized reading public that the advent of modernity heralded in Muslim societies.

[30] I will return to many of these points in chapter 4, under a discussion of the different economies of self-formation and bodily discipline.

opment of the women's mosque movement should, therefore, be understood as an organized attempt to address what has come to be conceived as a practical need, one grounded in recent historical and social circumstances. The key concept that has been most useful for the development of institutional practices conducive to virtuous conduct is *daʿwa*, a concept around which the women's mosque movement is organized. It is to the analysis of this concept that I now turn.

THE MOSQUE MOVEMENT IN A HISTORICAL CONTEXT

Few Islamic concepts capture the sensibility of modern socioreligious activism and the spirit of doctrinal innovation better than the concept of daʿwa. *Daʿwa* is the umbrella term under which the mosque movement, and the Islamist movement more generally, have organized many of their disparate activities. Daʿwa literally means "call, invitation, appeal, or summons." It is a Quranic concept associated primarily with God's call to the prophets and to humanity to believe in the "true religion," Islam.[31] Daʿwa did not receive much doctrinal attention in classical Sunni Islamic scholarship, and it was only in the late nineteenth and early twentieth centuries that it was given extensive elaboration.[32] The term *dāʿiya* literally means "one who practices daʿwa"—it is also the label used for the teachers in the women's mosque movement.[33]

While daʿwa may also be directed toward non-Muslims, the contemporary piety movement in Egypt primarily understands it to be a religious duty that requires all adult members of the Islamic community to urge fellow Muslims to greater piety, and to teach one another correct Islamic conduct. While the practice of daʿwa commonly takes the form of verbal admonishment, in Egypt

[31] See Canard 1999.

[32] Mendel has shown that during the early years of the Caliphate, *daʿwa* was used interchangeably with other terms, such as *sharīʿa* (Islamic Law), *dīn* (religion), *Sunna* (the tradition of the Prophet and his Companions), and sometimes even *jihād* (which means both "holy war" and "effort directed at a specified goal") (Mendel 1995, 289). In the Shiʿi tradition of Islam, however, the term *daʿwa* has a different history: it refers to a widespread Ismaili movement in the tenth century that later resulted in the establishment of the Fatimid dynasty in North Africa. See Kaabi 1972; Walker 1993. Since Egypt is primarily a Sunni country, my references are limited to the Sunni interpretation of daʿwa.

[33] Even though Arabic makes a distinction between male and female forms of the active participle, the word used in Egyptian colloquial and Modern Standard Arabic for someone who conducts daʿwa does not make this distinction: someone undertaking daʿwa—whether a man or a woman—is referred to as *dāʿiya*, the feminine form. The distinction is made in the plural: male practitioners of daʿwa are called *duʿāt*, and women *dāʿiyāt*. Gender distinction in the nominative singular is gradually emerging, however, as more women dāʿiyāt become active, and the Islamic press increasingly uses the term *dāʿi* to refer to men.

today it encompasses a range of practical activities that were once considered outside the proper domain of the classical meaning of the term. These activities include establishing neighborhood mosques, social welfare organizations, Islamic educational institutions, and printing presses, as well as urging fellow Muslims toward greater religious responsibility, either through preaching or personal conversation. While many of these institutionalized practices have historical precedents, they have, in the last fifty years, increasingly come to be organized under the rubric of daʿwa.[34] In many ways the figure of the dāʿiya exemplifies the ethos of the contemporary Islamic Revival, and people now often ascribe to this figure the same degree of authority previously reserved for religious scholars (Gaffney 1991; Haddad, Voll, and Esposito, 1991; Zeghal 1996).

Despite the fact that *daʿwa* has become a reigning organizational term for a range of activities, few historical works explore its semantic and institutional development.[35] This lacuna is all the more striking given the attention paid to other terms used by the Islamist movement, such as *al-jihād* or *al-daula*.[36] Where we do find some discussion of the notion of daʿwa is in relation to a sister concept, one whose semantic determination is tightly intertwined with that of daʿwa. This is the principle of *amr bil maʿrūf wal-nahi ʿan al-munkar* ("to enjoin others in the doing of good or right, and the forbidding of evil or wrong"), around which many of the daʿwa activities, especially those of religious exhortation and preaching, have been elaborated.[37] In fact, one could

[34] The Islamic Revival has been characterized by a proliferation of these activities. For example, there has been at least a 330 percent increase in the number of mosques built overall in Egypt between 1975 and 1995 (al-Ahram Center for Political and Strategic Studies 1996; Zeghal 1996). Similarly, the number of Islamic nongovernmental organizations grew by 17 percent in the 1960s, 31 percent in the 1970s, and 33 percent in the 1980s (al-Ahram Center for Political and Strategic Studies 1996, 236).

[35] For an exception to this rule, see the articles by Roest Crollius 1978; Hirschkind 2001a; Mendel 1995. While Roest Crollius and Mendel provide a historical background for the development of the Sunni concept of daʿwa in the Middle East, Hirschkind analyzes the effects of the contemporary practice of daʿwa on popular modes of sociability and public debate in Egypt. Also see the important work of Barbara Metcalf (1993, 1994, 1998) on the South Asian Tablīghi Jamāʿat, which is also organized around the concept of daʿwa, but more focused on the question of spiritual renewal than social welfare, which seems to be the hallmark of the Egyptian daʿwa movement.

[36] On the concept of *al-jihād*, see Kepel 2002; Peters 1996. For discussions of the concept of *al-daula*, see T. Asad 1980; Ayalon 1987; Zubaida 1993.

[37] The key words involved in this principle are *maʿrūf* and *munkar*: the former means "what is known and accepted according to acknowledged norms," whereas the latter means "what is disavowed or rejected" and therefore unacceptable. Notably, the former is considered to be consubstantial with what is mandated by God and the latter with iniquity. For the historical roots of the terms *maʿrūf* and *munkar*, both in pre-Islamic Jahili poetry and the Quran, see Izutsu 1966, 213–17.

argue that the modern doctrinal justification for daʿwa has been established primarily through the considerable moral scholarship conducted on the principle of amr bil maʿrūf. Since the principle of amr bil maʿrūf occurs in a number of places in the Quran that are concerned with the maintenance of public morality, Muslim reformers have paid close attention to its treatment within classical exegetical writings, especially in their attempts to rectify what they regard to be erroneous accretions to Islamic practices.[38]

Michael Cook, in his exhaustive survey of the Islamic scholarship on amr bil maʿrūf, notes that the interpretation of this principle has historically varied from school to school and scholar to scholar (Cook 2000). Cook's book is a remarkable synthesis of the diversity of opinions that have existed on the subject since early Islam. While I will draw upon his work, my concern here is more limited. I want to highlight those features of amr bil maʿrūf that undergird the daʿwa practices of the mosque movement, with particular attention to the shifts in the meaning of both these concepts that the modern Islamist movement has secured over the last century. My goal is to provide a brief genealogy of the figure of the dāʿiya, as she/he has come to lead the Islamic Revival, by drawing upon some of the contemporary popular uses of the term *daʿwa*—primarily within the mosque movement but also generally within the piety movement—and the particular interpretation this term has been given in the Egyptian Islamist literature.[39]

In contemporary Egypt, the activities denoted by the principle of amr bil maʿrūf can vary substantially, ranging from delivering a sermon or a mosque lesson to expressing a concern for the maintenance of pious comportment (for example, when a woman in a mosque, or on a bus, tells another woman that she should veil or pray) to addressing more general issues of moral and social conduct (as when someone tells a mother not to neglect her child while absorbed in a conversation with a friend). While many of these practices also fall under the rubric of daʿwa, there are activities—such as helping to build a mosque, or establishing an Islamic printing press—that are, strictly speaking, referred to through the concept of daʿwa more often than through the principle of amr bil maʿrūf. Given the overlapping contexts in which the two notions are used, I would summarize their interrelationship as manifesting itself

[38] The principle of *amr bil maʿrūf wal-nahi ʿan al-munkar* occurs in a number of places in the Quran. The most cited verses include verses 104 and 110 in Sūrat al-ʿImran, and verse 71 in Sūrat al-Tauba. The verse in Sūrat al-Tauba addresses women and men equally, and women dāʿiyāt frequently quote it to justify their involvement in the field of daʿwa. This verse reads: "And [as for] the believers, both men and women—they are close unto one another: they [all] enjoin the doing of what is right and forbid the doing of what is wrong, and are constant in prayer. . . ." All translations of Quranic verses are from M. Asad 1980.

[39] See, for example, Amin n.d.; al-Qaradawi 1991, 1993; Sultan 1996. On women's daʿwa, see al-Waʿi 1993.

in three different ways. Sometimes the terms are used synonymously, as in the case of someone offering verbal advice or admonishment. At other times, daʿwa is commonly understood as a kind of vocation (like that of a preacher, or a mosque teacher), while amr bil maʿrūf is regarded as a duty that a Muslim undertakes in the context of normal life. Finally, while both can be understood as involving enjoinders to piety, the notion of enjoining as it is used in amr bil maʿrūf extends beyond acts of encouragement to the use of force in prohibiting undesirable conduct (as suggested by the second part of the injunction, "the forbidding of evil and wrong").[40] Some have understood this to mean that the use of violence is justified in order to bring about moral good, as was the case when members of the militant group Takfīr wa Hijra killed President Anwar Sadat in 1981 for his alleged immoral conduct as a Muslim ruler.[41] Thus, we find that amr bil maʿrūf is more likely to be used to legitimate the use of physical force than is daʿwa; the latter remains primarily an instrument of moral exhortation and reform.

A contentious issue involved in the interpretation of amr bil maʿrūf turns on who is qualified to act as an agent of moral reform on the basis of this moral principle, especially in light of the tutelary role the state assigns to itself in relation to society and its exclusive claim on the use of violent force. Increasingly, as Islamic militants have used the principle of amr bil maʿrūf to justify their actions, the Egyptian state has mobilized its own network of religious scholars to argue, first, that it is the state that is primarily responsible for its correct implementation, and second, that it is best to forego this religious duty if it results in social discord or chaos.[42] The state has, in other words, sought to establish itself as the sole and legitimate undertaker of amr bil maʿrūf. The state's claim is widely rejected not only by the militants, but also by a number of those Muslim reformers who are strongly opposed to the use of violence as

[40] The particular logic of this interpretation draws upon a famous ḥadīth that says, "Whosoever among you sees a munkar must correct it by the hand, and if not able to, then by the tongue, and if unable to do [even] that, then by the heart, and this is the weakest [manifestation] of faith."

[41] A popular ḥadīth cited in support of the use of militant force against immoral rulers is: "The most excellent type of jihād [striving in the way of Allah] is speaking a true word in the presence of a tyrant ruler" (al-Nawawi n.d., 200). For an example of the use of this ḥadīth to urge militant action, see the pamphlet written by the famous Egyptian preacher Shaikh Umar Abd al-Rahman (now jailed in the United States for his alleged role in the 1991 bombing of the World Trade Center) (al-Rahman 1989). Those who oppose this interpretation use an alternative ḥadīth according to which Muhammed reportedly said that as long as rulers are effective in establishing the practice of worship or *ṣalāt* (one of the minimal conditions by which one qualifies as a Muslim) in the Muslim community (*umma*), people should not rebel against those rulers (al-Nawawi n.d., 196).

[42] See, for example, the widely circulated booklet put out by the Ministry of Religious Affairs (Daif 1995) in response to commentaries written by militant Islamists, such as Shaikh Umar Abd al-Rahman.

a means of bringing about moral transformation (Cook 2000, 526–28). These reformers include key intellectual figures of the contemporary Islamic Revival, such as Muhammed Umara (1989), Yusuf al-Qaradawi (1981), and Fahmi Huweidi (1993).[43]

historical imbrications

According to Roest Crollius, the first notable argument in the modern period that links daʿwa to amr bil maʿrūf probably occurs in the work of Rahid Rida (1865–1930), in his commentary on the Quranic verses pertaining to amr bil maʿrūf (Roest Crollius 1978).[44] This commentary is considered to be the combined work of Rida and his mentor Muhammed Abduh (1849–1905), both of whom participated in founding the Salafi movement widely regarded as the intellectual forebear of the contemporary Islamist movement.[45] Two elements of Rida's discussion are noteworthy for introducing a new perspective on classical discussions of daʿwa and amr bil maʿrūf wal-nahi ʿan al-munkar. The first is the emphasis he places on modern forms of knowledge and organizational practice—an emphasis that was absent in the work of earlier commentators (also see Cook 2000, 510).[46] Rida insists that, in addition to traditional knowledges, a familiarity with subjects such as history, sociology, psychology, and political science is necessary for the modern undertaking of daʿwa—even though these subjects did not exist in early Islamic history (Rida 1970, 39–45). The second noteworthy aspect of Rida's interpretation is his unequivocal

[43] The use of violence as a legitimate means to amr bil maʿrūf was also rejected by Ibn Taymiyya (d. 1328) and Hasan al-Banna (d. 1949), two key intellectual figures of the Islamist movement who are revered by the militants as well as the reformers. Both Ibn Taymiyya and al-Banna advocated that the practice of amr bil maʿrūf required civility (*rifq*) and gentle admonition (*al-mauʿiẓa al-ḥasana*) rather than militant force (Cook 2000, 153, 523).

[44] Rashid Rida compiled the lectures delivered by the then rector of al-Azhar, Muhammed Abduh, between 1899 and 1905, added his own commentary to the lectures, and published them in the journal *al-Manār*, which he edited from 1889 until his death (Rida 1970).

[45] The Salafi movement emerged at the end of the nineteenth century and the beginning of the twentieth in the context of European intellectual and political dominance in the Muslim world. The Salafis articulated a strong critique both of the secularizing trend among Muslim elites, and what they perceived to be the stagnation of thought among Muslim jurists and the *ʿulamāʾ* (religious scholars). The Salafi leadership argued for an interpretation of the founding sources of the tradition, the Quran and the Sunna, in accordance with principles of scientific rationality, liberal governance, and natural law (see Hourani 1983; Kerr 1966). The term *Salafi* derives from the term *al-Salaf al-Ṣāliḥ*, which refers to the virtuous forefathers who lived at the time of the Prophet and the early Caliphs.

[46] Rida was successful in establishing a short-lived school for daʿwa (1912–1914) for the training of Muslim missionaries, which attracted a considerable number of students from all over the Muslim world (Roest Crollius 1978, 278).

assertion that daʿwa activity is the obligation of every individual, and as such constitutes what is called *farḍ al-ʿain* in Islam (Rida 1970, 35).[47] Muslim jurists have made a distinction between individual obligations (farḍ al-ʿain) and those duties that are incumbent upon the community as a whole, but which, when fulfilled by some members of the community, then no longer oblige others (*farḍ al-kifāya*). While scholars have differed historically on whether amr bil maʿrūf falls under the former or the latter category, the common view has been that amr bil maʿrūf is a collective duty best undertaken by qualified religious scholars or Muslim leaders (Cook 2000, 17–18).[48] By departing from this older, more established position, Rida makes the conditions under which daʿwa and amr bil maʿrūf can be enacted fairly open: such an interpretation, as we shall see, has opened the space for women to speak in the name of daʿwa, as in the women's mosque movement I studied.

The two innovations that mark Rida's interpretation of daʿwa—its dependence on modern knowledge and organizational frameworks, and its status as an individual obligation—were crystallized further by the work of the Muslim Brotherhood (al-Ikhwān al-Muslimūn) under the leadership of its founder Hasan al-Banna (1906–1949).[49] Al-Banna established the Brotherhood in 1928. This organization has since grown into one of the key reform-oriented Islamist political groups of the twentieth century, and its activities have been at the forefront of daʿwa.[50] Al-Banna's elaboration of daʿwa was a key part of his larger program aimed at creating institutional structures and sensibilities capable of contesting Western cultural and political hegemony. Unlike Rida,

[47] At one point, for example, Rida argues, "Calling to excellence and the doing of good and the forbidding of evil [*al-daʿwa ʾila al-khair wa amr bil maʿrūf wal-nahi ʿan al-munkar*] is a definitive duty [*farḍ ḥatm*] incumbent upon every Muslim" (Rida 1970, 35).

[48] For a number of medieval theologians who are important to Salafi thought—such as Zamakhrashi, A. H. al-Ghazali, al-Razi, and Ibn Taymiyya—amr bil maʿrūf was a societal obligation (farḍ al-kifāya). Well aware of the threat such a calling entailed to social order, they went to great lengths to spell out a number of conditions that had to be met in order to perform this obligation correctly (see Cook 2000, 131–32, 153–55, 364–65; Roest Crollius 1978, 267–71). Even though Rida refers to A. H. al-Ghazali's work extensively in his commentary, he departs from A. H. al-Ghazali in treating the obligation as incumbent on every Muslim (farḍ al-ʿain).

[49] Hasan al-Banna was a product of the Salafi school of thought: he inherited the editorship of Rashid Rida's journal *al-Manār* upon Rida's death and edited it until 1940 (Skovgaard-Petersen 1997, 156).

[50] The Muslim Brotherhood was a part of the anticolonial struggle against the British, and had a relationship of mutual support with the Free Officers responsible for the 1952 coup. But soon after the 1952 revolution, sharp differences developed between the Brothers and President Gamal Adbul Nasser, who led the coup. Nasser banned the Muslim Brotherhood in 1954 and jailed the majority of its members. Not until Anwar Sadat came into power in 1971 was the Brotherhood allowed to function again, although officially it remains outlawed. For the early history of the Muslim Brotherhood (1928–1954), see R. Mitchell 1993.

whose primary focus was on missionary activity among non-Muslims, al-Banna directed his organizational efforts at the education and reform of fellow Muslims who, in his opinion, were becoming increasingly secularized and westernized under an indigenous leadership that had abandoned Islam in favor of Western values and lifestyles.[51] Various aspects of al-Banna's critique continue to be echoed by participants in the mosque movement, and their pedagogical activities have given a new life to his reconstructive project.

In extending the classical meaning of daʿwa, al-Banna incorporated many of the concepts and organizational strategies integral to the practice of modern politics and governance. For example, in his writings and public speeches he addressed fellow Muslims as citizens whose collective project was to sustain the Egyptian nation as an integral part of the *umma* (the Muslim community).[52] Similarly, the Muslim Brothers made the public spaces of urban life (cafés, clubs, and public squares) a key site of their daʿwa activity, and used aural and print media extensively to propagate their message.[53] They engaged in trade union activities and established professional syndicates, which to this day form the backbone of the Muslim Brotherhood's popular activism. The Brothers successfully transformed mosques from spaces reserved for worship to, what al-Banna described as "schools [for] the commoners, the popular universities and the colleges that lend educational services to the young and old alike" (al-Banna, quoted in Abu Rabiʿ 1996, 78)—a legacy that continues to thrive in the role mosques are playing in the current Islamic Revival.

The figure of the dāʿiya emerged from the confluence of two trends put into motion by reformers like al-Banna and the activities of the Muslim Brother-

[51] Hasan al-Banna held the Western-style education system (which had been gradually adopted since the late nineteenth century in Egypt) largely responsible for having turned indigenous elites into efficient vehicles for the propagation of Western and secular values. In pointing to the effects of this system of education, al-Banna wrote: "They [Western powers] founded schools and scientific institutes in the very heart of the Islamic domain, which cast doubt and heresy into the souls of its sons and taught them to demean themselves, disparage their religion and their fatherland, divest themselves of their traditions and beliefs, and to regard as sacred anything Western, in the belief that only that which had a European source could serve as a model to be emulated in this life" (al-Banna 1978, 28).

[52] For example, see al-Banna's open letter to King Faruq I of Egypt and a number of leaders of the Muslim world (al-Banna 1978, 103–132).

[53] Al-Banna wrote, "The methods of daʿwa today are not those of yesterday. The daʿwa of yesterday consisted of a verbal message given out in a speech or at a meeting, or one written in a tract or a letter. Today, it consists of publications, magazines, newspapers, articles, ordinary films, and radio broadcasting. All these have made it easy to influence the minds of all mankind, women as well as men, in their homes, places of business, factories and fields" (al-Banna 1978, 46). Note that even though the translator of al-Banna's work, Charles Wendell, translates *daʿwa* as "propaganda," here I have retained the original word, which captures the wider sense in which the term is used.

hood. On the one hand, the interpretation of daʿwa/amr bil maʿrūf as a religious duty that is incumbent upon every virtuous Muslim woman and man (farḍ al-ʿain) further strengthened the general propensity toward the individualization of moral responsibility so characteristic of modern Islam (al-Banna 1978, 80). The other trend that gained further ascendancy through al-Banna and his organizational activities was a trenchant critique launched against traditional religious education, in particular against religious scholars (*ʿulamā'*) and their institutions for making religion into a specialized field of knowledge that served only the interests of the ruling elite.[54] This critique of the ʿulamā' as a professional class only intensified after independence from colonial rule when the state took over many institutions of religious learning and training, harnessing their energies for its own nationalist project (see Gaffney 1991; Skovgaard-Petersen 1997; Zeghal 1999).[55] It was in the context of a growing perception that scholars and preachers trained within the government-administered religious institutions were no more than state functionaries and bureaucrats that there arose the figure of the self-trained preacher/dāʿiya, who took on daʿwa as a vocation rather than as a form of employment. Unencumbered by the patronage of the state, the dāʿiya could claim to act and speak in the name of pious commitment and not as a condition of his bureaucratic responsibility to the modernizing state. Significantly, it is not an accident that it is secular universities—not the state-run Islamic University of al-Azhar where the ʿulamā' are usually trained—that have produced the most prominent dāʿiyāt (both male and female) of the last century.[56]

WOMEN AND DAʿWA

It should come as no surprise that women have entered the field of religious pedagogy under the rubric of daʿwa, especially in light of how the practice has

[54] This critique had already been initiated by the Salafi thinkers, but gained a new valence through the work of the Muslim Brotherhood (Skovgaard-Petersen 1997, 155).

[55] In 1961 Nasser literally made traditional religious institutions, such as the division of Religious Endowments and the Islamic University of al-Azhar, parts of the state bureaucracy. Since then, the Egyptian government has also established a variety of governing bodies to oversee mosque activities, bringing them under the direct supervision of the Ministry of Religious Affairs. Similarly, the terminology of daʿwa became an integral part of the official enterprise of the state with the establishment in 1961 of the Department of Daʿwa and Islamic Culture (Qism al-Daʿwa wal-Thaqāfa al-Islāmiyya), which continues to train preachers for appointment to state-administered mosques.

[56] For example, both al-Banna and Sayyid Qutb (the ideologue of the militant wing of the Islamist movement) were graduates of the Department of Dār al-ʿUlūm (Faculty of Religious Sciences) at Cairo University—a department that has produced a number of key activists of the Islamist movement.

crystallized in the modern period. There are both theological and sociological bases for women's entrance into this field. Despite scant historical attention paid in the robust literature on amr bil maʿrūf to the role of women (Cook 2000, 286), modern interpretations of daʿwa often draw upon those verses of the Quran that enjoin women and men equally to undertake this duty.[57] Many religious scholars (male and female) associated with the Islamic Revival maintain that the requirements for women's performance of daʿwa are similar to those incumbent upon men: the dāʿiya must practice what she preaches, and her exhortations must be in accord with the Quran and the Sunna, undertaken with wisdom and sincerity of the heart (*ḥikma wa ḥasana*), and performed for the purpose of pleasing God rather than for personal gain or popularity (Z. al-Ghazali 1994a, 1996a; *al-Liwāʾ al-Islāmi* 1995; al-Qaradawi 1992; al-Waʿi 1993).[58] Since the prevalent interpretation of daʿwa holds that all those who are familiar with, and observant of, Islamic rules of conduct are qualified to engage in this activity, the ability to practice daʿwa has come to depend not so much on doctrinal expertise as on one's moral uprightness and practical knowledge of the tradition—this is particularly significant for women who have had little formal training in doctrinal issues.

Even though women's participation in the field of daʿwa has grown in recent years, it is important to realize that this participation is structured by certain limits. Foremost among these is the condition that women, while encouraged to carry out daʿwa among other women, are not allowed to do so among men. This is consistent with prohibitions forbidding women to deliver the Friday sermon or to guide men in the performance of collective prayer. Hence the terms *khaṭīb* (one who delivers a sermon) and *imam* (one who leads the prayers) are reserved for men. Women preachers are markedly called *dāʿiyāt* or *wāʿiẓāt* (nominative for *waʿẓ*, meaning "to preach, admonish, or give good advice"). The reasoning behind these restrictions is twofold. First is the general belief that since the Quran makes men the guardians of women, the latter should not serve in significant positions of leadership over men.[59] Second is the prevailing notion that a woman's voice can nullify an act of worship because it is capable of provoking sexual feelings in men—though it must be

[57] The most widely cited Quranic verses on this topic are verses 71 and 35 from Sūrat al-Tauba and Sūrat al-Aḥzāb, respectively. Many male leaders of the Islamic Revival support the participation of women in daʿwa. See, for example, M. al-Ghazali 1996; al-Qaradawi 1981; Abu Shuqqah 1995, vol. 1.

[58] In contrast, Cook reports that only two well-known medieval Sunni jurists—Ibn Hazam (d. 1064) and A. H. al-Ghazali (d. 1111)—specifically permitted women to undertake amr bil maʿrūf (Cook 2000, 485).

[59] The pertinent Quranic verse here is from Sūrat al-Nisāʾ: "Men shall take full care of women with the bounties which God has bestowed more abundantly on the former than on the latter" (verse 35).

noted that this view is not shared across all Muslim societies, and in places like Indonesia some of the most popular and respected Quranic reciters are women (see Hirschkind 2003).[60] Women dāʿiyāt in Egypt today do not challenge these conditions of participation. Yet despite their adherence to these limits, as we shall see later, the dāʿiyāt continue to evoke skepticism, if not outright condemnation, from the religious establishment.

Women's entry into the field of daʿwa is not solely the result of modern doctrinal innovations; it has also been facilitated by conditions of higher literacy and increased social mobility afforded to women in postcolonial Egypt. Since the 1950s, there has been a dramatic increase in the number of women being educated at the secondary and higher levels, and women have entered the paid work force in large numbers. The years between 1952 and 1970 witnessed a fifteenfold increase in women's enrollment in universities, and this trend has continued into the 1990s (Nelson 1984).[61] Since 1961, when the University of al-Azhar began admitting female students, women have been able to specialize in religious subjects (such as Islamic jurisprudence, exegesis of the Quran and the Sunna, and so on), although there is still no College of Daʿwa for women at the University of al-Azhar as there is for men. All of these developments have gradually opened doors for urban women to pursue religious study, and have endowed them with a sense of entitlement that they should be able to claim the Islamic tradition in a manner parallel (though not necessarily equal) to men. In light of this, it is not surprising that a large percentage of the participants in the mosque movement are either students or working women employed in a range of fields, including education, medicine, government bureaucracy, manufacturing, private enterprise, and so on.

The development of women's daʿwa, therefore, is part of a shared history of transformations that have occurred in secular and religious institutions in the modern period. As we have seen, it is almost impossible to track changes in the concepts of daʿwa and amr bil maʿrūf that are purely "religious" in scope. There is perhaps no better way to illustrate the intertwined role that secular and religious institutions have played in the articulation of women's daʿwa

[60] Despite the doctrinally contested nature of this position, many male religious figures who *support* women's daʿwa also, paradoxically, espouse this position. These figures include not only prominent intellectual Islamist figures (such as Abu Shuqqah, Muhammed al-Ghazali, and Yusuf al-Qaradawi), but also the leaders of the various nonprofit religious organizations that have played a pioneering role in the establishment of daʿwa training institutes for women in Egypt. See, for example, the statement made by the president of the nonprofit organization al-Jamʿiyya al-Sharʿiyya, which currently oversees the largest number of women's daʿwa institutes in Cairo (*al-Nūr* 1996).

[61] The UNESCO Statistical Yearbook reports that Egyptian women made up 36 percent of the total number of students enrolled in postsecondary institutions in 1996, including vocational and technical schools. This figure does not include enrollment at the University of al-Azhar and at private institutions of higher learning.

than through a brief examination of the life of Zaynab al-Ghazali. Al-Ghazali is believed to have been the first prominent female dāʿiya in Egypt, and her trajectory as a dāʿiya exemplifies key developments in the history of women's daʿwa since the 1940s. Ironically, her story is one that remains largely undocumented and, it would be fair to say, even unknown among the participants of the women's mosque movement.[62]

the secular/religious trajectory of the female dāʿiya

Zaynab al-Ghazali (b. 1917) is credited with establishing a women's organization called the Society of Muslim Ladies (Jamāʿat al-Sayyidāt al-Muslimāt) in the late 1930s, which was initially dedicated to providing charitable services to poor women and children. The Society later expanded its role to training women in the art of preaching so that they could instruct women in religious issues either in their homes or at mosques. During the first few years of the Society's operation, the institute (known as the "Center for Preaching and Advice") was affiliated with the University of al-Azhar, and many well-known ʿulamāʾ reportedly came to lecture on subjects such as exegesis of the Quran and the ḥadīth, the basic rules of Islamic jurisprudence (*fiqh*), and religious exhortation (al-Hashimi 1989, 205).[63] Women received six months of training and were then appointed to state-run mosques to provide religious lessons to other women. They were, at this point, referred to as wāʿiẓāt rather than dāʿiyāt.[64] Even after the institute's affiliation with al-Azhar ended (around 1938–39), al-Ghazali's organization continued to train women in the art of religious exhortation well into the late 1950s.

According to her biographers, al-Ghazali had no formal training in religious issues and never received an education beyond secondary school (al-

[62] While there are a few biographies of Zaynab al-Ghazali in Arabic (al-Arabi 1996; al-Hashimi 1989, 1990), and a couple of short entries on her life in English (Badran 1995; Hoffman 1985), to my knowledge there is no extensive history in English, Arabic, or French of the work conducted by al-Ghazali's organization, the Society of Muslim Ladies. I have been able to piece together a rough account of the work conducted under the auspices of this organization from a variety of sources, including al-Ghazali's own writings, Arabic and English commentaries on her published work, and personal interviews with Zaynab al-Ghazali and her secretary conducted over a period of several months in 1996. I have also drawn upon a series of tape-recorded interviews with al-Ghazali conducted in 1992 by a member of the Brotherhood that were part of her private collection, but which to my knowledge have not been disseminated or published to date.

[63] Significantly, al-Ghazali's institute had almost the same name as the state-run institute of preaching at al-Azhar University that was reserved for men. The former was called Maʿhad al-Waʿẓ wal-Irshād, and the latter Qism al-Waʿẓ wal-Irshād.

[64] Notably, al-Ghazali did not use the term daʿwa to describe her work at the time, and it was only when she became active in the Muslim Brotherhood that she assumed the title dāʿiya.

Arabi 1996, 17–62; al-Hashimi 1990, 29–30). She, like the male *du'āt*[65] of her time, was self trained in issues of religious doctrine and exhortation. Al-Ghazali had already become a powerful orator and public figure when Hasan al-Banna asked her to combine her efforts with those of the Muslim Brothers. Her participation would have been a boon to the Brothers since they did not have a significant history of public involvement with women's issues. Even though al-Ghazali never formally merged her organization with the Brotherhood, the Society of Muslim Ladies came to be perceived as part of the Islamic opposition to the government because of al-Ghazali's close ties with the Brotherhood. In the later years of the Society's association with the Brotherhood, al-Ghazali's organization published a journal entitled *al-Sayyidāt al-Muslimāt* (1954–56); a quick survey of this publication reveals that though the Society continued to train women in preaching, its public profile had become enmeshed in the political struggles Egypt was undergoing at the time.[66] The fate of the Society and the Muslim Brothers became further intertwined when al-Ghazali became one of the main coordinators of the Brotherhood after most of its leadership was jailed under President Gamal Abdul Nasser (Kepel 1986; Z. al-Ghazali 1995). In 1965 Nasser dissolved the Society of Muslim Ladies, and Zaynab al-Ghazali was imprisoned for six years.[67] After her release from prison, al-Ghazali was prohibited from speaking publicly, but she continued to hold religious lessons in private homes. She also wrote on the topic of women's da'wa and maintained a regular correspondence with young Muslim women and men from all over the Arab world who asked her for advice.[68]

Al-Ghazali's genealogy as a dā'iya was a product of the sociopolitical ethos of her times and the new possibilities that were opening up for women at the turn of the twentieth century. Al-Ghazali reached adulthood when there had already been almost three decades of women's activism in Egypt, much, but not all, of which was linked to the emergent nationalist movement of that time.[69] According to historian Beth Baron, a vigorous women's press had

[65] The term *du'āt* refers to men who undertake da'wa; see note 33 above.

[66] It remains unclear what the level of political involvement was for the women enlisted in the preaching institute of the Society. In speaking to al-Ghazali and her secretary, I got the impression that there was a small core of women, along with al-Ghazali, who were politically active, but that most of the women at the institute remained uninvolved.

[67] For an account of her years in prison, see Z. al-Ghazali 1995.

[68] Al-Ghazali remains one of the few contemporary women to have published commentaries on the Quran and the ḥadīth; see Z. al-Ghazali 1994a, 1994b, 1996a. For a compilation of her correspondence with young men and women, see Z. al-Ghazali 1996b, 1996c.

[69] Given the manner in which the "woman question" had become intertwined with the very definition and character of anticolonial politics, it is not surprising that this renaissance in women's activities coincided with the burgeoning of the nationalist movement in Egypt (Ahmed 1992; Haddad 1984). Yet, as historians of Egypt have been careful to point out, women's groups,

emerged during the period from 1892 to 1920, with nearly thirty journals "by, for, and about women" (*al-majallāt al-nisā'iyya*) representing a range of political positions (Baron 1994, 1). This was accompanied by an efflorescence of women's charitable associations, which served as the springboard for women's entry into public and political life, and which continued well into the 1940s.[70] At the same time, a broad urban culture emerged of women delivering speeches to other women, speeches that were published in the organizations' journals and by the emergent nationalist press (Baron 1994, 181–82).[71] Al-Ghazali's activism, therefore, occurred at the height of the early nationalist period in Egypt wherein the status of women and their visibility in public life was made a key signifier of the new nation, an emphasis that later declined once independence from colonial rule had been achieved.

Zaynab al-Ghazali's first exposure to women's activism came at the age of sixteen when she joined the Egyptian Feminist Union (EFU), an affiliation that she reportedly later terminated because of the EFU's "secular orientation" (al-Arabi 1996; al-Hashimi 1990, 33–34).[72] While a few women's organizations oriented around an Islamic framework had been established earlier in the century—a group called Tarqiyyat al-Mar'a (Society for Women's Progress) had been created as early as 1908 to promote the enforcement of the sharīʿa (Baron 1994, 176–77)—most of the early associations formed by women tended to privilege a secular-nationalist discourse. That said, it should be noted that even secular organizations, such as the EFU, never renounced religion or understood secularism to imply atheism. As Margot Badran has pointed out, the EFU and other feminists "shied away from a secularism which severed all links with religion" (Badran 1991, 210–11).

Despite the shared propensity of the Society of Muslim Ladies and organizations like the EFU to embrace some form of religiosity, there were important differences between them. To begin with, in contrast to the EFU, the Society was open only to Muslim women (and not, therefore, to Egypt's Christian and Jewish population). Secondly, the EFU's basic platform and the platforms of

---

from the late nineteenth century onward, were not simply mouthpieces for nationalist political parties but they in fact continued to adopt positions that opposed those of the male leadership of many of the groups with which they worked (Badran 1995; Baron 1994).

[70] See Salim 1984, 52–65; Badran 1995, 113–23; Baron 1994, 168–75.

[71] While many of the women engaged in these activities belonged to the elite strata of Egyptian society, some, like al-Ghazali, were from the middle or upper-middle class. See Baron's interesting discussion of the class composition of the Egyptian women's movement from 1892 to 1920 (1994, 116–21).

[72] Even though al-Ghazali discontinued her participation in the EFU, she claims she never opposed the EFU's activities and that there continued to be sporadic cooperation between the Society of Muslim Ladies and the EFU (Badran 1991).

other comparatively smaller organizations in the 1940s (such as the National Feminist Party and the Daughter of the Nile Union) highlighted liberal values and principles, such as equality between men and women, individual rights, and so on—issues that al-Ghazali treats with considerable ambivalence in her speeches and writing. Al-Ghazali has often portrayed the "woman question" (*qaḍiyyat al-mar'a*) as a "Western invention," and has continued to regard Muslim concern with this question as a reflection of their "colonized mentality" (al-Hashimi 1990, 231).[73] The principle of gender equality, while implicit in some of al-Ghazali's writings, never finds the prominent place it is accorded within the literature of other women's organizations and feminist figures of her time.

Nonetheless, it would be a mistake to disregard the extent to which al-Ghazali's Islamic activism was shaped by the liberal discourse of early nationalism, with its emphasis on women's public visibility. This influence is evident in al-Ghazali's position that Muslim women should play an active role in public, intellectual, and political life (such as running for public office or holding the position of a judge), with the important caveat that these responsibilities should not interfere with what she considers to be women's divinely ordained obligations to their immediate kin (al-Hashimi 1990).[74] In espousing this position, al-Ghazali departs from the views of the male religious establishment of her time. Similarly, the language of "women's rights" finds an important, if attenuated, place in al-Ghazali's speeches and writings and is often invoked to emphasize that Muslim women and men are equally called upon to serve God. Al-Ghazali's modernist religious activism illustrates how the histories of Islamism and secular liberalism are intimately connected, a connection that is, nonetheless, saturated with tensions and ambivalences.

al-ghazali and her legacy

Significant aspects of al-Ghazali's genealogy as a dāʿiya continue to characterize contemporary women's daʿwa activity in the mosque movement.[75] Doctrinal similarities exist between al-Ghazali and the dāʿiyāt of today, particularly

[73] Relatedly, al-Ghazali has long insisted that Islam does grant Muslim women all the rights that feminists are concerned with, and that what is missing is their proper implementation (al-Hashimi 1990). Note al-Ghazali's use of the term "women's rights" even as she condemns its invocation by feminists.

[74] Al-Ghazali is, however, against the idea that a woman should be allowed to hold the position of president or prime minister of a Muslim nation (al-Hashimi 1990, 242–56).

[75] Despite the significant continuity between the work of the Society of Muslim Ladies and the women's daʿwa movement, I was surprised that none of the women I worked with ever invoked either al-Ghazali or her organization in the context of mosque lessons or private conversations. When I mentioned al-Ghazali's work, many of the dāʿiyāt acknowledged her legacy but remained

in their adherence to those positions that represent the majority consensus among Muslim jurists. For example, like al-Ghazali, most of the dāʿiyāt I worked with do not dispute the prohibition on women's delivery of the Friday sermon, nor do they advocate for women to serve as imams for women (let alone men) in mosques. Similarly, like al-Ghazali, the dāʿiyāt seldom employ the rhetoric of women's equality: while they do invoke the language of rights to justify their access to sacred knowledge, the female bearer of these rights is not regarded as being on equal footing with her male counterpart. (See my discussion of these issues in chapter 3.)

Important continuities also exist in the organizational history of women's daʿwa between al-Ghazali's time and the present. Just as the University of al-Azhar and the Muslim Brotherhood were avenues for al-Ghazali's activism but never directly supported the establishment of the Society of Muslim Ladies, neither have these organizations been instrumental in organizing or promoting the contemporary women's mosque movement.[76] Despite the fact that the University of al-Azhar opened its doors to women in the study of religious sciences in the 1960s, none of the contemporary dāʿiyāt have come to the practice via this institutional trajectory, and only a very few of the mosque groups are affiliated with the Muslim Brothers. Moreover, the contemporary dāʿiyāt encounter the same neglect and skepticism from their male counterparts in regard to their considerable achievements as al-Ghazali did two generations prior. Just as the story of al-Ghazali's organization remains relatively obscure, the contemporary Islamic press bemoans the lack of women's participation "in the field of daʿwa" despite the proliferation of women's mosque groups (see, for example, *al-Liwāʾ al-Islāmi* 1995, 1996a, 1996b).[77] Similarly,

circumspect. Some of the dāʿiyāt, when pressed, explicitly said that they did not consider themselves to be working within a model of daʿwa similar to al-Ghazali's since they were not part of a political movement aimed at reforming the state. Such responses may reflect the nervousness many Egyptians feel about potential state reprisals against those who sympathize with the Muslim Brotherhood. Nonetheless, it seems to me that the earlier history of the Society of Muslim Ladies is not well known, and that neither the Brotherhood nor other religious associations have done much to publicize it.

[76] Recall that al-Ghazali had already attained considerable notoriety when the Muslim Brothers asked her to join them, and that, earlier, she had been able to continue her preaching activities successfully even after al-Azhar terminated its affiliation with her organization.

[77] During the period of my fieldwork (1995–97), it is significant that other than one small article in an Egyptian French newspaper (El-Imam 1996), I did not encounter any press on the ubiquitous women's daʿwa movement. Women writers have not addressed this omission either. For example, when I reviewed the list of Masters and Ph.D. theses produced by women at the College of Islamic Sciences (Kulliyat al-Dirāsāt al-Islāmiyya lil Banāt) at the University of al-Azhar between 1981 and 1996, I found none that addressed the role of women in daʿwa from either a theoretical or a sociological perspective.

despite the copious literature that currently addresses the techniques and skills of male duʿāt, hardly any publications focus on women's practice of daʿwa.[78]

The one institutional structure that continues to play a significant role in facilitating women's daʿwa activities is that of Islamic nonprofit organizations (*al-jamʿiyyāt*), whose focus has typically been on providing welfare and charitable services to the poor.[79] Just as it was al-Ghazali's nonprofit institute that initiated daʿwa lessons for women, the largest number of women's daʿwa training centers are run by Islamic nonprofit organizations in Egypt today. Chief among these is al-Jamʿiyya al-Sharʿiyya, established in 1912, which currently owns approximately seven thousand mosques in Egypt and is well known for providing an extensive array of services to the poor (including medical services, literacy classes, financial assistance, and remedial tutoring for children).[80] In 1997 al-Jamaʿiyya al-Sharʿiyya ran six training centers (Maʿāhid al-Daʿwa) for women in Cairo alone, in which eight hundred women were reportedly enrolled in two- to four-year daʿwa programs.[81] More modest in scope but providing a similar range of services are Anṣār al-Sunna, established in 1926, and Daʿwat al-Ḥaq, created in 1975, both of which also have institutes for training women and men in daʿwa.[82] Large numbers of women continue to enroll in these daʿwa centers: for example, in 1996 when I was conducting my fieldwork, the number of women enrolled at the training centers run by al-Jamʿiyya al-Sharʿiyya and Anṣār al-Sunna exceeded the number of men.[83]

[78] For an exception to this general rule, see Zaynab al-Ghazali's two books written on the topic of women's etiquette in the performance of daʿwa (1994a, 1996a), and one other publication to which I was repeatedly referred when I expressed puzzlement at this lacuna: *Nisā' al-dāʿiyāt* by Taufiq al-Waʿi (1993).

[79] The first Islamic charitable organization, al-Jamʿiyya al-Khairiyya, was established in 1892. It provided religious education, vocational training, and medical services to the poor, and was taken over by the Ministry of Health in 1965 (al-Ahram Center for Political and Strategic Studies 1996, 233).

[80] Al-Jamʿiyya al-Sharʿiyya's activities are almost entirely funded by voluntary donations collected from neighborhoods in which the organization is active; it receives only a nominal amount from the Egyptian government and accepts no donations from foreign countries. Yet the scope of its services is vast. For example, in 1996 alone the organization spent 1,914,460 Egyptian pounds on the provision of welfare services to poor children (*al-Nūr* 1996). For a brief history of al-Jamʿiyya al-Sharʿiyya, see al-Ahram Center for Political and Strategic Studies 1996, 238–42.

[81] Personal communication with the Secretary of al-Jamʿiyya al-Sharʿiyya, Cairo, 7 January 1997.

[82] Both these organizations publish popular monthly journals on daʿwa-related issues: Anṣār al-Sunna publishes *al-Tauḥīd* and Daʿwat al-Ḥaq publishes *al-Huda al-Nabawi*.

[83] Based on personal interviews with the program coordinators of these two organizations, 20 February 1997.

MODES OF SOCIABILITY

Nonprofit religious organizations of the kind I describe above have historically been concerned not only with the provision of religious instruction, but also with cultivating an Islamic ethos that makes them distinct from secular nonprofit organizations. If we take the example of the Society of Muslim Ladies, it is clear that even though it shared with the EFU some of the liberal-bourgeois and nationalist assumptions that permeated the Egyptian middle classes in the 1940s, there was a marked difference in the sources of authority and models of sociability each tried to emulate. While it was Europe that informed the sociocultural imagination of organizations like the EFU, the Society stressed a mode of living that was grounded in what they saw as Islamic values and ethics. If anything, this disparity between styles of conduct has grown even wider in Egypt today, and is manifest in the sharp lines drawn between those who conduct themselves in an "Islamic manner" and those who ground their sociability in what may be glossed as "Western-liberal" lifestyles. Women's mosque groups and Islamic nonprofit organizations (such as al-Jamʿiyya al-Sharʿiyya) believe that the formation of a virtuous society is critically dependent upon the regulation of everyday conduct in keeping with Islamic principles and values. As we saw earlier in this chapter, this not only includes performing religious obligations in a prescribed manner, but also includes regulating how one conducts oneself in public, how one maintains one's family and kinship relations, the kind of entertainment one consumes, and the terms on which public debate proceeds.

It would be a mistake to dismiss these concerns of the daʿwa movement as a preoccupation with superficial distinctions of style and form that have little impact on issues of "real import" (such as economics and electoral politics), or to assume that since piety movements do not confront the state directly, they are apolitical in character—as some scholars of the Middle East have recently argued (Göle 1996; Roy 1994).[84] As theorists of the public sphere have come to recognize, regulation of such quotidian practices is of eminent political concern because they play a crucial role in shaping the civic and public sensi-

[84] Roy, for example, makes a distinction between what he calls "political Islamism" and "nonpolitical" or "neofundamentalist" Islamism wherein he sees the former as a product of modernity and the latter as a rejection of modernity (1994). In my opinion, Roy subscribes to far too narrow an understanding of politics, and does not give adequate attention to the ways in which piety movements (which would fall under Roy's category of "nonpolitical" and "neofundamentalist" movements) are as much a product of modernity as are the state-oriented Islamist groups he regards as "political."

bilities essential to the consolidation of a secular-liberal polity.[85] The elaboration of the secular-liberal project in the Middle East has entailed a profound alteration in, and reorganization of, people's ethical and aesthetic sensibilities, life choices, and manner of public and personal conduct—not to mention a complete transformation of legal, educational, and political institutions. For example, Kemal Ataturk's project of secularizing Turkey critically rested on transforming modes of public sociability by making religious attire illegal, mandating European dress for women and men, abolishing the use of Arabic script (in light of its association with Islam), prohibiting the display of other public markers of religious practice, and banning religious education from schools (Göle 1996; Navaro-Yashin 2002).

Comparable changes, even if more limited in scope and ambition, can also be tracked in Egypt, since the Egyptian state has, at least since the nineteenth century, instituted a range of reforms targeted at the transformation of religious institutions and sensibilities (see T. Asad 2003; T. Mitchell 1991; Salvatore 1998; Skovgaard-Petersen 1997; Starrett 1998). These reforms have been aimed not so much at abolishing religion from Egyptian political and public institutions as at regulating Islamic practices in order to ensure that they take a particular form. In instances when Islamic practices depart from state-endorsed forms, they are met with the disciplinary force of the state apparatus. One recent example was the Ministry of Education's ban on the donning of the veil in primary schools (grades 1–5), which was ruled constitutional in 1994 when challenged in the Supreme Constitutional Court and subsequently enforced (Herrera 2003, 176–80). This regulation echoes similar decisions in Turkey and France, which also prohibit girls and women from wearing headscarves in public schools.[86] Even though there are important differences between the political cultures of these three countries, it is striking that a mundane article of clothing has provoked similar reactions among otherwise dissimilar liberal and would-be-liberal states. I would argue that the reason the veil elicits such strong responses is that

[85] Among the institutions that characterize modern society, social theorists have defined the public sphere as a critical space in which citizens come together to articulate and debate a variety of moral and political concerns (Calhoun 1992; Habermas 1991; Warner 2002). While the secular character of the public sphere is often taken for granted, an increasing number of scholars argue that long-standing religious sensibilities and institutions have played a crucial role both in the creation of the public sphere in various historical contexts and in the conceptualization of many of its ideals (see T. Asad 1999; Connolly 1999; Hirschkind 2001a; van der Veer 2001).

[86] For example, in March 1998, Istanbul University banned veiled students from attending classes, and later, in May 1999, an elected member of the Turkish parliament was denied permission to take office because she refused to remove her headscarf (Kinzer 1998, 1999). Similarly, the French government banned the wearing of headscarves by Muslim girls in public schools in 2004 as part of a broader ban on the display of religious symbols in schools (Sciolino 2004). For the 1994 debate about the veil in France, see Ibrahim 1994; Moruzzi 1994.

it continues to assert a kind of religiosity that is incommensurable with, and inimical to, those forms of public sociability that a secular-liberal polity seeks to make normative. Differently put, one can say that the forms of attire toward which secular-liberal morality claims indifference are indexical precisely of the kind of religiosity that makes such a secular-liberal morality possible in the first place. The indifference is put into question when nonliberal forms of religiosity claim the public space, and wittingly or unwittingly challenge the premise of this indifference. The fact that men's religious attire in the context of public schools—such as Jewish men's yarmulkes or Sikh men's turbans—does not elicit the same response further suggests that women's adoption of religious clothing is taken to be a sign of social coercion in a way that men's wearing of religiously symbolic clothing is not.[87]

Insofar as the secular-liberal project is aimed at the moral reconstruction of public and private life, it is not surprising that the Egyptian state has found a contentious rival in the piety movement, whose authority is grounded in sources that often elude and confound the state.[88] As part of the Egyptian government's ongoing efforts to regulate religious associational life (Gaffney 1991), in 1996 two laws were approved for implementation aimed at controlling the activities of the daʿwa movement. One aims to nationalize thirty thousand nongovernment mosques within five years—a process that was initiated in 1996 but continues (*al-Ḥayāt* 1997; *al-Nūr* 1997).[89] The second is directed at preaching activities: the state now requires that all male duʿāt and female dāʿiyāt, regardless of their prior religious training or experience, undergo a two-year training program in daʿwa administered by the Ministry of Religious Affairs (*al-Ḥayāt* 1996b). Upon completion of this training, the duʿāt and dāʿiyāt are conferred a state license to preach, and all those found preaching without this license may be punished by up to three months of imprisonment and a fine of one hundred Egyptian pounds (approximately thirty dollars). In addition, the government has stepped up its surveillance of women's mosque lessons, and it is now customary to see a government employee with a tape recorder sitting at the back of the mosque recording the lessons, which

[87] I am thankful to Jane Collier for urging me to take into account this aspect of the reaction to the veil.

[88] For example, even though the institution of al-Azhar is under the control of the Egyptian government, and legitimizes many of its policies, it has also continued to produce strong currents of resistance to state policies from time to time (Moustafa 2000; Zeghal 1999). In fact, the most vociferous opposition to the government legislation aimed at controlling preaching activities has come from the Azhar Scholars' Front (Jabhat ʿUlamāʾ al-Azhar). The government has responded by reorganizing the Front and dismissing many of its critical members (Moustafa 2000).

[89] This law was initially proposed in 1964 and has been on the books since (Gaffney 1991). Various governments, from Nasser's to Sadat's to Mubarak's, have made use of this law as they have sought to modulate their conflicts with the Islamist opposition.

are then examined for phrases and ideas considered objectionable from the state's point of view. Since I finished my fieldwork, all of the mosques where I worked have had lessons terminated for variable periods of time, and in the case of the Nafisa mosque, the government restricted the number of dāʿiyāt who could teach there, transferring some to lesser-known mosques.

The government has responded to increasing criticism of this legislation by arguing that it is the most effective means of weeding out "extremist elements" and preventing them from using mosques to spread their message (*al-Ḥayāt* 1997; *al-Muslimūn* 1996; *al-Wasaṭ* 1997).[90] Since the activities of the mosques have multiplied over the last two decades, the government worries that many men and women have used the authority conferred to them as preachers to propagate views critical of the state. This new legislation is an extension of state efforts to combat the Islamist movement on its cultural and pietistic fronts, having successfully put an end to the militant Islamist threat.[91] The Egyptian government hopes that by regulating the training that preachers receive and making them go through the licensing process, it will be able to control the kind of people who speak from the authoritative space of the mosque. The women dāʿiyāt have responded to this legislation by enrolling in the governmental training centers in order to procure the requisite license so that they can continue to preach. They are quite conscious, however, that the state lacks the resources to create the kind of institutional structure that could bring the vast resources of daʿwa networks under its control. They, therefore, intend to continue doing their work despite state surveillance.

egypt: a secular state?

Some readers may argue that I am wrong to describe the Egyptian state in secular-liberal terms because the Egyptian government violates the principal divide between religion and state that is so germane to normative models of secularism. According to such an argument, the Egyptian government's willingness to allow Islam an ongoing role in the administrative structure and

[90] There has been vociferous opposition to this legislation not only from popular male duāt, but also, surprisingly, from the ʿulamāʾ of al-Azhar, all of whom regard the law about preaching as the state's attempt to nationalize the field of daʿwa and turn preachers into government employees (*al-Ḥayāt* 1996b; *al-Shaʿb* 1997). The government has been criticized for muzzling those duʿāt who have had considerable experience in the field of preaching but who are trained at institutes other than those run by the Ministry of Religious Affairs.

[91] The Egyptian government was particularly successful in curtailing Islamist violence after the passage of an anti-terror law in July 1992, which expanded the power of the police to arrest and detain Egyptians suspected of terrorist activities. Since the attacks on the World Trade Center and the Pentagon in 2001, the Egyptian government has capitalized on the U.S.-sponsored "war on terrorism" to further quell Islamist opposition and to generally ban any form of political dissent.

policies of the state, and the state's financial support for and management of religious institutions (such as mosques and the University of al-Azhar), are all examples of the Egyptian state's departure from the model of secular governance best embodied in late-liberal Western societies.

By way of a response, let me first say that it is important not to conceptualize secularism on a single model whose skeletal structure has been fleshed out by Euro-American societies, a model by which the modernizing attempts of non-Western nations are to be assessed. Even if we understand secularism in its most narrow sense—as the doctrinal separation of religion and state—it is worth noting that this separation has been negotiated in a variety of ways even in Europe and the United States. Moreover, even in self-avowedly secular-liberal societies this doctrinal principle has not entailed the banishment of religion from the realm of politics, law, and public life. Various and contrasting imbrications of religion and politics within secular-liberal polities can be seen historically in the role Puritanism played in the United States in the eighteenth and nineteenth centuries, in the centrality of the Anglican Church in Britain, and in the place of the Catholic church in Spanish and Italian modernity. Within these contexts, secularism has entailed the legal and administrative intervention into religious life so as to construct "religion"—in its spatial entailments, in its worldly aspirations, and the scope of its reasoning—along certain lines (T. Asad 2003; Comaroff and Comaroff 1997; Connolly 1999; Jakobsen and Pellegrini 2003; van der Veer 2001).

From the late–nineteenth century to the present, the Egyptian state has been deeply involved in just such an intervention into the religious practices of the population it has governed.[92] Through the nationalization and direct management of religious institutions the state has attempted to redefine the locations and modalities of proper religious practice as part of the project of creating a modern polity. While the constitution heralds the sharīʿa as the basis of Egyptian law, in actual practice the sharīʿa has been restricted to the domain of personal status law in accord with the modernist logic of keeping religion domesticated within the private realm. Furthermore, Egyptian statecraft operates on the basis of an entire range of epistemological assumptions that

[92] One of the central challenge for scholars of postcoloniality lies, I believe, in the ability to conceptualize modes of secular-liberal governance in non-Western societies, societies that on the one hand follow the structural logic of what Foucault calls *governmentality* in the context of late-liberal Western societies, and that, on the other hand, have modified this logic in historically specific ways (Foucault 1991a). *Governmentality* in this sense refers not so much to the ruling capacities of the state apparatus as to the management of a social field whose operations ensure that citizens produce and monitor their own conduct as individual subjects. For discussions of governmentality in non-Western contexts, see Chatterjee 1995; Hansen 1999; T. Mitchell 1991; D. Moore 1999; D. Scott 1999.

are constitutive of the very idea of "the secular"—notions of causality, temporality, space, and the limits of verifiable knowledge (on these notions, see T. Asad 2003; Chakrabarty 2000; Chatterjee 1995). In these ways the Egyptian state cannot be analyzed outside the discursive logic of secular-liberal governance, just as it is impossible to describe the practices of the piety movement in religious terms alone.

The modernist project of the regulation of religious sensibilities, undertaken by a range of postcolonial states (and not simply Muslim states), has elicited in its wake a variety of resistances, responses, and challenges. One of the points that I will insist upon in the chapters that follow is that these challenges, while deeply indebted to the logic of secular-liberal governance, cannot be understood solely in relation to the practices of the modern state. This is in part due to the fact that many of the resistances posed to liberal secularity are the unintended consequences of a range of ethical practices that do not necessarily engage the state directly. Furthermore, insomuch as secular-liberal governance posits a putative separation between morality and politics, an analysis that remains focused on the agency of the state runs the risk of reinscribing this ideological separation without putting it to critical scrutiny. The analytical labor of the forthcoming chapters is directed precisely at exploring why and how movements of ethical reform—such as the piety movement—unsettle key assumptions of the secular-liberal imaginary even when they do not aim to transform the state.

3

Pedagogies of Persuasion

Contrary to expectations fostered by developments in European history, public education and urbanization have *not* led to a decline in religious observance in the Muslim world. Instead, the state-mandated system of secular education has served as an impetus for popular interest in various kinds of Islamic knowledges and forms of virtuous conduct (Eickelman 1992). Modern Muslim citizens, raised in a culture of mass media and public literacy, have become increasingly well versed in doctrinal arguments and theological concepts that were hitherto confined to the domain of religious specialists. This has fostered a market for reprints of old classical texts, as well as the creation of new genres of Islamic ethical literature—all of which are available at little expense to ordinary citizens (Eickelman and Anderson 1997; Messick 1997; Schulze 1987; Starrett 1995b, 1996). Furthermore, the advent of televisual and aural media has helped make many religious concepts from the classical tradition available even to unlettered Muslims, a development that has served to further stimulate interest in religious discourse (see Hirschkind 2001a, 2001b).

Because these popular Islamic materials are directed at ordinary Muslims rather than at scholars, the organization and presentation of Islamic themes in the materials are marked by a concern for ease of comprehension and practical applicability. Even classical texts are commonly reprinted in new formats with tables of contents, indexes, clearly marked topical subsections, and occasional comments to explain particularly difficult passages. Such characteristics make this literature easily accessible to nonscholarly audiences who have been brought up on modern protocols of reading and textual production.

A huge market also exists for Islamic ethical and pedagogical literature, in the form of booklets and pamphlets, the primary purpose of which is to provide information on practical rules of pietistic conduct. The topics of these publications range from laws that govern the performance of religious obligations, to issues of character formation and moral uprightness, to the training of oneself in aural conventions of Quranic recitation. These manual-like booklets represent a hybrid form of knowledge in which scholarly arguments and canonical sources are combined with vernacular commentaries on mundane concerns of modern existence. The voluminous demand for information on how to conduct oneself in accord with Islamic precepts in day-to-day life has also spawned an industry in tape-recorded sermons, religious lessons, and radio and television programs, which are available to those who lack the time or ability to consult the print literature.[1]

The pedagogy of the women's mosque movement is grounded in this genre of Islamic materials and shares its focus on practical questions of virtuous behavior. Even participants' engagement with classical commentaries on the Quran and the ḥadīth is geared not so much at developing abstract understanding of these texts but at a practical knowledge bearing on daily conduct. One example of the new Islamic literature widely used by the mosque participants are *fiqh* manuals. While *fiqh* is a technical term for the science of Islamic jurisprudence, it is used within such manuals as a general category referring to the collection of rules and regulations governing the performance of religious rituals and observances (ʿibadāt). It is common to find little booklets sold on Cairene sidewalks called *Fiqh al-mar'a* (Women's Fiqh) or *Fiqh al-ʿibādāt* (Fiqh of Worship), though the most widely used compendium, comprised of three volumes, is *Fiqh al-sunna*, by Sayyid Sabiq (d. 2000) (Sabiq 1994). *Fiqh al-sunna* was written in the 1940s and is reported to have been commissioned by the Muslim Brotherhood leader Hasan al-Banna (who wrote a short introduction to the book).[2] The collection condenses complicated juristic commentaries on regulations governing the performance of religious obligations

[1] While there are some superficial similarities between this literature and the self-help books that are published in the United States and Europe (both privilege the theme of self-improvement so characteristic of modern societies), there are also important differences between these two genres that will become clear in the course of this book. Not only are the sources of authority different on which these practices of the self are based, but also, as I will show in chapter 4, the architecture of the self and its sense of potentiality are dramatically different in these two genres.

[2] Sayyid Sabiq (1915–2000), a graduate of al-Azhar, was imprisoned innumerable times for his support of the Brotherhood in the 1940s. He briefly held the position of the Director of Mosques and Islamic Education in the Egyptian Islamic Affairs Ministry, taught at al-Azhar University for some time, and later spent a number of years in Saudi Arabia teaching the sharīʿa. On his return to Egypt, he lectured in various Egyptian mosques. See *al-Waʿi al-Islāmi* 2000 for a synopsis of Sayyid Sabiq's work.

into a list of straightforward rules that are easily understood, even by a person with limited literary skills, and that are applicable to practical situations—providing what the author himself called a "simplification of fiqh [protocols]" (*tabsīṭ al-fiqh*) (Abu Daud 1997).[3] Manuals such as this are also striking in another respect in that they do not reflect the doctrine of any single school of Islamic law (*madhhab*; plural: *madhāhib*),[4] but present the majority opinions of jurists from the four main schools, allowing readers to adopt any position they choose from those presented.[5] This doctrinal pluralism illustrates the "post-madhhab" character of modern religiosity that has been glossed as *talfīq*, namely, an increasing flexibility displayed toward one's fidelity to a madhhab in twentieth-century Islam.[6]

The fiqh manuals share many of these characteristics with other forms of Islamic pedagogical literature, including the popular *fatwas* (nonbinding religious opinions) that are widely circulated in print and media forms today.[7] Brinkley Messick has noted that in contrast to premodern times, when fatwas were primarily a technical means of resolving transactional and contractual issues and entailed a delimited interaction between the questioner and the *mufti* (juriconsult), they are now a popular medium through which scholars answer questions about practical problems of daily life (Messick 1996; also see Skovgaard-Petersen 1997). The focus of fatwas therefore has shifted from le-

[3] *Fiqh al-sunna* has been translated into multiple languages and is immensely popular among Muslims living in Europe and North America. I found multiple websites, geared toward the needs of diasporic Muslims, that make use of Sayyid Sabiq's compendium.

[4] Islamic law, or the sharīʿa, was consolidated between the second and ninth centuries A.D. In Sunni Islam, this consolidation is primarily attributed to four scholars—al-Shafiʿi (d. 820), Abu Hanifa (d. 767), Malik b. Anas (d. 795) and Ahmad Hanbal (d. 855)—whose names are now associated with the four dominant schools of Islamic law known as the Shafiʿi, Hanafi, Maliki, and Hanbali schools respectively. These founders developed structures of rules, based on the Quran and the ḥadīth, which were adopted by subsequent generations of jurists and address doctrinal and practical issues pertaining to the lives of Muslim communities. The academic discipline by which religious scholars describe, explore, and debate the sharīʿa is called *fiqh*. See Calder and Hooker 1999.

[5] Sayyid Sabiq discusses this aspect of his book in an interview conducted a few years before his death (Abu Daud 1997).

[6] According to the legal scholar Wael Hallaq, *talfīq* in modern "legal jargon . . . connotes the bringing together of certain elements of two or more doctrines in such a manner as to create therefrom yet another, different doctrine" (Hallaq 1998, 161). Hallaq notes the modern nature of the principle of talfīq, particularly its marked absence from classical and medieval juristic discourse.

[7] While there are fatwas issued by the office of the Chief Mufti of Egypt that deal with transactional and contractual matters, I am referring here to the vast majority of popular fatwas, which circulate in various mediatized forms (print or aural), but which are seldom documented in the manner that the former are. The topics addressed in Egyptian popular fatwas overlap significantly with those discussed by Messick in respect to Yemen (Messick 1996).

gal issues to questions about religious conduct in daily life (Messick 1996, 317–19). Importantly, new Islamic genres such as fatwas and fiqh manuals do not simply replace traditional concerns and modes of arguments; rather they point to a new set of conditions within which older commitments and themes have been given a new direction, shape, and form.[8]

A number of scholars have observed that the proliferation of Islamic pedagogical materials has led to a shift in the structures and sources of religious authority. One marker of this shift is, as I discussed in chapter 2, the increasing respect accorded to the figure of the dāʿiya and a concomitant decline in regard for the traditionally trained religious scholar, or *ʿālim*. Despite the ubiquity of this observation, however, we lack a clear picture of the kind of authority commanded by the complex figure of the dāʿiya, whose profile is not fixed in any single social, class, or gender location but traverses a wide terrain of the social landscape. Furthermore, we lack a robust sense of the pedagogical domain that has been created through the circulation of these new Islamic knowledges and ethical materials: What kind of authority does their use evoke? In what kinds of institutional settings are these sources used? And toward what end and under what circumstances? Since women's mosque lessons represent an important space where these materials are used and cited, by a variety of women from a range of social locations under the guidance of a dāʿiya, I want to explore these questions through an ethnographic analysis of the discussions that unfolded within the context of mosque lessons.

The ethnographic vignettes that follow are drawn so as to highlight three sets of issues. One, I focus on the different practical contexts in which women deployed diverse classical and popular genres of Islamic literature, and how disparate modes of argumentation drew upon a shared conception of discursive authority. Two, I explore how hierarchies of class, gender, and generation influenced the kinds of Islamic materials selected, the interpretations to which these materials were subjected, and the rhetorical techniques through which the interlocutors' authority was secured. In particular I am interested in understanding how members at the lower end of the social hierarchy—such as the younger members of the piety movement, and those with limited literacy skills—brought protocols of scholarly engagements with canonical sources to bear upon their daily struggles. Finally, in the last section of the chapter, I will focus on how patriarchal conceptions of women's sexuality, at the core of the juristic Islamic tradition, are debated, interpreted, and adapted by mosque participants from a range of socioeconomic and age backgrounds. For example, how did working women, students, and the dāʿiyāt abide by strict protocols of sex segregation (advocated by Muslim jurists) while at the same time

[8] On this point, also see T. Asad 1980; D. Brown 1999; Hirschkind 2001b; Messick 1996.

trying to meet the demands of an active public life? It is only through an exploration of questions such as these that we can even begin to get a sense of the practical problems women faced when trying to restore orthodox Islamic virtues in a social context that is saturated by the demands of a secular existence, one whose logic is often inimical to the project the mosque participants want to promote.

TEXTUAL INVOCATIONS

Hajja Faiza, a tall woman in her mid- to late forties, had been providing lessons at the upper-middle-class Umar mosque for over ten years when I first met her in 1995. Speaking in gentle and soft tones, she structures her lessons around the Quran and a well-known thirteenth-century compilation of the Prophet's sayings called *Riyāḍ al-ṣāliḥīn* (*Garden of the pious*) (al-Nawawi n.d.).[9] It takes Hajja Faiza a couple of years to guide her audience through a close reading of the two texts, at which point she begins the cycle again. Many women bring their own copies of the Quran and *Riyāḍ al-ṣāliḥīn*, often taking notes in the margins of their books as Hajja Faiza provides commentary on each verse and passage. No one is allowed to interrupt the flow of her explanation, and only fifteen minutes of the two-hour lesson are allocated to answering questions that women discreetly write on slips of paper and pass up to her. Seated on a podium facing the audience, Hajja Faiza speaks slowly and steadily into a microphone in colloquial Arabic, occasionally interjecting passages from various canonical sources in flawless classical Arabic. Her commentaries on the Quran and *Riyāḍ al-ṣāliḥīn* often include passages from the works of well-known jurists, both classical and modern (such as Ibn Kathir [d. 1373] and Yusuf al-Qaradawi [b. 1926]).[10] When asked about specific acts of worship and prayer, she refers her audience to the compendium I mentioned earlier, *Fiqh al-sunna*.

When I interviewed her about her trajectory as a dāʿiya, Hajja Faiza was clear that despite the two-year diploma she holds in Islamic studies from a pri-

[9] *Riyāḍ al-ṣāliḥīn* was assembled by the preeminent Shafiʿi scholar Abu Zakariyya Yahya al-Nawawi (1233–1277) in 1271–72. It draws upon the six most authoritative collections of aḥādīth.

[10] Yusuf al-Qaradawi is arguably the premier Muslim intellectual of the Islamic Revival in the Arab world today. Trained in the classical tradition at the University of al-Azhar, he has been jailed on a number of occasions by the Egyptian government for his support of the Muslim Brotherhood. He currently lives in Qatar whence he commands an international audience sympathetic to the goals of the Islamic Revival. For his various writings on the Islamic Revival and the practice of daʿwa, see Qaradawi 1981, 1991, 1992, 1993, and his website www.qaradawi.net.

vate institute in Cairo, her fluency in doctrinal issues is self-acquired.[11] She had already received a bachelor's degree in economics and political science from Cairo University when she developed an interest in religious pedagogy. When she tried to enroll in the University of al-Azhar, she, like many of the dāʿiyāt I worked with, was refused admission because she had no prior training in religious sciences. According to Hajja Faiza, she initially pursued her interest in religious pedagogy by teaching at one of the first Islamic schools established for primary and secondary education in a well-to-do neighborhood of Cairo. She later went on to become its chief administrator for a number of years, a period during which she also started to give informal lessons in Quranic recitation at the Umar mosque. This experience sparked her interest in further understanding the text—going beyond simply learning to recite it well. She therefore began to familiarize herself and her audience with the exegetical commentaries on the Quran, and soon thereafter, the ḥadīth. In so far as her interest in Quranic recitation (*tajwīd*) was an important precursor to her involvement in the provision of religious lessons, Hajja Faiza resembles the other dāʿiyāt I knew. (All of the mosques I worked with provided weekly lessons in Quranic recitation to adults and children.)

Once she had developed a following at the Umar mosque, Hajja Faiza quit her job at the Islamic school, and now, in addition to giving religious lessons at three upper-class mosques (including the Umar mosque), she also runs a small charitable nonprofit organization that provides services to poor women and children. Shortly after deciding to preach full time in mosques, Hajja Faiza procured the state-issued preaching license. She did this long before the Egyptian government made the license mandatory for preachers; this illustrates the caution with which Hajja Faiza has proceeded in becoming involved in the field of daʿwa. She seldom, if ever, makes any comments about political events in Egypt or elsewhere, and has become even more careful since the government increased its scrutiny and surveillance of mosque lessons post-1996. Despite her caution, the government has, since 1997 when I finished my fieldwork, periodically shut down her lessons without any public explanation.

Hajja Faiza's style of argumentation differs from that of the other dāʿiyāt I worked with, especially in her strict adherence to the scholarly sources she uses to structure her lessons, and in the learned commentary she provides to explain these texts. Hajja Faiza's style of argumentation draws upon the long tradition of scholarly commentary common among Muslim jurists, which she

[11] Most institutions of religious learning, outside of the University of al-Azhar, provide a two-year training program that, while sufficient to develop a familiarity with the basics of religious exhortation, is not rigorous enough to provide a thorough command of canonical sources.

integrates within the structure and protocols of a public lecture. These qualities give her lessons an air of scholarly sophistication that is consonant with the sensibilities of her well-educated audience. When answering questions posed to her about social and religious practices—such as how to conduct oneself in a social situation, or perform a religious ritual correctly—Hajja Faiza is careful to spell out several jurists' opinions on the subject without providing specific recommendations. By laying out the range of views among jurists on a particular topic, she trains her audience in a mode of interpretive practice that foregrounds the importance of individual choice and the right of the Muslim to exercise this choice. While Hajja Faiza's use of the notion of rights and choice reflects how the discourse of liberal humanism has come to inform religious arguments in present-day Egypt (particularly among the upper classes), it would be a mistake to ignore the ways in which her arguments depart from this discourse as well. As I will show, neither the field of choices nor the agents who exercise these choices simply reproduce the assumptions of the liberal-humanist tradition in Hajja Faiza's discourse. The range of choices Hajja Faiza outlines are determined by the scholarly opinions expressed within earlier traditions of juristic reasoning that provide the authoritative bases for any decision. As such, choice is understood not to be an expression of one's will but something one exercises in following the prescribed path to becoming a better Muslim.

During one of her lessons, for example, Hajja Faiza was asked about female circumcision (*khitān*), a practice that is quite common in Egypt and that has come under increasing criticism for being either un-Islamic or injurious to women's health and sexuality.[12] Hajja Faiza did not condone or condemn the practice in her answer. Instead she reasoned that the ḥadīth on which the practice of circumcision is based is actually *ḍaʿīf* (weak), a classificatory term in ḥadīth literature that refers to a Prophetic tradition of dubious authority. She explained that because the ḥadīth was weak, the practice of female circumcision was neither *wājib* (an obligatory act), nor *mustaḥabb* (a recommended act), nor Sunna (a custom of the Prophet and his Companions).[13]

[12] The debate about female circumcision had been raging in the media at the time. The Ministry of Health had just banned the practice, citing concern for women's health as the prime reason (*al-Ḥayāt* 1996a). The Shaikh al-Azhar, Muhammed Sayyid al-Tantawi, had come out in support of this decision, thereby rejecting the opinion of his predecessor in the office, Jad al-Haq, who was a strong supporter of female circumcision. Much of the debate occurred around the question of whether the ḥadīth used in support of female circumcision was authoritative or not. For an example of this debate, see the articles in the Islamist newspaper *al-Shaʿb* (al-Awwa 1996a, 1996b; Ismail 1996).

[13] Within Islamic jurisprudence, Sunna and mustaḥabb refer to categories of acts that are not mandatory but, if undertaken, accrue merit with God. Even though the categories of wājib and farḍ both refer to acts that are obligatory, they are also distinct in the authority each carries.

Since female circumcision falls outside these categories, she argued that it was an optional practice. Having spelled out her reasoning, Hajja Faiza continued, "There are people who support female circumcision [khitān] on the basis that it is good for the psychological health of the woman, and that it is prudent to follow even a weak ḥadīth since there must be wisdom [ḥikma] in it. It is up to you which opinion you want to choose, but make sure that you consult a medical doctor before doing it." Hajja Faiza's response stands in contrast to the styles of the other dāʿiyāt I worked with, most of whom propounded specific recommendations without discussing the range of interpretive positions that existed on any given topic.

Many of the women who attended Hajja Faiza's sessions appreciated her insistence that her role was simply that of a disseminator of correct information, and that each individual remained responsible for the choices she made and the actions she took. A number of the participants remarked to me that she "made people like their religion [*tikhalli in-nās tiḥibb dinha*]" because she did not invoke hell's fires and God's wrath to compel them into action; she tolerated the less-than-devout appearance of some of her audience; and she gave them a chance to change over time by listening to "God's speech" (*kalām al-lāh*). These participants were quick to point out, however, that Hajja Faiza did not compromise on the basic principles of God's message. She remained within the bounds of the four schools of Islamic law. For some, therefore, it was precisely Hajja Faiza's noninterventionist style that brought them closer to the implementation of divine will in their lives. Others were more critical, acknowledging her command of the canonical sources, but faulting her for not deploying a strong exhortatory style and for her tendency to desist from giving specific recommendations; if these things were remedied, they said, she would be more effective in impelling them toward pious behavior. Here, just as at the other mosques, attendees measured the effectiveness of a dāʿiya not only by her command of doctrinal knowledge, but also by the passional conditions of her rhetorical performance.

to lead or not to lead

Hajja Faiza has also become known in the mosque circles for some controversial practices, which she has been able to continue to uphold despite being criticized publicly for them. Key among these is her practice of leading women in the performance of collective prayer in mosques, even when there is a male

---

Whereas the status of farḍ is derived from clear injunctions based in either the Quran or the ḥadīth, the mandatory character of wājib is less certain because it is grounded in traditions with weaker authority.

imam available to perform this task.[14] While three of the four schools of Islamic law (Shafiʿi, Hanafi, and Hanbali) allow a woman to lead other women in the performance of the obligatory prayer ritual (*ṣalāt*), the common custom in Egypt is that if a man is present who is capable of leading the prayers, then women defer to him, especially when in a mosque where a male imam is always present.[15] Notably, the norm of custom differs in this case from majority juristic opinion. Hajja Faiza breaks the customary norm by holding a separate session of collective prayer for women in the mosques where she gives lessons (durūs). Thus when the call to prayer is issued at the Umar mosque, Hajja Faiza, unlike other dāʿiyāt, does not interrupt her lesson to allow women to join the male imam in praying, but waits until she is done with her lesson, at which point she herself conducts the prayer ritual.[16] Similarly, during the holy month of Ramadan, Hajja Faiza leads a two-hour session of supplicatory prayers (*tarāwiḥ*) immediately following those led by a male imam in the same mosque.[17] Around three hundred women show up night after night during Ramadan to pray with her. As far as I know, she is the only woman in the city of Cairo who leads such a session in a well-known mosque.

Hajja Faiza has been attacked for this practice by some of the women attendees, as well as by a famous male dāʿiya, Shaikh Karam, who gives lessons in the Umar mosque to men in the evenings. Hajja Faiza's critics claim that by leading women in prayer when there is a male imam available she is performing an act of *bidʿa*. *Bidʿa* is a term in Islamic doctrine that refers to unwarranted innovations, beliefs, or practices for which there was no precedent at the time of the Prophet, and which are therefore best avoided.[18] During one of the lessons I attended, a woman questioned Hajja Faiza's practice of leading women in prayer when a male imam was present because, she said, she had

[14] While all four schools of Islamic law recommend that, when possible, men pray collectively (*ṣalāt bil-jamāʿa*) in a mosque rather than alone at home, there is a difference of opinion among the jurists when it comes to women. The Maliki, Shafiʿi, and Hanafi schools hold that it is better if women perform their prayer at home than at a mosque; only Hanbali jurists recommend the opposite (Sabiq 1994, 1:171). In those instances when women do happen to pray collectively (at home, for example), the Shafiʿi, Hanbali, and Hanafi schools recommend that a woman lead the prayers.

[15] In the majority Sunni tradition, just as women are prohibited from issuing the call to prayer or delivering the Friday sermon, they are also prohibited from leading men and women together in prayer (al-Jumal 1981, 121–26). All four juristic schools hold that men may only be led by a male imam.

[16] Hajja Faiza has also been criticized for delaying the performance of prayer after the call is issued; however, it is her taking on the role of an imam that has drawn the most criticism.

[17] These prayers are supplementary to the obligatory prayers that are performed five times a day, and are undertaken as a special act of worship during the month of Ramadan.

[18] *Bidʿa* is distinct from heresy (*ilḥād*): the latter is considered to be an act of conscious rebellion, and the former the result of confusion, especially when it refers to disagreements about the authority of pertinent Prophetic traditions (see Robson 1999a).

heard from a well-respected shaikh that such an act was bidʿa. Hajja Faiza read the question aloud, smiled for a moment, and then responded, "This is, of course, the opinion of Shaikh Karam: did you hear it from him?" Without waiting for an answer, she continued:

> I respect his opinion, but it is based on the Maliki school. The other three schools [Shafiʿi, Hanafi, and Hanbali] say that it is permissible for a woman to lead other women in prayers, and is in fact better [*afḍal*]. There are three opinions on this matter [from among the four schools] that are in agreement, and the fourth is different. I follow the majority opinion in this case, and Shaikh Karam follows the minority one. He is within his rights to do so, just as I am, because remember that it is our right [*min ḥaqqina*] to select from any of the opinions available in the four schools, even if the opinion happens to be noncanonical or anomalous [*shādhdh*].

Hajja Faiza's response is striking for a number of reasons. Note that Hajja Faiza does not ground her justification for leading women in prayer rituals in an argument for gender equality, or women's equal capacity to perform such a task. Instead, she locates it within the space of disagreement among Muslim jurists about the conditions under which women may lead the prayer ritual. Her argument exemplifies two trends set into motion by modern Muslim reformers. First, her position on a Muslim's right to follow the opinion of any jurist from the four schools of Islamic law is one that has gained ascendancy in the modern period—glossed as *talfīq*, it connotes, as I indicated earlier, a de-emphasis on fidelity to any one school, and the freedom to choose from any of the opinions authorized by Muslim jurists.[19] The second position Hajja Faiza adopts in her argument against her critics is that she, like the shaikh she disagrees with, is within her rights to adopt even a minority opinion (shādhdh) from among the jurists.[20] In this she echoes a trend among modern Muslim re-

[19] The principle of talfīq not only informed the practices of upper-class mosque participants, but was also commonly evoked in poor neighborhoods. For example, a woman who wore the full body and face veil once challenged the male imam of the Ayesha mosque (from the humble Cairene suburb), asking whether it was appropriate for him to deliver a dars to women without a barrier between them. The imam responded that there was no clear ruling in the Quran or the ḥadīth on this issue; the woman, unsatisfied with this answer, posed the same question to other male imams of adjacent mosques. When attacked by her neighbors for sowing seeds of social discord (*fitna*) in the community by doubting their local imam's words, this woman defended herself by arguing that it was her right to determine the most correct ruling (*ḥukm ṣaḥīḥ*) on a religious issue, an argument that seemed to convince her critics.

[20] While *shādhdh* literally means "anomalous," in the ḥadīth classificatory literature it refers to a Prophetic tradition that is attributable to only a single source of authority, and which also differs from reports drawn from other transmitters. While one may choose to follow such a tradition, it must be rejected if it counters the wisdom of other traditions transmitted through sources of greater or more reliable authority. See Robson 1999b. Strictly speaking, Hajja Faiza is not referring here to a ḥadīth, and her use of *shādhdh* applies to juristic opinions.

formers toward making the adoption of even "weaker doctrines" legitimate, bestowing upon them a legitimacy that was previously restricted to sound doctrines (*ṣaḥīḥ*) (Hallaq 1997, 210). Hajja Faiza's ability to clearly articulate these two fairly complex positions within modern Islamic thought is as much a testimony to her command of canonical sources as it is indicative of the interpretive trends that are characteristic of Islamic debates in Egypt today.

What is rhetorically interesting about Hajja Faiza's use of scholarly arguments is that even though her own position is grounded in the majority opinion, and it is her critics who ascribe to the minority view, she is careful to spell out the doctrinal reasoning that secures her right to choose even unorthodox positions. Note that Hajja Faiza is criticized because she violates a popular Egyptian religious custom (which follows the Maliki school), even though her position is actually consonant with the majority juristic opinion. The considerable caution Hajja Faiza must exercise in challenging a well-regarded shaikh is illustrative of the precarious position women preachers occupy today, given the lack of institutional basis for women's daʿwa and the relative newness of the practice. She establishes her authority in part by demonstrating her command of canonical issues and debates, and goes to some length to show that she is well aware of the various interpretations that exist on the subject among jurists, customary practice in Egypt notwithstanding. It is precisely her knowledge of authoritative sources that enables Hajja Faiza to challenge the widespread Egyptian practice of deferring leadership of prayer to men; a dāʿiya with less command of such sources would not be able to accomplish such a task. It is interesting to note that, in the absence of religious institutions that train women in scholarly Islamic arguments, it is within the institutional space of daʿwa (exemplified by the mosque lessons) that women have come to acquire the requisite knowledge and create the conditions for their exercise of religious authority.

One important effect of Hajja Faiza's adherence to protocols of doctrinal reasoning is that her contestations of religious norms are limited to those issues that Muslim jurists have deemed debatable because of their unclear status in the Quran and the Sunna. On other topics, such as the wearing of the veil or women's subordination to their husbands, about which there is considerable consensus among religious scholars, Hajja Faiza's views are not that different from those of more orthodox dāʿiyāt.[21] There are two issues that are important to emphasize here. One, Hajja Faiza's views on the subject of female

[21] For example, as I will discuss in chapter 5, Hajja Faiza shared the view of the more orthodox dāʿiyāt that women should refrain from demanding a divorce from immoral husbands, even if this compromised their own standards of piety. This was in contrast to other dāʿiyāt who believed that a husband's persistent errant behavior was grounds for divorce because it posed an obstacle to the wife's ability to remain faithful to God.

circumcision and women's leadership in prayers should not be taken as a sign of a "moderate position" since her views vary widely in regard to women's place within Islam. If anything, she consistently emphasizes the importance of following the logic of juristic debates and forms of reasoning, which makes her position on the question of gender relations within Islam quite unpredictable.

Secondly, one must also note how Hajja Faiza's emphasis on the "right of Muslims to choose" from a range of juristic opinions, while informed by the discourse of rights and individual choice that permeates modern debates within Islam, inflects these notions in ways that are quite different from their treatment within liberal humanism. Hajja Faiza does not, for example, propose that personal preferences and inclinations be made the basis for how one chooses from among the juristic opinions. Rather, the form of reasoning one follows in exercising a choice must be guided by the requisite rationale and capacities that the jurists have deemed authoritative, thereby complicating the sovereign subject of liberal-humanist discourse. It was, for example, quite common to hear Hajja Faiza say, during the course of her lessons, "You cannot just choose from religion [al-dīn] what you like, and reject what you don't like. What is absolute [*ḥatmi*] in Islam is beyond dispute: our attitude toward it should be, 'We have heard, and we have obeyed' [from verse 285, Sūrat al-Baqara]. There can be no discussion [*munāqasha*] of God's commands [*aḥkām*]. But the Quran has left many issues unresolved, and it is our right to choose from any of the interpretations that the ʿulamāʾ have offered on these subjects." It was within this space of nonresolution that Hajja Faiza's emphasis on choice unfolds, thereby modifying the liberal notion of "individual choice" considerably.

Notably, Hajja Faiza's statements about "absolute commands" (*aḥkām ḥatmiyya*) entail an exercise of reason, assessment, and judgment that complicates a simple reading of what it means to follow these supposedly clear injunctions.[22] For example, even though Hajja Faiza concurs with the other dāʿiyāt that alcohol is prohibited in Islam, they all diverge in their opinions on how Muslims should deal with the presence of alcohol in their lives—especially since alcohol is sold openly in Egypt. Hajja Faiza holds that one may transact with commercial establishments that sell alcohol as long as it does not involve dealing with alcohol; others say that Muslims should avoid any interaction with such establishments; still others argue that alcohol should be

[22] *Aḥkām*, the plural of *ḥukm*, derives from the verb ḥakama which means "to withhold, prevent, and refrain." While *ḥukm* has specific meanings in Arabic philosophy and grammar, in Islamic jurisprudence it refers to a ruling of the sharīʿa. In the opinion of Muslim jurists, aḥkām about religious obligations (ʿibādāt) are absolute (*ḥatmi*). In common parlance, as in the case above (when Hajja Faiza refers to absolute commands), *ḥukm* is used to signify those commands that are derived from the Quran and the Prophetic tradition.

banned from a Muslim country like Egypt and direct their efforts at securing such a prohibition. In other words, even when dealing with what Hajja Faiza calls aḥkām ḥatmiyya (absolute commands), whose status is clearly established by the Quran, the Sunna, and the consensus of the jurists, there are a variety of ways in which these commands may be implemented.

CITATIONAL PRACTICES

If Hajja Faiza represents the scholarly end of the mosque movement, the preaching style at the Ayesha mosque in one of the poorest suburbs of Cairo is emblematic of the other end of the social and educational spectrum. The Ayesha mosque offers lessons several times a week to accommodate the schedules of the working-class women in this neighborhood. The lessons are delivered once by the male imam of the mosque, and twice by two women dāʿiyāt: one who was trained at the daʿwa center of the organization that runs this mosque (al-Jamʿiyya al-Sharʿiyya), and another who lacks formal training. In contrast to the Umar mosque, the lessons here are informal and unstructured; none of the three dāʿiyāt follow either a canonical text or any particular order of themes. Each dāʿiya decides what she or he wants to talk about that day, and the lessons cover a range of predictable topics, such as the correct performance of religious rituals, the proper manner of conducting oneself with one's kin and neighbors, and edificatory stories from the lives of the Prophet and his Companions.

The working-class (shaʿbi) flavor of the Ayesha mosque is evident in the speech of the dāʿiyāt: in the expressions and vocabulary they use, and in the rhythm and tenor of their delivery. Women attendees often interrupt the three dāʿiyāt (including the male imam) to ask for clarification, and a slow steady stream of conversation always permeates the air. The rhetorical style employed by the three dāʿiyāt relies heavily on the technique of invoking fear (*tarhīb*), an emotion invoked through colorful and graphic depictions of God's wrath, the contortions of death, and the tortures of hell. Women often react with loud exclamations, followed by loud incantations of the gory details of the torture and religious chants to ward off the anticipated pain and evil. In a sense, the lessons are a joint production in which both the dāʿiya and the listeners play a performative role. The participatory quality of the lessons is further accentuated by the permeability of the mosque to neighborhood sounds, due to the close proximity of residential and commercial activities. In a social space where everyone knows what is going on in the house next door, the questions put to the dāʿiyāt are frank; attendees frequently bring up issues of incest, sexual problems, and neighborhood skirmishes. The atmosphere is charged with intense energy and excitement, with women often shouting their questions to the dāʿiyāt, arguing with positions they regard as erroneous, and protesting when the lessons are finished sooner than scheduled.

The most popular of the three dāʿiyāt at the Ayesha mosque is a forty-year-old woman named Umm Faris who has no more than a high school diploma, and no formal training in daʿwa. Her religious knowledge comes from listening to sermons (both recorded and live), mosque lessons, and popular stories that recount events from the Prophet's life. When I met Umm Faris, she reported that her interest in religious pedagogy was fairly new, sparked by the difficulties she encountered in her marriage when her husband, one of the neighborhood butchers, took a second wife. In order to soothe her pain, she started to attend mosque sermons and lessons. Soon after, she felt she was called to serve God in daʿwa, a calling that was repeatedly revealed to her in the form of a dream. She responded by asking the imam of the Ayesha mosque if she could gather local women informally to talk about issues of piety (*taqwa*). She was granted permission based on her reputation in the neighborhood as a woman who "knew her religion": she had often helped to prepare dead bodies for a proper burial. Umm Faris soon developed a substantial following for her lessons. When I met her in 1996, she was preaching twice a week, drawing crowds of between fifty and one hundred women.

Umm Faris has been criticized for her lack of command over authoritative sources, and at times for imparting doctrinally incorrect advice. Some attendees have tried to have her removed as a dāʿiya from the mosque, but to no effect since she is immensely popular among the majority of the women. When I spoke to her supporters, they said they appreciated Umm Faris's admonitory style as well as her ability to effect changes in their behavior, changes that encompassed learning to perform a range of religious obligations correctly (such as ablutions, prayers, fasting, and so on) and becoming more observant of an Islamic manner of conduct in their day-to-day life. As was the case with Hajja Faiza, Umm Faris's audience too placed an emphasis on the passional conditions of the dāʿiya's performance in evaluating her effectiveness.

making up tradition?

Despite Umm Faris's lack of religious training, she often invoked authoritative canonical sources in her lessons (such as the Quran and the ḥadīth), even if her familiarity with these sources came from what many would consider nonauthoritative channels (such as orally transmitted stories, local sermons, and popular devotional literature). When Umm Faris recounted the same aḥādīth (singular: ḥadīth) as the more literate dāʿiyāt, her rendition of and engagement with the aḥādīth was distinctly different, marked by a form of colloquialism that corresponded with her audience's sensibility and level of literacy. Her lessons were punctuated by frequent incantations of devotional phrases and expressions that are popular in working-class neighborhoods of Cairo, and her audience would join her, imparting the air of a Baptist revival to her homilies. She often delivered her speeches in rhythmic tones, reminiscent of the style of certain storytellers in Egyptian cities and towns who are known to inhabit the tombs of Sufi saints, adapting the phrases to a lilting singsong pattern of high and low notes.

One practice that was particularly popular among the attendees was Umm Faris's habit of reciting short verses from the Quran and other supplicatory prayers (*aurād*), which members of the audience could memorize and repeat during the day to impart a sense of benediction to their chores. More educated members of the community criticized this practice, and other aspects of Umm Faris's durūs (singular: dars) for their doctrinal impreciseness. Umm Faris was aware of these criticisms and obliquely addressed them in her lessons. In one lesson, for example, Umm Faris recounted an exchange between the Prophet and his son-in-law Ali that centered around the popular theme of "torture of the grave" (*ʿadhāb al-qabr*)—in this instance, they were discussing the claustrophobic darkness that envelops one before the appearance of the angel of death who takes an accounting of the life one has led. What follows are excerpts from the fieldnotes I took when Umm Faris told the story; I have retained the Egyptian colloquial pronunciation in transcribing the Arabic in order to capture the flavor of her speech:

Umm Faris began, "Everyone hopes to have light [*nūr*] in their grave [*'abr*]. I will tell you five things: if you abide by them, act upon them, and follow them from the moment you hear them, there will be light in your grave [*lau iltazamtīhum wi ʿamaltīhum wi mishīti ʿalēhum min sāʿit ma simiʿtīhum yikūn nūr liki fi 'abrik*]. There is a ḥadīth that our beloved Prophet came to Ali and told him that he should do five things before he went to sleep if he wanted his grave to be lit." There were cries among the audience: "Praise be to God! [*subḥān allāh*]." Umm Faris continued, "Ali asked Muhammed: 'What are these, O Prophet of God [*'āl ʿali 'ma hum ya rasūl allāh*]?' The Prophet responded, 'First thing before you close your eyes is to read the whole Quran [*awwal ḥāga 'abl ma titghammaḍ ʿēnak, ti'ra il-qur'ān kullu*]; second thing before you close your eyes is to give charity of four thousand *dirham* [*tāni ḥāga 'abl ma titghammaḍ ʿēnak titṣadda' bi-arbaʿt alāf dirhim*]; third thing before you close your eyes is to visit Mecca [*kaʿba*]; fourth thing before you close your eyes is to protect what you have in heaven; and fifth thing, and this is between you and your God, you should make up with your adversaries [*khuṣūm*].'"

In her delivery of this story, Umm Faris set up a metrical beat by ending each sentence with a rhyming word, and by repeating a refrain that started with "before you close your eyes." She continued, "Ali was surprised. How do I say these things when I am going to sleep [since each requires considerable effort]? [*itʿaggib ʿali, izzāy ba'ūl il-ḥāgāt di wi ana gayy anām?*]. He asked the Prophet, 'How do I read the whole of the Quran before I go to sleep because the longest chapter in the Quran, Sūrat al-Baqara, is made up of 285 verses, and the shortest, Sūrat al-Kauthar, has three verses. How am I to do this?'" There were cries of "Oh God!" from the audience at the difficulty of the task, followed by a rustle of speculations.

Umm Faris silenced the whispers in her characteristic style by calling upon them to declare the oneness of God (*wāḥidu allāh*!), and the audience responded, "There is one and only one God!" She continued, "The Prophet said to Ali, if he recited Sūrat al-Ikhlāṣ [a short chapter of the Quran comprised of four verses] three times before going to sleep, it was as if he had recited the whole Quran [*lau 'arēt* Sūrat al-Ikhlāṣ *talat marrāt kā'innak 'arēt il-qur'ān kitāb allāh kullu*]." This engendered a commotion among the audience: many started to recite the verses aloud, and others repeated for each other the number of times they were to be performed before going to sleep. In this manner, Umm Faris went down the list, in each case providing a set of devotional formulas derived from the Quran that one could perform in lieu of the mammoth tasks Muhammed had asked Ali to perform, and which would earn them the same level of merit with God.

As she proceeded with her list, someone shouted from the crowd, "Can we recite these verses instead of performing the ritual prayers [*ṣalāt*]?" In midsentence, Umm Faris stopped, turned to this woman, and said emphatically, "No, no, O sister, you must perform all [religious duties] that [are] incumbent upon you [*la la yakhti, lāzim tiʿmili kull-il-farā'iḍ ʿalēki*]! You can't say this in lieu of the obligations. Listen, make yourself struggle and work hard all day long [in the path of God]: say the obligatory prayers, the supplicatory prayers, do the obligatory fasts and the supplicatory ones. But when you come to sleep, there is another ḥadīth! Now Shaikh Jibreel [the imam of the mosque] says that this ḥadīth is weak. Yes, he said that. But since in all the aḥādīth there is goodness, we should abide by them [*āh, huwwa 'āl kida wi lākin fi kullu khair wi iḥna niʿmil bi*]." She went on to support this claim further by saying, "Aren't we told that when we recite the Quran we accrue merit with God [*ḥasanāt*]? In every verse there is benefit and reward, isn't it so? [The audience responded, yes, of course.] So even if it's a weak ḥadīth, there is good in it, because it calls upon us to recite the Quran. Now do we want to trade with God [*nit'āgir maʿa allāh*], or do we just want to sit on our hands saying that I prayed and fasted and I don't have to do anything else? We have to bargain with God all the time. So if you do all these things, while getting merits with God you will also have your grave all lit up!"

There are several aspects of Umm Faris's dars that more literate members of the audience, and dāʿiyāt from middle- and upper-middle-class mosques, find objectionable. Umm Faris is criticized for trivializing piety in her liberal dispensation of devotional formulaic verses—investing short verses with an inordinate power, which might lead people to think they can recite these in lieu of performing the more difficult duties of Muslim worship. Similarly, the metaphor of trading (*tijāra*; colloquial Egyptian Arabic: *tigāra*) with God that Umm Faris uses at the end of the lesson described above offends the sensibilities of educated and well-to-do attendees. This metaphor is commonly used in the popular neighborhoods in Cairo, but the dāʿiyāt from other mosques criticize it, claiming that it diminishes one's relationship to the divine by rendering it in worldly terms. As Hajja Faiza from the Umar mosque once remarked, when asked about the appropriateness of the expression "trade" in regard to the divine, "It is not incorrect per se, but it does not capture the proper etiquette [*adab*] with which you should approach God Almighty." Indeed, some scholars might regard Umm Faris's preaching style and the criticisms it elicits as exemplary of a "folk Islam" that is assumed to characterize the practices of the poor and uneducated, and that is distinct from the "scriptural Islam" upheld by religious scholars and the elite classes (see, for example, Geertz 1968; Gellner 1981; Gilsenan 1982).

A closer analysis of Umm Faris's argumentative logic, however, reveals something more complex than a simple distinction between folk and elite Islam might suggest. To begin with, Umm Faris's defense against her critics is grounded in the same set of authoritative sources and doctrinal reasoning that the more educated dāʿiyāt use, and it evokes a consonant rationale. For example, in the passages quoted above, when someone asks Umm Faris whether the devotional verses whose virtues she is extolling could serve as a surrogate for the performance of other religious obligations, she resolutely answers that this is not the case. She in fact invokes the same doctrinal principle that informs the arguments of her critics, namely, that the prescribed ritual obligations are the sole means of fulfilling one's duty toward God. Similarly, when I asked Umm Faris what she thought of the objections raised against her use of the metaphor of trading with God, she was taken aback, and said that even though she did not remember the exact verses, she knew that this expression was used in several places in the Quran.

When I asked Shaikh Yusuf from al-Azhar, with whom I had been taking lessons in the principles of Islamic jurisprudence, about this issue, he concurred and said, "What is wrong with trading with God? It is not as if God benefits from our good deeds or worship, it is we who benefit! *He* does not need our acts of worship: *we* need them." He then proceeded to lay out what the logic of trading with God entailed by first quoting verse 40 from Sūrat al-Nisā', and then explaining, "We are awarded ten merits [ḥasanāt] for every good deed we perform with sincerity of intent [*al-ʿamal bil-ikhlāṣ*], but only one sin [*sayyiʿa*] is written against us for every bad deed we do. It is a testimony to His munificence that if we perform even ordinary tasks, but do them with the intent of pleasing Him, it will accrue us rewards with Him."[23]

It is clear that even though the metaphor of trade is well established among Islamic scholars, the authority it carries among elite and well-educated Egyptians today is diminished because it renders the relationship between the creator and the created in worldly terms in a way that conflicts with the deistic conception of God invoked by people from these classes.[24] Yet, as Umm Faris's usage above makes clear, the metaphor of trade is quite popular among poor and uneducated Muslims in Egypt. What this illustrates is that there is no direct correspondence between the views of religious scholars and elite classes, as the scriptural and folk dichotomy seems to suggest. Rather, there is a complex relationship between scholarly arguments, elite interpretations, and the practices of unlettered Muslims, which calls into question any simple correlation between the social position of a particular group and the religious interpretation that the group's members uphold.[25]

The interesting issue, therefore, is not how religious ideology reflects class interests, but the more complicated question of what forms scholarly opinions and arguments take when they traverse the hierarchical divisions of class, gender, education, and social status. Scholarly arguments are not simply frozen bodies of texts, but live through the discursive practices of both lettered and unlettered Muslims whose familiarity with these arguments is grounded in a variety of sources—not all of which are controlled by scholars. Moreover, scholarly arguments are often transformed by the contexts in which they are evoked, a process that imparts to the arguments new meanings, usages, and

[23] For the use of the term *tijāra* in the Quran, see verse 10 in Sūrat Al-Ṣaff: "You who have attained to faith! Shall I point out to you a bargain that will save you from grievous suffering [in this world and in the life to come]?"

[24] Competing translations of the Quranic term *ʿabd allāh* often provoke a similar reaction. The term literally means "slave of God," and for many Muslims it captures the unconditional obedience that is characteristic of the relationship between the creator and the created. In modern times, *ʿabd allāh* has come to be translated "servant of God, worshiper, or believer," a translation that avoids the idea of total subordination implied by "slave," which is incompatible with the humanist assumptions of many contemporary Muslims. On this issue, see T. Asad 1993, 221–22.

[25] This is a point that has been made eloquently, and demonstrated repeatedly, by well-respected historians of early and medieval Christianity. See, for example, P. Brown 1981; Bynum 1992.

valences not intended by the original authors. Even in those instances when what are termed "folk practices" go against scholarly opinions, it is important to pay attention to the reasoning, arguments, and terms used to justify and contest these practices, precisely because these terms reveal the set of assumptions that bind oppositional viewpoints into a shared discursive terrain broadly construed as "Islamic."

In order to elaborate this point, I would like to examine Umm Faris's usage of the ḥadīth in the excerpt from her lesson quoted above. Note the manner in which Umm Faris defends herself against the charge that she relies on stories about the Prophet and his Companions that are not considered to be reliable or authoritative by the guardians of the canon. To begin with, even though no one in the audience challenges the veracity of her account of the conversation between Ali and the Prophet, she voluntarily acknowledges that the ḥadīth on which it is based is considered "weak" (ḍaʿīf) by the imam of the mosque. Despite its dubious status, Umm Faris goes on to support her use of this ḥadīth by arguing that since the advice it proffers urges incorporating Quranic verses into one's daily life, it is in accord with general wisdom in Islam about the edificatory effects of Quranic recitation and its use is therefore warranted. Importantly, Umm Faris's argument resonates with a longstanding tradition among Muslim jurists who have justified the use of weak aḥādīth if they encourage or promote pious behavior.[26] I am not suggesting that Umm Faris was necessarily familiar with this scholarly argument. But what I want to draw attention to is the wide scope this kind of reasoning enjoys today, even among uneducated Muslims, facilitated in part by the kind of Islamic pedagogical materials (oral, visual, and print) that I discussed earlier, the production and circulation of which has only increased since the efflorescence of the Islamic Revival. The widespread distribution of such popular Islamic pedagogical materials has substantially changed the conditions of assessment essential to the classical distinction made within Islam between *ʿālim*, "one who has knowledge," and *jāhil*, "one who is ignorant."[27]

Umm Faris's engagement with the Prophetic tradition—the ḥadīth—calls into question any attempt to draw a firm boundary between folk Muslim practices and the scholarly or scriptural tradition. Doctrinally speaking, the ḥadīth is a collection of the Prophet's speech and actions that Muslim jurists com-

[26] For example, when well-known Muslim jurists such as al-Jawzi and al-Dhahabi criticized the twelfth-century theologian A. H. al-Ghazali for his use of weak aḥādīth, several ʿulamāʾ defended this usage on the principle that if the argument in which the weak ḥadīth is located inspires virtuous conduct, then its use is justified (Winter 1989, xx). Winter points out that this principle is generally well known among scholars of *uṣūl al-ḥadīth*, and is cited in al-Nawawi's authoritative twelfth-century text, *Sharḥ matn al-arbaʿūn al-nawawiyya* (1990).

[27] On this distinction, see Messick 1993, 152–67.

piled in the eighth century A.D./second century A.H.[28] A number of such compilations exist, but only six of these are considered to be the most authoritative. To understand the importance of the ḥadīth within lived practice, however, one has to move beyond these authorized compilations and consider the multiple relocations and embodiments of this scholarly genre. As historians of Islam have pointed out, the boundary between scholarly practices of ḥadīth compilation and popular stories has always been permeable (Berkey 2001). This border has become even more porous in the modern period, where contemporary ḥadīth materials now range from shorter versions excerpted from authorized collections, to booklets and pamphlets on aḥādīth about popular topics, to oral traditions that include devotional stories, sermons, and religious lessons that are both tape-recorded and publicly delivered. In other words, the practice of ḥadīth is not limited to the citational protocols of religious scholars, but comprises a field of proliferating discourse with multiple dislocations that, nonetheless, engages with scholarly procedures in some form or another.

Brinkley Messick's description of how the sharīʿa functioned prior to the modern period reveals certain similarities with contemporary citational practices involving ḥadīth (Messick 1993). Messick argues that prior to the introduction of the modern legal system in Yemen, the sharīʿa, while based on a set of founding texts, was not so much a system of codified rules as it was a set of discursive practices "lived in social relations, in human embodiers and interpretive articulations" (1993, 152). These discursive practices entailed not only secondary commentaries on the founding texts, but also the practical ways in which a variety of social actors used the sharīʿa to resolve a range of problems and settle arguments. Although the sharīʿa was abstracted from the fabric of daily life in Muslim societies as it increasingly came to be reconceptualized on the model of modern legal systems, the kind of ḥadīth practices I have described here, insomuch as they continue to inform a range of everyday practices and arguments, bear a certain similarity to the premodern sharīʿa practice described by Messick. Invocations of the ḥadīth constitute a genre of speech act that is constantly lived, reworked, and transformed in the context of daily interactions. The Islamic Revival has played a key role in embedding ḥadīth invocations into the social fabric of contemporary Cairene life, prolif-

[28] In the modern period, there have been serious challenges posed to the authority that Muslim jurists have historically accorded to the ḥadīth in the formulation of the sharīʿa. In the nineteenth century alone, a range of well-known Islamic thinkers—including Sayyid Ahmad Khan in India and Muhammad Abduh in Egypt—raised doubts about the authenticity of the ḥadīth literature. In the twentieth century, other scholars (such as Ali Abd al-Raziq [in Egypt] and Chiragh Ali [in India]) dramatically limited the scope of the Prophetic tradition to spiritual matters alone. On these debates, see D. Brown 1999.

erating and generating new forms of relationship between different genres of ḥadīth invocations.

Viewed in this way, Umm Faris's arguments about ḥadīth usage do not represent a dilution of pristine doctrine (or a kind of "folk Islam" that stands apart from a "scriptural Islam"); rather, these arguments and the transformative labor they perform on learned debates are precisely the means through which the discursive logic of a scholarly tradition comes to be lived by its ordinary adherents. As many examples in this chapter show, when a learned or unlettered Muslim quotes a ḥadīth in an argument, she does not simply repeat the memorized words from a fixed script. She also comments on the ḥadīth in response to the situation of utterance, thereby imparting new meanings to it. This process of interpretation, while it differs from one context to another, is not free-floating, but is structured by the authority ascribed to norms of usage that are grounded in scholarly discourse.[29] It is the presupposition of such authoritative norms that defines a speech act as a ḥadīth citation, and it is the deployment of these norms that places the comments of women like Umm Faris within this discursive field. One can say, in other words, that it is through practices of citations—such as those used by Umm Faris—that the authority of the ḥadīth is performatively constituted.

SEXUAL TRANSGRESSIONS AND THE FEMININE GAZE

In the section that follows, I want to trace some of the ways in which the scope and meanings of classical Islamic concepts have been extended in light of the fact that women now deploy these concepts to resolve practical problems generated by the exigencies of urban secular existence. Women's increasing familiarity and engagements with canonical sources—such as ḥadīth commentaries—tends to push forms of juristic reasoning to address new areas of "problematizations" (Rabinow 2003) and points of concern that had hitherto been outside the purview of scholarly debates. The mosque participants often encounter practical problems when trying to realize an ethical life based on orthodox readings of Islamic scriptures. For example, while a majority of the participants within the piety movement argue that women and men should abide by strict protocols of sex segregation, most working women and students find it impossible to follow this edict. The mosque participants often resolve such contradictions by returning to the juristic debates and reinter-

[29] To use Bakhtin's terminology, one might say that the practice of ḥadīth citation is a combination of both an "authoritative" and an "internally persuasive discourse" (Bakhtin 1981, 345–46).

preting these debates in light of their day-to-day struggles. Such attempts, while clearly bringing women's interpretive practices to bear upon the male exegetical tradition in new ways, also extend the logic and reach of this tradition into areas of practical and quotidian conduct that might have otherwise remained outside of its purview.

These two tendencies may be elaborated through an ethnographic account of a contentious exchange that occurred between the conservative Nafisa dāʿiyāt and a group of young students at the Nafisa mosque. As I mentioned earlier, the Nafisa dāʿiyāt are known for their intense admonitory and severe style of preaching, often selecting the most exacting position from a range of juristic opinions and delivering it with full exhortatory force. In this particular instance that I am about to recount, their young audience took exception to the Nafisa dāʿiyāt's insistence that the Quran and the ḥadīth require strict sex segregation based on the argument that such an interpretation is both impractical and incorrect in light of other readings of the tradition.

In June 1995 the dāʿiyāt at the Nafisa mosque had organized lessons for young women between the ages of fifteen and twenty-two during their summer vacations from school. These lessons were part of a "summer package" the dāʿiyāt had organized for the girls, a program that also included activities such as visits to important Islamic architectural sites and museums, and Quranic recitation and memorization contests. Many of the participants were the daughters of women who attended the Nafisa mosque regularly; others were girls who lived in the neighborhood but who did not have any particular attachment to the mosque. The dāʿiyāt believed that since young women were more susceptible to the fads and fashions of Egyptian urban life, they were most in need of instruction in Islamic modes of conduct (*al-ādāb al-islāmiyya*). By involving the young women in "Islamically-oriented" activities, the dāʿiyāt's intention was to provide an alternative source of information and socialization, different from what they were normally exposed to in their schools.

On this particular morning, the topic of discussion at hand was *ikhtilāṭ*, which literally means "mixing and blending," but which in Islamic ethical literature refers to rules of conduct that govern interactions between men and women who are not related by immediate kin ties (*ghair maḥārim*).[30] The dāʿiyāt started the session with the Quranic verse that has formed the basis for the Islamic injunction that requires Muslim women to veil and behave modestly when in public. The verse reads: "And tell the believing women to lower their gaze and to be mindful of their chastity, and not to display their charms

[30] Close male kin, according to Muslim jurists, include a woman's immediate kin (for example, father, brother, nephews), her husband, the husband's immediate male kin, and any male who was breast-fed by her mother (al-Jumal 1981, 93–95).

[in public] beyond what may be apparent thereof; hence, let them draw their head-coverings over their bosoms" (verse 31, Sūrat al-Nisā'). Since the young women attending the lesson were all veiled, the dā'iyāt used this verse to focus on how the girls should interact with men. What follows over the next several pages are excerpts, from the tape recording I made of the discussion, highlighting those moments when the exchange between the dā'iyāt and the young women became particularly intense. Hajja Samira, a forty-year-old woman with a severe facial expression, began the lesson by explaining the aforementioned Quranic verses in this manner:

> God Almighty has informed us that the correct way of understanding ikhtilāṭ is the abstention from the mixing of women and men *unless by necessity* [*illa bil ḍarūra*]. So the limit here [to the commingling of women and men] is necessity [*ḍarūra*]. But how do we understand necessity? Now [the pursuit of] education is a necessity. If a woman is able to acquire a university degree—like a masters or a doctorate—or any other level of education, this is considered necessity. This is because we must fight against ignorance, and this will not be possible unless we have the weapon of the world in our hands, which is education. So we are not saying to you that you should sit at home. . . . But when we exit from home for a purpose like education, it is required that we do so in accordance with the appearance that God has sketched for us [*fa la budda inni akhrug bi-ṣṣūra illi rasamhāli allāh subḥāna-ta'āla*], which is: I wear a ḥijāb that covers all but my face and hands so that my hair does not show, and I wear clothes that cover the shape of my body so that it is not apparent. Second thing, when I deal with men [*atṣarraf ma'a riggāla*], I do as the verse we started with says, "And tell the believing women to lower their gaze and to be mindful of their chastity" [verse 31, Sūrat al-Nisā']. I should lower my eyes as God has commanded when I speak with men because it is sight through which the devil enters you and incites you to fornication [*ash-shiṭān bi-yidkhul bil-naẓar wi yiwaswisik lil-zinā'*]. Now [the problem is that] there is no segregation between men and women in the universities. Our government does not respect Islam and has not created universities for women. Since you are compelled [*miḍṭarra*] to go to these universities, when you talk to male teachers and students you should "lower your eyes [*ghuḍḍu min abṣārukum*]." And remember, you should only speak to them out of necessity, and not for any other reason. . . . [Similarly] when you take private lessons from male tutors, as many of you do, avoid looking at them because this is what God has commanded. And it is much better if instead of having a male tutor, you ask your mother to get a woman teacher so that the question of *ghaḍḍ al-baṣar* [lowering the gaze] does not arise.

Hajja Samira and the other dā'iyāt spent considerable time dwelling on the intricacies involved in avoiding eye contact when taking private lessons from a male tutor—a practice that is quite common among middle-class families since both private and public schools often fail to prepare students to succeed in nationally administered annual examinations. At first, the young women objected to the dāʿiyāt's reading of the Quranic verses on the basis of the practical difficulties they would encounter if they avoided eye contact with male teachers: some said they would appear strange and awkward if they behaved in this manner; others said that it was difficult to find qualified women to provide private lessons; and still others argued that they would not understand what was being taught if they did not look their teachers in the eye. Maryam, a tall young woman between sixteen and eighteen years of age, raised another objection: "But if I know the [male] teacher well and he is well respected, and I know myself that I am responsible and pious [*mas'ūla wa mittaqiyya*], and my intention is pure [*niyyiti naqya*], then what is the problem with taking lessons with a male tutor?"

Hajja Iman, another dāʿiya, responded quickly, "Look, my daughter, who were the most pure and virtuous [*anqa wa aṭhar*] on the surface of this earth? These were the Companions of the Prophet and his wives. Right, isn't it? And yet God commanded *them*: 'Whenever you ask them [the Prophet's wives] for anything that you need, ask them from behind a screen' [verse 53, Sūrat al-Aḥzāb], meaning there should be no eye contact between the man and the woman. It is not about your or my intent, O Maryam, this is the command from God, we have no choice! [Moreover,] as you know, it is incumbent upon us to follow the Sunna of the Prophet and his household [*bait al-nabuwwa*]."

Maryam shot back, "But those verses were meant for the Prophet's wives, and they were not like other ordinary Muslims. There is another ḥadīth that says there are special issues, which only pertain to Muhammed's immediate female kin, that are different from those for the remainder of [Muslim] women [*yaʿni awāmir khāṣṣa bī-hum mukhtalifa ʿan bā'i an-nisā'*]." She concluded emphatically, "These verses are not meant for us!"

Before I proceed with the rest of the discussion, which got progressively more heated as the morning wore on, let me draw the reader's attention to certain aspects of the exchange so far that exemplify key trends within the Islamic Revival. First of all, note that the discussion surrounding ikhtilāṭ here is squarely situated within the expectations generated by women's access to public education in postcolonial Egypt, and the presumption of their right to higher education.[31] The dāʿiyāt's criticism is directed *not* at the fact that women are pursuing higher education, but at the failure of the educational institutions to provide the requisite conditions for the cultivation of pious conduct.

[31] For a historical analysis of debates about women's education in modern Egypt, see Ahmed 1992; Nelson 1984.

Their solution to this problem is not to prohibit girls from attending these institutions, but to train them in those sensibilities, thoughts, and modes of behavior that will help them combat what the dāʿiyāt consider to be the deleterious moral effects of such a system of education. Against their critics who fault the dāʿiyāt for their overly stringent ethical pronouncements (such as their advocacy of the full face and body veil), the dāʿiyāt argue that such severity is a necessary antidote to the institutional conditions that are corrosive of Islamic virtues and sensibilities.

The challenge Maryam poses to Hajja Iman's interpretation of the Quranic verses demonstrates how familiar the young members of the daʿwa movement are with scholarly arguments, and the remarkable dexterity they exhibit when using canonical sources to establish an argumentative point. Maryam's objection to the dāʿiyāt's argument for avoiding eye contact with male teachers, for example, invokes principles of both Quranic exegesis and ḥadīth interpretation. When the dāʿiya presents the Quranic verse about the Prophet's wives to counter Maryam's claim that she has pure intentions (and therefore does not need to avoid eye contact with male teachers), Maryam is quick to point to the inapplicability of these verses to the conduct of Muslim women like herself. In this Maryam implicitly invokes a well-known principle of Quranic exegesis, known as *asbāb al-nuzūl lil-āyāt al-qur'āniyya*, which Muslim jurists have used to determine the scope a particular verse commands in light of the conditions under which it was revealed, such as the immediate ends it served or to whom it was addressed.[32] Following this principle, Maryam argues that the Quranic verses that require a visual separation between men and women were directed at the Prophet's wives and therefore do not pertain to ordinary Muslims. She further buttresses her argument by citing a well-known ḥadīth in which the Prophet advises Muslims to distinguish between commands that are specific to him and his kin and those that apply to Muslims in general.[33]

Note that in making these counterarguments, Maryam does not challenge the principle of female modesty as divinely ordained, but contests the dāʿiyāt's ideas regarding how this principle should be lived in practice. Key to Maryam's argument is her insistence that the injunction to avoid interactions with men should be contextualized: not only should one's moral character be taken into account when determining the manner in which one interacts with the opposite sex, but also the conditions under which the Quranic verses used to regulate such interactions were revealed. In the latter point, Maryam unsettles the implicit but powerful assumption of the Nafisa dāʿiyāt that

[32] See Abedi and Fischer (1990) for a discussion of this principle of Quranic exegesis in the every day context of Iranian political debates, particularly chapter 2, entitled "Qur'anic Dialogics: Islamic Poetics and Politics for Muslims and for Us."

[33] For a discussion of this ḥadīth, see Abu Shuqqah 1995, 3:70–87.

Quranic verses are universally applicable regardless of context, and that the Prophet's life and that of his Companions and female kin must be emulated in all respects. At one level, most women in the mosque movement embrace this assumption but at another level, many participants, like Maryam, bring other considerations to bear upon this well-established and oft-repeated belief. It is within this space of disagreement that Maryam is able to raise her objections to the dāʿiyāt's interpretation of the Quranic verses.

Notably, Maryam's arguments resonate with a number of scholars active in the Islamic Revival who have written against the kind of views espoused by the Nafisa dāʿiyāt in order to correct what they perceive as a strong trend toward overly stringent and narrow interpretations of the Quran and the ḥadīth, particularly in those aspects that pertain to the conduct of women (see Abu Shuqqah 1995; M. al-Ghazali 1996; al-Qaradawi 1996). When I asked Maryam whether she had read these authors, she said she had not but had become familiar with their arguments through attending mosque groups such as these, and through discussions with her peers at school, where such topics enjoyed common currency. When I asked her why she continued to attend the Nafisa dāʿiyāt's lessons, given her disagreements, Maryam said that sessions such as these forced her to acknowledge the danger of not being vigilant enough in her interactions with men in institutional contexts, and sharpened her argumentative skills in presenting a counterposition to women like the Nafisa dāʿiyāt—one that remained, nonetheless, within the purview of Islamic reasoning. Maryam said that she considered this to be a part of her contribution to the work of daʿwa.

As is evident from the exchange between Maryam and Hajja Iman, the pedagogical space of daʿwa is often constituted by debate and disagreement, as much as it is a space of consensus, about what are deemed to be the proper terms and protocols of engagement with canonical sources. Consider, for example, an objection raised by another audience member, Rabia, who was fifteen years old. When one of the dāʿiyāt was in the midst of one of her long monologues about the dangers posed to pious conduct by worldly desires, Rabia interrupted her rather spontaneously, and said: "Okay, okay [*ṭayyib ṭayyib*], Hajja Samira, perhaps I can give a comment [*ana mumkin li taʿlīq*]. There are sound aḥādīth that show that women did sit with the Prophet and his [male] Companions. There is one that says a woman came to talk to the Prophet to ask for advice because by mistake she ate while she was fasting, and Abu Hurayra [a well-known Companion of the Prophet] was there and he admonished her before the Prophet replied [this implies that unrelated women and men interacted at the time of the Prophet]."

The dāʿiya Hajja Samira cut her off and argued back, "First of all, you don't know how this woman was related to Abu Hurayra;[34] second, you don't know if this incident was before the veil was made incumbent upon Muslims or after;[35] third, are you sure that this ḥadīth is sound [*ṣaḥīḥ*]?"

Rabia insisted that it was indeed a sound ḥadīth. Hajja Samira replied, "When we want to follow a ḥadīth, it's necessary that we see it in the context of the entire spirit of the religion [*iḥna lāzim nākhud id-dīn kullu*], and also see what is the consensus of the religious scholars [*ijmāʿ il-ʿulamāʾ*] [on the issue].[36] You see, there exists a consensus among the ʿulamāʾ that ikhtilāt should not be undertaken unless necessary."

This exchange is instructive because it reveals the contentious character of the pedagogical space of the mosque lessons. Note that despite the difference in age, and in experience in the use of canonical sources, between the dāʿiyāt and their audience, the conversation between these women proceeds along remarkably equitable lines. It would be rare, for example, to find this ease of debate and counterargument in a parallel setting at the University of al-Azhar, between a shaikh and his male students, because the boundaries are more strictly drawn. In contrast, the young attendees here challenge the dāʿiyāt not only by citing their own authoritative sources, but also by drawing upon the experience of their own lives in interpreting what are considered to be divine injunctions and indicators thereof. The young women and the dāʿiyāt both contribute to this milieu of debate, disagreement, and persuasion, even though the Nafisa dāʿiyāt have the reputation of being the most strict and stringent of all Cairene dāʿiyāt. Note, for example, that in response to Rabia's demonstration that women and men interacted at the time of the Prophet without a "barrier" (Modern Standard Arabic: *ḥājiz*; Egyptian Colloquial Arabic: *ḥāgiz*), the dāʿiya responds not by rejecting this account outright, but by *asking* the young woman a series of questions about its reliability. By doing this, she not only implicitly acknowledges that she herself does not know the story's authoritative status, but also demonstrates to the attendees the se-

[34] The dāʿiya is alluding here to the Islamic edict that women may interact with their immediate male kin without the same order of restrictions they have regarding other men. In this view, if the woman was the daughter, wife, or mother of Abu Hurayra, then she would, according to Islamic protocols, be able to interact with him without the same restraints.

[35] The dāʿiya is referring here to the understanding in Islamic tradition that the content of revelation changed dramatically over time, since the Quran was revealed *seriatim* over a period of twenty-three years. The verses that were revealed after Muhammed migrated to Medina form the basis of most Islamic laws dealing with economic, ritual, and social issues. Verses that pertain to women's modest dress and behavior, such as those in Sūrat al-Nūr, Sūrat al-Aḥzāb, and Sūrat al-Nisāʾ, were all revealed in the Medinan period.

[36] *Ijmāʿ* is one of the three most important means of debating and adapting various aspects of Islamic law, and refers to the unanimous opinion of recognized religious jurists about issues that are not clearly spelled out in the Quran and the Sunna.

ries of questions they need to ask in order to authenticate a Prophetic tradition. The dāʿiya's response gives the young woman the opportunity to come right back and assert her own evidentiary claims.[37] What I am suggesting here is that this kind of exchange presents a situation far more complex than any simple model of "religious indoctrination" would suggest, and requires an analysis of the micropractices of persuasion through which people are made to incline toward one view versus another.

Women from a variety of ages and background have come to acquire a familiarity with a wide range of scholarly procedures, terminologies, and modes of reasoning through involvement in precisely these kinds of interactions and open-ended discussions, and have in turn suffused these doctrinal debates with a new kind of urgency that stems from the exigencies of their daily lives. One result of women's increasing familiarity with the canonical sources is that it has brought aspects of their lives within the purview of the logic of this largely male-inscribed canon, expanding its scope and applicability to problems that were hitherto outside its purview. As I have stated before, these discussions are remarkably consistent in staying within the protocols and assumptions of debate established by Muslim jurists. This does not mean, however, that a uniformity of views exists, but rather that when contestations are launched, they tend to engage with a fairly consistent set of materials, protocols of debate, and reasoning—making these contestations an integral part of what currently constitutes the discursive field of Islamic daʿwa.

FEMALE SEXUALITY AND SOCIAL DISCORD

The Nafisa dāʿiyāt's position on ikhtilāṭ is predicated upon a key doctrinal position, upheld by the four schools of Islamic law, which accords female sexuality a significant weight in the provocation to illicit sexual desire and the establishment of relationships between men and women who are not married. This position is well captured in a popularly cited ḥadīth: "The woman, all of her, is unseemly/unprotected [*ʿaura*]; if she goes out from the house, the devil will oversee her [actions] [*al-mar'a kullaha ʿaura fa idha kharajit min baitīha istashrafha al-shaiṭān*]." This is one among a number of authoritative aḥādīth that, combined with certain Quranic verses, provide the basis for regulating women's appearance in public. The term *ʿaura*, used to describe women here, is complex and has a variety of meanings, including "weakness," "faultiness,"

[37] The dāʿiya could have lied about the status of the ḥadīth in order to assert her authority against the young woman's claim. But this would be unacceptable behavior since lying about anything, in particular about the status of a ḥadīth, is considered a cardinal sin.

"unseemliness," "imperfection," "disfigurement," and "genitalia." *ʿAura* is related to the term *ʿawir*, which Edward Lane translated as that which has "no keeper or guardian . . . literally having a gap, or an opening, or a breach, exposing it to thieves and the like" (Lane 1984). The English term *pudendum* (plural: *pudenda*) best captures the meaning of *ʿaura* as used in this ḥadīth because it refers not only to the genital organs of men and women, but also to that "of which one ought to be ashamed" (OED 1999).[38] According to the logic of this ḥadīth (and of the fiqh literature in general), "woman is ʿaura" because: (a) her exit from the house exposes her to dangers, requiring protection;[39] and (b) just as one is ashamed to expose one's genitalia, one is ashamed to have a woman appear in public. According to this view, all those parts of a woman's body that may cause embarrassment and shame should therefore be covered, which, in the majority view of Muslim jurists, includes everything except a woman's hands, feet, and face.[40]

A small number of participants in the daʿwa movement interpret this ḥadīth to mean that "correct" Islam prohibits interactions between women and men. Others—like the Nafisa dāʿiyāt—take this ḥadīth, along with certain Quranic verses, to mean that social interactions between men and women should be severely restricted. The vast majority of participants in the mosque movement, however, interpret these authoritative texts more loosely. For example, many women at the lower-class Ayesha mosque have no choice but to work in mixed-sex offices, and regard the aforementioned ḥadīth as an admonition to greater vigilance in their dealings with men rather than a prohibition against male-female interactions. Hajja Faiza, from the upper-middle-class Umar mosque, espouses a similar if somewhat more nuanced view on the subject. When asked by one of her audience whether she inter-

[38] In four different English translations of the Quran, when the term *ʿaura* occurs in conjunction with women, it is translated as "nakedness" or "women's private parts;" and when it occurs in conjunction with the term "houses," it is translated as something that is "exposed" and therefore requires protection.

[39] In the same spirit, the Quran says: "Verily our houses are ʿaura [i.e., exposed or open to attack]" (from verse 13, Sūrat al-Aḥzāb). The term is used four times in the Quran, and the only place where *ʿaura* is used to refer to women's genitalia (or private parts), it occurs in the plural (*ʿaurāt*), in verse 31 of Sūrat al-Nūr. Hoffman-Ladd argues that the idea that all of woman is ʿaura is not contained in the Quran, but only became hegemonic later in Islamic history, as the standards for women's modesty grew more strict (1987, 46 n. 34).

[40] The consensus among the four schools of Islamic law is that a woman should cover all her body, with the exception of face, hands, and feet. This position is justified by reference to Quranic verses 31 and 53 in Sūrat al-Nūr and Sūrat al-Aḥzāb, respectively, and two aḥādīth attributed to Muhammed's wife Ayesha (Abu Shuqqah 1995, 4:83–246). Some Muslim thinkers have challenged the conclusion that these verses and aḥādīth make the veil obligatory upon all Muslim women. See, for example, Ashmawi 1994a, 1994b. For a response that reiterates the majority position upheld by the ʿulamāʾ, see the state mufti's response to this interpretation, Tantawi 1994.

preted the ḥadīth about a woman being ʿaura to mean that interaction between men and women was prohibited, this is how she responded:

> Does this ḥadīth prove that ikhtilāṭ is prohibited in all its forms? Or that it should be severely restricted so that it becomes almost impossible for women and men to work together? In order to answer this, we must return to what the Prophet [*rasūl*] and his female Companions [*ṣaḥabiyyāt*] did because they are the ones we should refer to in all matters.[41] There are personal opinions or points of view [*hunāk wighāt an-naẓariyya shakhṣiyyan*] that refer to specific kinds of interests and fears. But as a community of Muslims, when we decide what is prohibited and permitted [*ḥarām wa ḥalāl*], we must return to the community of Muslims who lived around the Prophet. For everyone has the freedom [*ḥurriyya*] to prohibit unto himself what he does not like: for example, one may say I don't like to eat green beans so he does not eat it. But we can't say that the sharīʿa says that green beans are prohibited [ḥarām]. It depends on one's temperament, not the sharīʿa. . . . So our source of authority [*marjiʿiyya*] is not personal likes and dislikes, but it is what Allah and His Prophet have said.
>
> The issue of intermixing between men and women is very clear [in Islam]. There are etiquettes of mixing that the sharīʿa has spelled out. So when we say there are etiquettes, it also means that there is ikhtilāṭ, but it must be done in accord with certain rules. So when God says "*ghuḍḍu min abṣārukum*" [lower your gaze], it doesn't mean that a woman should not go out from her house. If she is not to go out of her house at all, then what is the point of having all the instructions about wearing modest dress [*libās muḥtashim*]? Neither does it mean that women and men cannot make eye contact when they work together, for example, or when they buy and sell from each other, or in an educational setting. Now, tell me, did the Prophet not meet and talk to women? Did women not pray directly behind men in the mosque without any partition/separation [ḥāgiz] between them? We know the answers to these questions because we have had lessons on this. What is prohibited, as you know, is a woman meeting a man alone [*khalwa*]. Yet we also know that the Prophet visited some of his female Companions [ṣaḥābiyyāt] when they were alone, and so did many of his male Companions, didn't they? So there is

[41] Note Hajja Faiza's unusual use of the term *ṣaḥabiyyāt* to refer to Muhammed's female kin as well as to other virtuous women who were not directly related to him but lived close to him. *Ṣaḥabiyyāt* is the female form of the more common term *ṣaḥāba*, which is used to refer to Muhammed's male Companions. The traditional term used for Muhammed's female kin and associates is *bait al-nabuwwa* (household of the Prophet). Hajja Faiza's usage of this new term indicates a growing awareness among the more educated dāʿiyāt that the women in the Prophet's life are an important source of information about his actions and should therefore be treated in the same manner as his male Companions.

> debate [*kalām*] even about this issue of a woman and man interacting alone without supervision [*khalwa*].

Here Hajja Faiza went through a long list of examples from Muhammed's and his Companions' lives that illustrated their interactions with women. Anticipating the audience's response to her argument, she said, "Of course we say that these were very pious people [*mittaqiyyin*] and we are not like them, but these examples also show that ikhtilāṭ is permitted [*jā'iz*]. . . . Yes, there are limits [*ḥudūd*] to and etiquettes for interaction between women and men. But if we were to say that there is no interaction between men and women, this would make for great hardship [*mashaqqa shadīda*]. God did not order us to do this, so why say He did?"

There are clear differences between Hajja Faiza's approach to the issue of ikhtilāṭ and the attitude of the Nafisa dāʿiyāt. Not only do they differ about whether women and men should avoid all eye contact when conducting business, but also about the role the social circumstances under which the early Muslim community lived should play in interpreting the ḥadīth. Hajja Faiza insists that a proper understanding of the Prophetic tradition does not depend solely upon the advice contained in the text of a particular ḥadīth, but must be understood in relation to the life of the Prophet in its entirety and, in this sense, to the whole body of the ḥadīth that makes that life available to generations of Muslims who have followed the Prophet. Thus, even though the Nafisa dāʿiyāt and Hajja Faiza share the idea that the authoritative source (marjiʿiyya) for structuring a Muslim life is the exemplary conduct of the Prophet and his Companions, they differ in the relative weight they accord to the immutability of the text of a ḥadīth.[42] Furthermore, in contrast to the Nafisa dāʿiyāt, Hajja Faiza is willing to acknowledge the ambiguity and contradictions entailed in the accounts given of the lives of the Prophet and his Companions, thereby implying that even those injunctions that seem to be immutable (such as the prohibition on a man and a woman interacting alone without others being present) may be more flexible than is often conceded.

The differences between these two points of view are significant, both for the dāʿiyāt and for members of the mosque movement who closely follow these debates. But there is also a substrate of assumptions and presuppositions, shared among these interlocutors, that must be examined because they reveal

[42] It would be a mistake to assume that the Nafisa dāʿiyāt are therefore "literalists," because they often take the larger context of the tradition into account. See, for example, the response Hajja Samira gives to Rabia above.

how these disparate positions constitute part of the same discursive field.[43] To begin with, note that Hajja Faiza does not cast doubt upon the validity of the ḥadīth that describes women as ʿaura; indeed, since the ḥadīth is attributed to a reliable source, questions regarding its legitimacy cannot be made the grounds for Hajja Faiza's disagreements, given her strict abidance by the terms of the juristic discourse.[44] Instead, she criticizes the conclusion that is derived from this ḥadīth and made the basis for either severely restricting the practice of ikhtilāṭ or prohibiting it. In her arguments, Hajja Faiza stresses the criteria that her middle- to upper-middle-class audience must bear in mind, and the measures they must take, when negotiating the contradictory demands of their lifestyles (including women's pursuit of professional careers, which brings them considerable public exposure) and the requisites of a virtuous life.

Far more significantly, however, Hajja Faiza shares with the Nafisa dāʿiyāt two interrelated assumptions that are at the core of the debate about ikhtilāṭ in the daʿwa circles. One is the principle, unanimously upheld by Muslim jurists, that interactions between women and men who are unrelated by immediate kin ties (ghair maḥārim) are a potential source of unvirtuous conduct and illicit relationships.[45] While women and men are both urged to discipline their sight, behavior, and thoughts so as to prevent the stirring of illicit sexual passions (see Quranic verse 30 of Sūrat al-Nūr), it is women who bear the primary responsibility for maintaining the sanctity of relations between the sexes. This is because the juristic Islamic tradition assumes that women are the objects of sexual desire and men the desiring subjects, an assumption that has come to justify the injunction that women should "hide their charms" when in public so as not to excite the libidinal energies of men who are not their immediate kin. It is noteworthy that Islam, unlike a number of other orthodox religious traditions (for example, strands of Buddhism, Hinduism, and Christianity), does not place a high premium on the practice of sexual abstinence and regards the pursuit of sexual pleasure (within the bounds of a marital relationship) a necessary virtue both for women and men. In this moral worldview, illicit sexual relationships are understood to create social discord and sedition (*fitna*) in a community, and are regarded as signs of its moral de-

[43] Moreover, an analysis of these shared assumptions also puts into question any simple parceling of Hajja Faiza's and the Nafisa dāʿiyāt's views into liberal or conservative categories, precisely because such an analysis demonstrates their mutual imbrication.

[44] This ḥadīth is part of one of the six most authoritative collections of Muhammed's deeds and sayings, *Ṣaḥīḥ al-Tirmazi*. For a scholarly opinion along the lines of Hajja Faiza's argument, see Abu Shuqqah 1995, 3:38.

[45] In Lane's *Lexicon* the word *maḥram* (plural: *maḥārim*) is conceptually related to that which signifies honor, possession, and a relationship in the name of which one can seek protection and hold another accountable for its violation (Lane 1984, 554–55). Note the linguistic connection between *ʿaura* and *maḥram*; both signify a certain relationship to honor and possession.

generacy.[46] The injunctions for women to veil, dress modestly, avoid eye contact with men, and so on, all constitute the practical strategies through which the danger women's sexuality poses to the sanctity of the Muslim community is deterred.

Even those religious scholars who provide extensive doctrinal elaboration in *support* of women's participation in the public realm regard these presumptions as immutable.[47] For example, Abd al-Halim Abu Shuqqah (d. 1995), a well-respected Islamic scholar, wrote an extensive six-volume study aimed at combating interpretations of Quranic verses and aḥādīth, popular among contemporary Muslims, that restrict women's participation in economic, political, and social domains (Abu Shuqqah 1995).[48] Abu Shuqqah meticulously goes through scholarly debates and counterexamples from the lives of Muhammed, his female kin, and his Companions, questioning the authenticity of many of the canonical sources used to buttress these claims in order to show that women have the right to participate in the umma's productive life, to have sexual pleasure, and to pursue various kinds of social relationships that are often considered to be reserved only for men in popular culture. It is striking, however, that even though Abu Shuqqah makes these arguments, he continues to uphold the principle that women's physical appearance is a threat to the integrity of the Muslim community and that men are more libidinal and sexually charged than women.[49]

[46] One of the primary meanings of *fitna* is "rebellion against divine law," or "civil war and revolt" in which the believers' faith and unity of community is put in grave danger. *Fitna* can also mean "temptation," "attractiveness," or "infatuation." Muslim jurists, in discussing female sexuality, use the verb *yuftinu* (from the root *fatana*, the same root from which *fitna* is derived), which literally means "to charm or enamor someone"; these jurists thereby intimately connect seduction with sedition. For an insightful discussion of the layered meanings entailed in the term *fitna*, see Pandolfo 1997, 156–62.

[47] In addition to Abu Shuqqah, see, for example, M. al-Ghazali 1996; Z. al-Ghazali 1996b; al-Qaradawi, 1996.

[48] Abu Shuqqah, an Egyptian by birth, lived most of his adult life in Doha and Qatar. He was well known in Islamist circles, and founded the well-respected Islamist intellectual journal *al-Muslim al-Muʿāṣir*. According to Yusuf al-Qaradawi (see note 10 above), in his introduction to Abu Shuqqah's six-volume compendium, Abu Shuqqah was, in his youth, close to Hasan al-Banna (the founder of the Muslim Brotherhood), was imprisoned under Nasser (as was al-Qaradawi) for his support of the Brothers, and continued to be a loyal supporter of the Brotherhood throughout his life. This six-volume study, which reportedly took Abu Shuqqah twenty years to finish, is the only complete manuscript he authored. For a review of Abu Shuqqah's book, published upon his death, see Huwedi 1995.

[49] For example, when arguing for the rights of a woman to participate in the political, economic, and social life of her community, Abu Shuqqah is careful to spell out the conditions of her physical appearance in accordance with the majority juristic tradition: she must not be perfumed, she must wear dark-colored and loose clothing that does not draw attention to her body, she must not behave in beguiling ways, and so on (1995, 3:38–39).

There seems to be a contradiction here in that even though women and men are both acknowledged to have sexual desire, which they are encouraged to pursue within the private space of matrimonial life, in public it is only male sexuality that is accorded a force. Since men are understood to be more sexually excitable in public than women, it follows that various kinds of social rules are set up to protect against men's propensity to commit sexual transgressions. This is only one illustration of how these ideas about male-female sexuality provide the necessary ground upon which much of the current Islamist debate proceeds; those who challenge these presumptions are often treated as being outside the fold of Islam: as being either "un-Islamic" or "secularist."[50]

As a number of feminist scholars have pointed out, these kinds of arguments assign the burden of maintaining a community's purity and integrity to women, a task that necessitates their subordination to men, who are entrusted to oversee and control women's sexuality and mobility, as well as their access to a community's symbolic and material resources. In a system of inequality predicated on this view of male-female sexuality, differential gender roles are rooted in the naturalized topography of female and male nature in which the former is regarded as passive and the latter as agentival. Feminist cultural anthropologists have offered various explanations for why certain societies invest women's sexuality with this valence. Some scholars have focused on the logic of sexual symbology that reproduces and naturalizes gender subordination (Delaney 1991; Pitt-Rivers 1977); others have analyzed the socioeconomic organization of systems of kinship and inheritance that are at the root of sexually differentiated relations of gender inequality (Abu-Lughod 1986; Collier 1988; Ortner 1978).[51] While this work is crucial in offering various analytical paradigms to explain why and how female sexuality is linked to the production of gender subordination, my focus—in this chapter in particular, and in this book in general—is somewhat different.

My goal is not to explain why this particular system of gender inequality exists, but to ask: How did the women of the mosque movement practically work

[50] In this respect, the debate in Egypt about male-female interactions differs significantly from what is happening currently in Iran, where Muslim activists have begun to argue that since women and men are equal in the eyes of God, they equally share the burden of guarding against illicit sexual desire and conduct. See Mir-Hosseini 1999; Najmabadi 1998.

[51] Jane Collier, for example, argues, "Female chastity is not a single, coherent idiom with a single cause. Rather, it is a complex, multiply-determined symbol. In a world where legitimate heirs are distinguished from illegitimate non-heirs, a mother's chastity guarantees her children the right to inherit. Where only virgins are eligible to become mothers of legitimate children, a daughter's virginity may represent her family's hopes of upward mobility and political patronage" (Collier 1986, 106). Collier thus locates inheritance from fathers (whether in patrilineal or bilateral systems) as the key factor that gives a particular cast and form to practices and relations of gender.

upon themselves in order to become the desirous subjects of this authoritative discourse? What were the forms of reasoning and modes of persuasion they used to convince themselves and others of the truth of this discourse? And what were the practical consequences that followed when the truth of this discourse was argumentatively established? Clearly the women with whom I worked regarded the logic of feminine chastity and modesty as divinely ordained. Yet the task of living in accordance with this understanding was not a simple matter; it was mediated not only by debates internal to the Islamic tradition, particularly in its modernist reincarnation, but also by the practical conditions of the women's lives. In the foregoing analysis, part of my goal has been to explore the limits of this discursive tradition, its assumptions and presuppositions, and the day-to-day context through which these limitations were enacted, contested, and lived.

THE MODERNITY OF TRADITIONAL PRACTICES

I would like to conclude by making some observations about the notion of tradition that has informed this chapter, in particular its relationship to what is sometimes considered to be the opposite of tradition, modernity. It is fashionable these days to interpret any invocation of tradition, any claim to continuity with the past, as a nostalgic event, an "auratic" gesture that under the disillusioned (or hyperrealist?) modernist gaze crumbles to reveal the illusory character of such forms of (be)longing. Walter Benjamin's two essays, "The Storyteller" and "The Work of Art in the Age of Mechanical Reproduction," are sometimes used to give credence to this judgment.[52] In these essays, Benjamin argues that the fragmentary character of modern existence makes traditional crafts and modes of knowledge impossible to practice, rendering any access to these past practices impracticable under the new perceptual regimes of "the modern" (Benjamin 1969a, 1969b). Indeed, the informational nature of

[52] For two recent formulations of this use of Benjamin's argument, see Ivy 1995 and Mufti 2000. A closer reading of Benjamin's argument reveals, however, that Benjamin's interpretation of the terms "aura" and "authenticity" is far more complicated than these readings suggest. What is often missed in discussions of the aura and its loss is that for Benjamin what was at stake was not simply tradition but a sense of historicity itself (see Asad on this point in Shaikh 2002). Hannah Arendt, who is also known for remarks similar to Benjamin's about the loss of tradition in the modern age, exhibits a similar ambivalence about this loss: "it cannot be denied that without a securely anchored tradition—and the loss of this security occurred several hundred years ago—the whole dimension of the past has also been endangered. We are in danger of forgetting, and such oblivion—quite apart from the contents themselves that could be lost—would mean that, humanly speaking, we would deprive ourselves of one dimension, the dimension of depth in human existence" (Arendt 1977, 94).

the pedagogical Islamic materials I have described in this chapter, materials that are the mainstay of the Islamic Revival and the mosque movement, may well be regarded as emblematic of what Benjamin regards as the necessary character of modern knowledge: that it be gleaned from disparate sources, be promptly verifiable, and be of immediate practical application (Benjamin 1969a). It follows from Benjamin's argument that the practitioners of these forms of knowledge, despite their claims to the contrary, are only tenuously connected to past practices and modes of reasoning, since the institutional conditions that made these practices possible (such as guilds, or organized forms of apprenticeship and discipleship) no longer exist.[53]

Another related version of the same argument, commonly used within the social sciences and the humanities, suggests that a claim for the traditional status of a practice is a particularly modern mode of asserting its legitimacy: this mode uses the past as a reservoir of symbols, idioms, and languages to authorize political and social projects that are in fact quite recent in origin. Historians Eric Hobsbawm and Terrance Ranger popularized this notion by coining the term "invented tradition" to describe how the past is used to authenticate a novel set of practices that in fact lack historical antecedents (Hobsbawm 1983).[54] Several scholars of the Arab-Muslim world implicitly or explicitly use the idea of "invented tradition" to show how Islamists clothe a range of modern concepts—such as the nation-state, nuclear family, economics, and so on—in a vesture of authenticity and traditionalism in order to justify their uniquely modern sociopolitical projects (Abu-Lughod 1998; Gilsenan 1982; Zubaida 1993). These scholars conclude that such attempts at positing continuity with the past do not stand up under the analytical gaze, precisely because none of these concepts and institutions actually existed in premodern Islamic history: these invocations of the past are authenticating moves that lack sociohistorical facticity.

Even though I think these critiques raise important points about the disjunctural and fragmented character of modern existence and about the variable deployments of the past to legitimize current projects, I would suggest there are other ways of thinking about tradition that privilege a somewhat different set of analytical questions. Tradition may also be understood along the lines of what Foucault calls a "discursive formation," a field of statements and

[53] Olivier Roy (1994) and Malika Zeghal (1999) make similar arguments in regard to popular Islamic knowledges.

[54] Hobsbawm defines "invented tradition" as a "set of practices, normally governed by overtly or tacitly accepted rules and of a ritual or symbolic nature, which seek to inculcate certain values and norms of behavior by repetition, which automatically implies continuity with the past" (1983, 1). Invented traditions, in this view, use history to authenticate actions and claims, and to cement "group cohesion" (Hobsbawm 1983, 12).

practices whose structure of possibility is neither the individual, nor a collective body of overseers, but a form of relation between the past and present predicated upon a system of rules that demarcate both the limits and the possibility of what is sayable, doable, and recognizable as a comprehensible event in all its manifest forms.[55]

Talal Asad, in drawing upon the work of Alisdair MacIntyre (MacIntyre 1984, 1988), proposes a notion of tradition that is commensurable with Michel Foucault's work on discursive formations (T. Asad 1986).[56] Asad suggests that Islam is best regarded as a "discursive tradition" whose pedagogical practices articulate a conceptual relationship with the past, through an engagement with a set of foundational texts (the Quran and the ḥadīth), commentaries thereon, and the conduct of exemplary figures. Tradition, in this sense, may be conceived as a particular modality of Foucault's discursive formation in which reflection upon the past is a constitutive condition for the understanding and reformulation of the present and the future. Islamic discursive practices, in this view, link practitioners across the temporal modalities of past, present, and future through pedagogy of practical, scholarly, and embodied forms of knowledges and virtues deemed central to the tradition (T. Asad 1986, 14). Clearly indebted to Foucault's conception of power and discourse, Asad's formulation of tradition draws attention both to micropractices of interpersonal pedagogy, through which the truth of a particular discursive practice is established, and to the macrolevel of historically sedimented discourses, which determine the possibility of what is debatable, enunciable, and doable in the present.

Tradition, viewed in this way, is not a set of symbols and idioms that justify present practices, neither is it an unchanging set of cultural prescriptions that stand in contrast to what is changing, contemporary, or modern. Nor is it a historically fixed social structure. Rather, the past is the very ground through which the subjectivity and self-understanding of a tradition's adherents are constituted. An Islamic discursive tradition, in this view, is therefore a mode of discursive engagement with sacred texts, one effect of which is the creation of sensibilities and embodied capacities (of reason, affect, and volition) that in turn are the conditions for the tradition's reproduction. Significantly, such a concept does not assume all-powerful voluntary subjects who manipulate

[55] On discursive formation, see Dreyfus and Rabinow 1982; Foucault 1972, 1991b.

[56] Despite important overlaps, there are two critical differences, as I see it, between MacIntyre's notion of tradition and that of Talal Asad. One, Asad places an emphasis on relations of power that are necessary both for the propagation of a tradition in relation to other discursive traditions and to the process by which certain practices and arguments become hegemonic within a tradition. In MacIntyre's theory of tradition, there is no discussion of power. Asad also differs from MacIntyre in that he emphasizes the role embodied capacities (in addition to rational argumentation) play in the reproduction of a tradition.

the tradition for their own ends, but inquires into those conditions of discursive formulation that require and produce the kind of subjects who may speak in its name. The central question privileged by such an understanding of tradition is: how is the present made intelligible through a set of historically sedimented practices and forms of reasoning that are learned and communicated through processes of pedagogy, training, and argumentation?

The conceptual role that foundational texts play in Asad's notion of tradition is particularly relevant to the ways in which the participants of the mosque movement used the canonical sources (the Quran, the ḥadīth, and juristic commentaries). For Asad, an engagement with the founding texts of Islam is not limited to scholarly commentaries alone, but entails the practices of ordinary Muslims, such as when an unlettered Muslim invokes the authority of sacred texts to solve a practical problem, or a child argues with a parent about the correct (or incorrect) nature of an Islamic practice. By emphasizing the practical context through which foundational texts gain their specific meaning, Asad shifts from an understanding of scripture as a corpus of authoritatively inscribed scholarly opinions that stand for religious truth, to one in which divine texts are one of the central elements in a discursive field of relations of power *through which* truth is established. Thus the process by which a particular interpretation of a canonical source comes to be authorized depends not only upon one's knowledge of the scholarly tradition, but also upon the practical context of power relations (including hierarchies of age, class, gender, and knowledge) under which textual authority is invoked.[57]

As should be apparent by now, I have found Asad's conception of tradition eminently useful, for analytical as well as descriptive reasons, in exploring the practices of the movement I studied. Asad's notion of tradition is analytically useful because it helps me foreground questions of subject formation as a means of understanding how a particular discourse establishes its authority and truth within a historical moment. Descriptively speaking, many aspects of the mosque movement resonate with key aspects of this notion of tradition. The women I worked with understood their activities in terms of a recuperation of a set of traditional practices they saw as grounded in an exemplary past and in classical notions of Islamic piety. The modality of instruction through which they honed their skills involved a type of argumentation that was critically dependent on various types of historical reference. Yet, while certain continuities with earlier practices were evident, it was also clear that the mod-

[57] These various elements do not interact in a determinate way, and an established order of hierarchy may be challenged depending upon the particular context of power relations. For example, given the popularity of the daʿwa movement among younger generations, age hierarchy is often reversed when young duʿāt invoke higher moral authority and greater Islamic knowledge than their elders to criticize them for their lax religious lifestyles.

ern adaptations of classical Islamic notions did not mirror their historical precedents, but were modulated by, and refracted through, contemporary social and historical conditions.

In analyzing the renewed attention given to historical forms of ethical listening under the Islamic Revival, Charles Hirschkind provides an important corrective to Walter Benjamin's comments on the difficulty of practicing older forms of knowledges under modern conditions (Hirschkind 2001b). It is worth keeping his admonition in mind as we move into the next chapter, which focuses on the embodied character of Islamic knowledge practiced by the mosque movement. Hirschkind argues that the fractured space and temporality of modernity do not simply efface older forms of perception and knowledges, as Benjamin seems to suggest, but that these aspects of modernity also make possible the retrieval and maintenance of traditional practices and perceptual regimes, giving these practices a renewed life and novel form. Indeed, one of his points is that the adoption of what are termed "modern" ways of being do not signify a wholesale replacement of preexisting sensibilities, but are structured by, and embedded in, ongoing historical traditions. It therefore becomes critical to ask what types of relationships are established between newly emergent practices and knowledges, and those of the past, with special attention to elucidating the limits and possibilities of such articulations.

4

Positive Ethics and Ritual Conventions

Within the vast literature produced on the topic of contemporary Islam, Islamist movements have often been analyzed through the lens of identity politics. In such analyses, the increasing emphasis on Islamic forms of behavior among Muslims in the postcolonial Middle East has been commonly read as a recoding of nationalist sentiments in religious idioms, a recoding that does not so much replace Arab nationalism as recast its political sentiment in Islamic symbols. The increasing interest of Muslims in Islamic rituals and practices such as donning the veil, performing collective prayers, and listening to sermons is understood to enfold existent forms of Arab nationalism into particularistic forms of religious belonging, a development that has, if anything, narrowed the scope of nationalist politics by making the figure of the Muslim paradigmatic of the citizen subject. This continuity between Islamism and nationalism would appear to be all the more pronounced in regard to the question of gender, insomuch as both ideologies seem to cast women as the repositories of tradition and culture, their bodies made the potent symbols of collective identity.

Indeed, it is not difficult to find examples of the laminated character of Islamist-nationalist discourse in Egypt today. A number of Egyptian Islamists, for instance, speak of the veil as an expression of Arab identity (see chapter 2), while many of their secular-oriented critics view Islam as an essential part of the cultural terrain upon which the Egyptian nation has acquired its unique historical character.[1] In contrast to these views, however, a large number of those

[1] Consider, for example, how a primary-school textbook, widely used in Egypt today, recruits the ritual of Muslim prayer to the task of nation-building, "because in prayer there is rising and

who are part of the daʿwa movement are highly critical of such a nationalist-identitarian understanding of Islam, and direct their organizational efforts at combating the practical effects of this interpretation. The critique put forward by the daʿwa movement is not simply that the nationalist-identitarian view vitiates the religious character of Islam in rendering it a political ideology. Rather, as I suggested in chapter 2, their criticism is that such a position reduces Islamic ritual practices to the status of cultural customs, a kind of Muslim folklore, thereby radically transforming the role such practices have played historically in the realization of a pious life. However abstruse this might sound to secular ears, debates about how to interpret and enact the variety of embodied Islamic injunctions pervade Egyptian public life today, and even political discussions often devolve upon questions about the proper role ascribed to the performance of these practices.

To date, debates about the proper interpretation of religious obligations (such as veiling, fasting, or praying) have been treated as inconsequential in most analyses of the sociopolitical landscape created by the Islamic Revival over the last forty years. Scholars have tended to treat questions of bodily form as superficial particularities through which more profound cultural meanings find expression. Even in those instances where bodily practices (like veiling and praying) are considered within political analyses, they are understood as symbols deployed by social movements toward political ends, serving at most as vehicles for the expression of group interests or political differences. The specific conception of bodily practices and the forms they take are not in themselves seen to have political implications. This tendency is in part a product of the normative liberal conception of politics, one separate from the domain of ethics and moral conduct, and is in part a reflection of how the field of ethics has been conceptualized in the modern period. In regard to the latter, as I suggested in chapter 1, there is a general lack of attention paid within post-Enlightenment thought to what I earlier referred to as the morphology of moral actions, an omission reflecting the legacy of humanist ethics, particularly in its Kantian formulation. Since the Kantian tradition conceives of ethics as an abstract system of regulatory norms, values, and principles, it tends to disregard the precise shape moral actions take. In this view, ethical practices may elucidate a moral rule, or even symbolize the value a moral code exemplifies, but the manifest form of an ethical practice does not help elabo-

---

bowing and prostration, all actions that invigorate the body, and the Muslim devotes himself to work with zeal and energy, and increases production and spreads the good, and promotes [the progress of] the nation. . . . Prayer accustoms us to order, and the keeping of appointments, and the binding together of Muslims with cooperative ties and love and harmony" (quoted in Starrett 1995a, 962).

rate the substance of a moral system. It is therefore not surprising, for example, that even those scholars who write on the subject of Islamic ethics focus on Islamic doctrinal and legal arguments, while much of the literature that falls under the heading of *fiqh al-ʿibādāt* (the pedagogical aspects of religious obligations) remains outside of their purview.[2]

I would like to pursue a somewhat different approach to ethics here, glossed as "positive ethics" (the skeletal structure of which was laid out in chapter 1), in which the particular form that ethics takes is not a contingent but a necessary aspect of understanding its substantive content. Originally grounded in the tradition of ancient Greek philosophy, and more recently expanded by Michel Foucault, ethics in this formulation is founded upon particular forms of discursive practice, instantiated through specific sets of procedures, techniques, and exercises, through which highly specific ethical-moral subjects come to be formed (Colebrook 1998; Davidson 1994; Foucault 1997c; Hadot 1995, 2002; Martin, Gutman, and Hutton 1988). An inquiry into ethics from this perspective requires that one examine not simply the values enshrined in moral codes, but the different ways in which people live these codes—something anthropologists are uniquely situated to observe. What is consequential in this framework is not necessarily whether people follow the moral norms or not, but what relationships they establish between the various constitutive elements of the self (body, reason, emotion, volition, and so on) and a particular norm. In this view, the specific gestures, styles, and formal expressions that characterize one's relationship to a moral code are not a contingent but a necessary means to understanding the kind of relationship that is established between the self and structures of social authority, and between what one is, what one wants, and what kind of work one performs on oneself in order to realize a particular modality of being and personhood. (See my discussion of ethics in chapter 1.)

An obvious resonance exists between my exploration of processes of self-formation and anthropology's historical concern with the cultural construction of personhood, as represented in the work of scholars like Marcel Mauss, Margaret Mead, Erving Goffman, and Marilyn Strathern. However, two important differences distinguish my approach from this tradition of anthropological scholarship. First, the approach I have outlined here does not assume a homogeneous notion of a self that is coextensive with a given culture or temporality. Rather, as I will show, very different configurations of personhood can cohabit the same cultural and historical space, with each configuration the product of a specific discursive formation rather than of the culture at

[2] See, for example, Carney 1983; Hashmi 2002.

large.[3] One need only think of the different conceptions of self that operate within economic, legal, familial, and medical realms in the United States (however complexly intertwined and overlapping) to understand the analytical purchase of this presupposition (see, for example, Rorty 1987).[4] This insight is particularly germane to the fault line that exists in Egypt today between those who promote a nationalist-identitarian understanding of Islam, and those members of the daʿwa movement who oppose it. As I will show, different ways of understanding ritual obligations among Egyptian Muslims actually reveal radically different conceptualizations of the role bodily behavior plays in the construction of the self, a difference that in turn has consequences for how the horizon of individual freedom and politics is imagined and debated.

My analytical framing differs from anthropological studies of cultural constructions of personhood (particularly the work of Mead and Goffman)[5] in another respect: I do not begin my inquiry from the vantage point of an individuated consciousness that uses various corporeal techniques to acquire a cultural specificity. Rather, my investigation treats the empirical character of bodily practices as the terrain upon which the topography of a subject comes to be mapped, and I elaborate the architecture of the self through the immanent form bodily practices take—an analytical move that productively reverses the usual routing from interiority to exteriority in which the uncon-

[3] Consider, for example, Foucault's remarks on the different forms an ethical subject may take: "[The subject] is not a substance. It is a form, and this form is not primarily or always identical to itself. You do not have the same type of relationship to yourself when you constitute yourself as a political subject who goes to vote or speaks at a meeting and when you are seeking to fulfill your desires in a sexual relationship. Undoubtedly there are relationships and interferences between these different forms of the subject; but we are not dealing with the same type of subjects. In each case, one plays, one establishes a different type of relationship to oneself" (1997a, 290). See Nikolas Rose's comments on this aspect of Foucault's work (Rose 1998, 31–33).

[4] In this respect my argument differs from that of James Faubion, who has also argued for the productive application of Foucault's work on ethics to anthropology. Faubion suggests that Foucault's elaboration of ethics can be usefully mapped onto culturally specific notions of the self—such as the Haagen and Greek conceptions of personhood (2001, 90). In contrast, I am suggesting that there is no single conception of the self that corresponds to the discursive practices of a given culture, but that many different conceptions may exist simultaneously and perhaps in tension with one another, depending upon the particular regimes of truth to which they accede.

[5] As will become evident to the reader, my arguments share certain aspects of Marcel Mauss and Marilyn Strathern's work from this tradition of scholarship. With the former, I share an interest in how bodily techniques help construct specific conceptions of personhood (Mauss 1979), and with the latter I share a concern with the role different articulations of interiority and exteriority play in securing a particular sense of the self and its relationship to "the social" (Strathern 1988).

scious manifests itself in somatic forms. My understanding of bodily practices resonates with what Pierre Hadot calls "spiritual exercises"—a term he coined to elaborate a conception of life and ethics endemic to ancient Greek philosophy (Hadot 2002), and that was influential in Foucault's formulation of "technologies of the self" (Foucault 1997c). Hadot describes the notion of spiritual exercises as "practices which could be physical, as in dietary regimes, or discursive, as in dialogue and meditation, or intuitive, as in contemplation, but which were all intended to effect a modification and transformation in the subject who practiced them" (Hadot 2002, 6). What is striking about this approach to the explication of the self is that the *work* bodily practices perform in crafting a subject—rather than the *meanings* they signify (Bowen 1993; Starrett 1995a)—carries the analytical weight. In other words, the "how" of practices is explored rather than their symbolic or hermeneutical value.

Toward the end of the chapter, I will show how such an analysis of bodily practices helps us understand the question of politics, particularly the relationship between social authority and individual freedom. Specifically, I will argue that, far from being inconsequential, differential understandings of performative behavior and ritual observance among contemporary Egyptian Muslims enfold contrasting conceptions of individual and collective freedom—conceptions that have radically different implications for the organization of political life within public and personal domains. My ethnographic account of current debates about the formal requirements of bodily comportment will show that what is at stake in these debates are different imaginaries of personal and collective freedom, presupposing different relations to forms of social authority (whether enshrined in scripture, national citizenship, or exemplary models). As I will make clear, my argument differs from one made by certain liberal and communitarian philosophers who maintain that different conceptions of the individual depend upon the social milieus that produce and sustain these conceptions. In contrast, my argument is that the mosque movement's activities require a much deeper questioning of the weight accorded to the distinction between the individual and the social within theories of moral and political action in liberal and communitarian philosophies. In order to explicate these issues, let me turn to an analysis of the debates about ritual that saturate the contemporary political scene in Egypt.

PIETY AND PRAYER

The women I worked with described the condition of piety as the quality of "being close to God": a manner of being and acting that suffuses all of one's acts, both religious and worldly in character. Although the consummation of a pious comportment entails a complex disciplinary program, at a fundamental level it requires that the individual perform those acts of worship made incumbent upon Muslims by God (al-farā'iḍ),[6] as well as Islamic virtues (*faḍā'il*) and acts of beneficence that secure God's pleasure (*al-aʿmāl al-ṣāliḥa*). The attitude with which these acts are performed is as important as their prescribed form: sincerity (*al-ikhlāṣ*), humility (*khushūʿ*), and feelings of virtuous fear and awe (*khashya* or taqwa) are all emotions by which excellence and virtuosity in piety are measured and marked. Many of the mosque attendees noted that though they had always been aware of these basic Islamic duties, it was only through attending mosque lessons that they had acquired the necessary skills to perform them regularly and with diligence.

According to the mosque participants, one of the minimal requirements critical to the formation of a virtuous Muslim is the act of praying five times a day. The performance of ritual prayer (singular: *ṣalāt*; plural: *ṣalawāt*) is considered so centrally important in Islam that the question of whether someone who does not pray regularly qualifies as a Muslim has been a subject of intense debate among theologians.[7] The correct execution of ṣalāt depends on the following elements: (a) an intention to dedicate the prayer to God; (b) a prescribed sequence of gestures and words; (c) a physical condition of purity; and (d) proper attire. While fulfilling these four conditions renders prayer acceptable (*maqbūl*), I was told it is also desirable that ṣalāt be performed with all the feelings, concentration, and tenderness of the heart appropriate to the state of being in the presence of God—a state called *khushūʿ*.

While it is understandable that an ideal such as khushūʿ would have to be learned through intense devotion and training, it was surprising to me that mosque participants considered the desire to pray five times a day (with its minimal conditions of performance) an object of pedagogy. Many of the participants acknowledged that they did not pray diligently and seemed to lack the requisite will to accomplish what was required of them. They often held the general social and cultural ethos in which they lived to be responsible for the erosion of such a will, claiming that it instead fostered desires and dispositions that were quite inimical to the demands of piety. Because such states of will were *not* assumed to be natural by the teachers, or by their followers, women took extra care to teach one another the means by which the desire to pray could be cultivated and strengthened in the course of performing the sort of routine, mundane actions that occupied most women during the day.

The complicated relationship between the performance of ṣalāt and one's

[6] These include verbal attestation to faith (*shahāda*), praying five times a day (ṣalāt), fasting (*ṣaum*), the giving of alms (*zakāt*), and pilgrimage to Mecca (ḥajj).

[7] See the debate between two preeminent theologians—al-Shafiʿi (d. 820) and Ahmad Hanbal (d. 855)—on this issue (reported in Sabiq 1994, 72).

daily activities was revealed to me in a conversation that I observed among three women, all of whom regularly attended lessons in different mosques of their choice in Cairo. These women were among a small number of women whom I had come to regard as experienced in the cultivation of piety. My measure for coming to such a judgment was none other than the one used by the mosque participants: they not only carried out their religious duties (al-farāʾiḍ) diligently, but also attested to their faith (imān) by continuously doing good deeds (al-aʿmāl al-ṣāliḥa)[8] and practicing virtues (al-faḍāʾil). As the following exchange makes clear, these women pursued the process of honing and nurturing the desire to pray through the performance of seemingly unrelated deeds during the day (whether cooking, cleaning, or running an errand), until that desire became a part of their condition of being (also see footnote 20).

The setting for this conversation was a mosque in downtown Cairo. Since all of the three women worked in the same building as clerks for the local state bureaucracy, it was convenient for them to meet in the neighboring mosque in the late afternoons after work on a weekly basis. Their discussions sometimes attracted other women who had come to the mosque to pray. In this instance, a young woman in her early twenties had been sitting and listening intently when she suddenly interrupted the discussion to ask a question about one of the five basic prayers required of Muslims, a prayer known as *al-fajr*. This prayer is performed right after dawn breaks, before sunrise. Many Muslims consider it the most demanding and difficult of prayers because it is hard to leave the comfort of sleep to wash and pray, and also because the period within which it must be performed is very short. This young woman expressed the difficulty she encountered in performing the task of getting up for the morning prayer and asked the group what she should do about it.

Mona, a member of the group in her mid-thirties, turned to the young woman with a concerned expression on her face and asked, "Do you mean to say that you are unable to get up for the morning prayer *habitually and consistently*?" The young woman nodded yes. Bearing the same concerned expression on her face, Mona said, "You mean to say that you forbid yourself the reward [*ṣawāb*] of the morning prayer? This *surely* is an indication of *ghafla* on your part?" The young woman looked somewhat perturbed and guilty, but persisted and asked, "What does *ghafla* mean?" Mona replied that it refers to what you do in the day: if your mind is mostly occupied with things that are not related to God, then you are in a state of ghafla (carelessness, negligence). According to Mona, such a condition of negligence results in inability to say the morning prayer.

[8] Examples of al-aʿmāl al-ṣāliḥa include doing good deeds for the elderly, treating one's parents with respect, helping the needy, giving charity, and so on.

Looking puzzled, the young woman asked, "What do you mean what I do in the day? What does my saying of the prayer [ṣalāt] have to do with what I do in the day?" Mona answered:

> It means what your day-to-day deeds are. For example, what do you look at in the day? Do you look at things that are prohibited to us by God, such as immodest images of women and men? What do you say to people in the day? Do you insult people when you get angry and use abusive language? How do you feel when you see someone doing acts of disobedience [*maʿāṣi*]? Do you get sad? Does it hurt you when you see someone committing a sin or does it not affect you? These are the things that have an effect on your heart [*qalbik*], and they hinder or impede [*taʿaṭṭal*] your ability to get up and say the morning prayer. [The constant] guarding against disobedience and sins wakes you up for the morning prayer. Ṣalāt is not just what you say with your mouth and what you do with your limbs. It is a state of your heart. So when you do things in a day for God and avoid other things because of Him, it means you're thinking about Him, and therefore it becomes easy for you to strive for Him against yourself and your desires. If you correct these issues, you will be able to rise up for the morning prayer as well.

Perhaps responding to the young woman's look of concentration, Mona asked her, "What is it that annoys you [*bitghīẓik*] the most in your life?" The young woman answered that her sister fought with her a lot, and this bothered her and made her angry most days. Mona replied, "You, for example, can think of God when your sister fights with you and not fight back with her because He commands us to control our anger and be patient. For if you do get angry, you know that you will just gather more sins [*dhunūb*], but if you are quiet then you are beginning to organize your affairs on account of God and not in accord with your temperament. And then you will realize that your sister will lose the ability to make you angry, and you will become more desirous [*rāghiba*] of God. You will begin to notice that if you say the morning prayer, it will also make your daily affairs easier, and if you don't pray it will make them hard."

Mona looked at the young woman, who had been listening attentively, and asked: "Do you get angry and upset [*tizʿali*] when you don't say your morning prayer?" The young woman answered yes. Mona continued, "But you don't get upset enough that you don't miss the next morning prayer. Performing the morning prayer should be like the things you can't live without: for when you don't eat, or you don't clean your house, you get the feeling that you *must* do this. It is this feeling I am talking about: there is something inside you that makes you want to pray and gets you up early in the morning to pray. And you're angry with yourself when you don't do this or fail to do this." The young woman looked on and listened, not saying much. At this point, we moved back to our previous discussion, and the young woman stayed with us until the end.

The answer Mona gave this young woman was not a customary answer, such as invoking the fear of God's retribution for habitually failing to perform one's daily prayers. Mona's response reflects the sophistication and elaboration of someone who has spent considerable time and effort familiarizing herself with an Islamic interpretive tradition of moral discipline.[9] I would like to draw attention here to the economy of discipline at work in Mona's advice to the young woman, particularly the ways in which ordinary tasks in daily life are made to attach to the performance of consummate worship. Notably, when Mona links the ability to pray to the vigilance with which one conducts the practical chores of daily living, *all* mundane activities—such as getting angry with one's sister, the things one hears and looks at, the way one speaks—become a place for securing and honing particular moral capacities. As is evident from the preceding discussion, the issue of punctuality clearly entails more than the simple use of an alarm clock; it encompasses an entire attitude one cultivates in order to create the desire to pray. Of significance is the fact that Mona does not assume that the desire to pray is natural, but that it *must be created* through a set of disciplinary acts. That is to say, desire in this model is not the *antecedent* to, or cause of, moral action, but *its product*.[10] The techniques through which pious desires are cultivated include practices such as avoiding seeing, hearing, or speaking about things that make faith (imān) weaker, and engaging in those acts that strengthen the ability to enact obedience to God's will. The repeated practice of orienting all acts toward securing God's pleasure is a cumulative process, the net result of which is, on one level, the ability to pray regularly and, on another level, the creation of a pious self.

conventional behavior and pragmatic activity

Anthropological literature on ritual is a productive site to which one can turn to bring out the peculiarity of Mona's understanding of ritual prayer; it is a

[9] This tradition differs from other traditions of moral discipline within Islam such as the Sufi and Shīʿi traditions.

[10] This economy of action and desire reverses the Enlightenment model in which desires (sometimes along with volition) were considered to be the necessary antecedents to action. Susan James has traced the complex history of the changing status of passions and volition in theories of action within Western philosophical thought (1997). She argues that, following Descartes, the understanding of appetites and passions became more narrow, so that desire came to be regarded as the primary passion leading to action. Locke is interesting in this respect because, in contrast to Hobbes, he reintroduces the Scholastic understanding of volition as a mediating force against passions, but retains, nonetheless, the Hobbesian view that actions are explained by beliefs and desires (James 1997, 268–94).

site, moreover, that maps some familiar ways of thinking about the relationship between ritual behavior and pragmatic action,[11] and between conventional behavior[12] and spontaneous actions. To begin with, note that Mona's understanding of ritual prayer posits an ineluctable relationship between rule-governed or socially prescribed action and routine conduct. In Mona's formulation, ritual prayer is conjoined and interdependent with the pragmatic actions of daily life, actions that must be monitored and honed as conditions necessary for the felicitous performance of the ritual itself. This conjoining of ritual action with pragmatic activity problematizes a key distinction at the center of anthropological theories of ritual: the distinction between formal or conventional behavior, and routine, informal, or mundane activity. Even among those anthropologists who disagree about whether ritual action is a *type* of human behavior (e.g., Bloch 1975; Douglas 1973; Turner 1969) or an *aspect* of all kinds of human action (e.g., Leach 1964; Moore and Myerhoff 1977), there seems to be consensus that ritual activity is conventional and socially prescribed, setting it apart from mundane activities (Bell 1992, 70–74). Malinowski, for example, acknowledged the instrumental aspects of certain rituals, but then made this the basis for a distinction between "magical" and "religious" rites, wherein it was the former and not the latter that had an instrumental and pragmatic quality (Malinowski 1922).[13] Later anthropologists such as Victor Turner and Stanley Tambiah, even though they propose contrastive theories of ritual, tend to share this conception of ritual as distinct from pragmatic activity. Thus Turner's statement that ritual is "prescribed formal behavior for occasions not given over to technological routine" (1976, 504) is in keeping with Tambiah's view that "if we postulate a continuum of behavior, with intentional behavior at one pole and conventional behavior at

[11] Within anthropological discussions of ritual, the terms "pragmatic" and "technical" are frequently used interchangeably and should not be confused with the Aristotelian distinction between *praxis* (practical action) and *techne* (skill or craft). For Aristotle, *praxis* referred to a type of action defined in terms of goods and standards internal to the action itself, and *techne* referred to actions instrumentally applied to achieve a goal not internal to the actions themselves. Anthropologists of ritual, in contrast, use both terms—"pragmatic action" and "technical action"—to refer to routine mundane activities that one performs during the course of the day but which have no symbolic value associated with them.

[12] The term "conventional" is sometimes used to refer to ordinary or standard ways of doing things, and at other times to indicate behavior that is constrained by custom or social rules. I have used "conventional" in the latter sense, sometimes alternating it with phrases like "rule-governed and socially prescribed behavior."

[13] Later, with the decline of structural functionalism, anthropologists increasingly interpreted ritual as an expressive and communicative act, the meaning of which was to be deciphered by the analyst (see, for example, Clifford Geertz, Edmund Leach, and Stanley Tambiah). For a critical examination of this genealogy, see T. Asad 1993, 55–82; and Bell 1992, 182–96.

the other, we shall have to locate formalized ritual near the latter pole" (1985, 134).[14]

As is evident from Mona's discussion with the young woman, the mosque movement's understanding of ritual prayer stands in contrast to this view: according to participants in the mosque movement, ritualized behavior is one among a continuum of practices that serve as the necessary means to the realization of a pious self, and that are regarded as the critical instruments in a teleological program of self-formation. One might say that for women like Mona, ritual performances are understood to be disciplinary practices through which pious dispositions are formed, rather than symbolic acts that have no relationship to pragmatic or utilitarian activity.[15] This understanding is well captured in a comment I often heard in the mosque circles: that an act of prayer performed for its own sake, without adequate regard for how it contributes to the realization of piety, is "lost power" (*quwwa mafqūda*).

spontaneity and theatricality

Mona's discussion of ritual prayer also problematizes another polarity within anthropological discussions of ritual and conventional behavior: the polarity between the spontaneous expression of emotion and its theatrical performance (see Bloch 1975; Evans-Pritchard 1965; Obeyesekere 1981; Radcliffe-Brown 1964; Tambiah 1985; Turner 1969). Drawing on depth psychology, Victor Turner, for example, has argued that ritual action is a means of, and space for, channeling and divesting the antisocial qualities of powerful emotions.[16] Following this line of thought, other anthropologists have suggested that ritual is a space of "conventional" and not "genuine" (that is, personal or individual) emotions (Bloch 1975; Kapferer 1979; Tambiah 1985).[17] Ritual, in these views, is either understood to be the space where individual psychic

[14] Bloch expresses a similar view when he argues, "The reason why the formalized code is unsuitable for practical day-to-day maneuvering is because formalization creates an uncharted distance between specific things or situations and the communication" (1974, 65).

[15] See T. Asad 1993 for a discussion of this understanding of ritual action and how it came to be marginalized within anthropological theories of ritual.

[16] According to Victor Turner, "Powerful drives and emotions associated with human physiology, especially the physiology of reproduction, are divested in the ritual process of their antisocial quality and attached to components of the normative order, energizing the latter with a borrowed vitality, and thus making the Durkheimian 'obligatory' desirable" (1969, 52–53).

[17] See Scheff, who draws upon Turner's work to argue that ritual is the "distanced reenactment of situations which evoke collectively held emotional stress" such as fear, grief, anger, and embarrassment (1977, 489). None of the seventeen scholars responding to Scheff's argument in *Current Anthropology* take issue with his proposition that ritual facilitates the catharsis of universally valid emotions and produces a distance between the performers and their feelings (1977, 490–500).

drives are channeled into conventional patterns of expression, or where they are temporarily suspended so that a conventional social script may be enacted. Common to both these positions is the understanding that ritual activity is where emotional spontaneity comes to be controlled.[18]

At first blush, it may seem that Mona's understanding of the role emotions play within a ritual performance is consistent with the view that formal conventional behavior forecloses the possibility of the expression of spontaneous emotions (as, for example, when she advises the young woman to suppress her anger). Yet there are many ways in which Mona's understanding of prayer belies the neat separation of spontaneous emotions from disciplined behavior that anthropologists have taken for granted. A close examination of Mona's advice to the young woman reveals that the enactment of conventional gestures and behaviors devolves upon the *spontaneous* expression of *well-rehearsed* emotions and individual intentions, thereby directing attention to how one learns to express "spontaneously" the "right attitudes." For women like Mona, ritual (that is, conventional, formal action) is understood as the space par excellence for making their desires act spontaneously in accord with pious Islamic conventions.

This was brought home to me further in the considerable attention the mosque attendees paid to the act of crying during prayer as a mark of one's devotion to God. The ultimate sign of ṣalāt performed with consummate excellence (that is, with khushūʿ) is the act of weeping during the course of prayer, especially at the time of supplication (*duʿāʾ*). Yet this was not something that came naturally to the mosque participants, and they often discussed various ways of inducing this emotion in themselves while performing the prayers. One of the widely circulated booklets among the mosque groups, entitled "How Can You Feel Humility and Submission [khushūʿ] in Prayer?" provides various

[18] Much of this discussion assumes a particular model of the relation between the inner life of individuals and their outward expressions, a model predicated on a Cartesian understanding of the self as it was developed in early modern and Romantic thought in Europe. As a theatrical mode of self-presentation emerged as a legitimate and necessary form of commercial sociability in eighteenth-century Europe, Romantic thinkers, for example, came to see this development in terms of the need for a necessary detachment between the inner life of individuals and their social performances. Historian E. J. Hundert discusses this attitude in the work of Rousseau, who drew a clear separation between an inner self and its social performances, saying that "expressions of inner life resisted all attempts to encode it as a feature of social practices theatrically conceived, precisely because such a life was [regarded as] singular and self-defining" (1997, 82). Hundert quotes Rousseau from *The Confessions*: "I know my own heart. . . . I am made unlike anyone I have ever met. I will even venture to say that I am like no one in the whole world. I may be no better, but at least I am different" (1997, 82). This view of the unique privatized subject whose essence cannot be captured in the social conventions of a given society seems to resonate with the conception of ritual action as necessarily devoid of "authentic, individualized" emotions.

techniques that help develop one's capacity to cry spontaneously during ṣalāt (Maharib 1991). These entail various exercises of the body and the imagination geared toward exciting one's emotions, evoking the pious tenderness that khushūᶜ entails and that should ideally lead to weeping. Many of the women I knew advised one another to envision that they were being physically held between the hands of God during prayer in order to induce khushūᶜ, or to visualize crossing the legendary bridge (*al-ṣirāṭ*), narrow as a sharp blade, that all Muslims will be required to walk in the Hereafter but that only the pious will be able to traverse successfully, avoiding the fires of hell that lie beneath. Other women talked about imagining the immensity of God's power and their own insignificance.[19] As I will discuss later in the chapter, the principle underlying these exercises is that repeated invocations of weeping, with the right intention, habituate the cardinal virtue of fear of God (taqwa) to the point that it infuses all of one's actions, of which ritual obligations are an important part. Virtuous fear becomes, in other words, a part of one's "natural" disposition such that one does not have to simulate it but it issues forth spontaneously.

As the booklet and discussions among the mosque attendees make clear, weeping during the course of prayer is not tantamount to crying provoked by the pain of personal suffering. Nor must it be undertaken for the sake of impressing fellow Muslims, an act that some Muslim theologians explicitly identify as idolatrous (*shirk*). This weeping must instead issue forth out of a sense of being overwhelmed by God's greatness, and must be enacted with the intention of pleasing Him.[20] Thus, the mosque participants do not consider fear and weeping, within the context of ritual action, to be generic expressions or acts devoid of intentionality; they are specific to the economy of motivation and action of which they are a constitutive part and, in an important sense, impart to the ritual action its distinctive quality.

It might be tempting to explain such a reorientation of emotions as simply a performance of social obligations in the delimited context of acts of worship and, in keeping with anthropological theories of ritual, as an enactment of a socially authorized discourse that has little to do with what one "genuinely" or

[19] There is a strong resonance here with Epicurean practices of self-formation in which imagery and affect played a central role. See Hadot 2002, 113–26.

[20] There is a large body of literature in Islam that deals with the importance of intention (*al-niyya*) in the performance of religious and worldly acts. Thus the same act (such as slaughtering an animal) can acquire a different status depending on the intention with which it is undertaken—from an act of worship, to an ordinary act of tending to one's hunger, to an idolatrous act (al-Nawawi 1990, 23). Many of the mosque participants' discussions focused on how to render mundane tasks of daily living virtuous by dedicating the intention accompanying these acts to God, a process that oriented one's "secular" acts toward securing His pleasure. For a contrastive reading of similar debates about the proper role of intention in Muslim prayer in Indonesia, see Bowen 1989, 2000.

"truly" feels (as, for example, when one cries out of distress) (Bloch 1975; Scheff 1977; Tambiah 1985; Turner 1969).[21] However tempting such a reading may be, I would argue that it would be a mistake to reduce the practice of weeping in prayer to a cross-cultural example of conventionalized behaviors that are assumed to achieve the same goal in all contexts (see Mahmood 2001b). Such a view does not give adequate attention to those performances of conventional behavior that are aimed at the development and formation of the self's spontaneous and effortless expressions. As is clear from the examples I give above, the pedagogical program among the mosque participants was geared precisely toward making prescribed behavior natural to one's disposition, and one's virtuosity lay in being able to spontaneously enact its most conventional aspects in a ritual context as much as in ordinary life, thereby making an a priori separation between individual feelings and socially prescribed behavior unfeasible. Thus, ritual worship, for the women I worked with, was both *enacted through*, and *productive of*, intentionality, volitional behavior, and sentiments—precisely those elements that a number of anthropologists assume to be dissociated from the performance of ritual. Importantly, in this formulation, ritual is not regarded as the theater in which a preformed self enacts a script of social action; rather, the space of ritual is one among a number of sites where the self comes to acquire and give expression to its proper form.

RITUAL PERFORMANCE AS A MEANS AND AN END

Let me consider a different understanding of ritual prayer that contrasts sharply with the one captured in Mona's advice to the young woman, but that enjoys common currency among Egyptian Muslims. In what follows, I will quote a passage on the performance of ṣalāt written by Mona Hilmi, a woman columnist who contributes regularly to the weekly magazine *Rūz al-Yūsuf*, which represents a liberal-nationalist perspective in the Egyptian press. Hilmi's article was prompted by the arrest of several teenagers from upper-middle-class and upper-class families for allegedly participating in "devil worship" (*ʿibādat al-shaiṭān*). This incident was widely reported in the Egyptian

[21] Stanley Tambiah, for example, argues that "ordinary acts 'express' attitudes and feelings directly (for example, crying denotes distress in Western society) and 'communicate' that information to interacting persons (the person crying wishes to convey to another his feeling of distress). But ritualized, conventionalized, stereotyped behavior is construed in order to express and communicate, and is publicly construed as expressing and communicating certain attitudes congenial to an ongoing institutionalized intercourse. . . . *Stereotyped conventions . . . code not intentions but 'simulations' of intentions*" (1985, 132; emphasis added).

press and prompted a discussion about the appropriate role of religion—in particular ritual worship—in Egyptian society. Hilmi wrote:

> The issue is not whether people perform rituals and acts of worship [ʿibādāt] either to get recompense or reward [ṣawāb], or out of fear of God, or the desire to show off in front of other people. The issue instead is how rituals [*ṭuqūs*] and worship [ʿibādāt] prepare for the creation of a type of person who thinks freely, is capable [*mu'ahhal*] of enlightened criticism on important daily issues, of distinguishing between form and essence, between means and ends, between secondary and basic issues. The biggest challenge is how to transform love for God inside every citizen [*muwāṭin wa muwāṭina*] into continuous self-criticism of our daily behaviors and manners, and into an awakening of innovative/creative revolutionary thought that is against the subjugation of the human being and the destruction of his dignity. (Hilmi 1997, 81)

Clearly Hilmi's argument engages with the significance of religious practice in Egyptian society, but her interpretation of ritual practice is quite distinct from the one that Mona and her friends espoused. For one thing, Hilmi's ideas about what kind of person should be created in the process of performing rituals are clearly different from the ideas of the women I worked with. Hilmi imbues her view of what a human being should become with the language and goals of liberal-nationalist thought: the highest goal of worship for her is to create a human being capable of "enlightened criticism on important daily issues" and "revolutionary thought that is against the subjugation of human beings" (1997, 81). As a result, Hilmi addresses "the citizen" (muwāṭin wa muwāṭina) in her call to duty rather than "the faithful" (mu'min wa mu'mina) or "slaves of God" (*ʿibād allāh*), the terms more commonly used by the women with whom I worked. In contrast, for many of the mosque participants, the ultimate goal of worship was the natural and effortless performance of the virtue of submission to God. Even though women like Mona subjected their daily activities to self-criticism (as Hilmi recommends), they did so in order to secure God's approval and pleasure rather than to hone those capacities referred to by Hilmi and central to the rhetoric of liberal citizenship.

I do not mean to suggest that the discourses of nationalism have been inconsequential in the development of the mosque movement or that the modern state and its forms of power (social, political, and economic) have not shaped the lives of the women I worked with in important ways. My point is simply that the inculcation of the ideals of enlightened citizenship is *not* the aim of worship for the women I worked with as it seems to be for Hilmi. Note that Hilmi does not abide by a deistic and deontologized conception of religiosity, one in which embodied rituals play no role in the creation of the religious subject. (In this sense, Hilmi and Mona agree that rituals like ṣalāt *should* play a role in the creation of a proper Muslim subjectivity.) But where the two women disagree sharply is in their ideas of what this end ("proper Muslim subjectivity") actually entails, that is, what *kind* of Muslim one should ideally become through the performance of these rituals.

Furthermore, the different models of an ends-and-means relationship that Mona's and Hilmi's understandings of ṣalāt presuppose mark a critical disjuncture between the two perspectives. For Hilmi, it seems, the goal of creating modern autonomous citizens remains independent of the means she proposes (Islamic rituals); indeed, one may argue, various modern societies have accomplished the same goal through other means. In Hilmi's schema, the means (ritual or ṣalāt) and the end (the model liberal citizen) can be characterized without reference to each other, and a number of quite different means may be employed to achieve one and the same end. In other words, whereas rituals such as ṣalāt may, in Hilmi's view, be usefully enlisted for the project of creating a self-critical citizenry, they are not necessary but *contingent* acts in the process. Hence Hilmi emphasizes the citizen's ability to distinguish between essence and form—that is, between an inner meaning conceptually independent from the outward performances that express it—and the dangers of conflating the two.

In contrast, for women like Mona, ritual acts of worship are the sole and ineluctable means of forming pious dispositions. A central aspect of ritual prayer, as understood by most mosque participants and captured in Mona's discussion above, is that it serves both as a *means* to pious conduct and an *end*. In this logic, ritual prayer (ṣalāt) is an end in that Muslims believe God requires them to pray, and a means insofar as it transforms daily action, which in turn creates or reinforces the desire for worship. Thus, the desired goal (pious worship) is also one of the means by which that desire is cultivated and gradually made realizable. Moreover, in this worldview, neither consummate worship nor the acquisition of piety are possible without the performance of prayer in the prescribed (that is, codified) manner and attitude. As such, outward bodily gestures and acts (such as ṣalāt or wearing the veil) are indispensable aspects of the pious self in two senses: first in the sense that the self can acquire its particular form only through the performance of the precise bodily enactments; and second in the sense that the prescribed bodily forms are necessary attributes of the self.

Notably, Hilmi and Mona's understandings of ritual action entail very different articulations of interiority and exteriority, despite their shared reliance on this dichotomy. Indeed, as Marilyn Strathern has astutely observed, what is analytically interesting is not so much the binary nature of the inner/outer distinction when found in a particular cultural context, but the relation between these two terms, the particular form their articulation takes (Strathern 1988, 88).[22] In what follows I will reflect further upon the relationship between inwardness and outwardness articulated within the practices of the mosque participants, in particular on the techniques and exercises through which this relationship was secured. My aim in pursuing this is to analyze how different conceptions of interiority and exteriority are predicated upon different arrangements of power and authority, which in turn enfold contrastive visions of what it means to act politically in this world.

EXTERIORITY AS A MEANS TO INTERIORITY

The ongoing contestation in Egypt about the proper understanding of ritual performance is reminiscent of similar debates about worship in a variety of historical and cultural contexts.[23] One debate that has strong parallels with the one taking place in Egypt today occurred in Renaissance England over the question of whether or not Protestant Christian notions of devotional practice required a prescribed form of collective prayer. Literary critic Ramie Targoff challenges the established scholarship on the Renaissance which has traditionally argued that the separation between a public exteriority and a privatized interiority, so characteristic of modernity, was secured in this period. Targoff explores a counterdiscourse within the Renaissance that was critical of such a separation and sought to reentrench the link between outward behavior and the interiorized subjectivity of the individual (Targoff 1997, 2001).

In making her argument, Targoff focuses on debates that were spurred by the Church of England's adoption of a formalized structure of public prayer, conducted in the vernacular. The prescribed form of this public prayer was spelled out in the *Book of Common Prayer*, a manual that came to be widely used in the late sixteenth- and early seventeenth-century English churches. Such a move toward standardization may seem surprising given the Protestant tendency to emphasize individualized forms of devotional practice that, in contrast to Catholicism's emphasis on sacraments and liturgy, were considered

[22] Thus we find that even though Plato and Aristotle both used the body/soul distinction, they had very different conceptions of the relationship between the two terms. Plato accorded the soul a metaphysical priority over the body, whereas for Aristotle the two were part of an inseparable unity in which the soul became the form of the body's matter. In keeping with this language, one might say that the women I worked with seemed to regard the body almost as the material enactment of the soul whereby the latter was a condition for the former.

[23] See, for example, Garrett 1993; Keane 1997, 2002; Nuttall 1992.

to be the "original and spontaneous" expression of one's spiritual experience.[24] Targoff explains this seeming discordance by examining two key assumptions that undergirded the Protestant leadership's decision to adopt a uniform model for public worship. First, the ecclesiasts in the Church of England regarded visible forms of public prayer—manifest in "the worshipper's physical posture, the tone of her words, and the nature of her expression"—as markers and measures of her sincerity and devotion, not only to outside observers but also for the worshiper herself (1997, 57). Second, they also believed in the power of public performance to transform the worshiper's soul, and regarded performative behavior (in this case, collective prayer) as a vehicle of inward change. What to their critics seemed to be a misplaced faith in outward behavioral forms as reflections of a corresponding interiority, was for the Church officials a logical extension of the necessary interdependence of body and soul (Targoff 2001, 17). Targoff astutely points out that the debates about these formal prayer structures turned upon contrastive understandings of performative behavior and its relationship to interiority, the contentious nature of which is elided if we read the Church's policy as nothing more than ecclesiastical ambition.[25] For the ecclesiasts, prescribed forms of collective prayer, manifest in specific bodily gestures and behaviors, were a necessary means of creating the requisite devotional attitudes and dispositions among the worshipers (Targoff 2001, 10).

There are multiple levels of resonance between the Church of England's faith in the power of public prayer and the mosque movement's conception of ṣalāt as a disciplinary practice. One in particular that I want to explore in some depth is the Aristotelian model of ethical pedagogy undergirding both conceptions, in which external performative acts (like prayer) are understood to create corresponding inward dispositions. Among a range of ancient Greek concepts adopted by early Christians as well as Muslims is the Aristotelian formulation of *habitus*, which is concerned with ethical formation and presupposes a specific pedagogical process by which a moral character is secured.[26]

[24] This move toward standardization does not appear to be surprising at all, of course, if we take into account the role Protestantism played in the formation of the nation-state in England. Similar attempts at standardization exist in other places in early modern Europe where religion played a role in the creation of the modern state.

[25] Targoff points out that these contrasting notions of the linkage between interiority and exteriority were not limited to religious circles alone in Renaissance England, but were also extant in secular culture—particularly among the theatricalists and their critics (1997).

[26] For discussions of the Christian adaptation and reformulation of the Aristotelian notion of habitus, see Carruthers 1990; Inglis 1999; and Nederman 1989–90. For historical discussions of how ancient Greek ideas came to be adopted and developed in the Islamic tradition, see Fakhry 1983; Sherif 1975; and Watt 1985.

The term *habitus* has become best known in the social sciences through the work of Pierre Bourdieu, who uses it as a theoretical concept to explain how the structural and class positions of individual subjects come to be embodied as dispositions—largely through unconscious processes (Bourdieu 1977). My own work draws upon a longer and richer history of this term, however, one that addresses the centrality of gestural capacities in certain traditions of moral cultivation and that is therefore analytically more useful for my purposes. *Habitus* in this older Aristotelian tradition is understood to be an acquired excellence at either a moral or a practical craft, learned through repeated practice until that practice leaves a permanent mark on the character of the person. Thus, moral virtues (such as modesty, honesty, and fortitude) are acquired through a coordination of outward behaviors (e.g., bodily acts, social demeanor) with inward dispositions (e.g., emotional states, thoughts, intentions) through the repeated performance of acts that entail those particular virtues.

In *Nicomachean Ethics*, Aristotle makes a distinction between intellectual and moral virtues, and it appears that the pedagogical principle of habitus pertains to the latter but not the former:

> Virtue, then, being of two kinds, intellectual and moral, intellectual virtue in the main owes both its birth and its growth to teaching (for which reason it requires experience and time), while moral virtue comes about as a result of habit, whence also its name *ethike* is one that is formed by a slight variation from the word *ethos* (habit). From this it is also plain that none of the moral virtues arise in you by nature; for nothing that exists by nature can form a habit contrary to nature. . . . For the things we have to learn before we can do them, we learn by doing them, e.g. men become builders by building and lyre players by playing the lyre; so too we become just by doing just acts, temperate by doing temperate acts, brave by doing brave acts. . . . By doing the acts we do in our transactions with other men we become just or unjust, and by doing the acts that we do in the presence of danger, and being habituated to feel fear or confidence, we become brave or cowardly. (Aristotle 1941, 592–93)

While a virtuous habitus is acquired through virtuous habits, the two are not to be confused because habitus—unlike habits—once acquired through assiduous practice, takes root in one's character and is considered largely unchangeable. What is noteworthy is that *habitus* in this tradition of moral cultivation implies a quality that is acquired through human industry, assiduous practice, and discipline, such that it becomes a permanent feature of a person's character. In other words, "a habitus can be said to exist only when someone has actively formed it" (Nederman 1989–90, 96).[27] Premeditated learning is a teleological process in this sense, aimed at making moral behavior a nondeliberative aspect of one's disposition. Both vices and virtues in this understanding—insofar as they are considered products of human endeavor, rather than revelatory experience or natural temperament—are acquired through the repeated performance of actions that entail a particular virtue or vice, until all behavior comes to be regulated by the habitus. The appeal of this notion to Christian and Muslim theologians is not hard to understand given its emphasis on human activity and deliberation, rather than divine grace or divine will, as determinants of moral conduct.

This Aristotelian understanding of moral formation influenced a number of Islamic thinkers, foremost among them the eleventh-century theologian Abu Hamid al-Ghazali (d. 1111), but also al-Miskawayh (d. 1030), Ibn Rushd (d. 1198), and Ibn Khaldun (d. 1406). Historian Ira Lapidus draws attention to this genealogy in his analysis of Ibn Khaldun's use of the Arabic term *malaka*.[28] Lapidus argues that although Ibn Khaldun's use of the term *malaka* has often been translated as "habit," its sense is best captured in the Latin term *habitus*, which Lapidus describes as "that inner quality developed as a result of outer practice which makes practice a perfect ability of the soul of the actor" (Lapidus 1984, 54). Consider, for example, Ibn Khaldun's remarks in *The Muqadimmah*, which bear remarkable similarity to Aristotle's discussion: "A habit[us] is a firmly rooted quality acquired by doing a certain action and repeating it time after time, until the form of that action is firmly fixed [in one's disposition]. A habit[us] corresponds to the original action after which it was formed" (Ibn Khaldun 1958, 346). In terms of faith, *malaka*, according to Lapidus, "is the acquisition, from the belief of the heart and the resulting actions, of a quality that has complete control over the heart so that it commands the action of the limbs and makes every activity take place in submissiveness to it to the point that all actions, eventually, become subservient to this affirmation of faith. This is the highest degree of faith. It is perfect faith" (1984, 55–56).

This Aristotelian legacy continues to live within the practices of the contemporary daʿwa movement in Egypt. It is evident in the frequent invocation of Abu Hamid al-Ghazali's spiritual exercises and techniques of moral cultivation, found in popular instruction booklets on how to become pious, and often referred to in ordinary conversations within the daʿwa circles (see, for ex-

[27] Nederman notes, "Aristotle does not . . . construe the permanence and stability of moral character as the product of an in-bred or natural inheritance. Nature bestows upon man only a capacity . . . to be good or evil. The capacity must be actualized through moral education" (1989–90, 90).

[28] See Leaman 1999 for a discussion of the term *malaka* in the Islamic tradition.

ample, Farid 1990, 1993; Hawwa 1995).[29] Even though the term *malaka* is not used in these publications and discussions, the role outward behavioral forms play in shaping moral character is clearly indebted to Islamic reformulations of Aristotle's notion of habitus, as will become clear below.

Since it is almost impossible to discuss the term *habitus* in the social sciences without evoking the work of Pierre Bourdieu, it is best to clarify how the older Aristotelian genealogy differs from Bourdieu's use of the term and why I have found the older formulation more useful for analyzing the practices of the mosque movement. Bourdieu proposed the notion of habitus as a means to conceptually integrate phenomenological and structuralist approaches in order to elucidate how the supraindividual structure of society comes to be lived in human experience (Bourdieu 1977, 1990). For Bourdieu, habitus is a "generative principle" through which "objective conditions" of a society are inscribed in the bodies and dispositions of social actors (1977). According to Bourdieu, structured dispositions that constitute habitus correspond to an individual's class or social position and are engendered "in the last analysis, by the economic bases of the social formation in question" (1977, 83). While Bourdieu acknowledges that habitus is learned—in the sense that no one is born with it—his primary concern is with the unconscious power of habitus through which objective social conditions become naturalized and reproduced. He argues that "practical mimesis" (the process by which habitus is acquired) "has nothing in common with an *imitation* that would presuppose a conscious effort to reproduce a gesture, an utterance or an object explicitly constituted as a model . . . [instead] the process of reproduction . . . tend[s] to take place below the level of consciousness, expression and the reflexive distance which these presuppose. . . . What is 'learned by the body' is not something that one has, like knowledge that can be brandished, but something that one is" (Bourdieu 1990, 73).

Apart from the socioeconomic determinism that characterizes Bourdieu's discussion of bodily dispositions,[30] what I find problematic in this approach is

[29] While A. H. al-Ghazali was critical of the neo-Platonist influence on Islam (Fakhry 1983, 217–33), his ethical thought retained a distinctly Aristotelian influence. On this point, see Sherif 1975, and the introduction by T. J. Winter in A. H. al-Ghazali 1995, xv–lxxi. For A. H. al-Ghazali's seminal work on practices of moral self-cultivation, see A. H. al-Ghazali 1984, 1992, 1995.

[30] The correspondence Bourdieu draws between the class and social position of social actors and their bodily dispositions needs to be complicated by the fact that in any given society there are traditions of discipline and self-formation that cut across class and social positions. See Cantwell 1999 for an excellent discussion of this point. Indeed, my work with mosque groups from a wide range of socioeconomic backgrounds shows that the tradition of moral formation I have described, with its corresponding pedagogical program, while inflected by relations of social hierarchy, did not in any simple way reflect the social and class position of the participants. For a discussion of this point in the context of other traditions of discipline, see Foucault 1997c; Hadot 1995; and Rose 1998.

its lack of attention to the pedagogical process by which a habitus is learned. In the ethnographic account I have presented of the mosque movement, the body was thematized by the mosque participants as a site of moral training and cultivation; the intentional nature of this cultivation problematizes the narrow model of unconscious imbibing that Bourdieu assumes in his discussion of habitus. Consistent with the Aristotelian conception of habitus, conscious training in the habituation of virtues itself was undertaken, paradoxically, with the goal of making consciousness redundant to the practice of these virtues. This was evident in Mona's advice to the young woman when she said that one should become so accustomed to the act of praying five times a day that when one does not pray one feels just as uncomfortable as when one forgets to eat: at this stage, the act of prayer has attained the status of an almost physiological need that is fulfilled without conscious reflection. Yet it would be a mistake to say that mosque participants believe that once a virtue has taken root in one's disposition, it issues forth perfunctorily and automatically. Since the point is not simply *that* one acts virtuously but also *how* one enacts a virtue (with what intent, emotion, commitment, and so forth), constant vigilance and monitoring of one's practices is a critical element in this tradition of ethical formation. This economy of self-discipline therefore draws attention to the role self-directed action plays in the learning of an embodied disposition and its relationship to "unconscious" ways of being.[31]

In summary, even though Bourdieu draws upon the Aristotelian tradition in retaining the sense that habitus, once acquired, is a durable aspect of one's disposition, he leaves aside the pedagogical aspect of the Aristotelian notion as well as the context of ethics within which the notion of habitus was formulated. One result of Bourdieu's neglect of the manner and process by which a person comes to acquire a habitus is that we lose a sense of how specific conceptions of the self (there may be different ones that inhabit the space of a single culture) require different kinds of bodily capacities. In contrast, the Aristotelian notion of habitus forces us to problematize how specific kinds of bodily practice come to articulate different conceptions of the ethical subject, and how bodily form does not simply express the social structure but also endows the self with particular capacities through which the subject comes to enact the world.

[31] Gregory Starrett (1995a) has drawn attention to Bourdieu's neglect of the role explicit discourse plays in fixing the ideological meaning of embodied practices. While I agree with Starrett's critique, my point here is somewhat different in that I am interested in conscious action that is directed at making certain kinds of behaviors unconscious or nondeliberative. See my response to Starrett's argument, Mahmood 2001b. For an argument similar to Starrett's from a different cultural context, see Bowen 1989, 2000.

FEAR, FELICITY, AND MORAL ACTION

Perhaps no other theme of the mosque lessons better captures the Aristotelian principle of ethical formation than that of the classical triad of fear (*al-khauf*), hope (*al-rajā'*), and love (*al-ḥubb*) invoked by the attendees and the dāʿiyāt.[32] The process of cultivating and honing a pious disposition among the mosque participants centered not only on the practical tasks of daily living, as we have seen, but also on the creation and orientation of the emotions such a disposition entailed. As elaborated in the mosque lessons, fear (al-khauf) is the dread one feels from the possibility of God's retribution (such as, fires of hell), an experience that leads one to avoid indulging in those actions and thoughts that may earn His wrath and displeasure; hope (al-rajā') is the anticipation of the closeness to God one would achieve if one were to act piously; and love (al-ḥubb) is the affection and devotion one feels for God, which in turn inspires one to pursue a life in accordance with His will and pleasure. Thus, each emotion is tied to an economy of action that follows from the experience of that particular emotion.

For a long period during my work with the mosques, I understood this tripartite matrix of emotion and action in terms of the "carrot and stick" of religious discipline. It appeared to me that the elements of hope and love were the "carrot" of religion insomuch as the promise of gaining merit with or recompense (*ḥasanāt*) from God inspired one to undertake religious duties. Likewise, fear of God's wrath was the "stick" that motivated one to abstain from sins and vices. It was only toward the end of my two-year period of fieldwork that I began to realize the triad's complex relationship to the larger system of pedagogy, wherein these emotions are constituted not simply as motivational devices, but as integral aspects of pious action itself. Moreover, it became apparent to me that the argument that people are driven to behave piously because of the fear of hell or the promise of rewards leaves unexplained what it seeks to answer: specifically, how these emotions are acquired and come to command authority in the topography of a particular moral-passional self. In what follows, therefore, I want to attend to the specific texture of these emotions—in particular, fear—and to understand how they came to be constituted as motives for, and modalities of, pious conduct in the realization of a virtuous life.

Consider the following excerpt from a mosque lesson delivered by Hajja Samira, mentioned in the earlier chapters of this book, who often draws an audience of five hundred women at the Nafisa mosque. Hajja Samira was well

[32] For a discussion of the triad of fear-hope-love in the Sunni tradition, see McKane 1965.

known for her repeated evocations of fear in her weekly lessons, and was sometimes criticized by her audience for these evocations. In response, she had the following to say one morning as she wrapped up her hour-long lesson (dars):

> People criticize us for evoking fear in our lessons [durūs]. But look around you: Do you think ours is a society that is afraid of God? If we were afraid of Him and His fury [*qahr*], do you think we would behave in the way we do? We are all humans and commit mistakes, and we should ask for forgiveness from Him continually for these. But to commit sins *intentionally*, as a habit, is what is woeful! Do we feel remorse and cry at this condition of the Islamic community [umma]? No! We do not even know we are in this condition. The last shred of fear in our hearts has been squeezed out by the countless sins we commit, so that we don't even know the difference between what is permissible and what is not [ḥarām wa ḥalāl]. Remember that if we cannot cry out of fear of the fires of hell, then we should certainly cry at the condition of our souls!

These remarks are striking for the ineluctable relationship Hajja Samira draws between the ability to fear God and capacities of moral discernment and action. In this formulation, the emotion of fear does not simply serve as a motivation for the pursuit of virtue and avoidance of vice, but has an epistemic value: it enables one to know and distinguish between what is good for oneself and for one's community and what is bad (in accordance with God's program). Notably, according to Hajja Samira, the repeated act of committing sins intentionally and habitually has the cumulative effect of making one into the kind of person who has lost the capacity to fear God, a loss that in turn is understood as the ultimate sign of the inability to judge the status of one's moral condition.[33] For many Muslims, the ability to fear God is considered to be one of the critical registers by which one monitors and assesses the progress of the moral self toward virtuosity, and the absence of fear is regarded as the marker of an inadequately formed self. Hajja Samira, therefore, interprets the incapacity of Egyptian Muslims today to feel frightened of the retribution of God as both the *cause* and the *consequence* of a life lived deliberately without virtue.

The various elements of this economy of emotion and action were clarified to me further by one of the longtime attendees of Hajja Samira's lessons.

[33] This logic is captured well in the Quranic phrase (often repeated by the mosque participants) that describes those who commit sins habitually as doing "injustice to themselves" (*ẓalama nafsahu*). Hence Hajja Samira's statement that the condition of habitual sinners deserves the utmost pity because their real punishment is their deficient and ill-formed characters for which they will not only pay in the Hereafter, but also in this world. For an excellent discussion of the concept of "doing injustice to oneself" as it occurs in the Quran, see Izutsu 1966, 164–72.

Umm Amal, a gentle woman in her late fifties, had recently retired after having worked as an administrator for the Egyptian airline most of her life. Having raised two children single-handedly and through adversity, she had acquired a forgiving and accommodating temperament that seemed quite the opposite of Hajja Samira, who was often strict and unrelenting in her criticisms of the impious behavior of Egyptian women. It came as a surprise to me, therefore, when Umm Amal defended Hajja Samira's emphasis on fear in her lessons, in particular her evocations of themes such as the tortures of hell and the pain of death. I asked Umm Amal what she meant when she said that she feared God, and how she thought it affected her ability to feel close to God. She responded:

> I feel fear of God not simply because of threats of hell and torments of the grave [*ʿadhāb al-qabr*], though these things are also true because God mentions them in the Quran. But for me the real fear of God stems from two things: from the knowledge that He is all powerful [*qudratihi*], and from the knowledge of the sins that we have committed in our lives and continue to commit without knowing. Imagine God is the Lord of all worlds. And knowing this engenders fear and awe [khashya wa khushūʿ] in you. This is different from fear [al-khauf] that paralyzes you, because it is fear that motivates you to seek His forgiveness and come closer to Him. Because fear that paralyzes you, or makes you feel despondent about His kindness [*raḥma*], is objectionable and reprehensible [*madhmūm*]. But fear that propels you toward Him is commendable and praiseworthy [*maḥmūd*]. So one who fears is not someone who cries all the time *but one who refrains from doing things that make him afraid of punishment*. . . . So yes, when I hear talk about fear [*kalām ʿan al-khauf*], it has an effect on me because it reminds me of the acts of disobedience I have committed unknowingly, given how absorbed I have been in my life with raising my children and working, and makes me want to seek forgiveness for them. You see if I am not reminded, then I forget, and I become accustomed to making these mistakes and sins. Most of us don't sin intentionally, but we do so without knowing. Talk of fear reminds us of this and forces us to change our behaviors [*taṣarrufātina*]. But the greatness of my Lord [*rabbi*] is that He continually forgives us. This causes me to love Him as much as I fear His capacity for greatness.

Umm Amal's answer is remarkable for its delineation of the economy of fear and love undergirding virtuous action. Notably, these emotions are not simply subjective states in this economy, but are linked to action. Umm Amal therefore draws a distinction between fear that results in inaction (considered reprehensible, madhmūm) and fear that compels one to act virtuously (perceived as desirable or praiseworthy, maḥmūd). Fear of God in this conception is a cardinal virtue the force of which one must feel subjectively and act on in accord with its dictates. Umm Amal also draws a distinction between ordinary fear (khauf) and fear with reverence or awe (khashya). Khauf is what you feel, as another mosque participant put it, when you walk alone into a dark unknown space, but khashya is what you feel when you confront something or someone whom you regard with respect and veneration—in particular, when you confront that aspect of God that Umm Amal calls "His omnipotence" (qudratihi).[34] She goes on to say that it is precisely the qualities that inspire khashya in her that also inspire her to love God. Thus, in Umm Amal's view, love and fear of God are integrally related to her ability to recognize God's greatness: both in His capacity to punish and in His capacity to forgive and sustain His creatures despite their tendency to err.

Umm Amal's response also speaks to the roles fear and love play in the habituation of both virtues and vices. Note that the concept of vice does not represent the privation of virtue here; rather, vices and virtues are parallel qualities and can cohabit a single disposition simultaneously (notably, unlike Christianity, there is no notion of "original sin" in Islam). Unlike Hajja Samira in the lesson described earlier, Umm Amal is talking about Muslims who commit acts of disobedience (*maʿāṣi*) out of negligence rather than conscious intention. Yet even vices committed out of negligence, according to her, if done repeatedly, have the same effect as intentionally committed vices in that once they have acquired the status of habits they can come to corrode the requisite will to obey God.[35] This logic assumes that while someone with a pious disposition can err, the repeated practice of erring from God's program results in the sedimentation of this quality in one's character. This accords with the behaviorist philosophy at the core of Aristotle's notion of habitus in that the repeated performance of vices (as well as virtues) results in the formation of an unvirtuous (or virtuous) disposition.[36] Fear of God is the capacity by which one becomes cognizant of this state and begins to correct it. Thus, repeated invocations of fear, and practices that evoke and express that fear, train one to live piously (act as a spur to virtuous action) and are also a permanent condition of the pious self (*al-nafs al-muttaqi*).

[34] Isutzu also spells out this difference in his discussion of the terms *khauf* and *khashya* as they occur in the Quran (1966, 195–97). He shows that in most instances when *khashya* is used in the Quran, its proper object is God rather than human beings.

[35] This is also the reasoning implicit in the phrase often repeated by the mosque participants: "*mafīsh ṣaghīra baʿd al-istimrār wa mafīsh kabīra baʿd al-istighfār*," which means "vices done repeatedly and continually acquire the status of grave sins, and a grave sin if repented properly loses its gravity (in the eyes of God)."

[36] See Nederman's discussion of this point in his exegesis of Aristotle's notions of virtue and habitus (1989–90, 91).

fear as a modality of action

While the examples above make clear the importance of fear in this tradition of ethical formation, the question arises as to how this emotion is acquired and cultivated, particularly since the mosque participants do not consider fear of God to be natural, but something that must be learned. According to the women I worked with, there are many avenues for pursuing training in fear. One is the space of the mosque lessons. There were a number of women attendees who were familiar with the scholarly and gentle style of the dāʿiya Hajja Faiza—who delivered lessons at the upper-middle-income Umar mosque near their homes—but preferred Hajja Samira's admonitory manner, and often went to the extra trouble of commuting to the Nafisa mosque. When I asked one of these women why she preferred Hajja Samira's severe and strident (*mutashaddid*) style of delivery, she responded:

> We live in a society in which it is hard to remain pious and to be protective of our religion [*niḥfuẓ ʿala dinīna*]. When we hear this kind of talk, it startles us and keeps us from getting lost in the attractions of the world. You see, the path to piety [taqwa] is very difficult. Hajja Samira and others are afraid that unless they use [the rhetorical style of] *takhwīf* [to cause to fear], people will have wasted all the effort they exerted in getting there. They want people to hold on to their efforts in the path of piety [taqwa] and this is why they use takhwīf.

It is clear from this response that Hajja Samira's audience appreciated her not so much for her scholarly knowledge or argumentative logic, but for her ability to transform moral character through engendering in her audience various emotions associated with the divine.[37] Hajja Samira, it seems, did not simply prescribe fear as a necessary condition for piety, but deployed a discourse and rhetorical style that elicited it as well.[38] In doing so, she punctuated her lessons with evocations of the fires of hell, the trials faced in death, and the final encounter with God after death, all of which served as evocative techniques for the creation of virtuous emotions.

This style of preaching, aimed at the creation of fear in the listeners, is termed *tarhīb* (and at times *takhwīf*, as the woman interviewed above indicates); its antonym, *targhīb*, refers to the evocation of love for God in the audience. Most dāʿiyat stress the importance of maintaining a fine balance between

[37] I am reminded here of Pierre Hadot's admonishment to those who fault Plato's dialogues for doctrinal inconsistencies. Hadot argues that this is a judgment inconsistent with Plato's own intent, which was to "form" people rather than "inform" them (Hadot 2002, 73).

[38] Rhetoric in this usage refers to the process by which the orator recruits her listeners to participate in a shared economy of action and response (Burke 1969; McKeon 1987). For an excellent discussion of how rhetoric, within a particular tradition of Yemeni poetry, both expresses and constructs emotions, see Caton 1990.

these two rhetorical strategies. In addition to the space of the mosque lessons where the women learn to acquire virtuous fear, tape-recorded sermons that use the takhwīf style are also widely popular among the women I worked with.[39] Another crucial space for the inculcation and realization of virtuous fear is the ritual act of prayer (ṣalāt), and, as I mentioned earlier, weeping in prayer is an expression of virtuous fear as much as a means of its acquisition. Fear is, therefore, not only something that motivates one to pray but is also a necessary aspect of the act itself, an "adverbial virtue" that imparts to the act of prayer the specific quality through which it becomes consummate.[40]

Notably, the understanding that the emotion of fear motivates a person to act accords with the belief in certain cultural traditions that emotions are causative of action, an understanding that has been analyzed in considerable detail by some historians and anthropologists of emotion (James 1997; Lutz and White 1986; Rosaldo 1980). What is significant here, however, is that the emotion of fear not only propels one to act, but is also considered to be integral to action. Thus, fear is an element internal to the very structure of a pious act, and as such it is a condition for (to use J. L. Austin's terms) the "felicitous" performance of the act.[41] In other words, what this understanding draws attention to is not so much how particular emotions as modes of action constitute different kinds of social structure (Abu-Lughod 1986; Caton 1990; Myers 1986), but more how particular emotions are constitutive of specific actions and are the conditions by which those actions attain their excellence. The connection between the emotion of fear and practices of piety (such as prayer) is further borne out by the way they are semantically intertwined in the Arabic term *taqwa*, which is used in the Quran for both "piety" and "fear of God." In the Quran, the eschatological fear of God and the Day of Judgment is held to be almost synonymous with true belief, and piety is at times almost indistinguishable from the capacity to fear (Izutsu 1966, 164–72).[42]

[39] For an extended analysis of the rhetorical practice of Islamic sermons in contemporary Egypt among male preachers and listeners, see Hirschkind 2001a, 2001b.

[40] "Adverbial virtue" is an expression used by political theorist Michael Oakeshott (1975) to describe a conception of virtue that emphasizes the manner or sensibility with which a virtue is undertaken, as compared to an emphasis on the ends and purposes for which a virtue is undertaken. A particular virtue can, of course, emphasize both aspects—as was the case with regnant understandings of virtue in the tradition I studied.

[41] The English philosopher J. L. Austin calls a speech act "felicitous" when nothing "goes wrong" in its execution, that is, when the conditions that enable it to achieve its intended effect are met (Austin 1994, 14–15).

[42] It is for this reason that, depending upon the context, I have translated the term *taqwa* at times as "piety," and at other times as "virtuous fear" or "fear of God." For an analysis of the conceptual and linguistic relationship between piety and fear, see Izutsu's excellent discussion of the use of the terms *taqwa, khauf, khashya,* and *rahiba* (all of which are used interchangeably) in the Quran (1966, 195–200).

emulation and reflexivity

The mosque participants are often disparaged for their abidance by a behaviorist model of virtuous emotions wherein their emulation of exemplary standards stands in, their critics argue, for a more "sincere" and "personal connection" with God. Among these critics was a group of women I had come to know through my visits to a middle-class social club (*nādi*) in Cairo, where the group met to practice Quranic recitation. A number of them had experimented with mosque lessons but had not pursued them because they felt that the dāʿiyāt were "distorting the teachings of Islam." They often told me that one of the problems with the mosque teachers and attendees was that they exaggerated the role religious rituals play in a Muslim's life; this was a problem not because these rituals were unimportant, they said, but because the mosque participants thought that the "mere performance of rites and rituals" (*mujarrad al-ṭuqūs wal-ʿibādāt*) would make them pious. Amna, a medical student in her mid-twenties, gave the example of the mosque participants' practice of weeping publicly in prayer as something she found particularly objectionable:

> I cannot stand to go to these mosques anymore for Friday prayers because I find it offensive that so many people start to sob when the time for supplication [duʿā] comes. I am not saying that these women are not moved by real love for God. How can I say that? It is only He who knows what is in the heart. But I know from talking to many of these people that when they cry in prayer they do not really feel it from within; they do it because they think they will gain merits [ḥasanāt] with God. Or they think that "Oh, Abu Bakr [the first caliph and Muhammed's close Companion] did this, so should I." Where is sincerity of intent [*ikhlāṣ al-niyya*] here? You should cry not because you want recompense from God, or you want to follow the Companions blindly without thinking. You should cry for God because you really feel inside you what Abu Bakr felt, and cannot prevent yourself from crying, whether you are alone or in public. And I am telling you, it *never* happens to *me* when I am in the company of others.

When compared with the views of the mosque participants, comments such as these suggest a very different understanding of the relationship between public behavior and interiority, and of the role exemplary models should play in shaping the pious self. Amna's skepticism about the public display of emotions registers a detachment between the inner life of a self and its outward expressions wherein the experience of the former cannot be adequately captured in the latter, and where its true force can only be felt within the valorized space of personal self-reflection. Amna questions the mosque participants' sincerity precisely because they place undue weight on performative behavior and social conventions as a measure of their religiosity; indeed, if the proper location of religion and emotions is the inner life of the individual, as Amna seems to suggest, then it follows that one's sincerity in these two domains cannot be measured in one's outward performances. In contrast, for the women I worked with, outward behavioral forms were not only expressions of their interiorized religiosity but also a necessary means of acquiring it.[43]

The difference between these two views turns upon contrastive understandings of the relationship between bodily behavior and the pious self: for Amna, performative behavior may signify a pious self but does not necessarily form it. For the women I worked with, bodily acts (like weeping in prayer), when performed repeatedly, both in public and private, endowed the self with certain qualities: bodily behavior was therefore not so much a sign of interiority as it was a means of acquiring its potentiality. I use the term "potentiality" here in its Aristotelian meaning, in which it does not suggest a generic faculty or power, but is linked to the abilities one acquires through specific kinds of training and knowledge.[44] This usage of "potentiality" implies that in order to be good at something one undergoes a teleological program of volitional training that presupposes an exemplary path to knowledge—knowledge that one comes to acquire through assiduous schooling and practice.

Another crucial difference between Amna's understanding of performative behavior and that of the mosque movement participants lies in their conception of the role authoritative role models (such as Abu Bakr who is legendary for his ability to cry profusely during prayers) play in the shaping of the virtuous self. Note how emphatic Amna is about the kind of reflection that should inform one's emulation of Abu Bakr's behavior: one cries not simply because Abu Bakr cried, but because through reflection upon Abu Bakr's conduct one finds those spaces within oneself that identify with his ability to cry. In other words, according to Amna, Abu Bakr's conduct should not be unthinkingly reproduced but should serve as the ground upon which reflection about the "true I" proceeds. In contrast, for the women I worked with, an exemplary

[43] It should be clear by now that my argument is not concerned with whether this was the attitude of all the mosque participants. Rather I am interested in explicating the ideals inherent in different discourses on piety among the mosque participants and their critics. In this sense, I am not interested so much in what a given person "really did" versus "what she said she should do" but in the different ideals of behavior, with their attendant notions of authority and personhood, that the mosque movement is popularizing in Egypt today.

[44] Giorgio Agamben, in commenting upon this concept of potentiality in Aristotle, says, "The potentiality that interests him [Aristotle] is one that belongs to someone who, for example, has knowledge or an ability. In this sense, we say of the architect that he or she has the *potential* to build, of the poet that he or she has the *potential* to write poems. It is clear that this *existing* potentiality differs from the *generic* potentiality of the child. The child, Aristotle says, is potential in the sense that he must suffer an alteration (a becoming other) through learning" (1999, 179).

model was not where one discovered the "true I" but was a means to *transcend* the "I" that is invested in ephemeral pleasures and pursuits. Moreover, in contrast to Amna, many of the mosque participants believed that to emulate Abu Bakr's habit of weeping during prayers was not wrong precisely because it was through this mimetic reproduction that one eventually came to acquire the moral character of the exemplar. Note that self-reflection plays a different role in this conception in that it is aimed toward molding the "I" to approximate an authoritative model whose immanent form is the necessary means to the substance the "I" is to become. In other words, bodily form in this view does not simply represent the interiority (as it does for women like Amna), but serves as the "developable means" (T. Asad 1993) through which certain kinds of ethical and moral capacities are attained.

POLITICS AND CONVENTIONS

In order to interrogate the political implications of these distinct economies of moral action, let me focus for a moment on the relationship between the interiority and exteriority of the subject that informed the pedagogical model of the pietists I worked with. As I have described, the mosque participants did not regard authorized models of behavior as an external social imposition that constrained the individual. Rather, they viewed socially prescribed forms of conduct as the potentialities, the "scaffolding," if you will, through which the self is realized. It is precisely this self-willed obedience to religiously prescribed social conventions—what is often criticized as blind and uncritical emulation—that elicits the critique that such movements only serve to reproduce the existing patriarchal order and to prevent women from distinguishing their "own desires and aspirations" from those that are "socially dictated." For some scholars of gender, women of the kind I worked with are often seen as depriving themselves of the ability to enact an ethics of freedom, one founded on their capacity to distinguish their own (true) desires from (external) religious and cultural demands.

Such a criticism turns upon an imaginary of freedom, one deeply indebted to liberal political theory, in which an individual is considered free on the condition that she act autonomously: that her actions be the result of her own choice and free will, rather than of custom, tradition, transcendental will, or social coercion. As I discussed in chapter 1, autonomy in this conception of freedom is a procedural principle, and not an ontological or substantive feature of the subject, in that it delimits the necessary condition for the enactment of the ethic of freedom. Under this principle, even illiberal actions can arguably be tolerated if it is determined that they are undertaken by a freely consenting individual who "acted on her own accord." Political theorist John Christman gives the example of a person who chooses out of her own free will to be someone else's slave (1991). In keeping with liberal precepts, as Christman argues, the only way in which we can consider such a person free is if we can make a determination that the process by which she acquired her desire for slavery was indeed the result of her "own thinking and reflection," unencumbered by social and cultural influences (see my discussion in chapter 1). In other words, it is not the substance of desires but its "origin that matters in liberal judgments about autonomy" (Christman 1991, 359).

It is in keeping with this logic that I am often told that the women of the mosque movement exemplify the liberal autonomous subject precisely because they are enacting their own desires for piety, despite the social obstacles they face, and not following the conventional roles assigned to women. Hence a true liberal, I am told, should be tolerant of this movement even if she disagrees with the movement's larger goals. In such a view, well captured in Christman's formulation of the "voluntary slave," it is not only assumed that conventional forms of behavior can be distinguished from one's true desires, but also that such a distinction is universal. (As I suggested earlier, the same assumption often animates anthropological theories of conventional or ritual behavior.) What I would like to emphasize here is that this model of human action presupposes that there is a natural disjuncture between a person's "true" desires and those that are socially prescribed. The politics that ensues from this disjuncture aims to identify moments and places where conventional norms impede the realization of an individual's real desires, or at least obfuscate the distinction between what is truly one's own and what is socially required.

The model of self presupposed by this position dramatically contrasts with the one that conceptually and practically shaped the activities of the women I worked with. The account I have presented of the mosque movement shows that the distinction between the subject's real desires and obligatory social conventions—a distinction at the center of liberal, and at times progressive, thought—cannot be assumed, precisely because socially prescribed forms of behavior constitute the conditions for the emergence of the self as such and are integral to its realization. One of the issues such a conception of self raises is: How does one rethink the question of individual freedom in a context where the distinction between the subject's own desires and socially prescribed performances cannot be so easily presumed, and where submission to certain forms of (external) authority is a condition for the self to achieve its potentiality? What kind of politics would be deemed desirable and viable in a discursive tradition that regards conventions (socially prescribed performances) as necessary to the self's realization?

The argument I am making here should not be confused with the one made by communitarian philosophers (Sandel 1998; Taylor 1985a, 1985c) and their feminist interlocutors (Benhabib 1992; Friedman 1997; Meyers 1989; Nedelsky 1989; Young 1990) who have argued that liberalism has an anemic and anomic model of the individual, one that does not take full account of the ways in which the individual is socially produced and personifies the social within herself. According to many of these thinkers, recognition of the socially embedded character of the individual would rectify the autonomizing tendency within liberalism. But what remains unproblematized by these critics is the distinction between the individual and the social: even among the communitarians and their feminist interlocutors, the interiority of the subject remains a valorized space to which one turns in order to realize one's interests and to distinguish those fears and aspirations that are one's own from those that are socially imposed.

For example, Charles Taylor, in criticizing the concept of atomism underlying various strands of liberal theory,[45] argues that the capacity for freedom requires not only "a certain understanding of self, one in which the aspirations to autonomy and self-direction become conceivable," but also requires that this self-understanding be sustained and defined "in conversation with others or through the common understanding which underlies the practices of our society" (Taylor 1985a, 209). What is notable here is that Taylor does not discard the notion that autonomy is central to the exercise of freedom, but rather emphasizes the social conditions that are necessary for its production and flourishing. Furthermore, autonomy, for Charles Taylor, means not simply acting as one wants (the Hobbesian requirement of negative freedom), but consists in achieving "a certain condition of self-clairvoyance and self-understanding" in order to be able to prioritize and assess conflicting desires, fears, and aspirations within oneself, and to be able to sort out what is in one's best interest from what is socially required (1985c, 229). In other words, the exercise of freedom for Taylor turns not only on the ability to distance oneself from the social, but also, more importantly, on the capacity to turn one's gaze critically to reflect upon oneself in order to determine the horizon of possibilities and strategies through which one acts upon the world.

Seyla Benhabib, as a critical interlocutor of communitarians, proposes a feminist communicative ethics that builds upon the work of philosophers like Sandel and Taylor, and deontological liberal theorists like Rawls and Haber-

[45] Taylor describes atomism as "a vision of society as in some sense constituted by individuals for the fulfillment of ends which [are] primarily individual"—a notion that underlies social contract theory in particular, but also informs other traditions of thought in liberalism (1985a, 187).

mas, who have argued for the priority of the right over the good (1992).[46] What Benhabib finds useful in the communitarian critique is the recognition of the socially embedded quality of the individual, and the necessity of a particular structure of the social that makes the ideal of autonomy possible and sustainable in the first place. Benhabib is right to point out, however, that this view is not limited to the communitarians alone but shares something critical with a conception of communicative ethics that is Habermasian and Rawlsian in origin but is often assumed to be the opposite of communitarian views of the social and the individual (1992, 71–76). What these contentious ethical traditions share, Benhabib argues, is an understanding of the self that upholds moral autonomy as a necessary "right of the self to challenge religion, tradition and social dogma, but also the right of the self to distance from social roles and their content or to assume 'reflexive social distance'" (Benhabib 1992, 73). Benhabib finds this bridge between the communitarians and the deontologists to be of critical importance in building a feminist conception of ethics that is predicated upon a critique of an ahistorical and atomistic conception of self and society. What Benhabib's argument makes evident is that even feminist renditions of the communitarian point of view aim to establish a balance between social belonging and critical reflection wherein critical reflection is understood fundamentally as an autonomous exercise.[47]

It should be clear by now that the liberal communitarian framework is not appropriate for the analysis of conceptions of the self and its relationship to authority that were prevalent among the women of the mosque movement. Ultimately a person for whom self-realization is a matter of excavating herself (developing what Taylor calls "self-clairvoyance"), or sorting out her own interests from those that are social and collective (what Benhabib calls "the right of the self to distance from social roles and their content"), looks to a different set of strategies and horizons than a subject for whom the principle ideals and tools of self-reference reside outside of herself. This is one reason I have tried to use the analytical language of ethical formation to describe the process of moral cultivation (note the relevant term here is "cultivation" and

[46] The emphasis Rawls and Habermas place on the concept of individual rights stands in contrast to the view of communitarian philosophers like Taylor and Sandel who argue for the primacy of a shared vision of the collective good in a given society. The latter connect their critique of the impoverished notion of the unencumbered self in liberalism to what they think is an exaggerated importance given to the concept of individual rights in liberal societies.

[47] The fact that communitarian views embody this tension between the social and the individual is not entirely surprising given their Romantic legacy. As Charles Larmore points out, a range of Romantics—from Burke to Herder to Rousseau—seem to have embraced, to varying degrees, the notion of a private interiorized subjectivity, which, even though it was recognized to be a product of the larger community, nonetheless had to be distinct from the community in order to be "true to itself" (Larmore 1996, 66–85).

not "inculcation"). My argument therefore has not focused on contextualizing the individual within a particular structure of the social. Rather, I have tried to map the contours of the kind of subject presumed to be necessary to the political imaginary of the piety movement (of which the mosque movement is an important part) and the various embodied practices through which such a subject is produced. If the desire for freedom from social conventions is not an innate desire, as I have argued, but assumes a particular anthropology of the subject, then it is incumbent upon us to analyze not only hierarchical structures of social relations, but also the architecture of the self, the interrelationship between the constituent elements of the self, that make a particular imaginary of politics possible.

This analytical framework is particularly helpful in grasping the ethical and political force of nonliberal movements such as the one I worked with. This is because, as I suggested in chapter 1, their political agency does not consist in engaging the usual forms and institutions of politics (such as making claims on the state or the judicial system, using the language of rights and identity, and public protest). Instead their ethical practices are a necessary condition of their political agency insomuch as these practices have produced unanticipated effects in the prevailing social field. One sign of their political effectivity is the ire the pious activists have provoked from the Egyptian state (as we saw in chapter 2) and the criticism they have elicited from fellow Islamists as well as secular-liberal Muslims. Notably, these critics of the piety movement share an orientation toward nationalist-identitarian politics, one that is called into question by the practices of the mosque movement in particular and the piety movement in general. In order to understand what precisely this movement unsettles about the nationalist-identitarian imaginary *and* how it has transformed the sociopolitical landscape of Egypt, it is essential to analyze the architecture of ethical practices through which this movement has produced a particular form of embodied sociability. My analysis of the practices of the mosque movement in this chapter invites us to seriously explore what it means to acknowledge that politics involves not simply rational argumentation and evaluation of moral principles, but issues forth from intersubjective levels of being and acting—requiring us to think through the problematic of politics in a way that is adequate to the variable understandings of the self and its embodied powers.

5

Agency, Gender, and Embodiment

While in the earlier chapters of this book I explored how the ethical practices of the mosque movement have been shaped by, and in turn transformed, the social field of Egyptian secularity in unexpected ways, here I want to focus on how we might think about these ethical practices in the context of relations of gender inequality. Given the overwhelming tendency of mosque movement participants to accept the patriarchal assumptions at the core of the orthodox Islamic tradition, this chapter is animated by the following questions: What were the terms the mosque participants used to negotiate the demands of the orthodox Islamic tradition in order to master this tradition? What were the different modalities of agency that were operative in these negotiations? What difference does it make analytically if we attend to the terms internal to this discourse of negotiation and struggle? And what challenges do these terms pose to notions of agency, performativity, and resistance presupposed within liberal and poststructuralist feminist scholarship?

In chapter 1, I argued for uncoupling the analytical notion of agency from the politically prescriptive project of feminism, with its propensity to valorize those operations of power that subvert and resignify the hegemonic discourses of gender and sexuality. I have argued that to the extent that feminist scholarship emphasizes this politically subversive form of agency, it has ignored other modalities of agency whose meaning and effect are not captured within the logic of subversion and resignification of hegemonic terms of discourse. In this chapter, I want to attend not only to the different meanings of agency as they emerge within the practices of the mosque movement, but also to the kinds of analytical questions that are opened up when agency is analyzed in some of its other modalities—questions that remain submerged, I would contend, if agency is analyzed in terms of resistance to the subordinating function of power.

I should make clear that my exploration of the multiple forms agency takes is not simply a hermeneutical exercise, one that is indifferent to feminism's interest in theorizing about the possibility of transforming relations of gender subordination. Rather, I would argue that any discussion of the issue of transformation must begin with an analysis of the specific practices of subjectivation that make the subjects of a particular social imaginary possible.[1] In the context of the mosque movement, this means closely analyzing the scaffolding of practices—both argumentative and embodied—that secured the mosque participants' attachment to patriarchal forms of life that, in turn, provided the necessary conditions for both their subordination and their agency. One of the questions I hope to address is: how does the particularity of this attachment challenge familiar ways of conceptualizing "subordination" and "change" within liberal and poststructuralist feminist debates?

Finally, since much of the analytical labor of this book is directed at the specificity of terms internal to the practices of the mosque movement, I would like to remind the reader that the force of these terms derives not from the motivations and intentions of the actors but from their inextricable entanglement within conflicting and overlapping historical formations. My project is therefore based on a double disavowal of the humanist subject. The first disavowal is evident in my exploration of certain notions of agency that cannot be reconciled with the project of recuperating the lost voices of those who are written out of "hegemonic feminist narratives," to bring their humanism and strivings to light—precisely because to do so would be to underwrite all over again the narrative of the sovereign subject as the author of "her voice" and "her-story."

My project's second disavowal of the humanist subject is manifest in my refusal to recuperate the members of the mosque movement either as "subaltern feminists" or as the "fundamentalist Others" of feminism's progressive agenda. To do so, in my opinion, would be to reinscribe a familiar way of being human that a particular narrative of personhood and politics has made available to us,

[1] I am in agreement with anthropologists such as Jane Collier, Marilyn Strathern, and Sylvia Yanagisako who have argued that all cultures and societies are predicated upon relations of gender inequality, and that the task of the anthropologist is to show how a culturally specific system of inequality (and its twin, equality) is constructed, practiced, and maintained (Collier 1988, 1997; Collier and Yanagisako 1989; Strathern 1988). My only caveat is that I do not believe that there is a single arrangement of gender inequality that characterizes a particular culture; rather, I believe that different arrangements of gender inequality often coexist within a given culture, the specific forms of which are a product of the particular discursive formation that each arrangement is a part of.

forcing the aporetic multiplicity of commitments and projects to fit into this exhausted narrative mold. Instead, my ruminations on the practices of the women's mosque movement are aimed at unsettling key assumptions at the center of liberal thought through which movements of this kind are often judged. Such judgments do not always simply entail the ipso facto rejection of these movements as antithetical to feminist agendas (e.g., Moghissi 1999); they also at times seek to embrace such movements as forms of feminism, thus enfolding them into a liberal imaginary (e.g., Fernea 1998). By tracing in this chapter the multiple modalities of agency that informed the practices of the mosque participants, I hope to redress the profound inability within current feminist political thought to envision valuable forms of human flourishing outside the bounds of a liberal progressive imaginary.

ETHICAL FORMATION

In order to begin tugging at the multiple twines that hold this object called agency in its stable locution, let me begin with an ethnographic vignette that focuses on one of the most feminine of Islamic virtues, *al-ḥayā'* (shyness, diffidence, modesty), a virtue that was considered necessary to the achievement of piety by the mosque participants I worked with. In what follows, I want to examine the kind of agency that was involved when a novice tried to perfect this virtue, and how its performance problematizes certain aspects of current theorizations within feminist theory about the role embodied behavior plays in the constitution of the subject.

In the course of my fieldwork, I had come to spend time with a group of four working women, in their mid- to late thirties, who were employed in the public and private sectors of the Egyptian economy. In addition to attending the mosque lessons, the four also met as a group to read and discuss issues of Islamic ethical practice and Quranic exegesis. Given the stringent demands their desire to abide by high standards of piety placed on them, these women often had to struggle against the secular ethos that permeated their lives and made their realization of piety somewhat difficult. They often talked about the pressures they faced as working women, which included negotiating close interactions with unrelated male colleagues, riding public transportation in mixed-sex compartments, overhearing conversations (given the close proximity of their coworkers) that were impious in character and tone, and so on. Often this situation was further compounded by the resistance these women encountered in their attempts to live a pious life from their family members—particularly from male members—who were opposed to stringent forms of religious devotion.

When these women met as a group, their discussions often focused on two challenges they constantly had to face in their attempts to maintain a pious lifestyle. One was learning to live amicably with people—both colleagues and immediate kin—who constantly placed them in situations that were far from optimal for the realization of piety in day-to-day life. The second challenge was in the internal struggle they had to engage in within themselves in a world that constantly beckoned them to behave in unpious ways.

On this particular day, the group had been reading passages from the Quran and discussing its practical significance for their daily conduct. The Quranic chapter under discussion was "The Story" (Surat al-Qaṣaṣ), which discusses the virtue of shyness or modesty (al-ḥayāʾ), a coveted virtue for pious Muslims in general and women in particular. To practice al-ḥayāʾ means to be diffident, modest, and able to feel and enact shyness. While all of the Islamic virtues are gendered (in that their measure and standards vary when applied to men versus women), this is particularly true of shyness and modesty (al-ḥayāʾ). The struggle involved in cultivating the virtue of shyness was brought home to me when, in the course of a discussion about the exegesis of "The Story," one of the women, Amal, drew our attention to verse 25. This verse is about a woman walking shyly—with al-ḥayāʾ—toward Moses to ask him to approach her father for her hand in marriage. Unlike the other women in the group, Amal was particularly outspoken and confident, and would seldom hesitate to assert herself in social situations with men or women. Normally I would not have described her as shy, because I considered shyness to be antithetical to qualities of candidness and self-confidence in a person. Yet, as I was to learn, Amal had learned to be outspoken in a way that was in keeping with Islamic standards of reserve, restraint, and modesty required of pious Muslim women. The conversation proceeded as follows.

Contemplating the word *istiḥyāʾ*, which is form ten of the substantive ḥayāʾ,[2] Amal said, "I used to think that even though shyness [al-ḥayāʾ] was required of us by God, if I acted shyly it would be hypocritical [*nifāq*] because I didn't actually feel it inside of me. Then one day, in reading verse 25 in Surat al-Qaṣaṣ ["The Story"] I realized that al-ḥayāʾ was among the good deeds [*huwwa min al-aʿmāl al-ṣaliḥa*], and given my natural lack of shyness [al-ḥayāʾ], I had to make or create it first. I realized that making [*ṣanaʿ*] it in yourself is not hypocrisy, and that eventually your inside learns to have al-ḥayāʾ too." Here she looked at me and explained the meaning of the word *istiḥyāʾ*: "It means making oneself shy, even if it means creating it [*Yaʿni ya Saba, yiʿmil nafsu yitkisif ḥatta lau ṣanaʿti*]." She continued with her point, "And finally I under-

[2] Most Arabic verbs are based on a triconsonantal root from which ten verbal forms (and sometimes fifteen) are derived.

stood that once you do this, the sense of shyness [al-ḥayāʾ] eventually imprints itself on your inside [*as-shuʿūr yiṭbaʿ ʿala guwwaki*]."

Another friend, Nama, a single woman in her early thirties, who had been sitting and listening, added: "It's just like the veil [ḥijāb]. In the beginning when you wear it, you're embarrassed [*maksūfa*] and don't want to wear it because people say that you look older and unattractive, that you won't get married, and will never find a husband. But you *must* wear the veil, first because it is God's command [*ḥukm allah*], and then, with time, because your inside learns to feel shy without the veil, and if you take it off, your entire being feels uncomfortable [*mish rāḍī*] about it."

To many readers this conversation may exemplify an obsequious deference to social norms that both reflects and reproduces women's subordination. Indeed, Amal's struggle with herself to become shy may appear to be no more than an instance of the internalization of standards of effeminate behavior, one that contributes little to our understanding of agency. Yet if we think of "agency" not simply as a synonym for resistance to social norms but as a modality of action, then this conversation raises some interesting questions about the kind of relationship established between the subject and the norm, between performative behavior and inward disposition. To begin with, what is striking here is that instead of innate human desires eliciting outward forms of conduct, it is the sequence of practices and actions one is engaged in that determines one's desires and emotions. In other words, action does not issue forth from natural feelings but *creates* them. Furthermore, pursuant to the behaviorist tradition of Aristotelian moral philosophy discussed in chapter 4, it is through repeated *bodily acts* that one trains one's memory, desire, and intellect to behave according to established standards of conduct.[3] Notably, Amal *does not* regard simulating shyness in the initial stages of her self-cultivation to be hypocritical, as it would be in certain liberal conceptions of the self where a dissonance between internal feelings and external expressions would be considered a form of dishonesty or self-betrayal (as captured in the phrase: "How can I do something sincerely when my heart is not in it?"). Instead, taking the absence of shyness as a marker of an incomplete learning process, Amal further develops the quality of shyness by synchronizing her outward behavior with her inward motives until the discrepancy between the two is dissolved. This is an example of a mutually constitutive relationship between

[3] It is interesting to note that the women I worked with did not actually employ the body-mind distinction I use in my analysis. In referring to shyness, for example, they talked about it as a way of being and acting such that any separation between mind and body was difficult to discern. I have retained the mind-body distinction for analytical purposes, the goal being to understand the specific relation articulated between the two in this tradition of self-formation.

body learning and body sense—as Nama says, your body literally comes to feel uncomfortable if you do *not* veil.

Secondly, what is also significant in this program of self-cultivation is that bodily acts—like wearing the veil or conducting oneself modestly in interactions with people (especially men)—do not serve as manipulable masks in a game of public presentation, detachable from an essential interiorized self. Rather they are the *critical markers* of piety as well as the *ineluctable means* by which one trains oneself to be pious. While wearing the veil serves at first as a means to tutor oneself in the attribute of shyness, it is also simultaneously integral to the practice of shyness: one cannot simply discard the veil once a modest deportment has been acquired, because the veil itself is part of what defines that deportment.[4] This is a crucial aspect of the disciplinary program pursued by the participants of the mosque movement, the significance of which is elided when the veil is understood solely in terms of its symbolic value as a marker of women's subordination or Islamic identity.

A substantial body of literature in feminist theory argues that patriarchal ideologies—whether nationalist, religious, medical, or aesthetic in character—work by objectifying women's bodies and subjecting them to masculinist systems of representation, thereby negating and distorting women's own experience of their corporeality and subjectivity (Bordo 1993; Göle 1996; Mani 1998; E. Martin 1987). In this view, the virtue of al-ḥayāʾ (shyness or modesty) can be understood as yet another example of the subjection of women's bodies to masculinist or patriarchal valuations, images, and representational logic. A feminist strategy aimed at unsettling such a circumscription would try to expose al-ḥayāʾ for its negative valuation of women, simultaneously bringing to the fore alternative representations and experiences of the feminine body that are denied, submerged, or repressed by its masculinist logic.

A different perspective within feminist theory regards the recuperation of "women's experience" to be an impossible task, since the condition for the possibility of any discourse, or for that matter "thought itself" (Colebrook 2000b, 35), is the rendering of certain materialities and subjectivities as the

[4] This concept can perhaps be illuminated by analogy to two different models of dieting: an older model in which the practice of dieting is understood to be a temporary and instrumental solution to the problem of weight gain; and a more contemporary model in which dieting is understood to be synonymous with a healthy and nutritious lifestyle. The second model presupposes an ethical relationship between oneself and the rest of the world and in this sense is similar to what Foucault called "practices of the care of the self." The differences between the two models point to the fact that it does not mean much to simply note that systems of power mark their truth on human bodies through disciplines of self-formation. In order to understand the force these disciplines command, one needs to explicate the conceptual relationship articulated between different aspects of the body and the particular notion of the self that animates distinct disciplinary regimes.

constitutive outside of the discourse. In this view, there is no recuperable ontological "thereness" to this abjected materiality (such as "a feminine experience"), because the abject can only be conceived in relation to hegemonic terms of the discourse, "at and as its most tenuous borders" (Butler 1993, 8). A well-known political intervention arising out of this analytic aims to demonstrate the impossibility of "giving voice" to the subalterity of any abject being—thereby exposing the violence endemic to thought itself. This intervention is famously captured in Gayatri Spivak's rhetorical question, "Can the Subaltern Speak?" (Spivak 1988).

The analysis I have presented of the practice of al-ḥayāʾ (and the practice of veiling) departs from both these perspectives: I do not regard female subjectivity as that which belies masculinist representations; nor do I see this subjectivity as a sign of the abject materiality that discourse cannot articulate. Rather, I believe that the body's relationship to discourse is variable and that it seldom simply follows either of the paths laid out by these two perspectives within feminist theory. In regard to the feminist argument that privileges the role representations play in securing male domination, it is important to note that even though the concept of al-ḥayāʾ embeds a masculinist understanding of gendered bodies, far more is at stake in the practice of al-ḥayāʾ than this framework allows, as is evident from the conversation between Amal and her friend Nama. Crucial to their understanding of al-ḥayāʾ as an embodied practice is an entire conceptualization of the role the body plays in the making of the self, one in which the outward behavior of the body constitutes both the potentiality and the means through which interiority is realized (see chapter 4). A feminist strategy that seeks to unsettle such a conceptualization cannot simply intervene in the system of representation that devalues the feminine body, but must also engage the very armature of attachments between outward behavioral forms and the sedimented subjectivity that al-ḥayāʾ enacts. Representation is only one issue among many in the ethical relationship of the body to the self and others, and it does not by any means determine the form this relationship takes.

Similarly, I remain skeptical of the second feminist framing, in which the corporeal is analyzed on the model of language, as the constitutive outside of discourse itself. In this framework, it would be possible to read al-ḥayāʾ as an instantiation of the control a masculinist imaginary must assert over the dangerous supplement femininity signifies in Islamic thought. Such a reading is dissatisfying to me because the relationship it assumes between the body and discourse, one modeled on a linguistic theory of signification, is inadequate to the imaginary of the mosque movement. Various aspects of this argument will become clear in the next section when I address the notion of performativity underlying the Aristotelian model of ethical formation the mosque participants followed. Suffice it to say here that the mosque women's practices of modesty and femininity do not signify the abjectness of the feminine within Islamic discourse, but articulate a positive and immanent discourse of being in the world. This discourse requires that we carefully examine the *work that bodily practices perform* in creating a subject that is pious in its formation.

To elucidate these points, it might be instructive to juxtapose the mosque participants' understanding of al-ḥayāʾ with a view that takes the pietists to task for making modesty dependent upon the particularity of attire (such as the veil). The contrastive understanding of modesty or al-ḥayāʾ (also known as *iḥtishām*) that results from such a juxtaposition was articulated forcefully by a prominent Egyptian public figure, Muhammad Said Ashmawi, who has been a leading voice for "liberal Islam" in the Arab world.[5] He is a frequent contributor to the liberal-nationalist magazine *Rūz al-Yūsuf*, which I quoted from earlier. In a series of exchanges in this magazine, Ashmawi challenged the then-mufti of Egypt, Sayyid Tantawi, for upholding the position that the adoption of the veil is obligatory upon all Muslim women (farḍ) (Ashmawi 1994a, 1994b; Tantawi 1994). Ashmawi's general argument is that the practice of veiling was a regional custom in pre-Islamic Arabia that has mistakenly been assigned a divine status. His writings represent one of the more eloquent arguments for separating the virtue of modesty from the injunction to veil in Egypt today:

> The real meaning of the veil [ḥijāb] lies in thwarting the self from straying toward lust or illicit sexual desires, and keeping away from sinful behavior, without having to conjoin this [understanding] with particular forms of clothing and attire. As for modesty [iḥtishām] and lack of exhibitionism [*ʿadam al-tabarruj*] in clothing and outward appearance [*maẓhar*], this is something that is imperative, and any wise person would agree with it and any decent person would abide by it. (Ashmawi 1994b, 25)

Note that for Ashmawi, unlike for the women I worked with, modesty is less a divinely ordained virtue than it is an attribute of a "decent and wise person," and in this sense is similar to any other human attribute that marks a person as respectable. Furthermore, for Ashmawi the proper locus of the attribute of modesty is the interiority of the individual, which then has an effect on outward behavior. In other words, for Ashmawi modesty is not so much an attribute of the body as it is a characteristic of the individual's inte-

[5] Ashmawi served as the chief justice of the Criminal Court of Egypt and as a professor of Islamic and Comparative Law at Cairo University. For an overview of his work on Islamic legal theory, see Hallaq 1997, 231–54.

riority, which is then expressed in bodily form. In contrast, for the women I worked with, this relationship between interiority and exteriority was almost reversed: a modest bodily form (the veiled body) did not simply express the self's interiority but was the means by which it was acquired. Since the mosque participants regarded outward bodily markers as an ineluctable means to the virtue of modesty, the body's precise movements, behaviors, and gestures were all made the object of their efforts to live by the code of modesty.

performativity and the subject

It might seem to the reader that the differences between these two perspectives are minor and inconsequential since, ultimately, both understandings of modesty have the same effect on the social field: they both proscribe what Ashmawi calls "illicit sexual desires and sinful behavior." Disagreement about whether or not one should veil may appear to be minor to those who believe it is the moral principle of the regulation of sexuality, shared by Ashmawi and the mosque participants, that matters. The idea that such differences are minor accords with various aspects of the Kantian model of ethics discussed in chapters 1 and 4; however, from an Aristotelian point of view, the difference between Ashmawi's understanding of modesty and that of the mosque participants is immense. In the Aristotelian worldview, ethical conduct is not simply a matter of the effect one's behavior produces in the world but depends crucially upon the precise form that behavior takes: both the acquisition and the consummation of ethical virtues devolve upon the proper enactment of prescribed bodily behaviors, gestures, and markers (MacIntyre 1966). Thus, an act is judged to be ethical in this tradition not simply because it accomplishes the social objective it is meant to achieve but also because it enacts this objective in the manner and form it is supposed to: an ethical act is, to borrow J. L. Austin's term, "felicitous" only if it achieves its goals in a prescribed behavioral form (Austin 1994).

Certain aspects of this Aristotelian model of ethical formation resonate with J. L. Austin's concept of the performative, especially as this concept has been conjoined with an analysis of subject formation in Judith Butler's work (1993, 1997a), which I touched upon briefly in chapter 1. It is instructive to examine this resonance closely for at least two reasons: one, because such an examination reveals the kinds of questions about bodily performance and subjectivity that are important to foreground in order to understand the force this Aristotelian tradition of ethical formation commands among the mosque participants; and two, because such an examination reveals the kind of analytical labor one needs to perform in order to make the ethnographic particularity of a social formation speak generatively to philosophical concepts—concepts whose anthropological assumptions are often taken for granted.

A performative, which for Austin is primarily a speech act, for Butler includes both bodily and speech acts through which subjects are formed. Butler, in her adoption of Derrida's interpretation of performativity as an "iterable practice" (Derrida 1988), formulates a theory of subject formation in which performativity becomes "one of the influential rituals by which subjects are formed and reformulated" (1997a, 160). Butler is careful to point out the difference between performance as a "bounded act," and performativity, which "consists in a reiteration of norms which precede, constrain, and exceed the performer and in that sense cannot be taken as the fabrication of the performer's 'will' or 'choice'" (Butler 1993, 234).[6] In *Excitable Speech*, Butler spells out the role bodily performatives play in the constitution of the subject. She argues that "bodily habitus constitutes a tacit form of performativity, a citational chain lived and believed at the level of the body" (1997a, 155) such that the materiality of the subject comes to be enacted through a series of embodied performatives.[7]

As I discussed earlier, Butler's conception of performativity is also at the core of her theory of agency: she claims that the iterable and repetitive character of the performatives makes the structure of norms vulnerable and unstable because the reiteration may fail, be resignified, or be reappropriated for purposes other than the consolidation of norms. This leads Butler to argue: "That no social formation can endure without becoming reinstated, and that every reinstatement puts the 'structure' in question at risk suggests the possibility of its undoing is at once the condition of possibility of the structure itself" (1997b, 14). In other words, what makes the structure of norms stable—the reiterative character of bodily and speech performatives—is also that which makes the structure susceptible to change and resignification.[8]

Butler's notion of performativity and the labor it enacts in the constitution of the subject may at first glance seem to be a useful way of analyzing the mosque participants' emphasis on embodied virtues in the formation of a pious self. Both views (the mosque participants' and Butler's) suggest that it is through the repeated performance of virtuous practices (norms in Butler's terms) that the subject's will, desire, intellect, and body come to acquire a par-

[6] An important aspect of Butler's formulation of performativity is its relationship to concepts in psychoanalytic theory. On this relationship, see the chapter "Critically Queer" in Butler 1993.

[7] See Amy Hollywood's excellent discussion of Butler's analysis of embodied performativity and its relationship to the concept of ritual (2002).

[8] While Butler remains indebted to Derrida in this formulation, she also departs from him by placing a stronger emphasis on the historically sedimented quality of performatives. See Butler 1997a, 147–50.

ticular form. The mosque participants' understanding of virtues may be rendered in Butlerian terms in that they regard virtuous performances not so much as manifestations of their will but more as actions that produce the will in its particularity. In this conception, one might say that the pious subject does not precede the performance of normative virtues but is enacted through the performance. Virtuous actions may well be understood as performatives; they enact that which they name: a virtuous self.

Despite these resonances between Butler's notion of performativity and the mosque participants' understanding of virtuous action, it would be a mistake to assume that the logic of piety practices can be so easily accommodated within Butler's theoretical language. Butler herself cautions against such a "technological approach" to theory wherein "the theory is articulated on its self-sufficiency, and then shifts register only for the pedagogical purpose of illustrating an already accomplished truth" (Butler, Laclau, and Žižek 2000, 26). Such a perfunctory approach to theory is inadequate, Butler argues, because theoretical formulations often ensue from particular examples and are therefore constitutively stained by that particularity. In order to make a particular theoretical formulation travel across cultural and historical specificities, one needs to rethink the structure of assumptions that underlies a theoretical formulation and perform the difficult task of translation and reformulation.[9] If we take this insight seriously, then the question we need to ask of Butler's theorization of performativity is: how does a consideration of the mosque participants' understanding of virtuous action make us rethink the labor performativity enacts in the constitution of the pious subject?

To address this question, I believe that it is necessary to think through three important dimensions of the articulation of performativity in regard to subject formation: (a) the sequencing of the performatives and their interrelationship; (b) the place of language in the analysis of performativity; and (c) different articulations of the notions of "subversion," "change," or "destabilization" across different models of performativity. One of the crucial differences between Butler's model of the performative and the one implicitly informing the practices of the mosque movement lies in how each performative is related to the ones that follow and precede it. The model of ethical formation followed by the mosque participants emphasizes the sedimented and cumulative char-

[9] Butler argues this point eloquently in her recent work: "no assertion of universality takes place apart from a cultural norm, and, given the array of contesting norms that constitute the international field, no assertion can be made without at once requiring a cultural translation. Without translation, the very concept of universality cannot cross the linguistic borders it claims, in principle, to be able to cross. Or we might put it another way: without translation, the only way the assertion of universality can cross a border is through colonial and expansionist logic" (Butler, Laclau, and Žižek 2000, 35).

acter of reiterated performatives, where each performative builds on prior ones, and a carefully calibrated system exists by which differences between reiterations are judged in terms of how successfully (or not) the performance has taken root in the body and mind. Thus the mosque participants—no matter how pious they were—exercised great vigilance in scrutinizing themselves to gauge how well (or poorly) their performances had actually taken root in their dispositions (as Amal and Nama do in the conversation described earlier in this chapter).

Significantly, the question of the disruption of norms is posed differently in the model governing the mosque movement from how it is posed in the model derived from the examples that Butler provides. Not only are the standards by which an action is perceived to have failed or succeeded different, but the practices that *follow* the identification of an act (as successful or failed) are also distinct. Consider for example Butler's discussion of drag queens (in "Gender Is Burning") who parody dominant heterosexual norms and in so doing expose "the imitative structure by which hegemonic gender is itself produced and disputes heterosexuality's claim on naturalness and originality" (Butler 1993, 125). What is significant here is that as the drag queen becomes more successful in her approximation of heterosexual norms of femininity, the challenge her performance poses to the stability of these norms also increases. The excellence of her performance, in other words, exposes the vulnerability of heterosexual norms and puts their naturalized stability at risk. For the mosque participants, on the other hand, excellence at piety does not put the structure that governs its normativity at risk but rather consolidates it.

Furthermore, when, in Butler's example, a drag queen's performance fails to approximate the ideal of femininity, Butler reads this failure as a sign of the intrinsic inability of the performative structure of heteronormativity to realize its own ideals. In contrast, in the model operative among the mosque participants, a person's failure to enact a virtue successfully is perceived to be the marker of an inadequately formed self, one in which the interiority and exteriority of the person are improperly aligned. The recognition of this disjuncture in turn requires one to undertake a specific series of steps to rectify the situation—steps that build upon the rooted and sedimented character of prior performances of normative virtues. Amal, in the conversation cited above, describes how she followed her initial inability to simulate shyness successfully with repeated acts of shyness that in turn produced the cumulative effect of a shy interiority and disposition. Drag queens may also expend a similar kind of effort in order to better approximate dominant feminine norms, but what is different is that they take the disjuncture between what is socially performed and what is biologically attributed as necessary to the very structure of their performance. For the mosque participants, in contrast, the relevant disjuncture is that between a religious norm (or ideal) and its actual performance: their actions are aimed at precisely *overcoming* this disjuncture.

One reason these two understandings of performative behavior differ from each other is based in the contrastive conceptions of embodied materiality that underlie them. Butler understands the materiality of the body on the model of language, and analyzes the power of bodily performatives in terms of processes of signification whose disruptive potential lies in the indeterminate character of signs. In response to those who charge her with practicing a kind of linguistic reductionism, Butler insists that the body is not reducible to discourse or speech, since "the relationship between speech and the body is that of a chiasmus. Speech is bodily, but the body exceeds the speech it occasions; and speech remains irreducible to the bodily means of its enunciation" (Butler 1997a, 155–56). So how are we to understand this chiasmus? For Butler, the answer lies in formulating a theory of signification that is always operative—whether acknowledged or not—when one tries to speak about this chiasmus, because in speaking one renders discursive what is extra- or nondiscursive (Butler 1993, 11). The discursive terms, in turn, become constitutive of the extra-discursive realms of the body because of the formative power of language to constitute that which it represents.[10] Butler remains skeptical of approaches that leave the relationship between discursive and extra-discursive forms of materiality open and untheorized, and seeks to demonstrate the power of an analysis that foregrounds the significatory aspects of the body.[11]

It is important to point out here that there are a range of theorists who may agree with Butler about the chiasmic relationship between the body and discourse, but for whom a theory of signification does not quite address a basic problem: how do we develop a vocabulary for thinking conceptually about forms of corporeality that, while efficacious in behavior, do not lend themselves

[10] Note that Butler's focus on the formative power of discourse posits a strong critique of a representational model of language. Her objections are twofold: one, that this model incorrectly presupposes that language is anterior to the object it represents, when it in fact constitutes the object as well; two, that this model presumes a relationship of exteriority between language and power, when, in essence, language is not simply a tool for power but is itself a form of power. On these points, see Butler's critique of Bourdieu's representational theory of language in Butler 1997c; also see Butler and Connolly 2000.

[11] In response to a question posed by William Connolly about the nondiscursive character of bodily practices, Butler argues: "To focus on linguistic practice here and non-linguistic practice there, and to claim that both are important is still not to focus on the relation between them. It is that relation that I think we still do not know how to think. . . . It will not be easy to say that power backs language when one form that power takes is language. Similarly, it will not be possible to look at non-discursive practices when it turns out that our very way of delimiting and conceptualizing the practice depends on the formative power of a certain conceptual discourse. We are in each of these cases caught in a chiasmus relation, one in which the terms to be related also partake of one another, but do not collapse into one another" (Butler and Connolly 2000).

easily to representation, elucidation, and a logic of signs and symbols (see, for example, T. Asad 1993; Connolly 1999; Grosz 1994; Massumi 2002). For these scholars, a theory of linguistic signification does not quite apprehend the power that corporeality commands in the making of subjects and objects. These scholars, of course, speak from within a long philosophical tradition that extends from Spinoza to Bergson to Merleau-Ponty and, more recently, to Deleuze.

In light of this ongoing debate, a consideration of the mosque participants' understanding of virtuous action raises yet another set of interesting questions regarding Butler's emphasis on the significatory aspects of bodily performatives. As I mentioned earlier, the mosque participants do not understand the body as a sign of the self's interiority but as a means of developing the self's potentiality. (Potentiality here refers not to a generic human faculty but to the abilities one acquires through specific kinds of embodied training and knowledge, see p. 147.) As described in chapter 4, the mosque participants are in fact strongly critical of the nationalist-identitarian interpretations of religiosity because these views treat the body primarily as a sign of the self rather than as a means to its formation. One might say that for the mosque participants, therefore, the body is not apprehensible through its ability to function as a sign but encompasses an entire manner of being and acting in which the body serves as the developable means for its consummation. In light of this, it is important to ask whether a theory of embodied performativity that assumes a theory of linguistic signification (as necessary to its articulation) is adequate for analyzing formulations of the body that insist on the inadequacy of the body to function as a sign?

The fact that the mosque participants treat the body as a medium for, rather than a sign of, the self also has consequences for how subversion or destabilization of norms might operate within such an imaginary. Note that the mosque participants regard both *compliance to* and *rebellion against* norms as dependent upon the teachability of the body—what I called the "docility of the body" in chapter 1—such that both virtuous and unvirtuous dispositions are neccesarily learned. This means that the possibility for disrupting the structural stability of norms depends upon *literally* retutoring the body rather than on destabilizing the referential structure of the sign, or, for that matter, positing an alternative representational logic that challenges masculinist readings of feminine corporeality. Thus, anyone interested in reforming this tradition cannot simply assume that resignifying Islamic practices and virtues (like modesty or donning the veil) would change the meaning of these practices for the mosque participants; rather, what is required is a much deeper engagement with the architecture of the self that undergirds a particular mode of living and attachment, of which modesty/veiling are a part.

The recalcitrant character of the structure of orthodox Islamic norms contrasts dramatically with the politics of resignification that Butler's formulation of performativity presupposes. Butler argues that the body is knowable through language (even if it is not reducible to language); corporeal politics for her often ensue from those features of signification and reference that destabilize the referential structure. In Butler's conception, insofar as the force of the body is knowable through the system of signification, challenges to the system come from interventions in the significatory features of that system. For example, Butler analyzes the reappropriation of the term "queer," which was historically used as a form of hate speech against lesbians and gays, but which has now come to serve as a positive term of self-identification. For Butler the appropriation of the term "queer" works by redirecting the force of the reiterative structure of homophobic norms and tethering the term to a different context of valences, meanings, and histories. What is notable for the purpose of my argument here is that it is a change in the referential structure of the sign that destabilizes the normative meaning and force of the term "queer." In the case of the mosque movement, as I have argued above, a change in the referential structure of the system of signs cannot produce the same effect of destabilization. Any attempt to destabilize the normative structure must also take into account the specificity of embodied practices and virtues, and the kind of work they perform on the self, recognizing that any transformation of their meaning requires an engagement with the technical and embodied armature through which these practices are attached to the self.

My somewhat long foray into Butler's theory of embodied performativity elucidates, I hope, the range of productive questions that are generated through an encounter between philosophical "generality" and ethnographic "particularity"—an encounter that makes clear the constitutive role "examples" play in the formulation of theoretical concepts. Moreover, an analysis of the historical and cultural particularity of the process of subjectivation reveals not only distinct understandings of the performative subject but also the perspectival shifts one needs to take into account when talking about politics of resistance and subversion.

TO ENDURE IS TO ENACT?

In this section I would like to return to the exploration of different modalities of agency whose operations escape the logic of resistance and subversion of norms. In what follows I will investigate how suffering and survival—two modalities of existence that are often considered to be the antithesis of agency—came to be articulated within the lives of women who live under the pressures of a patriarchal system that requires them to conform to the rigid demands of heterosexual monogamy. Given that these conditions of gender inequality uniformly affect Egyptian women, regardless of their religious persuasion, I am particularly interested in understanding how a life lived in accordance with Islamic virtues affects a woman's ability to inhabit the structure of patriarchal norms. What resources and capacities does a pious lifestyle make available to women of the mosque movement, and how do their modes of inhabiting these structures differ from women for whom the resources of survival lie elsewhere? In particular I want to understand the practical and conceptual implications of a religious imaginary in which humans are considered to be only partially responsible for their own actions, versus an imaginary in which humans are regarded as the sole authors of their actions. It is not so much the epistemological repercussions of these different accounts of human action that interest me (cf. Chakrabarty 2000; Hollywood 2004), but how these two accounts affect women's ability to survive within a system of inequality and to flourish despite its constraints.

In what follows, I will juxtapose an example drawn from the life of a woman who was part of the mosque movement with another taken from the life of a woman who considered herself a "secular Muslim," and who was often critical of the virtues that the mosque participants regard as necessary to the realization of their ability to live as Muslims. I want to highlight the strikingly different ways in which these two women dealt with the pressures of being single in a society where heterosexual marriage is regarded as a compulsory norm. Even though it would be customary to consider one of these strategies "more agentival" than the other, I wish to show that such a reading is in fact reductive of the efforts entailed in the learning and practicing of virtues—virtues that might not be palatable to humanist sensibilities but are nonetheless constitutive of agency in important ways.

The full extent to which single women in Egypt are subjected to the pressure to get married was revealed to me in a conversation with Nadia, a woman I had come to know through her work in the mosques. Nadia was in her mid-thirties and had been married for a couple of years, but did not have any children; she and her husband lived in a small apartment in a lower-middle-income neighborhood of Cairo. She taught in a primary school close to her home, and twice a week after work she taught Quranic recitation to young children in the Nafisa mosque as part of what she considered her contribution to the ongoing work of daʿwa. Afterward, she would often stay to attend the lesson at the mosque delivered by one of the better-known dāʿiyat. Sometimes, after the lesson, I would catch a bus back with her and her friends. The ride was long and we would often have a chance to chat.

During one of these rides, I observed a conversation between Nadia and her longtime friend Iman, who was in her late twenties and who also volunteered at the mosque. Iman seemed agitated that day and, upon getting on the bus, immediately spoke to Nadia about her dilemma. A male colleague who was married to another woman had apparently approached her to ask her hand in marriage.[12] By Egyptian standards Iman was well over the marriageable age. Iman was agitated because although the man was very well respected at her place of work and she had always held him in high regard, he already had a first wife. She was confused about what she should do, and was asking Nadia for advice. Much to my surprise, Nadia advised Iman to tell this man to approach her parents formally to ask for her hand in marriage, and to allow her parents to investigate the man's background in order to ascertain whether he was a suitable match for her.

I was taken aback by this response because I had expected Nadia to tell Iman not to think about this issue any further, since not only had the man broken the rules for proper conduct by approaching Iman directly instead of her parents, but he was also already married. I had come to respect Nadia's ability to uphold rigorous standards of pious behavior: on numerous occasions I had seen her give up opportunities that would have accrued her material and social advantages for the sake of her principles. So a week later, when I was alone with Nadia, I asked her the question that had been bothering me: why did she not tell Iman to cut off any connection with this man?

Nadia seemed a little puzzled and asked me why I thought this was proper advice. When I explained, she said, "But there is nothing wrong in a man approaching a woman for her hand in marriage directly as long as his intent is serious and he is not playing with her. This occurred many times even at the time of the Prophet."

I interrupted her and said, "But what about the fact that he is already married?" Nadia looked at me and asked, "You think that she shouldn't consider marriage to an already married man?" I nodded yes. Nadia gave me a long and contemplative look, and said, "I don't know how it is in the United States, but this issue is not that simple here in Egypt [*il-mas'ila di mish sahla fi maṣr*]. Marriage is a very big problem here. A woman who is not married is rejected by the entire society as if she has some disease [*il-maraḍ*], as if she is a thief [*ḥarāmi*]. It is an issue that is very painful indeed [*hadhahi mas'ila muẓlima jiddan, jiddan ḥaqīqi*]."

I asked Nadia what she meant by this. She replied: "If you are unmarried after the age of say late teens or early twenties—as is the case with Iman—everyone around you treats you like you have a defect [*al-naqṣ*]. Wherever you go, you are asked, 'Why didn't you get married [*matgawwaztīsh ley*]?' Everyone knows that you can't offer to marry a man, that you have to wait until a man

[12] Islamic jurisprudence permits men to have up to four wives.

approaches you. Yet they act as if the decision is in your hands! You know I did not get married until I was thirty-four years old: I stopped visiting my relatives, which is socially improper, because every time I would go I would encounter the same questions. What is even worse is that your [immediate] family starts to think that you have some failing [*il-ʿēb*] in you because no man has approached you for marriage. They treat you as if you have a disease."

Nadia paused reflectively for a moment and then continued: "It's not as if those who are married necessarily have a happy life. For marriage is a blessing [*naʿma*], but it can also be a trial/problem [fitna]. For there are husbands who are cruel [*qāṣi*]: they beat their wives, bring other wives into the same house, and don't give each an equal share. But these people who make fun of you for not being married don't think about this aspect of marriage, and only stress marriage as a blessing [naʿma]. Even if a woman has a horrible husband, and has a hard married life, she will still make an effort to make you feel bad for not being married."

I was surprised at Nadia's clarity about the injustice of this situation toward women and the perils of marriage. I asked Nadia if single men were treated in the same way. Nadia replied resoundingly, "Of course not! For the assumption is that a man, if he wanted to, could have proposed to any woman: if he is not married it's because he *didn't want* to, or there was no woman who deserved him. But for the woman it is assumed that no one wanted *her* because it's not up to her to make the first move." Nadia shook her head again, and went on, "No, this situation is very hard and a killer [*il-mauḍūʿ ṣaʿb wi qātil*], O Saba. You have to have a very strong personality [*shakhṣiyya qawiyya*] for all of this not to affect you because eventually you also start thinking that there is something deeply wrong with you that explains why you are not married."

I asked her what she meant by being strong. Nadia said in response, "You must be patient in the face of difficulty [*lāzim tikūni ṣābira*], trust in God [*tawwakali ʿala allah*], and accept the fact that this is what He has willed as your fate [*qaḍāʾ*]; if you complain about it all the time, then you are denying that it is only God who has the wisdom to know why we live in the conditions we do and not humans." I asked Nadia if she had been able to achieve such a state of mind, given that she was married quite late. Nadia answered in an unexpected manner. She said, "O Saba, you don't learn to become patient [*ṣābira*] or trust in God [*mutawakkila*] only when you face difficulties. There are many people who face difficulties, and may not even complain, but they are not *ṣābirīn* [patient, enduring]. You practice the virtue of patience [*ṣabr*] because it is a good deed [al-ʿamal al-ṣāliḥ], regardless of your situation: whether your life is difficult or happy. In fact, practicing patience in the face of happiness is even more difficult."

Noting my look of surprise, Nadia said: "Yes, because think of how often people turn to God only when they have difficult times, and often forget Him in times of comfort. To practice patience in moments of your life when you are happy is to be mindful of His rights [*ḥaqqahu*] upon you at all times." I asked Nadia, "But I thought you said that one needs to have patience so as to be able to deal with one's difficulties?" Nadia responded by saying, "It is a secondary consequence [*al-natīja al-thānawiyya*] of your doing good deeds, among them the virtue of patience. God is merciful and He rewards you by giving you the capacity to be courageous in moments of difficulty. But you should practice ṣabr [patience] because this is the right thing to do in the path of God [*fi sabīl lillah*]."

I came back from my conversation with Nadia quite struck by the clarity with which she outlined the predicament of women in Egyptian society: a situation created and regulated by social norms for which women were in turn blamed. Nadia was also clear that women did not deserve the treatment they received, and that many of those she loved (including her kin) were equally responsible for the pain that had been inflicted on her when she was single. While polygamy is allowed in Islam, Nadia and other participants of the mosque movement would often point out that, according to the Quran, marriage to more than one woman is conditional upon the ability of a man to treat all his wives equally (emotionally and materially), a condition almost impossible to fulfill.[13] For this reason, polygamous marriages are understood to create difficult situations for women, and the mosque participants generally advise against it.[14] Nadia's advice to Iman that she consider marriage to a married man, however, was based on a recognition of the extreme difficulty entailed in living as a single woman in Egypt.

While Nadia's response about having to make such choices resonated with other, secular, Egyptian friends of mine, her advocacy of the cultivation of the virtue of ṣabr (roughly meaning "to persevere in the face of difficulty without complaint") was problematic for them.[15] Ṣabr invokes in the minds of many the passivity women are often encouraged to cultivate in the face of injustice. My friend Sana, for example, concurred with Nadia's description of how diffi-

[13] Both the Hanbali and Maliki schools of Islamic jurisprudence permit a woman to stipulate in her marriage contract that if the husband takes a second wife, she has the right to seek divorce. What is quite clear is that none of the schools give the woman the legal right to prevent her husband from taking a second wife. For recent debates on polygamy among contemporary religious scholars in Egypt, see Skovgaard-Petersen 1997, 169–70, 232–33.

[14] This is further augmented by the liberal ideal of nuclear family and companionate marriage, which, as Lila Abu-Lughod points out (1998), has increasingly become the norm among Islamists as well as secular-liberal Egyptians.

[15] I have retained the use of *ṣabr* in this discussion rather than its common English translation, "patience," because *ṣabr* communicates a sense not quite captured by the latter: one of perseverance, endurance of hardship without complaint, and steadfastness.

cult life could be for a single woman in Egypt, but strongly disagreed with her advice regarding ṣabr.

Sana was a single professional woman in her mid-thirties who came from an upper-middle-class family—a self-professed "secular Muslim" whom I had come to know through a group of friends at the American University in Cairo. In response to my recounting of the conversation with Nadia, Sana said, "Ṣabr is an important Islamic principle, but these religious types [*mutadayyinīn*] think it's a solution to everything. It's such a passive way of dealing with this situation." While Sana, too, believed that a woman needed to have a "strong personality" (*shakhṣiyya qawiyya*) in order to be able to deal with such a circumstance, for her this meant acquiring self-esteem or self-confidence (*thiqa fil-nafs wal-dhāt*). As she explained, "Self-esteem makes you independent of what other people think of you. You begin to think of your worth not in terms of marriage and men, but in terms of who you *really are*, and in my case, I draw pride from my work and that I am good at it. Where does ṣabr get you? Instead of helping you to improve your situation, it just leads you to accept it as fate—passively."

While Nadia and Sana shared their recognition of the painful situation single women face, they differed markedly in their respective engagements with this suffering, each enacting a different modality of agency in the face of it. For Sana the ability to survive the situation she faced lay in seeking self-empowerment through the cultivation of self-esteem, a psychological capacity that, in her view, enabled one to pursue self-directed choices and actions unhindered by other people's opinions. In this view, self-esteem is useful precisely because it is a means to achieving self-directed goals.[16] For Sana one of the important arenas for acquiring this self-esteem was her professional career and achievements. Nadia also worked, but clearly did not regard her professional work in the same manner.

Importantly, in Nadia's view, the practice of ṣabr does not necessarily make one immune to being hurt by others' opinions: one undertakes the practice of ṣabr first and foremost because it is an essential attribute of a pious character, an attribute to be cultivated regardless of the situation one faces. Rather than alleviating suffering, ṣabr allows one to bear and live hardship *correctly* as prescribed by one tradition of Islamic self-cultivation.[17] As Nadia says, if the practice of ṣabr fortifies one's ability to deal with social suffering, this is a secondary, not essential, consequence. Justification for the exercise of ṣabr, in other

[16] In the language of positive freedom, Sana may be understood to be a "free agent" because she appears to formulate her projects in accord with her own desires, values, and goals, and not those of others.

[17] For contemporary discussions of *ṣabr* among leaders of the Islamic Revival, see M. al-Ghazali 1990; al-Qaradawi 1989.

words, resides neither in its ability to reduce suffering nor in its ability to help one realize one's self-directed choices and/or goals. When I pressed Nadia for further explanation, she gave me the example of Ayyub, who is known in Islam for his exemplary patience in the face of extreme physical and social hardship (Ayyub is the equivalent of Job in the Judeo-Christian tradition). Nadia noted that Ayyub is famous *not* for his ability to rise above the pain, but precisely for the manner in which he *lived* his pain. Ayyub's perseverance did not decrease his suffering: it ended only when God had deemed it time for it to end. In this view, it is not only the lack of complaint in the face of hardship, but the way in which ṣabr infuses one's life and mode of being that makes one a *ṣābira* (one who exercises ṣabr). As Nadia notes in the conversation reported earlier, while ṣabr is realized through practical tasks, its consummation does not lie in practice alone.

Importantly, Nadia's conception of ṣabr is linked to the idea of divine causality, the wisdom of which cannot be deciphered by mere human intelligence. Many secular-oriented Muslims,[18] like Sana above, regard such an approach to life as defeatist and fatalist—as an acceptance of social injustice whose real origins lie in structures of patriarchy and social arrangements, rather than in God's will manifest as fate (qaḍā'). According to this logic, holding humans responsible for unjust social arrangements allows for the possibility of change, which a divine causality forecloses. Note, however, that the weight Nadia accords to fate does not absolve humans from responsibility for the unjust circumstances single women face. Rather, as she pointed out to me later, predestination is one thing and choice another (*al-qadr shai' wal-ikhtiyār shai' ākhir*): while God determines one's fate (for example, whether someone is poor or wealthy), human beings still choose how to deal with their situations (for example, one can either steal or use lawful means to ameliorate one's situation of poverty). What we have here is a notion of human agency, defined in terms of individual responsibility, that is bounded by both an eschatological structure *and* a social one. Importantly, this account privileges neither the relational nor the autonomous self so familiar to anthropologists (Joseph 1999), but a conception of individual ethics whereby each person is responsible for her own actions.[19]

[18] As I indicated in chapter 1, I am using "secular-oriented Muslims" as shorthand to refer to those for whom religious practice has limited relevance outside of personal devotion. See chapter 2 for my discussion of how the term "secularism" is used by the mosque participants in Egypt today.

[19] Notably, Sunni Islam shares with Protestantism two central ideas. First, they both share the assumption that each follower of the tradition is potentially capable of inculcating the highest virtues internal to the tradition and is responsible for the self-discipline necessary to achieve this goal (even though divine grace plays a central role in both traditions). Second, they both share

Just as the practice of self-esteem structured the possibilities of action that were open to Sana, so did the realization of ṣabr for Nadia, enabling certain ways of being and foreclosing others. It is clear that certain virtues (such as humility, modesty, and shyness) have lost their value in the liberal imagination and are considered emblematic of passivity and inaction, especially if they don't uphold the autonomy of the individual: ṣabr may, in this view, mark an inadequacy of action, a failure to act under the inertia of tradition. But ṣabr in the sense described by Nadia and others does not mark a reluctance to act. Rather, it is integral to a constructive project: it is a site of considerable investment, struggle, and achievement. What Nadia's and Sana's discussions reveal are two different modes of engaging with social injustice, one grounded in a tradition that we have come to value, and another in a nonliberal tradition that is being resuscitated by the movement I worked with.

Note that even though Nadia regarded herself as only partially responsible for the actions she undertook (the divine being at least equally responsible for her situation), this should not lead us to think that she was therefore less likely to work at changing the social conditions under which she lived. Neither she nor Sana, for a variety of reasons, could pursue the project of reforming the oppressive situation they were forced to inhabit. The exercise of ṣabr did not hinder Nadia from embarking on a project of social reform any more than the practice of self-esteem enabled Sana to do so. One should not, therefore, draw unwarranted correlations between a secular orientation and the ability to transform conditions of social injustice. Further, it is important to point out that to analyze people's actions in terms of realized or frustrated attempts at social transformation is necessarily to reduce the heterogeneity of life to the rather flat narrative of succumbing to or resisting relations of domination. Just as our own lives don't fit neatly into such a paradigm, neither should we apply such a reduction to the lives of women like Nadia and Sana, or to movements of moral reform such as the one discussed here.

THE PARADOXES OF PIETY

As I suggested in chapter 1, it is possible to read many of the practices of the mosque participants as having the effect of undermining the authority of a va-

---

the assumption that the highest virtues of the tradition must be pursued while one is immersed in the practicalities of daily life, rather than through seclusion in an enclosed community (of nuns, priests, or monks), or a predefined religious order (as is the case in certain strains of Christianity, Hinduism, and Buddhism). Consequently all of life is regarded as the stage on which these values and attitudes are enacted, making any separation between the secular and the sacred difficult to maintain.

riety of dominant norms, institutions, and structures. Indeed, my analysis of the overall aims of the mosque movement shows that challenging secular-liberal norms—whether of sociability or governance—remains central to the movement's self-understanding. Moreover, regardless of the movement's self-understanding, the objective effects that the movement has produced within the Egyptian social field de facto pose stiff impediments to the process of secularization. Despite this acknowledgment, as I suggested before, it would be a mistake to analyze the complexity of this movement through the lens of resistance insomuch as such a reading flattens out an entire dimension of the force this movement commands and the transformations it has spawned within the social and political fields.

This caution against reading the agency of this movement primarily in terms of resistance holds even more weight when we turn our attention to the analysis of gender relations. In what follows, I want to show why this is the case through ethnographic examples in which women may be seen as resisting aspects of male kin authority. While conceding that one of the effects of the mosque participants' pursuit of piety is the destabilization of certain norms of male kin authority, I want to argue that attention to the terms and concepts deployed by women in these struggles directs us to analytical questions that are closed off by an undue emphasis on resistance. The discourse of the mosque movement is shot through, of course, with assumptions that secure male domination: an analysis that focuses on terms internal to the discourse of piety must also engage the entire edifice of male superiority upon which this discourse is built. Indeed, my analysis of the mosque participants' practices of pedagogy and ritual observance (in chapters 3 and 4) is in part an exposition of this point. But the fact that discourses of piety and male superiority are ineluctably intertwined does not mean that we can assume that the women who inhabit this conjoined matrix are motivated by the desire to subvert or resist terms that secure male domination; neither can we assume that an analysis that focuses on the subversive effects their practices produce adequately captures the meanings[20] of these practices, that is, what these practices "do" within the discursive context of their enactment. Let me elaborate.

The pursuit of piety often subjected the mosque participants to a contradictory set of demands, the negotiation of which often required maintaining a delicate balance between the moral codes that could be transgressed and those that were mandatory. One common dilemma the mosque participants faced was the opposition they encountered to their involvement in daʿwa activities from their immediate male kin, who, according to the Islamic juristic tradition, are supposed to be the guardians of women's moral and physical well-being. In

[20] Obviously, my use of the term "meaning" here goes well beyond mere sense and reference.

order to remain active in the field of daʿwa, and sometimes even to abide by rigorous standards of piety, these women often had to go against their male kin, who exercised tremendous authority in their lives, authority that was sanctioned not only by divine injunctions but also by Egyptian custom.

Consider for example the struggles a woman called Abir had with her husband regarding her involvement in daʿwa activities. I had met Abir during one of the lessons delivered in the low-income Ayesha mosque and, over a period of a year and a half, came to know her and her family quite well. Abir was thirty years old and had three children at the time. Her husband was a lawyer and worked two jobs in order to make ends meet. Abir would sew clothes for her neighbors to supplement their income, and also received financial help from her family, who lived only a few doors down from her. Like many young women of her class and background, Abir was not raised to be religiously observant, and showed me pictures from her youth when she, like other neighborhood girls, wore short skirts and makeup, flaunting the conventions of modest comportment. Abir recounted how, as a young woman, she had seldom performed any of the obligatory acts of worship and, on the occasions when she did, she did so more out of custom (*ʿāda*) than out of an awareness of all that was involved in such acts. Only in the last several years had Abir become interested in issues of piety, an interest she pursued actively by attending mosque lessons, reading the Quran, and listening to taped religious sermons that she would borrow from a neighborhood kiosk. Over time, Abir became increasingly more diligent in the performance of religious duties (including praying five times a day and fasting during Ramadan). She donned the headscarf, and then, after a few months, switched to the full body and face veil (niqāb). In addition, she stopped socializing with Jamal's male friends and colleagues, refusing to help him entertain them at home.

Abir's transformation was astonishing to her entire family, but it was most disturbing to her husband, Jamal. Jamal was not particularly religious, even though he considered himself a Muslim—if an errant one. He seldom performed any of his religious obligations and, much to Abir's consternation, sometimes drank alcohol and indulged his taste for X-rated films. Given his desire for upward mobility—which required him to appear (what Abir called) "civilized and urbane" (*mutahaḍḍir*) in front of his friends and colleagues—Jamal was increasingly uncomfortable with the orthodox Islamic sociability his wife seemed to be cultivating at an alarming rate, the full face and body veil (niqāb) being its most "backward" (*mutakhallif*) sign. He was worried, and let Abir know in no uncertain terms that he wanted a more worldly and stylish wife who could facilitate his entry and acceptance into a class higher than his own.

Things became far more tense between them when Abir enrolled in a two-year program at a nongovernmental institute of daʿwa so she could train to become a dāʿiya. She had been attending the local mosque lessons, and felt that she would make a more effective teacher than the local dāʿiyāt if she had the proper training. Jamal did not take her seriously at first, thinking that she would soon grow tired of the study this program required, coupled with the long commute and daily child care and housework. But Abir proved to be resolute and tenacious: she knew that if she was lax in her duties toward the house, her children, or Jamal, she did not stand a chance. So she was especially diligent in taking care of all household responsibilities on the days she attended the daʿwa institute, and even took her son with her so that Jamal would not have to watch him when he returned from work.

Jamal tried several tactics to dissuade Abir. He learned quickly that his sarcastic remarks about her social "backwardness" did not get him very far: Abir would retort by pointing out how shortsighted he was to privilege his desire for worldly rewards over those in the Hereafter. She would also ridicule his desire to appear "civilized and urbane," calling it a blind emulation of Western values. Consequently, Jamal changed his tactic and started to use religious arguments to criticize Abir, pointing out that she was disobeying Islamic standards of proper wifely conduct when she disobeyed the wishes and commands of her husband. He would also occasionally threaten to take a second wife, as part of his rights as a Muslim man, if she did not change her ways. On one occasion, when he had just finished making this threat in front of her family and myself, Abir responded by saying, "You keep insisting on this right God has given you [to marry another woman]. Why don't you first take care of *His* rights over *you* [*ḥaqq allāh ʿēlaik*]?" It was clear to everyone that she was talking about Jamal's laxity in the performance of prayers, particularly since just an hour before, Abir had asked him, as the man of the household, to lead the evening prayer (*ṣalāt al-maghrib*)—a call he had ignored while continuing to watch television. Abir had eventually led the prayers herself for the women present in the house. Jamal was silenced by Abir's retort, but he did not refrain from continuing to harass her. At one point, after a particularly harsh argument between the two of them, I asked Abir, when we were alone, if she would consider giving up her daʿwa studies due to Jamal's opposition. She answered resolutely, "No! Even if he took an absolute stand on the issue [*hatta lau kān itmassik il-mauqif*], I would not give up daʿwa."

In response to Jamal's increasing pressure, Abir adjusted her own behavior. Much to her family's surprise, she became uncharacteristically gentle with Jamal, while using other means of persuasion with him. In particularly tense moments, she would at times cajole or humor him, and at times embarrass him by taking the higher moral ground (as in the scene just described). She also started to pray regularly for Jamal to his face, pointedly asking for God's pardon (*maghfira*) and blessings (*baraka*), not only in this life but in the Hereafter. The phrase "rabbinna yihdīk, ya rabb!" ("May our Lord show you the straight path, O Lord!") became a refrain in her interactions with Jamal. Sometimes she would play tape-recorded sermons at full volume in the house, especially on Fridays when he was home, that focused on scenes of death, tortures in hell, and the day of final reckoning with God. Thus, in order to make Jamal feel vulnerable, Abir invoked destiny and death (reminding him of the Hereafter when he would face God), urging him to accord these their due by being more religiously observant.

All of these strategies eventually had a cumulative effect on Jamal and, even though he never stopped pressuring Abir to abandon her studies at the daʿwa institute, the intensity with which he did so declined. He even started to pray more regularly, and to visit the mosque occasionally with her. More importantly for Abir, he stopped indulging his taste for alcohol and X-rated films at home.

What is important to note in this account is that none of Abir's arguments would have had an effect on Jamal had he not shared with her some sort of a commitment to their underlying assumptions—such as belief in the Hereafter, the inevitability that God's wrath will be unleashed on those who habitually disobey His commands, and so on. Abir's persuasion worked with Jamal in part because he considered himself to be a Muslim, albeit one who was negligent in his practice and prone to sinful acts. As an example of this, even when he did not pray in response to her repeated enjoinders, he did not offer a reasoned argument for his refusal in the way an unbeliever might have when faced with a similar situation. Certain shared moral orientations structured the possibilities of the argument, and thus the shape of the conflict, between them. When confronted with the moral force of Abir's arguments, Jamal could not simply deny their truth. As Abir once explained to me, for Jamal to reject her moral arguments would be tantamount "to denying God's truth, something even he is not willing to risk." The force of Abir's persuasion lay partly in her perseverance, and partly in the tradition of authority she invoked to reform her husband, who was equally—if errantly—bound to the sensibilities of this tradition. In other words, Abir's effectiveness was not an individual but a collaborative achievement, a product of the shared matrix of background practices, sensibilities, and orientations that structured Jamal and Abir's exchanges.

Secondly, it is also important to note that Abir's enrollment in the daʿwa institute against the wishes of her husband would not be condoned by majority of the dāʿiyāt and Muslim jurists. This is because, as I explained in chapter 2, while daʿwa is regarded a voluntary act for women, obedience to one's husband is considered an obligation to which every Muslim woman is bound.[21] Abir was aware of the risks she was taking in pursuing her commitment to daʿwa: Jamal's threats to divorce her, or to find a second wife, were not entirely empty since he was within his rights as a Muslim man to do so in the eyes of the sharīʿa. Abir was able to hold her position in part because she could claim a higher moral ground than her husband. Her training in daʿwa had given her substantial authority from which to speak and challenge her husband on issues of proper Islamic conduct. For example, as she learned more about the modern interpretation of daʿwa from the institute where she attended classes, she started to justify her participation in daʿwa using the argument, now popular among many Islamist thinkers (see chapter 2), that daʿwa was no longer considered a collective duty but an individual duty that was incumbent upon each and every Muslim to undertake—a change that had come about precisely because people like Jamal had lost the ability to know what it meant to live as Muslims.[22] Paradoxically, Abir's ability to break from the norms of what it meant to be a dutiful wife were predicated upon her learning to perfect a tradition that accorded her a subordinate status to her husband. Abir's divergence from approved standards of wifely conduct, therefore, did not represent a break with the significatory system of Islamic norms, but was saturated with them, and enabled by the capacities that the practice of these norms endowed her with.

It is tempting to read Abir's actions through the lens of subordination and resistance: her ability to pursue daʿwa work against her husband's wishes may well be seen as an expression of her desire to resist the control her husband was trying to exert over her actions. Or, from a perspective that does not privilege the sovereign agent, Abir's use of religious arguments may be understood as a simultaneous reiteration and resignification of religious norms, whereby patriarchal religious practices and arguments are assigned new meanings and valences. While both analyses are plausible, they remain inadequately attentive to the forms of reasoning, network of relations, concepts, and practices that were internal to Abir's actions. For example, what troubled Abir was not the authority Jamal commanded over her (upheld by divine injunctions), but

[21] Even among those writers who argue that daʿwa in the modern period has acquired the status of an individual duty (farḍ al-ʿain) rather than a collective duty (farḍ al-kifāya), daʿwa is still considered, for women, an obligation secondary to their duties as wives, mothers, and daughters. This position is upheld not only by men but also by women, like Zaynab al-Ghazali, who have advocated for women's increased participation in the field of daʿwa (see Z. al-Ghazali 1996a, 39; al-Hashimi 1990, 237).

[22] Jamal could have countered this argument by pointing out that most proponents of daʿwa consider it to be a woman's duty only if daʿwa does not interfere with her service to her husband and children (see note above). But since Jamal was unfamiliar with these debates about daʿwa, he was unable to make this argument.

his impious behavior and his attempts to dissuade her from what she considered to be her obligations toward God. For Abir, the demand to live piously required the practice of a range of Islamic virtues and the creation of optimal conditions under which they could be realized. Thus Abir's complicated evaluations and decisions were aimed toward goals whose sense is not captured by terms such as *obedience* versus *rebellion*, *compliance* versus *resistance*, or *submission* versus *subversion*. These terms belong more to a feminist discourse than to the discourse of piety precisely because these terms have relevance for certain actions but not others. Abir's defiance of social and patriarchal norms is, therefore, best explored through an analysis of the ends toward which it was aimed, and the terms of being, affectivity, and responsibility that constituted the grammar of her actions.[23]

daʿwa and kinship demands

The significance of an analysis that attends to the grammar of concepts within which a set of actions are located may be further elaborated through another example, one that is well known and often cited among those who are familiar with the figure of Zaynab al-Ghazali. As I mentioned in chapter 2, Zaynab al-Ghazali is regarded as a pioneering figure in the field of women's daʿwa in Egypt; she is also well known for having served as a leader of the Islamist political group the Muslim Brotherhood in the 1950s and 1960s. Given her public profile and political activism, al-Ghazali has been seen as a paradoxical figure who urged other women to abide by their duties as mothers, wives, and daughters, but lived her own life in a manner that challenged these traditional roles (Ahmed 1992; Hoffman 1985). An often-cited example of this seeming contradiction is al-Ghazali's account of how she divorced her first husband whom she claimed interfered with her "struggle in the path of God" (*jihād fi sabīl lillāh*), and then married her second husband on the condition that he not intervene in her work of daʿwa (Z. al-Ghazali 1995; Hoffman 1985, 236–37).

In her well-known autobiographical account, *Days from My Life* (*Ayyām min ḥayāti*), al-Ghazali reports an exchange with her second husband, who,

[23] My insistence throughout this book that we attend to the terms and concepts informing the actions of the mosque participants does not aim to simply reproduce "folk categories." Rather, my argument is that attention to these terms and concepts is necessary to rethinking analytical questions about regnant notions of agency in the social sciences and feminist theory. In this sense, my approach to the analysis of concepts is informed by the philosopher Ian Hacking who notes, "a concept is nothing other than a word in its sites. That means attending to a variety of types of sites: the sentences in which the word is actually (not potentially) used, those who speak those sentences, with what authority, in what institutional settings, in order to influence whom, with what consequences for the speakers" (Hacking 2002, 17).

upon seeing the frequency of her meetings with male members of the Muslim Brotherhood increase, had inquired about the nature of her work. According to al-Ghazali, since the Brotherhood was under strict government surveillance, with many of its leaders in Egyptian jails, her work with the Brotherhood had to be performed clandestinely, and she refused to share the exact nature of this work with her husband. When he probed, she conceded that her work with the Brotherhood could endanger her life, but reminded him of the agreement they had come to before their marriage:

> I cannot ask you today to join me in this struggle [jihād] but it is within my rights to stipulate [*ashtaraṭ ʿalayka*] that you not prevent me from my struggle in the path of God [jihādi fi sabīl lillāh], and that the day this [task] places upon me the responsibility of joining the ranks of the strugglers [*mujāhidīn*] you do not ask me what I am doing. But let the trust be complete between us, between a man who wanted to marry a woman who has offered herself to the struggle in the name of God and the establishment of the Islamic state since she was eighteen years old. If the interests of marriage conflict with the call to God [*al-daʿwa ʾila allāh*], then marriage will come to an end and the call [to God] [daʿwa] will prevail in my whole being/existence. . . . I know it is within your rights to order me, and it is incumbent upon me to grant you [your wishes], but God is greater in us than ourselves and His call is dearer to us than our existence. (Z. al-Ghazali 1995, 34–35)

In commenting on this passage, feminist historian Leila Ahmed points out that al-Ghazali's own choices in life "flagrantly undercut her statements on the role of women in Islamic society" (Ahmed 1992, 199–200). This contradiction is most apparent, in Ahmed's view, when al-Ghazali gives herself permission to place her work above her "obligations to raise a family," but does not extend the same right to other Muslim women (Ahmed 1992, 200).[24] While I do not deny that al-Ghazali's life has entailed many contradictions,[25] I think it is possible to understand her prescriptions for Muslim women as

[24] Hoffman (1985) offers a similar reading of these passages.

[25] In her two-volume book addressed to Muslim women in Egypt, al-Ghazali calls on women to enter the field of daʿwa (Z. al-Ghazali 1994a, 1996a). However, she advises a woman dāʿiya to concentrate her efforts on other women because "she can understand their temperaments, circumstances and characteristics, and therefore will succeed in reaching their hearts and solving their problems, and [be able] to follow their issues" (1994a, 2). While al-Ghazali conducted daʿwa among women for a period of thirteen years, she also worked with men when she joined the Muslim Brotherhood as part of what she considered her work in daʿwa. She rose to a position of leadership among the Muslim Brothers during a period when the majority of its top leaders were in jail and played a key role in coordinating the activities of the Brothers, a role for which she was later imprisoned. Clearly, her advice to women dāʿiyāt—to primarily focus on other women—was not something she followed in her own life.

consistent with the conditions she stipulated in her own marriage. Notably, al-Ghazali does not argue that the pursuit of *any* kind of work in a woman's life permits her to excuse herself from familial duties (as Ahmed suggests): only her work "in the path of God" (fi sabīl lillāh) allows her to do so, and only in those situations where her kinship responsibilities interfere with her commitment to serving God. According to al-Ghazali, had she been able to bear children, her choices would have been more complicated because, as she expressed to me in one of my interviews with her, this would not have left her "free to devote herself to the path of God" (Cairo, 22 July 1996). She also talks about this in an interview that was published in a Saudi women's magazine called *Sayyidati* (Hindawi 1997). In this interview, al-Ghazali explains her decision to seek divorce from her first husband by saying, "It was God's wisdom that He did not divert me from my [religious] activities by endowing me with a son, or blessing me with children. I was, however, and still am, a mother to all Muslims. Thus, confronted with the treasure and ardor of this call [to daʿwa], I was not able to keep myself from responding to it. When my [first] husband refused to let me continue my daʿwa activities, I asked him for a divorce and this was how it happened" (Hindawi 1997, 72).

Two doctrinal presuppositions are at the core of Zaynab al-Ghazali's argument. One is the position within Islamic jurisprudence, and commonly espoused by contemporary dāʿiyāt and the ʿulamāʾ, that a woman's foremost duty is to her parents before marriage, and to her husband and offspring after marriage, and that this responsibility is second only to her responsibility toward God. Only in situations where a woman's loyalty to God is compromised by her obligations toward her husband and family is there space for debate on this issue, and it is within this space that al-Ghazali formulates her dissent against her husband.

Zaynab al-Ghazali's argument also turns upon another important distinction made by Muslim jurists between one's *material* and *spiritual* responsibilities toward one's kin—both of which are organized along lines of age, gender, and kinship hierarchy. In this moral universe, while women are responsible for the *physical well-being* of both their husbands and children in the eyes of God, they are accountable only for their own and their children's *moral conduct*—not that of their husbands. Husbands, on the other hand, by virtue of the authority they command over their wives and children, are accountable for their *moral conduct* as well as their *social and physical well-being*. Thus, while inferiors and superiors have mutual *material* responsibilities toward each other (in the sense that wives, husbands, and children are obligated to care for one another's material comforts, albeit in different ways), it is husbands who are accountable for their wives' virtue, while wives are accountable only for the moral conduct of their children. This distinction allowed al-Ghazali to argue that her inability to bear children had "freed her" to pursue daʿwa activities, something she would have been unable to do if she were encumbered by the responsibility for her children's moral and physical well-being.

Al-Ghazali's ability to break successfully from traditional norms of familial duty should be understood, as I suggested in chapter 2, within the context of her considerable exposure to a well-developed discourse of women's rights at the turn of the twentieth century, a discourse that had been crucial to her formation as an activist. Indeed, it is quite possible to read al-Ghazali's ability to stipulate conditions in both her marriages as a function of the opportunities that were opened up for women of her socioeconomic background in the 1930s and 1940s in Egypt and the new consciousness this had facilitated regarding the role women had come to play in the public domain.

While this social and historical context is undoubtedly important for explicating al-Ghazali's actions in her personal and public life, it would be a mistake to ignore the specificity of doctrinal reasoning and its governing logic that accorded her actions a particular force—a force whose valence would be quite different if her arguments had relied upon the claim that women should be granted rights equal to those enjoyed by men within Islam in regard to marriage, divorce, and other kinship responsibilities. Al-Ghazali's actions and her justifications for her actions did not, in fact, depend on such an argument for equal rights. Instead her argument pivoted upon the concept of "moral and physical responsibility" that she as a Muslim woman owed to her immediate kin. In al-Ghazali's reasoning, her ability to break from these responsibilities was a function of her childless status. Whether we agree with the politics this reasoning advances or not, the discursive effects that follow from her invocation of this concept of moral responsibility explain both the power she commands as an "Islamic" (rather than a "feminist") activist in the Muslim world today and the immense legitimacy her life story has accorded juristic Islamic discourse on kinship—particularly for those who want to pursue a lifestyle that breaks from the traditional demands of this discourse while at the same time abiding by its central tenets and principles.

Here I do not mean to suggest that the effect of al-Ghazali's abidance by the terms of juristic discourse is best understood in terms of the lifestyles it has legitimized; rather, my point is that her narrative account should be analyzed in terms of the particular field of arguments it has made available to Muslim women and the possibilities for action these arguments have opened and foreclosed for them. It is this dimension of al-Ghazali's reasoning that I have wanted to emphasize, particularly because it is often ignored and elided in accounts that explain her actions in terms of the universal logic of "structural changes" that modernity has heralded in non-Western societies like Egypt. While these "structural changes" provide an important backdrop for understanding al-Ghazali's speech and actions, they have little power when it comes to explicating the force her life story commands in the field of Islamist activism.

doctrinal (ir)resolutions

While many of the problems that al-Ghazali and Abir faced in their pursuit of piety were related to their goal of becoming trained dāʿiyāt, women who did not have such ambitions also encountered structurally similar problems. Given that Islamic jurisprudence regards men to be the moral and physical guardians of women,[26] participants in the mosque movement often complained that living with male kin who were not as religiously devout compromised their own standards of piety. The problem seemed to be particularly acute for a woman who was married to what the mosque participants called "al-zauj al-ʿāṣi" (a disobedient husband)—this concern was widely discussed not only in the mosque circles but also in religious advice columns in newspapers. In the eyes of the sharīʿa, even though a woman is not responsible for her husband's moral conduct but only her own and her children's, her husband's behavior nonetheless profoundly affects her own pursuit of a virtuous life, given the moral authority he commands over her and his offspring as their custodian. Faced with such a situation, it is not easy for a woman to challenge her husband's conduct or to seek divorce, given the stigma of being a divorcée in Egyptian society and the restrictions Islamic law places on a woman's right to divorce. It was, therefore, very common during the mosque lessons to hear the audiences ask the dāʿiyāt what a woman should do if she was married to a husband who lived a sinful existence by the standards of virtuous Muslim conduct.

There is no simple doctrinal resolution to this problem. The responses of the dāʿiyāt varied and the women were urged to pursue a variety of means to come to terms with the contradictions posed by the conflicting demands of loyalty to God versus fidelity to one's (sinful) husband. Most dāʿiyāt, whether at the upper-middle-, middle-, or lower-income mosques, argued that since men are the custodians (*auliyāʾ*; singular: *wali*) of female kin in Islam, and not the other way around, women are not accountable in the eyes of God for the actions of their adult male kin. They advised women to try persuading their "disobedient husbands" to reform their behavior, and in the event they failed, to continue living with them with the understanding that they would have to be extra vigilant in monitoring their own conduct.

[26] The Quranic verse often cited to support this position states, "Men shall take full care of women with the bounties which God has bestowed more abundantly on the former than on the latter" (*al-rijāl qawwamūn ʿala al-nisāʾ*, verse 34 from Sūrat al-Nisāʾ ["The Woman"]).

I questioned some of the dāʿiyāt and the mosque participants about the contradictions this advice generated in a woman's life, since living with an impious husband would force her into situations that compromised her ability to live by acceptable standards of virtuous conduct. Most of them acknowledged that their recommendations did not constitute the best solution to the problem at hand, but insisted that most women had no choice. Some of the dāʿiyāt said, "If we advised women to seek divorce from disobedient husbands, we would de facto be asking half the population of married Egyptian women to be divorcées!"—implying that they thought a large number of Egyptian men were impious. Some argued that the fact that women are not held accountable for their husband's conduct is a blessing God has bestowed upon women—one that frees them to pursue piety without having to worry about the conduct of male kin—while men are burdened with having to account for their wives' actions as well as their own.

Other dāʿiyāt, such as Hajja Asma, who had been Zaynab al-Ghazali's student and now served as a dāʿiya in a local mosque, answered the question very differently.[27] During an afternoon lesson, when Hajja Asma was presented with this question by a woman in her mid-thirties from among a group of twelve middle-class housewives, she started by inquiring about the nature of the husband's sins. Once it was established that they were "grave sins" (*al-kabā'ir*)—such as refusing to pray regularly (*qaṣr al-ṣalāt qāṣiran*), engaging in illicit sexual activity (zinā'), and drinking alcohol—she advised the woman to employ a variety of strategies to convince her husband to change his conduct. She said:

> The first step is to cry in front of your husband, and make him realize that you are worried for him because of what God will do to him given his conduct. Don't think that this crying is in vain [*mafish fā'ida bi*] because crying is known to have melted the hearts of many. One of my neighbors convinced her husband to start praying regularly this way. She also brought other pressures to bear on him by having me talk to him, because she knows that he respects me and would be embarrassed [*maksūf*] if I were to question him about prayers. But if you find that crying does not seem to have results, then the next step you can take is to stop sharing meals with him [*baṭṭali it-taʿm maʿa*]. Eventually this is bound to have an effect, especially because men usually have stronger willpower than women and when a man sees a woman stronger than him he is moved by her persistence and strength [*istimrāriha wi quwwatiha*].

[27] Hajja Asma was the only dāʿiya I worked with who talked openly about her sympathies with the Muslim Brotherhood. As a result, she often had to move from mosque to mosque under government pressure and was only able to offer lessons sporadically.

At this point one of the women listening to Hajja Asma asked, "What if none of this has an effect on him [*matitʿashirīsh bi*]?" Hajja Asma replied, "The final and last thing you can try is to refuse to sleep with him [*baṭṭali al-ishrʿa maʿa*]." There was a palpable silence among the women at this point, and then a woman in her early thirties said in a low voice, "What if that doesn't work?" An older woman in her late sixties added loudly in response, "Yes, this happens a lot! [*ʿaiwa, da ḥaṣal kitīr*]." Hajja Asma nodded in agreement and said, "If none of this works, and you are certain that you have tried everything—and *only you can judge how hard you have tried*—and he still does not change his ways, then you have the right to demand a divorce from him [*ʿalēyki ḥaqq tuṭlubi it-ṭalāq minnu*]."

Some of the women gasped in surprise: "Yā!" ("Yā!" is an expression of surprise women often use in Egyptian colloquial Arabic). Noting this reaction, Hajja Asma responded, "Of course—what else can you do [*ḥatiʿmli ʾēh*]? Live with a sinning husband, raise your children in a sinful atmosphere—who will then grow up to be like him? How can you be obedient to God if you are living with a man like this [*tikūni fi-ṭ-ṭāʿat allāh izāy lamma tikūni maʿa rāgil zayyu*]?" She continued, "If it was only a matter of him being harsh with you [*lau kān qāṣi maʿaki*], or having a rough temperament [*tabīʿatu kān khishn*], then you could have endured it [*titṣabbiri ʿalēy*]. But this is something you cannot be patient about or forebear: it is an issue between you and your God."

Hajja Asma's words were received with somber silence, since divorce is not something that is easy for Egyptian women to contemplate given the social taboos associated with it, the bias against women in Egyptian law regarding child custody, and the economic hardship a divorcée must face in raising her children. Moreover, as I mentioned earlier, Islamic law does not make it easy for a woman to seek divorce, even in such a situation. In talking to Hajja Asma later, it was obvious to me that divorce was not something she took lightly either. Notably, Hajja Asma emphasized (as she does above) that if a woman was faced with a husband who had a harsh temperament, it was her obligation to be patient, given that patience (ṣabr) is an Islamic virtue that she should cultivate as a pious Muslim. But to practice forbearance in a situation where *God's claims over her* were being compromised, was to place her own interests (in terms of the security and safety marriage provides) above her commitment to God. When I asked the other dāʿiyāt and their audiences what they thought of Hajja Asma's response, they argued that not all women would have the courage and strength to risk the scorn and hardship a divorcée would be subjected to in Egyptian society in order to uphold high standards of virtuous conduct. Among the dāʿiyāt who took such a position, some of them said that women like Hajja Asma "were true slaves of God [*humma ʿibād allāh ḥaqīqiyyan*]!"

As is clear from these disparate answers, the choice between submission to

God's will and being obedient to one's husband did not follow a straightforward rule, and at times placed contradictory demands on the mosque participants. As a result, women were called upon to make complex judgments that entailed an interpretation of the Islamic corpus as well as their own sense of responsibility in the situation.[28] The questions the audience members posed, and the answers the dāʿiyāt provided, assumed that a woman is responsible for herself and her moral actions; the anguish underlying these queries was a product of both the sense of moral responsibility these women felt and the limited scope of choices available to them within orthodox Islamic tradition.

Within the moral-ethical framework articulated by Hajja Asma, a woman must, prior to asking for divorce, have a clear understanding of the order of priorities entailed in God's commands so that she challenges her husband only on those issues that compromise her ability to live as a dutiful Muslim. According to Hajja Asma's framework, if husbands interfere with matters pertaining to voluntary, rather than obligatory, acts (such as praying in a mosque instead of at home, practicing supererogatory fasts, undertaking daʿwa, or wearing the full face and body veil), then women are advised to give up these practices and to not disobey their husbands' wishes and commands. Similarly, a husband's harsh treatment of his wife is not regarded as sufficient reason to seek a divorce (although Egyptian women have been known to do so). Only when the nature of a husband's conduct is such that it violates key Islamic injunctions and moral codes, making it impossible for a woman to realize the basic tenets of virtuous conduct in her own and her children's lives, is she allowed to resort to divorce.

When viewed from a feminist perspective, the choices open to the mosque participants appear quite limited. The constraining nature of these alternatives notwithstanding, I would argue that they nonetheless represent forms of reasoning that must be explored on their own terms if one is to understand the structuring conditions of this form of ethical life and the forms of agency they entail. Note that the various paths followed by the women do not suggest the application of a universal moral rule (in the Kantian sense), but are closer to what Foucault calls ethics: the careful scrutiny one applies to one's daily actions in order to shape oneself to live in accordance with a particular model of behavior. Thus, Hajja Asma's advice entails a variety of techniques of introspection and argument, including: examining oneself to determine whether one has exhausted all possible means of persuading one's husband prior to ask-

[28] To make informed decisions about such an issue, Muslims often turn to a mufti (juriconsult) who, after consulting various established opinions and evaluating the individual situation, issues a fatwa that is legally nonbinding. In the context of the mosque lessons, the dāʿiyāt, though not trained to be muftis, in practice enact this role by helping women interpret the sharīʿa in light of their personal situations. For more complex issues, the dāʿiyāt often refer their audiences to a qualified mufti.

ing for a divorce; being honest with oneself in such an examination, since no one else can make such a judgment; and employing a variety of techniques of persuasion, both oral and embodied, to change the immoral ways of the husband. This stands in contrast to the kind of self-scrutiny applied by a woman who chooses to stay with an impious husband: such a woman must constantly watch that she does not use her husband's behavior as an excuse for her own religious laxity, assess her intentions and motivations for the actions she pursues, make sure she does everything in her capacity to raise her children in accord with standards of pious conduct, and so on. In both situations, moral injunctions are not juridically enforced but are self-monitored and entail an entire set of ascetic practices in which the individual engages in an interpretive activity, in accord with sharīʿa guidelines, to determine how best to live by Islamic moral codes and regulations.

Only through attention to these kinds of specificities can we begin to grasp the different modalities of agency involved in enacting, transgressing, or inhabiting ethical norms and moral principles. The analysis I have presented here should not be confused with a hermeneutical approach, one that focuses on the meanings that particular utterances, discourses, and practices convey. Rather, the framework I have suggested analyzes the *work* that discursive practices perform in making possible particular kinds of subjects. From this perspective, when assessing the violence that particular systems of gender inequality enact on women, it is not enough to simply point out, for example, that a tradition of female piety or modesty serves to give legitimacy to women's subordination. Rather it is only by exploring these traditions in relation to the practical engagements and forms of life in which they are embedded that we can come to understand the significance of that subordination to the women who embody it.

Finally, in respect to agency, my arguments in this chapter show that the analytical payback in detaching the concept of agency from the trope of resistance lies in the series of questions such a move opens up in regard to issues of performativity, transgression, suffering, survival, and the articulation of the body within different conceptions of the subject. I have insisted that it is best not to propose *a* theory of agency but to analyze agency in terms of the different modalities it takes and the grammar of concepts in which its particular affect, meaning, and form resides. Insomuch as this kind of analysis suggests that different modalities of agency require different kinds of bodily capacities, it forces us to ask whether acts of resistance (to systems of gender hierarchy) also devolve upon the ability of the body to behave in particular ways. From this perspective, transgressing gender norms may not be a matter of transforming "consciousness" or effecting change in the significatory system of gender, but might well require the retraining of sensibilities, affect, desire, and sentiments—those registers of corporeality that often escape the logic of representation and symbolic articulation.

EPILOGUE

No study of Islamist politics situated within the Western academy can avoid engaging with the contemporary critique of Islamic ethical and political behavior, and with the secular-liberal assumptions that animate this critique. This owes to the fact that the "problem" giving rise to current scholarly concern surrounding Islam centers on this tradition's (potentially dangerous) divergence from the perceived norms of a secular-liberal polity. The force this framing commands is apparent not only in the writings of those who are critical of Islamist politics but also in the posture of defense that many Islamist writers must adopt in order to make their case in the court of international public opinion. Even the concepts I have had to rely on in describing the mosque movement incorporate this evaluative purview. The neologism "Islamism," for example, frames its object as an eruption of religion outside the supposedly "normal" domain of private worship, and thus as a historical anomaly requiring explanation if not rectification. The events of September 11, 2001, have only served to strengthen the sense that it is a secular-liberal inquisition before which Islam must be made to confess.

A study that focuses on "Muslim women" carries the burden of this judgment even more because of all the assumptions this dubious signifier triggers in the Western imagination concerning Islam's patriarchal and misogynist qualities. Far more than issues of democracy and tolerance, the "Woman Question" has been key within the development of the Western critique of Islam, even for writers who express distinctly antifeminist views when it comes to women in the West. A long history of colonialism has of course helped secure this essential framing: colonialism rationalized itself on the basis of the "inferiority" of non-Western cultures, most manifest in their patriarchal customs and practices, from which indigenous women had to be rescued through the agency of colonial rule (Abu-Lughod 2002; Ahmed 1992; Lazreg 1994; Mohanty 1991; Spivak 1987). Western Europeans were not the only ones to deploy this trope within a colonial context; the Soviet Union also foregrounded a similar set of arguments in executing its civilizing mission among Muslim populations in Central Asia.[1] Today the force of this evaluative framing remains glaringly apparent in the fact that women's active participation in contemporary Islamist movements, rather than constituting a challenge to such long-standing assumptions, is taken instead as further evidence of the profound subjugation of Muslim women (see Mahmood 2003). My point in mentioning the tenacity of such views is not to suggest that there is no violence against women in the Muslim world, but that it is the reductive character of this framing, one that orchestrates an entire chain of equivalences associated with Islam, that needs to be questioned.

Admittedly, this evaluative stance I have described is not limited to Islam but, to varying extents, has long been a structural feature of the anthropological enterprise itself, as many anthropologists have pointed out. Marilyn Strathern, for example, has written eloquently about the historical understanding of Melanesia (her area of study) in the Western imagination as a space of "cultural primitiveness" that helped secure the West's own self-understanding as "modern, civilized, and scientific" (1988). Strathern deals with the weight this prior framing exerts on her work by employing a textual strategy that begins by acknowledging the constructed quality of what stands in for Melanesia in Western discourse. She writes, "I am constrained by the fact that there is, of course, no 'Melanesian case' that is not a Western projection. I therefore deliberately 'reveal' it through a binarism firmly located in an us/them contrast that works by inversion and negation. These are my means. Not the infinite strategy of third (mediating) terms, but a strategy of displacements. I thus try to present Western discourse as a form through which Melanesian discourse can appear. If one thinks about it, 'Melanesian discourse' can, of course, have no other locus" (Strathern 1992b, 75). Note that Strathern's strategy is not an attempt at cultural translation (through the use of "third mediating terms"); instead it seeks to displace Western analytical categories by staging inversions of familiar ways of thinking and conceptualizing.

[1] As Rosalind Morris has perceptively shown in a recent article, Muslim women in the Central Asian republics came to be regarded by a number of early Marxist theorists (key among them Lenin and Trotsky) as a "surrogate proletariat" whose enslaved status made them supposedly more receptive to the emancipatory promises of communism (Morris 2002). Ironically, his opposition to Trotsky notwithstanding, it was Stalin who put these ruminations into practice; Gregory Massell (1974) documents the immense human disaster that the Soviet policy of recruiting Muslim women into the communist project unleashed in what were then called "the Eastern states."

My project in this book partakes in some aspects of Strathern's arguments. Like the Melanesian case, my discussion of Islamist politics perforce must also engage the terms through which Islamism has come to be understood in popular Euro-American discourse. My juxtapositions of the practices of the pietists against secular-liberal understandings of agency, body, and authority in this book therefore take on a necessary quality: it is not a task I choose so much as one that is thrust upon me. It is clear that, regardless of whether I stage such juxtapositions or not, the horizon of secular-liberal presuppositions about the proper role religiosity should play in the constitution of a modern subjectivity, community, and polity will inevitably structure my audience's reading of this book. Not wanting to promote the particular assumptions that such a framing entails, I have attempted to circumvent these predictable modes of reading by parochializing the terms my readership is likely to bring to this material, displacing them through a combination of narrative description and analytical preemption.

There is a further layer of complication to my exploration of the Islamist movement in Egypt that is perhaps different from the dilemmas that Strathern faced. It has to do with the fact that North Atlantic geopolitical interests in the Middle East have long made it a primary site for the exercise of Western power, and thus for the deployment of the secular-liberal discourses through which that power often operates. What is at stake in Western critiques of Islam, in other words, is not simply a question of ideological bias, but rather the way these critiques function within a vast number of institutional sites and practices aimed at transforming economic, political, and moral life in the Middle East—from international financial institutions to human rights associations to national and local administrative bureaucracies. The transformations brought about within the context of this vast modernizing project have enveloped the entire social fabric of the Middle East, impacting everything from pedagogical techniques to conceptions of moral and bodily health to patterns of familial and extra-familial relations.

In light of this, secular liberalism cannot be addressed simply as a doctrine of the state, or as a set of juridical conventions: in its vast implications, it defines, in effect, something like a form of life. It is precisely for this reason that the knowledges, ethics, and sensibilities of even nonstate movements like the women's mosque movement necessarily engage its broad and diffuse agency. As I have sought to demonstrate in this book, this engagement cannot be analyzed in terms of a conflict between two historically distinct opponents. While contemporary Islamist activities identify secular liberalism as a powerful corrosive force within Muslim societies, the discourses in which they do so also presuppose practical and conceptual conditions that are indebted to the extension of the secular-liberal project itself.[2] As the preceding chapters have made clear, however, the inextricable intertwining between these two formations is not without its tensions and ruptures. One of the basic premises of this book is that in order to understand Islamism's enmeshment within, and challenges to, assumptions at the core of the secular-liberal imaginary, one must turn not to the usual spaces of political struggle (such as the state, the economy, and the law) but to arguments about what constitutes a proper way of living ethically in a world where such questions were thought to have become obsolete. In Egypt today, the primary topoi for this ethical labor are the body, ritual observances, and protocols of public conduct.

POLITICS IN UNUSUAL PLACES

It is customary to analyze debates about religious markers of public behavior through the lens of identity politics, a politics that presupposes that each individual and group seeks to express its authenticity through symbols of ethnic, religious, and other forms of particularistic belonging so as to achieve recognition and respect from other members of the social collectivity. To the extent that claims on the state for rights, goods, and services must be made on the basis of social identity, it comes to be politicized as a key site of contestation. In this view, contemporary movements of multiculturalism and queer identity in Western liberal democracies, and ethnic and religious movements in the non-Western world, all exemplify this form of politics in that they are seen to be making claims on the state in particular, and the social collectivity in general, on the basis of certain shared characteristics that the participants consider essential to their self-definition as a group.

The uniquely modern character of identity politics has been analyzed from a variety of perspectives. Charles Taylor, for example, argues that identity politics is a result of the intertwining of two different discourses that the culture of liberal modernity has made available: the universalist discourse of equal rights and dignity on the one hand, and the particularistic discourse of the ideal of authenticity on the other (Taylor 1992). Other theorists, following Jacques Lacan, regard identity politics as an expression of a fundamental psychological process through which an individual comes to define herself in opposition to the Other (see, for example, Laclau 1990). On this view, new social movements are an expression of the constitutive lack that haunts all

[2] As I describe in chapter 2, the emergence and proliferation of Islamist movements are deeply indebted to modern mass education, practices of media consumption, and forms of political and associational life characteristic of civil society—all of which are crucial elements within the historical trajectory of secular liberalism across the globe.

processes of identity formation, a lack that on the symbolic level (which is also the realm of culture and language) manifests itself as a condition of possibility for these movements. Despite theoretical differences between these two perspectives as to how identity is constituted, there is agreement that contemporary (or "new") social movements are best analyzed in terms of a politics of identity that manifests itself in claims of rights, recognition, distributive justice, and political representation.

If we examine the material I have presented in this book about the character of the piety movement, it is quite apparent that this particular strand of the Islamist movement is only marginally organized around questions of rights, recognition, and political representation. Indeed, as I have shown, the mosque participants are quite ambivalent about the question of identity and are, in fact, emphatically critical of those Muslims who understand their religious practices as an expression of their Muslim or Arab identity rather than as a means of realizing a certain kind of virtuous life (see chapters 2 and 4). In this sense, it is not toward *recognition* that the activities of the mosque or the piety movement are oriented but rather toward the *retraining* of ethical sensibilities so as to create a new social and moral order. In light of this, it would therefore be a mistake to assume that all contemporary social movements find their genesis in a politics of identity and should be analyzed as responses to the juridical language of rights, recognition, and distributive justice.

The fact that the piety movement does not directly engage the state and its juridical discourses, however, should not lead us to think that it has no direct political implications.[3] To the extent that all aspects of human life (whether they pertain to family, education, worship, welfare, commercial transactions, instances of birth and death, and so on) have been brought under the regulatory apparatuses of the nation-state, the piety movement's efforts to remake any of these activities will necessarily have political consequences. As Charles Hirschkind has argued persuasively, "Modern politics and the forms of power it deploys have become a [necessary] condition for the practice of many of our more personal activities. As for religion, to the extent that the institutions enabling the cultivation of religious virtue have become subsumed within (and transformed by) the legal and administrative structures linked to the state, then the (traditional) project of preserving those virtues will necessarily be political if it is to succeed" (1997, 13). In other words, it is not that the pietists have "politicized" the spiritual domain of Islam (as some scholars of Islamism claim) but that conditions of secular-

[3] This is a position, as I suggested earlier, that is upheld by a number of scholars of Islamic reform movements. See, for example, Beinin and Stork 1997; Göle 1996; Metcalf 1993, 1994, 1998; Roy 1994.

liberal modernity are such that for any world-making project (spiritual or otherwise) to succeed and be effective, it must engage with the all-encompassing institutions and structures of modern governance, whether it aspires to state power or not. It is not surprising, therefore, that the supposedly apolitical practices of the piety movement have been continually targeted by the disciplinary mechanisms of the Egyptian state.

While acknowledging the constitutive role practices of governance continue to play in the formation of the piety movement, it is nonetheless crucial to point out that the full sociopolitical force of this movement cannot be apprehended in terms of an analysis solely focused on conditions of postcolonial governance. The discursive logic that has sustained this movement, and the contingent effects it has produced in the social field, are in no way coterminous with the operations of state power. Yet it seems to me that we have few conceptual resources available for analyzing sociopolitical formations that do not take the nation-state and its juridical apparatuses as their main points of reference. Partha Chatterjee expresses a similar dissatisfaction with our conceptual vocabulary when he argues that even though affiliations of lineage, religion, caste, and language (all of which exceed national forms of belonging) continue to command a powerful force within contemporary postcolonial societies, they remain poorly theorized within contemporary discussions of postcolonial modernity. Chatterjee glosses these affiliations under the "fuzzy" notion of "community" and argues:

> I do not believe that the imaginative possibilities afforded by the fuzziness of the community have disappeared from the domain of popular political discourse. On the contrary, I suspect that with the greater reach of the institutions and processes of the state into the interiors of social life, the state itself is being made sense of in the terms of that other discourse, far removed from the conceptual terms of liberal political theory. (1993, 225)

What Chatterjee discusses under the rubric of "community" has a certain resonance with my thematization of ethics in this book insomuch as my analysis of the ethical practices of the piety movement makes explicit those modalities of action through which embodied attachments to historically specific forms of belonging are forged. These ethical practices, as I have suggested, are also practices of subjectivation whose logic, while clearly shaped by modes of secular-liberal governance, is not reducible to its operations. It seems to me that such an understanding of the ethical in terms of the political, and vice versa, is crucial if we are to understand the power that extra-national forms of belonging currently command in the postcolonial world.

FEMINIST POLITICS AND ETHICAL DILEMMAS

Finally, in conclusion, I want to revisit some of the questions regarding feminism with which I opened this book: How does my analysis of this movement complicate the analytical and politically prescriptive projects of feminism? What does it mean for feminists like myself to take the mosque participants' concepts of human flourishing into account? What are the ethical demands that a consideration of nonliberal movements such as the mosque movement imposes on us? What are the analytical resources that feminist theory offers to help us think through these questions?

As I suggested above, for a scholar of Islam, none of these questions can be adequately answered without encountering the essential tropes through which knowledge about the Muslim world has been organized, key among them the trope of patriarchal violence and Islam's (mis)treatment of women. The veil, more than any other Islamic practice, has become the symbol and evidence of the violence Islam has inflicted upon women. I have seldom presented my arguments in an academic setting, particularly my argument about the veil as a disciplinary practice that constitutes pious subjectivities, without facing a barrage of questions from people demanding to know why I have failed to condemn the patriarchal assumptions behind this practice and the suffering it engenders. I am often struck by my audience's lack of curiosity about what else the veil might perform in the world beyond its violation of women. These exhortations are only one indication of how the veil and the commitments it embodies, not to mention other kinds of Islamic practices, have come to be understood through the prism of women's freedom and unfreedom such that to ask a different set of questions about this practice is to lay oneself open to the charge that one is indifferent to women's oppression. The force this coupling of the veil and women's (un)freedom commands is equally manifest in those arguments that endorse or defend the veil on the grounds that it is a product of women's "free choice" and evidence of their "liberation" from the hegemony of Western cultural codes.

What I find most troubling about this framing is the analytical foreclosure it effects and the silence it implicitly condones regarding a whole host of issues—issues that demand attention from scholars who want to productively think about the Islamic practices undergirding the contemporary Islamic Revival. I understand the political demand that feminism imposes to exercise vigilance against culturalist arguments that seem to authorize practices that underwrite women's oppression. I would submit, however, that our analytical explorations should not be reduced to the requirements of political judgment, in part because the labor that belongs to the field of analysis is different from that required by the demands of political action, both in its temporality and its social impact. It is not that these two modalities of engagement—the political and the analytical—should remain deaf to each other, only that they should not be collapsed into each other.[4] By allowing theoretical inquiry some immunity from the requirements of strategic political action, we leave open the possibility that the task of thinking may proceed in directions not dictated by the logic and pace of immediate political events.

Wendy Brown has written eloquently about what is lost when analysis is subjected to the demands of political attestation, judgment, and action. She argues:

> It is the task of theory . . . to "make meanings slide," while the lifeblood of politics is made up of bids for hegemonic representation that by nature seek to arrest this movement, to fix meaning at the point of the particular political truth—the nonfluid and nonnegotiable representation—that one wishes to prevail. . . . [L]et us ask what happens when intellectual inquiry is sacrificed to an intensely politicized moment, whether inside or outside an academic institution. What happens when we, out of good and earnest intentions, seek to collapse the distinction between politics and theory, between political bids for hegemonic truth and intellectual inquiry? We do no favor, I think, to politics or to intellectual life by eliminating a productive tension—the way in which politics and theory effectively interrupt each other—in order to consolidate certain political claims as the premise of a program of intellectual inquiry. (W. Brown 2001, 41)

I read Wendy Brown here as insisting on the importance of practicing a certain amount of skepticism, a suspension of judgment, if you will, toward the normative limits of political discourse. "Intellectual inquiry" here entails pushing against our received assumptions and categories, through which a number of unwieldy problems have been domesticated to customary habits of thought and praxis.

This argument gains particular salience in the current political climate, defined by the events of September 11, 2001, and the subsequent war of terror that the United States government has unleashed on the Muslim world. The long-

[4] The distinction between these two forms of human labor, as Judith Butler points out, goes back to at least Aristotle, who argues that "theoretical wisdom" is not the same as "practical wisdom" since each are oriented toward different ends: the former pursues what Aristotle calls "happiness," and the latter "virtue" (Butler, Laclau, and Žižek 2000, 264–66). For contemporary reformulations of this argument, see Wendy Brown's discussion of the work of Benedetto Croce, Maurice Merleau-Ponty, and Michel Foucault (W. Brown 2001, 40–44).

standing demand that feminists stand witness to the patriarchal ills of Islam has now been enlisted in the service of one of the most unabashed imperial projects of our time. Consider, for example, how the Feminist Majority's international campaign against the Taliban regime was an essential element in the Bush administration's attempt to establish legitimacy for the bombing of Afghanistan—aptly called "Operation Enduring Freedom" (on this, see Hirschkind and Mahmood 2002). It was the burka-clad body of the Afghan woman—and *not* the destruction wrought by twenty years of war funded by the United States through one of the largest covert operations in American history—that served as the primary referent in the Feminist Majority's vast mobilization against the Taliban regime (and later the Bush administration's war). While the denial of education to Afghan women and the restrictions imposed on their movements were often noted, it was this visual image of the burka more than anything else that condensed and organized knowledge about Afghanistan and its women, as if this alone could provide an adequate understanding of their suffering. The inadequacy of this knowledge has today become strikingly evident as reports from Afghanistan increasingly suggest that the lives of Afghan women have not improved since the ouster of the Taliban and that, if anything, life on the streets has become more unsafe than it was under the old regime due to conditions of increased sociopolitical instability (Amnesty International 2003; Badkhen 2002; Human Rights Watch 2002). Perhaps we need to entertain the possibility that had there been some analytical complexity added to the picture that organizations such as the Feminist Majority presented of Afghan women's situation under Taliban rule, had the need for historical reflection not been hijacked by the need for immediate political action, then feminism might have been less recruitable to this ill-conceived project.

The ethical questions that imperial projects of this proportion pose for feminist scholars and activists are also relevant to the more sedate context of the women's mosque movement that has been the focus of this book. To the degree that feminism is a politically prescriptive project, it requires the remaking of sensibilities and commitments of women whose lives contrast with feminism's emancipatory visions. Many feminists, who would oppose the use of military force, would have little difficulty supporting projects of social reform aimed at transforming the attachments, commitments, and sensibilities of the kind that undergird the practices of the women I worked with, so that these women may be allowed to live a more enlightened existence. Indeed, my own history of involvement in feminist politics attests to an unwavering belief in projects of reform aimed at rendering certain life forms provisional if not extinct. But the questions that I have come to ask of myself, and which I would like to pose to the reader as well, are: Do my political visions ever run up against the responsibility that I incur for the destruction of life forms so that "unenlightened" women may be taught to live more freely? Do I even fully comprehend the forms of life that I want so passionately to remake? Would an intimate knowledge of lifeworlds distinct from mine ever lead me to question my own certainty about what I prescribe as a superior way of life for others?

In his provocative and disturbing book *Liberalism and Empire*, Uday Mehta argues that one of the reasons a number of liberal thinkers, committed to ideals of equality, liberty, fraternity, and tolerance, were able to actively endorse the project of the Empire—a project not simply of conquest and pillage but also of profound political and moral paternalism—had to do with a broad orientation inherent within liberal thought regarding how one responds to "the experiences of the unfamiliar" (Mehta 1999, 201). As Mehta argues, for those who share this orientation, any given present is to be understood in terms of its contribution to an unbounded future. Insomuch as unfamiliar ways of life are judged by reference to their projection into such a future, one defined by the unfolding of the liberal project itself, the particularities of these forms are rendered provisional, moments of difference subsumed within a teleological process of improvement (Mehta 1999, 201–210). A similar orientation is also operative, I believe, in our feminist certainty that women's sensibilities and attachments, particularly those that seem so paradoxically inimical to what we take to be their own interests, *must* be refashioned for their own well-being.

Personally, it was this certainty that came to dissolve before my eyes as I became enmeshed within the thick texture of the lives of the mosque participants, women whose practices I had found objectionable, to put it mildly, at the outset of my fieldwork. I had approached the study of this movement with a sense of foreknowledge of what I was going to encounter, of how I was going to explain these women's "intransigent behavior" in regard to the ideals of freedom, equality, and autonomy that I myself have held so dear. Over time, I found these ideals could no longer serve as arbiters of the lives I was studying because the sentiments, commitments, and sensibilities that ground these women's existence could not be contained within the stringent molds of these ideals. My prejudices against their forms of life (or, for that matter, theirs against mine) could not be reconciled and assimilated within "a cosmopolitan horizon" (Mehta 1999, 22); the unseemliness of differences could not be synthesized. Nor did I find myself capable of factoring this difference into my old calculus of what in their behavior had more "feminist potential" and what was hopelessly irrecuperable. This language of assessment, I realized, is not neutral but depends upon notions of progressive and backward, superior and inferior, higher and lower—a set of oppositions frequently connected with a compelling desire to erase the second modifier even if it means implicitly forming alliances with coercive modes of power.

In this absence of familiar milestones, I came to reckon that if the old feminist practice of "solidarity" had any valence whatsoever, it could not be grounded in the ur-languages of feminism, progressivism, liberalism, or Islamism, but could only ensue within the uncertain, at times opaque, conditions of intimate and uncomfortable encounters in all their eventuality. I say this not to resurrect a redemptive narrative of anthropological reckoning or universal humanism that claims the power to break through the thicket of prejudices and find a common human essence. To do so would be to reduce yet again all that remains irreconcilable into the trope of a shared humanity and its assumed teleological futurity. Rather what I mean to gesture at is a mode of encountering the Other which does not assume that in the process of culturally translating other lifeworlds one's own certainty about how the world should proceed can remain stable. This attitude requires the virtue of humility: a sense that one does not always know *what* one opposes and that a political vision at times has to admit its own finitude in order to even comprehend what it has sought to oppose.

As must be apparent to the sensitive reader, I have avoided the strategy of rendering the Other through its traces and absences—a strategy pursued by postcolonial writers sensitive to the violence a hegemonic discourse commits when it tries to assimilate the Other to a language of translatability.[5] On this view, to render unfamiliar lifeworlds into conceptual or communicable form is to domesticate that which exceeds hegemonic protocols of intelligibility. I have avoided this strategy of narrativization because I fear that it engenders a certain recursivity that ends up privileging the hegemonic terms of discourse by failing to engage—and be engaged by—the systemacity and reason of the unfamiliar, the strange, or the intransigent. Furthermore, to the extent that the tilt of the current political climate is such that all forms of Islamism (from its more militant to its more quiescent) are seen as the products of a roving irrationality, I feel a certain responsibility to render to reason that which has been banished from its domain. Perhaps more importantly, it is through this process of dwelling in the modes of reasoning endemic to a tradition that I once judged abhorrent, by immersing myself within the thick texture of its sensibilities and attachments, that I have been able to dislocate the certitude of my own projections and even begin to comprehend why Islamism, at least in one of its renditions, exerts such a force in people's lives. This attempt at comprehension offers the slim hope in this embattled and imperious climate, one in which feminist politics runs the danger of being reduced to a rhetorical display of the placard of Islam's abuses, that analysis as a mode of conversation, rather than mastery, can yield a vision of coexistence that does not require making others lifeworlds extinct or provisional.

[5] See, for example, Bhabha 1996; Chakrabarty 2000; Spivak 1987.

Glossary of Commonly Used Arabic Terms

Adab. — Etiquette.

ʿAlmana or *ʿalmāniyya.* — Secularization.

ʿAlmāniyyin. — Secularists.

al-Aʿmāl al-ṣāliḥa. — Good deeds.

Amr bil maʿrūf wal-nahi ʿan al-munkar. — To enjoin someone in the doing of good or right, and the forbidding of evil or wrong.

ʿAura. — Linguistically means "weakness," "faultiness," "unseemliness," "imperfection," "disfigurement," and "genitalia"; also used in Islamic juristic discourse to signify women.

Bidʿa. — In Islamic doctrine, this refers to unwarranted innovations, beliefs or, practices for which there was no precedent at the time of the Prophet and that are therefore best avoided.

Dāʿiya (plural: *dāʿiyāt*). — Preacher/religious teacher; one who undertakes *daʿwa.*

Dars (plural: *durūs*). — Lesson; in the context of the mosque movement, this term refers to a religious lesson.

Daʿwa. — Literally means "call, invitation, appeal, or summons"; in the twentieth century, the term has come to be associated with prosleytization activity among Muslims and non-Muslims alike. In the last fifty years, it refers primarily to those activities that urge fellow Muslims to greater piety.

Faḍāʾil. — Islamic virtues.

Fatwa. (plural: *fatāwi*) — Nonbinding religious opinion.

Ghafla. — Carelessness, negligence.

Ḥadīth (plural: *aḥādīth*). — The authoritative record of the Prophet's exemplary speech and actions.

Ḥadīth ṣaḥīḥ; ḥadīth daʿīf. — A sound Prophetic tradition; a weak Prophetic tradition.

Ḥajja. — Literally means a woman who has performed the pilgrimage to Mecca (the *ḥajj*), but it is also used in Egyptian colloquial Arabic to respectfully address an older woman.

Ḥalāl. — That which is permissible and legal.

Ḥarām. — That which is forbidden and unlawful.

Ḥasanāt. — Merits accrued with God.

Ḥayā'. — Shyness, diffidence, modesty, timidity.

Ḥijāb. — Veil; note that even though the term *ḥijāb* refers to the headscarf (which is distinct from other forms of the veil such as the *khimār* or the *niqāb*), it is also used as a general term for the veil in Egyptian colloquial and Modern Standard Arabic.

Ḥubb. — Love.

Ḥukm (plural: *aḥkām*). — Literally means "to withhold, prevent, and refrain"; while ḥukm has specific meanings in Arabic philosophy and grammar, in Islamic jurisprudence it refers to a ruling of the sharīʿa.

ʿIbādāt. — Acts of worship; in the sharīʿa this term refers to religious observances and devotional practices.

Iḥtishām. — Shyness, modesty, decency.

Ikhtilāṭ. — Literally means "mixing and blending," but in Islamic ethical literature, it refers to rules of conduct that govern interactions between men and women who are not related by immediate kin ties.

Khashya. — Fear, anxiety, apprehension.

Khauf. — Fear.

Khimār. — A form of veil that covers the head and extends over the torso.

Khitān. — Circumcision.

Khushūʿ. — Submission, humility; a state particularly cultivated during acts of worship.

Madhhab (plural: *madhāhib*). — School of Islamic law. There are four primary juristic schools in Sunni Islam known as the Shafaʿi, Hanafi, Maliki, and Hanbali schools each of which is associated with the name of the Muslim jurist who founded the school.

Maḥram (plural: *maḥārim*). — Close male kin, which, according to Muslim jurists, include a woman's immediate family (for example, father, brother, nephews), her husband, the husband's immediate male kin, and any male who was breastfed by her mother.

Malaka. — It has often been translated as "habit," but its sense is best captured in the Latin term habitus.

Maʿṣiyya (plural: *maʿāṣi*). — Act of disobedience, sin.

Muʿāmalāt. — Social transactions; sections of the sharīʿa concerned with transactions, including bilateral contracts and unilateral dispositions.

Mufti. — Juriconsult.

Niqāb. — A form of the veil that covers the head, face, and torso.

Rajā'. — Hope, anticipation.

Ṣabr. — Patience, fortitude.

Ṣaḥābiyyāt. — The Prophet's female companions.

al-Ṣaḥwa al-Islāmiyya. — Islamic Revival.

Ṣalāt (plural: *ṣalawāt*). — Islamic prayer ritual that is considered obligatory within the *sharīʿa.*

Shādhdh. — Literally means "anomalous"; in the ḥadīth classificatory literature, it refers to a Prophetic tradition that is attributable to only a single source of authority and differs from reports drawn from other transmitters.

Sharīʿa. — Moral discourses and legal procedures that are often glossed as "Islamic Law."

Sunna. — Describes the practices of the Prophet and his Companions, and is considered the second most important source for the derivation of Islamic laws after the Quran in Islamic jurisprudence.

Tagharrub. — Westernization.

Talfīq. — In Islamic jurisprudence, it refers to the tendency in twentieth-century Islam to combine various opinions from the four schools of Islamic law and a de-emphasis on fidelity to any one school.

Tarhīb/takhwīf. — Literally means intimidation; in Islamic homiletic literature, it refers to a rhetorical style that invokes fear of God in the listener (its antonym is *targhīb*, meaning to invoke desire for or love of God in the listener).

Taqwa. — Piety or virtuous fear; *taqwa* is used in the Quran for both "piety" and "fear of God" and often used interchangeably with the terms *khashya* and *khauf.*

ʿUlamāʾ. — Islamic religious scholars.

Zināʾ. — Adultery, fornication.

REFERENCES

Abedi, Mehdi, and Michael M. J. Fischer. 1990. *Debating Muslims: Cultural dialogues in postmodernity and tradition*. Madison: University of Wisconsin Press.

Abu Daud, al-Sayyid. 1997. al-Shaikh Sayyid Sābiq fi ḥadīth. *al-Waʿi al-Islāmi*, no. 372:50–51.

Abu-Lughod, Lila. 1986. *Veiled sentiments: Honor and poetry in a Bedouin society*. Berkeley and Los Angeles: University of California Press.

———. 1990a. Anthropology's orient: The boundaries of theory on the Arab world. In *Theory, politics, and the Arab world: Critical responses*, ed. H. Sharabi, 81–131. New York: Routledge.

———. 1990b. The romance of resistance: Tracing transformations of power through Bedouin women. *American Ethnologist* 17 (1): 41–55.

———. 1993. *Writing women's worlds: Bedouin stories*. Berkeley and Los Angeles: University of California Press.

———. 1998. The marriage of feminism and Islamism in Egypt: Selective repudiation as a dynamic of postcolonial cultural politics. In *Remaking women: Feminism and modernity in the Middle East*, ed. L. Abu-Lughod, 243–69. Princeton, NJ: Princeton University Press.

———. 2002. Do Muslim women really need saving? Anthropological reflections on cultural relativism and its others. *American Anthropologist* 104 (3): 783–90.

Abu-Rabiʿ, Ibrahim. 1996. *Intellectual origins of Islamic resurgence in the modern Arab world*. Albany: State University of New York Press.

Abu Shuqqah, Abd al-Halim Muhammed. 1995. *Taḥrīr al-mar'a fi ʿaṣr al-risāla: Dirāsa ʿan al-mar'a jamiʿat li-nuṣūṣ al-Qur'ān al-karīm wa Ṣaḥīḥ al-Bukhāri wa Muslim*. 6 vols. Kuwait: Dār al-qalam wal-nashr lil-tauzīʿ bil-Kuwait.

Adams, Parveen, and Jeff Minson. 1978. The "subject" of feminism. *m/f* 2:43–61.

Afshar, Haleh. 1998. *Islam and feminisms: An Iranian case study*. New York: St. Martin's Press.

Agamben, Giorgio. 1999. *Potentialities: Collected essays in philosophy*. Ed. and trans. D. Heller-Roazen. Stanford, CA: Stanford University Press.

Ahmed, Leila. 1982. Western ethnocentrism and perceptions of the harem. *Feminist Studies* 8 (3): 521–34.

———. 1992. *Women and gender in Islam: Historical roots of a modern debate*. New Haven, CT: Yale University Press.

al-Ahram Center for Political and Strategic Studies. 1996. Taqrīr al-ḥāla al-dīniyya fi Miṣr. Cairo: Center for Political and Strategic Studies.

Altorki, Soraya. 1986. *Women in Saudi Arabia: Ideology and behavior among the elite*. New York: Columbia University Press.

Amin, Said. n.d. *al-Daʿwa al-islāmiyya: fariḍa sharʿiyya wa ḍarūra bashariyya*. Cairo: Dār al-tauzīʿ wal-nashr al-islāmiyya.

Amnesty International. 2003. *Afghanistan: "No one listens to us and no one treats us as human beings": Justice denied to women*. Amnesty International reports, AI Index: ASA 11/023/2003. http://www.web.amnesty.org/library/index/engasa110232003.

Anscombe, G.E.M. 1981. Modern moral philosophy. In *Ethics, religion and politics*, vol. 3 of *The collected philosophical papers of* G.E.M *Anscombe*, 26–42. Minneapolis: University of Minnesota Press.

al-Arabi, Sherezad. 1996. *Zaynab al-Ghazali: min al-burneyṭa ila al-ḥijāb*. Cairo: Bait al-ḥikma.

Arendt, Hannah. 1977. What is authority? In *Between past and future: Eight exercises in political thought*, 91–141. New York: Penguin Books.

Aristotle. 1941. *The basic works of Aristotle*. Ed. R. McKeon. New York: Random House.

Asad, Muhammad. 1980. *The message of the Qur'ān*. Gibraltar: Dar al-Andalus.

Asad, Talal. 1980. Ideology, class and the origin of the Islamic state. *Economy and Society* 9 (4): 450–73.

———. 1986. The idea of an anthropology of Islam. *Occasional Papers Series*. Washington, DC: Center for Contemporary Arab Studies, Georgetown University.

———. 1993. *Genealogies of religion: Discipline and reasons of power in Christianity and Islam*. Baltimore, MD: Johns Hopkins University Press.

———. 1999. Religion, nation-state, secularism. In *Nation and religion: Perspectives on Europe and Asia*, ed. P. van der Veer and H. Lehmann, 178–96. Princeton, NJ: Princeton University Press.

———. 2003. *Formations of the secular: Christianity, Islam, modernity*. Stanford, CA: Stanford University Press.

Ashmawi, Said Muhammed. 1994a. Fatwa al-ḥijāb ghair sharʿiyya. *Rūz al-Yūsuf*, August 8, 28.

———. 1994b. al-Ḥijāb laisa farīḍa. *Rūz al-Yūsuf*, June 13, 22.

Atiya, Nayra. 1982. *Khul-Khaal: Five Egyptian women tell their stories*. Syracuse, NY: Syracuse University Press.

Austin, J. L. 1994. *How to do things with words*. Ed. J. O. Urmson and M. Sbisà. Cambridge, MA: Harvard University Press.

al-Awwa, Muhammed Salim. 1996a. Kalima akhīra fi khitān al-banāt. *al-Shaʿb*, November 22, 9.

———. 1996b. Khitān al-ināth: mafāhīm maghlūṭa!! *al-Shaʿb*, November 1, 9.

Ayalon, Ami. 1987. *Language and change in the Arab Middle East: The evolution of modern political discourse*. New York: Oxford University Press.

Badkhen, Anna. 2002. Afghan women still shrouded in oppression: Widespread abuse, restrictions on freedom continue almost a year after fall of Taliban. *San Francisco Chronicle*, October 14.

Badran, Margot. 1991. Competing agendas: Feminists, Islam and the state in nineteenth- and twentieth-century Egypt. In *Women, Islam and the State*, ed. D. Kandiyoti. Philadelphia: Temple University Press.

———. 1995. *Feminists, Islam, and nation: Gender and the making of modern Egypt*. Princeton, NJ: Princeton University Press.

Bakhtin, M. M. 1981. *The dialogic imagination: Four essays*. Ed. M. Holquist, trans. C. Emerson and M. Holquist. Austin: University of Texas Press.

al-Banna, Hasan. 1978. *Five tracts of Ḥasan al-Bannā': A selection from the Majmū'āt Rasā'il al-Imām al-Shahīd Ḥasan al-Bannā'*. Trans. C. Wendell. Berkeley and Los Angeles: University of California Press.

Baron, Beth. 1994. *The women's awakening in Egypt: Culture, society, and the press*. New Haven, CT: Yale University Press.

Bartky, Sandra. 1990. *Femininity and domination: Studies in the phenomenology of oppression*. New York: Routledge.

Beinin, Joel, and Joe Stork, eds. 1997. *Political Islam: Essays from* Middle East Report. Berkeley and Los Angeles: University of California Press.

Bell, Catherine. 1992. *Ritual theory, ritual practice*. New York: Oxford University Press.

Benhabib, Seyla. 1992. *Situating the self: Gender, community and postmodernism in contemporary ethics*. New York: Routledge.

Benhabib, Seyla, Judith Butler, Drucilla Cornell, and Nancy Fraser. 1995. *Feminist contentions: A philosophical exchange*. New York: Routledge.

Benjamin, Walter. 1969a. The storyteller: Reflections on the works of Nikolai Leskov. In *Illuminations*, ed. H. Arendt, trans. H. Zohn, 83–109. New York: Schocken.

———. 1969b. The work of art in the age of mechanical reproduction. In *Illuminations*, ed. H. Arendt, trans. H. Zohn, 217–51. New York: Schocken.

Berger, Peter. 1973. *The social reality of religion*. Harmondsworth, UK: Penguin Books.

Berkey, Jonathan. 2001. *Popular preaching and religious authority in the medieval Islamic Near East*. Seattle: University of Washington Press.

Berlin, Isaiah. 1969. *Four essays on liberty*. Oxford: Oxford University Press.

Bhabha, Homi. 1996. *The Location of Culture*. New York: Routledge.

Bloch, Maurice. 1974. Symbols, song, dance and features of articulation *or* Is religion an extreme form of traditional authority? *Archives Européennes de Sociologie* XV (1): 55–81.

———, ed. 1975. *Political language and oratory in traditional society*. New York: Academic Press.

Boddy, Janice. 1989. *Wombs and alien spirits: Women, men, and the Zār cult in Northern Sudan*. Madison: University of Wisconsin Press.

Bordo, Susan. 1993. *Unbearable weight: Feminism, Western culture, and the body*. Berkeley and Los Angeles: University of California Press.

Bourdieu, Pierre. 1977. *Outline of a theory of practice*. Trans. R. Nice. Cambridge: Cambridge University Press.

———. 1990. *The logic of practice*. Trans. R. Nice. Stanford, CA: Stanford University Press.

Bowen, John. 1989. *Salat* in Indonesia: The social meanings of an Islamic ritual. *Man* 24 (4): 600–19.

———. 1993. *Muslims through discourse: Religion and ritual in Gayo society*. Princeton, NJ: Princeton University Press.

———. 2000. Imputations of faith and allegiance: Islamic prayer and Indonesian politics outside the mosque. In *Islamic prayer across the Indian Ocean: Inside and outside the mosque*, ed. D. Parkin and S. Headley, 23–38. Richmond, UK: Curzon Press.

Brant, Beth, ed. 1984. *A gathering of spirit: Writing and art by North American Indian women*. Rockland, ME: Sinister Wisdom Books.

Brown, Daniel. 1999. *Rethinking tradition in modern Islamic thought*. Cambridge: Cambridge University Press.

Brown, Peter. 1981. *The cult of the saints: Its rise and function in Latin Christianity*. Chicago: University of Chicago Press.

Brown, Wendy. 2001. *Politics out of history*. Princeton, NJ: Princeton University Press.

Brusco, Elizabeth. 1995. *The reformation of machismo: Evangelical conversion and gender in Colombia*. Austin: University of Texas Press.

Burgat, François, and William Dowell. 1997. *The Islamic movement in North Africa*. Austin: Center for Middle Eastern Studies, University of Texas.

Burke, Kenneth. 1969. *A rhetoric of motives*. Berkeley and Los Angeles: University of California Press.

Butler, Judith. 1993. *Bodies that matter: On the discursive limits of "sex."* New York: Routledge.

———. 1997a. *Excitable speech: A politics of the performative*. New York: Routledge.

———. 1997b. Further reflections on conversations of our time. *Diacritics* 27 (1): 13–15.

———. 1997c. *The psychic life of power: Theories in subjection*. Stanford, CA: Stanford University Press.

———. 1999. *Gender trouble: Feminism and the subversion of identity*. New York: Routledge.

———. 2001. Doing justice to someone: Sex reassignment and allegories of transsexuality. *GLQ: A Journal of Lesbian and Gay Studies* 7 (4): 621–36.

Butler, Judith, and William Connolly. 2000. Politics, power and ethics: A discussion between Judith Butler and William Connolly. *Theory and Event* 24 (2), http://muse.jhu.edu/journals/theory_and_event/v004/4.2butler.html.

Butler, Judith, Ernesto Laclau, and Slavoj Žižek. 2000. *Contingency, hegemony, universality: Contemporary dialogues on the left*. London: Verso Press.

Bynum, Caroline. 1992. The mysticism and asceticism of medieval women: Some comments on the typologies of Max Weber and Ernst Troeltsch. In *Fragmentation and redemption: Essays on gender and the human body in medieval religion*, 53–78. New York: Zone Books.

Calder, N., and M. B. Hooker. 1999. Sharīʿa. In *The Encyclopedia of Islam*. CD-ROM, version 1.0. Leiden: Brill.

Calhoun, Craig, ed. 1992. *Habermas and the public sphere*. Cambridge, MA: MIT Press.
Canard, M. 1999. Daʿwa. In *The Encyclopedia of Islam*. CD-ROM, version 1.0. Leiden: Brill.
Cantwell, Robert. 1999. Habitus, ethnomimesis: A note on the logic of practice. *Journal of Folklore Research* 36 (2/3): 219–34.
Carney, Frederick. 1983. Some aspects of Islamic ethics. *Journal of Religion* 63 (2): 159–74.
Carruthers, Mary. 1990. *The book of memory: A study of memory in medieval culture*. Cambridge: Cambridge University Press.
Casanova, José. 1994. *Public religions in the modern world*. Chicago: University of Chicago Press.
Caton, Steven. 1990. *"Peaks of Yemen I summon": Poetry as cultural practice in a North Yemeni tribe*. Berkeley and Los Angeles: University of California Press.
Cavell, Stanley. 1995. What did Derrida want of Austin? In *Philosophical passages: Wittgenstein, Emerson, Austin, Derrida*, 42–65. Oxford: Blackwell.
Chakrabarty, Dipesh. 1992. Provincializing Europe: Postcoloniality and the critique of history. *Cultural Studies* 6 (3): 337–57.
———. 2000. *Provincializing Europe: Postcolonial thought and historical difference*. Princeton, NJ: Princeton University Press.
Chatterjee, Partha. 1993. *The nation and its fragments: Colonial and postcolonial histories*. Princeton, NJ: Princeton University Press.
———. 1995. Religious minorities and the secular state: Reflections on an Indian impasse. *Public Culture* 8 (1): 11–39.
Chodorow, Nancy. 1978. *The reproduction of mothering: Psychoanalysis and the sociology of gender*. Berkeley and Los Angeles: University of California Press.
Christman, John. 1991. Liberalism and individual positive freedom. *Ethics* 101: 343–59.
Colebrook, Claire. 1997. Feminism and autonomy: The crisis of the self-authoring subject. *Body and Society* 3 (2): 21–41.
———. 1998. Ethics, positivity, and gender: Foucault, Aristotle, and the care of the self. *Philosophy Today* 42 (1/4): 40–52.
———. 2000a. From radical representations to corporeal becomings: The feminist philosophy of Lloyd, Grosz, and Gatens. *Hypatia* 15 (2): 76–93.
———. 2000b. Incorporeality: The ghostly body of metaphysics. *Body and Society* 6 (2): 25–44.
Collier, Jane. 1986. From Mary to modern woman: The material basis of Marianismo and its transformation in a Spanish village. *American Ethnologist* 13 (1): 100–107.
———. 1988. *Marriage and inequality in classless societies*. Stanford, CA: Stanford University Press.
———. 1997. *From duty to desire: Remaking families in a Spanish village*. Princeton, NJ: Princeton University Press.
Collier, Jane, and Sylvia Yanagisako. 1989. Theory in anthropology since feminist practice. *Critique of Anthropology* IX (2): 27–37.
Collins, Patricia Hill. 1991. *Black feminist thought: Knowledge, consciousness, and the politics of empowerment*. New York: Routledge.

Comaroff, Jean and John Comaroff. 1997. *Of revelation and revolution*. Chicago: University of Chicago Press.
Connolly, William. 1999. *Why I am not a secularist*. Minneapolis: University of Minnesota Press.
Cook, Michael. 2000. *Commanding right and forbidding wrong in Islamic thought*. Cambridge: Cambridge University Press.
Daif, Nashat Abd al-Jawar. 1995. *Amr bil-maʿrūf wal-nahi ʿan al-munkar*. Cairo: Wizārat al-auqāf.
Davidson, Arnold. 1994. Ethics as ascetics: Foucault, the history of ethics, and ancient thought. In *Foucault and the writing of history*, ed. J. Goldstein, 63–80. Cambridge: Blackwell.
Davis, Angela. 1983. *Women, race and class*. New York: Vintage Books.
Davis, Susan. 1983. *Patience and power: Women's lives in a Moroccan village*. Cambridge, MA: Schenkman.
Delaney, Carol. 1991. *The seed and the soil: Gender and cosmology in Turkish village society*. Berkeley and Los Angeles: University of California Press.
Derrida, Jacques. 1988. Signature event context. In *Limited Inc*, 1–23. Evanston, IL: Northwestern University Press.
Douglas, Mary. 1973. *Natural symbols: Explorations in cosmology*. New York: Random House.
Dreyfus, Hubert, and Paul Rabinow. 1982. *Michel Foucault: Beyond structuralism and hermeneutics*. Chicago: University of Chicago Press.
Durkheim, Emile. 1965. *The elementary forms of the religious life*. Trans. J. W. Swain. New York: Free Press.
Dwyer, Daisy. 1978. *Images and self-images: Male and female in Morocco*. New York: Columbia University Press.
Early, Evelyn. 1993. *Baladi women of Cairo: Playing with an egg and a stone*. Boulder, CO: Lynne Rienner.
Eickelman, Dale. 1992. Mass higher education and the religious imagination in contemporary Arab societies. *American Ethnologist* 19 (4): 643–55.
Eickelman, Dale, and Jon Anderson. 1997. Print, Islam, and the prospects for civic pluralism: New religious writings and their audiences. *Journal of Islamic Studies* 8 (1): 43–62.
Eickelman, Dale, and James Piscatori. 1996. *Muslim politics*. Princeton, NJ: Princeton University Press.
El Guindi, Fadwa. 1981. Veiling *infitah* with Muslim ethic: Egypt's contemporary Islamic movement. *Social Problems* 28 (4): 465–85.
El-Imam, Soheir. 1996. Le docteur Abdel Rachid Abdel Aziz Salem assuré: "Les femmes ne peuvent pas être des prédicateurs." *Le Progrès Égyptien*, January 17, 2.
Esposito, John. 1992. *The Islamic threat: Myth or reality?* New York: Oxford University Press.
Evans-Pritchard, E. E. 1965. *Theories of primitive religion*. Oxford: Clarendon Press.
Fakhry, Majid. 1983. *A history of Islamic philosophy*. New York: Columbia University Press.
Farid, Ahmed. 1990. *al-Baḥr al-rāʾiq*. Alexandria: Dār al-imān.

———. 1993. *Tazkiyyat al-nufūs*. Alexandria: Dār al ʿaqīda lil-turāth.
Faubion, James. 2001. Toward an anthropology of ethics: Foucault and the pedagogies of autopoiesis. *Representations* 74:83–104.
Fernea, Elizabeth, ed. 1985. *Women and family in the Middle East: New voices of change*. Austin: University of Texas Press.
———. 1998. *In search of Islamic feminism: One woman's global journey*. New York: Doubleday Press.
Foot, Philippa. 1978. *Virtues and vices and other essays in moral philosophy*. Berkeley and Los Angeles: University of California Press.
Foucault, Michel. 1972. *The archaeology of knowledge*. Trans. A. M. Sheridan Smith. New York: Harper & Row.
———. 1978. *The history of sexuality: An introduction*. Trans. R. Hurley. New York: Pantheon Books.
———. 1980. Truth and power. In *Power/knowledge: Selected interviews and other writings 1972–1977*, ed. and trans. C. Gordon, 109–33. New York: Pantheon Books.
———. 1983. The subject and power. In *Michel Foucault: Beyond structuralism and hermeneutics*, ed. H. Dreyfus and P. Rabinow, 208–26. Chicago: University of Chicago Press.
———. 1990. *The use of pleasure*. Vol. 2 of *The history of sexuality*.Trans. R. Hurley. New York: Vintage Books.
———. 1991a. Governmentality. In *The Foucault effect: Studies in governmentality*, ed. G. Burchell, C. Gordon, and P. Miller, 87–104. Chicago: University of Chicago Press.
———. 1991b. Politics and the study of discourse. In *The Foucault effect: Studies in governmentality*, ed. G. Burchell, C. Gordon, and P. Miller, 53–72. Chicago: University of Chicago Press.
———. 1997a. The ethics of the concern of the self as a practice of freedom. In *Ethics: Subjectivity and Truth*: Vol. 1 of *Essential Works of Foucault, 1954–1984*, Vol. 1, ed. P. Rabinow, trans. R. Hurley et al., 281–301. New York: New Press.
———. 1997b. On the genealogy of ethics: An overview of work in progress. In *Ethics: Subjectivity and Truth*: Vol. 1 of *Essential Works of Foucault, 1954–1984*, ed. P. Rabinow, trans. R. Hurley et al., 253–80. New York: New Press.
———. 1997c. *Ethics: Subjectivity and Truth*: Vol. 1 of *Essential Works of Foucault, 1954–1984*, Vol. 1. Ed. P. Rabinow, trans. R. Hurley et al. New York: New Press.
Friedman, Marilyn. 1997. Autonomy and social relationships: Rethinking the feminist critique. In *Feminists rethink the self*, ed. D. T. Meyers, 40–61. Boulder, CO: Westview Press.
———. 2003. *Autonomy, gender, politics*. New York: Oxford University Press.
Gaffney, Patrick. 1991. The changing voices of Islam: The emergence of professional preachers in contemporary Egypt. *Muslim World* LXXXI (1): 27–47.
Garrett, Cynthia. 1993. The rhetoric of supplication: Prayer theory in seventeenth-century England. *Renaissance Quarterly* XLVI (2): 328–57.
Gatens, Moira. 1996. *Imaginary bodies: Ethics, power, and corporeality*. London: Routledge.
Geertz, Clifford. 1968. *Islam observed: Religious development in Morocco and Indonesia*. Chicago: University of Chicago Press.

Gellner, Ernest. 1981. *Muslim society*. Cambridge: Cambridge University Press.

al-Ghazali, Abu Hamid. 1984. *The recitation and interpretation of the Qur'ān: al-Ghazālī's theory*. Trans. M. Abul Quasem. London: KPI Press.

———. 1992. *Inner dimensions of Islamic worship*. Trans. M. Holland. Leicester, UK: Islamic Foundation.

———. 1995. *On disciplining the soul (kitāb riyāḍat al-nafs) and on breaking the two desires (kitāb kasr al-shahwatayn). Books XXII and XXIII of the revival of the religious sciences (iḥyā' 'ulūm al-dīn)*. Trans. T. J. Winter. Cambridge, UK: Islamic Texts Society.

al-Ghazali, Muhammed. 1990. *al-Jānib al-'āṭifi min al-Islām*. Alexandria: Dār al-da'wa.

———. 1996. *Qaḍāya' al-mar'a baina taqlīd al-risāla wal-wāfida*. Cairo: Dār al-shurūq.

al-Ghazali, Zaynab. 1994a. *'ila ibnati: al-juz' al-awwal*. Cairo: Dār al-tauzī' wal-nashr al-islāmi.

———. 1994b. *Naẓarāt fi kitāb allāh*. Cairo: Dār al-shurūq.

———. 1995. *Ayyām min ḥayāti*. Cairo: Dār al-shurūq.

———. 1996a. *'ila ibnati: al-juz' al-thāni*. Cairo: Dār al-tauzī' wal-nashr al-islāmiyya.

———. 1996b. *Min khawāṭir Zaynab al-Ghazali*. Cairo: Dār al-i'tisām.

———. 1996c. *Mushkilāt al-shabāb wal-fatayāt fi marḥalat al-murāhiqa: Rudūd 'ala al-rasā'il*. Cairo: Dār al-tauzī' wal-nashr al-islāmiyya.

Gilligan, Carol. 1982. *In a different voice: Psychological theory and women's development*. Cambridge, MA: Harvard University Press.

Gilsenan, Michael. 1982. *Recognizing Islam: Religion and society in the modern Arab world*. New York: Pantheon Books.

Göle, Nilüfer. 1996. *The forbidden modern: Civilization and veiling*. Ann Arbor: University of Michigan Press.

Gray, John. 1991. On negative and positive liberty. In *Liberalisms: Essays in political philosophy*, 45–68. New York: Routledge.

Green, Thomas Hill. 1986. *Lectures on the principles of political obligation and other writings*. Ed. P. Harris and J. Morrow. Cambridge: Cambridge University Press.

Grosz, Elizabeth. 1994. *Volatile bodies: Toward a corporeal feminism*. Bloomington: Indiana University Press.

Guha, Ranajit. 1996. The small voice of history. In *Subaltern Studies IX: Writings on South Asian History and Society*, ed. S. Amin and D. Chakrabarty, 1–12. Delhi: Oxford University Press.

Guha, Ranajit, and Gayatri Spivak, eds. 1988. *Selected subaltern studies*. Delhi: Oxford University Press.

Habermas, Jurgen. 1991. *The structural transformation of the public sphere: An inquiry into a category of bourgeois society*. Trans. T. Burger. Cambridge, MA: MIT Press.

Hacking, Ian. 1995. *Rewriting the soul: Multiple personality and the sciences of memory*. Princeton, NJ: Princeton University Press.

———. 2002. *Historical ontology*. Cambridge, MA: Harvard University Press.

Haddad, Yvonne. 1984. Islam, women and revolution in twentieth-century Arab thought. *Muslim World* LXXIV (3–4): 137–60.

Haddad, Yvonne, John Voll, and John Esposito, eds. 1991. *The contemporary Islamic revival: A critical survey and bibliography*. New York: Greenwood Press.

Hadot, Pierre. 1995. *Philosophy as a way of life: Spiritual exercises from Socrates to Foucault*. Ed. A. Davidson, trans. M. Chase. Oxford: Blackwell.

———. 2002. *What is ancient philosophy?* Trans. M. Chase. Cambridge, MA: Belknap University.

Hale, Sondra. 1986. Sudanese women and revolutionary parties: The wing of the patriarch. *MERIP Middle East Report* 16 (1): 25–30.

———. 1987. Women's culture/men's culture: Gender, separation, and space in Africa and North America. *American Behavioral Scientist* 31 (1): 115–34.

Hallaq, Wael. 1997. *A history of Islamic legal theories: An introduction to Sunnī usūl al-fiqh*. Cambridge: Cambridge University Press.

———. 1998. Talfīq. In *The encyclopedia of Islam*, vol. 10, ed. Th. Bianquis, C. E. Bosworth, E. van Donzel, and W. P. Heinrichs, 161. Leiden: Brill.

Hansen, Thomas Blom. 1999. *The saffron wave: Democracy and Hindu nationalism in modern India*. Princeton, NJ: Princeton University Press.

Harb, al-Ghazali. 1984. *Istiqlāl al-mar'a fi al-Islām*. Cairo: Dār al-mustaqbal al-ʿarabi.

Harding, Susan. 1991. Representing fundamentalism: The problem of the repugnant cultural other. *Social Research* 58 (2): 373–93.

———. 2000. *The book of Jerry Falwell: Fundamentalist language and politics*. Princeton, NJ: Princeton University Press.

Hartsock, Nancy. 1983. *Money, sex, and power: Toward a feminist historical materialism*. Boston: Northeastern University Press.

Hasan, Zoya, ed. 1994. *Forging identities: Gender, communities and the state in India*. Boulder, CO: Westview Press.

al-Hashimi, Ibn, ed. 1989. *al-Dāʿiya Zaynab al-Ghazali: Maṣīrat jihād wa ḥadīth min al-dhikrayāt min khilāl kitābatiha*. Cairo: Dār al-iʿtiṣām.

———, ed. 1990. *Humūm al-mar'a al-muslima wal-dāʿiya Zaynab al-Ghazali*. Cairo: Dār al-iʿtiṣām.

Hashmi, Sohail, ed. 2002. *Islamic political ethics: Civil society, pluralism, and conflict*. Princeton, NJ: Princeton University Press.

Hawwa, Said. 1995. *al-Mustakhlaṣ fi tazkiyyat al-anfus*. Cairo: Dār al-salām.

al-Ḥayāt. 1996a. Mashrūʿ qānūn yuḥarrim khitān al-ināth fi Miṣr. October 17, 1.

———. 1996b. Miṣr: tattajih naḥwa taṣāʿud al-ʿazma baina wazīr al-auqāf wa jabhat ʿulamā' al-Azhar. September 6, 1.

———. 1997. Wazīr al-auqāf al-maṣri lil-Ḥayāt: mu'assasāt al-Azhar tuʿayyid tanẓīm al-khaṭāba fil-masājid. January 25, 7.

Hefner, Robert. 2000. *Civil Islam: Muslims and democratization in Indonesia*. Princeton, NJ: Princeton University Press.

Hegland, Mary. 1998. Flagellation and fundamentalism: (Trans)forming meaning, identity, and gender through Pakistani women's rituals of mourning. *American Ethnologist* 25 (2): 240–66.

Heller, Thomas, Morton Sosna, and David Wellbery, eds. 1986. *Reconstructing individualism: Autonomy, individuality, and the self in Western thought*. Stanford, CA: Stanford University Press.

Herrera, Linda. 2003. Islamization and education in Egypt: Between politics, culture and the market. In *Modernizing Islam: Religion in the public sphere in the Middle East and Europe*, ed. J. Esposito and F. Burgat, 167–89. New Brunswick, NJ: Rutgers University Press.

Hill, Enid. 1987. *Al-Sanhuri and Islamic law: The place and significance of Islamic law in the life and work of 'Abd al-Razzaq Ahmad al-Sanhuri, Egyptian jurist and scholar, 1895–1971*. Cairo: The American University in Cairo Press.

Hilmi, Mona. 1997. ʿibādat al-shaiṭān wa ʿibādat al-siramīk. *Rūz al-Yūsuf*, January 26, 80.

Hindawi, Khayriyya. 1997. Naṣīḥat Zaynab al-Ghazali lil-mar'a al-muslima: al-Zauja la taqūl "la" li-zaujiha abadan illa fi ma yaghḍab allāh. *Sayyidati*, January 24, 70–75.

Hirschkind, Charles. 1997. What is political Islam? *Middle East Report* 27 (4): 12–14.

———. 2001a. Civic virtue and religious reason: An Islamic counterpublic. *Cultural Anthropology* 16 (1): 3–34.

———. 2001b. The ethics of listening: Cassette-sermon audition in contemporary Egypt. *American Ethnologist* 28 (3): 623–49.

———. 2003. Media and the Quran. *The encyclopedia of the Quran*, Volume 3, 341–49, ed. J. McAuliffe. Leiden: Brill.

———. 2004. Hearing modernity. In *Hearing cultures: Essays on sound, listening, and modernity*, ed. V. Erlmann, 191–216. Oxford: Berg.

Hirschkind, Charles, and Saba Mahmood. 2002. Feminism, the Taliban, and politics of counter-insurgency. *Anthropological Quarterly* 75 (2): 339–54.

Hobsbawm, Eric, ed. 1980. *Peasants in history: Essays in honour of Daniel Thorner*. Calcutta: Oxford University Press.

———. 1983. Introduction: Inventing traditions. In *The invention of tradition*, ed. E. Hobsbawm and T. Ranger, 1–14. Cambridge: Cambridge University Press.

Hoffman, Valerie. 1985. An Islamic activist: Zaynab al-Ghazali. In *Women and the family in the Middle East: New voices of change*, ed. E. Fernea, 233–54. Austin: University of Texas Press.

Hoffman-Ladd, Valerie. 1987. Polemics on the modesty and segregation of women in contemporary Egypt. *International Journal of Middle East Studies* 19:23–50.

Hollywood, Amy. 2002. Performativity, citationality, ritualization. *History of religions* 42 (2): 93–115.

———. 2004. Gender, agency, and the divine in religious historiography. *The journal of religion* 84 (4).

Hourani, Albert. 1983. *Arabic thought in the liberal age 1798–1939*. Cambridge: Cambridge University Press.

Hull, Gloria, Patricia Bell-Scott, and Barbara Smith, eds. 1982. *All the women are white, all the blacks are men, but some of us are brave: Black women's studies*. New York: Feminist Press.

Human Rights Watch. 2002. *"We want to live as humans": Repression of women and girls in western Afghanistan*. Human Rights Watch reports, vol. 14, no. 11 (C). http://www.hrw.org/reports/2002/afghnwmn1202.

Hundert, E. J. 1997. The European Enlightenment and the history of the self. In *Rewriting the self: Histories from the Renaissance to the present*, ed. R. Porter, 72–83. New York: Routledge.

Hunt, Ian. 1991. Freedom and its conditions. *Australasian Philosophy* 69 (3): 288–301.

Huwedi, Fahmi. 1993. *Lil-Islām wa dīmuqrāṭiyya.* Cairo: Markaz al-ahrām lil-tarjama wal-nashr.

———. 1995. ʿan fiqh al-ḥubb wal-muʿāshira. *al-Ahrām*, September 26, 11.

Ibn Khaldun. 1958. *The Muqaddimah: An introduction to history.* Trans. F. Rosenthal. New York: Pantheon Books.

Ibrahim, Youssef. 1994. France bans Muslim scarf in its schools: Says girls' attire violates secularism. *New York Times*, September 11, 4.

Inglis, John. 1999. Aquinas's replication of the acquired moral virtues. *Journal of Religious Ethics* 27 (1): 3–27.

Ismail, Yahya. 1996. Taʿqīb mashfūʿ bi-aʿtāb. *al-Shaʿb*, November 8, 9.

Ivy, Marilyn. 1995. *Discourses of the vanishing: Modernity, phantasm, Japan.* Chicago: University of Chicago Press.

Izutsu, Toshihiko. 1966. *Ethico-religious concepts in the Qur'ān.* Montreal: McGill University Press.

Jakobsen, Janet, and Ann Pellegrini. 2003. *Love the sin: Sexual regulation and the limits of religious tolerance.* New York: New York University Press.

James, Susan. 1997. *Passion and action: The emotions in seventeenth-century philosophy.* Oxford: Clarendon Press.

Joseph, Suad, ed. 1999. *Intimate selving in Arab families: Gender, self, and identity.* Syracuse: Syracuse University Press.

al-Jumal, Ibrahim. 1981. *Fiqh al-mar'a al-muslima: ʿibādāt wa muʿāmalāt.* Cairo: Maktabat al-Qurʾān.

Kaabi, Mongi. 1972. Les origines Ṭāhirides dans la *daʿwa* ʿAbbāside. *Arabica Revue d'Études Arabes* XIX:145–64.

Kant, Immanuel. 1998. *Religion within the boundaries of mere reason and other writings.* Ed. and trans. A. Wood and G. Di Giovanni. Cambridge: Cambridge University Press.

Kapferer, Bruce. 1979. Emotion and feeling in Sinhalese healing rites. *Social Analysis* 1:153–76.

Keane, Webb. 1997. From fetishism to sincerity: On agency, the speaking subject, and their historicity in the context of religious conversion. *Comparative Studies in Society and History* 39 (4): 674–93.

———. 2002. Sincerity, "modernity," and the protestants. *Cultural Anthropology* 17 (1): 65–92.

Kepel, Gilles. 1986. *Muslim extremism in Egypt: The prophet and the pharaoh.* Trans. J. Rothschild. Berkeley and Los Angeles: University of California Press.

———. 2002. *Jihad: The trail of political Islam.* Trans. A. Roberts. Cambridge, MA: Harvard University Press.

Kerr, Malcolm. 1966. *Islamic reform: The political and legal theories of Muḥammad ʿAbduh and Rashīd Riḍā.* Berkeley and Los Angeles: University of California Press.

Kinzer, Stephen. 1998. A woman, her scarf and a storm over secularism. *New York Times*, March 17.

———. 1999. Turkish president strips a Muslim parliamentarian of citizenship. *New York Times*, May 16.

Laclau, Ernesto. 1990. *New reflections on the revolution of our time*. London and New York: Verso.

Lane, Edward William. 1984. *Arabic-English lexicon*. Cambridge, UK: Islamic Texts Society.

Lapidus, Ira. 1984. Knowledge, virtue and action: The classical Muslim conception of *adab* and the nature of religious fulfillment in Islam. In *Moral conduct and authority: The place of adab in South Asian Islam*, ed. B. D. Metcalf, 38–61. Berkeley and Los Angeles: University of California Press.

Larmore, Charles. 1996. *The Romantic legacy*. New York: Columbia University Press.

Lazreg, Marnia. 1994. *The eloquence of silence: Algerian women in question*. New York: Routledge.

Leach, Edmund. 1964. *Political systems of highland Burma: A study of Kachin social structure*. London: Athlone Press.

Leaman, O. N. 1999. Malaka. In *The Encyclopedia of Islam*. CD-ROM, version 1.0. Leiden: Brill.

al-Liwā' al-Islāmi. 1995. Hal istaṭā'at al-mar'a an taqūm bi daur mu'aththir fi majāl al-da'wa? September 28.

———. 1996a. Aina daur kharījāt jamā'at al-Azhar fi al-majāl? August 15.

———. 1996b. Aina kharījāt al-da'wa? December 19.

Lorde, Audre. 1984. *Sister outsider: Essays and speeches*. Trumansburg: Crossing Press.

Lovibond, Sabina. 2002. *Ethical formation*. Cambridge, MA: Harvard University Press.

Lutz, Catherine, and Geoffrey White. 1986. The anthropology of emotions. *Annual Review of Anthropology* 15:405–36.

MacCallum, Gerald. 1967. Negative and positive freedom. *Philosophical Review* LXXVI (3): 312–34.

MacIntyre, Alisdair. 1966. *A short history of ethics: A history of moral philosophy from the Homeric to the twentieth century*. New York: Macmillan.

———. 1984. *After virtue: A study in moral theory*. Notre Dame, IN: University of Notre Dame Press.

———. 1988. *Whose justice? Which rationality?* Notre Dame, IN: University of Notre Dame Press.

MacKinnon, Catharine. 1989. *Toward a feminist theory of the state*. Cambridge, MA: Harvard University Press.

———. 1993. *Only words*. Cambridge, MA: Harvard University Press.

MacLeod, Arlene Elowe. 1991. *Accommodating protest: Working women, the new veiling and change in Cairo*. New York: Columbia University Press.

Maharib, Ruqaiyya Bint Muhammad Ibn. 1991. *Kayfa takhsha'īna fi al-ṣalāt?* Cairo: Dār al-'ulūm al-islāmiyya.

Mahmood, Saba. 1996. Cultural studies and ethnic absolutism: Comments on Stuart Hall's "Culture, community, nation." *Cultural Studies* 10 (1): 1–11.

———. 2001a. Feminist theory, embodiment, and the docile agent: Some reflections on the Egyptian Islamic revival. *Cultural Anthropology*, 6 (2): 202–36.

———. 2001b. Rehearsed spontaneity and the conventionality of ritual: Disciplines of *ṣalāt*. *American Ethnologist* 28 (4): 827–53.

———. 2003. Anthropology and the study of women in Islamic cultures. In *The encyclopedia of women and Islamic cultures*, 307–14. Leiden: Brill.

Malinowski, Bronislaw. 1922. *Argonauts of the Western Pacific: An account of native enterprise and adventure in the archipelagoes of Melanesian New Guinea*. London: G. Routledge and Sons.

Mani, Lata. 1998. *Contentious traditions: The debate on sati in colonial India*. Berkeley and Los Angeles: University of California Press.

Martin, David. 1978. *A general theory of secularization*. Oxford: Blackwell.

Martin, Emily. 1987. *The woman in the body: A cultural analysis of reproduction*. Boston: Beacon Press.

Martin, Luther, Huck Gutman, and Patrick Hutton, eds. 1988. *Technologies of the self: A seminar with Michel Foucault*. Amherst: University of Massachusetts Press.

Massell, Gregory. 1974. *The surrogate proletariat: Moslem women and revolutionary strategies in Soviet Central Asia, 1919–1929*. Princeton, NJ: Princeton University Press.

Massumi, Brian. 2002. *Parables for the virtual: Movement, affect, sensation*. Durham, NC: Duke University Press.

Mauss, Marcel. 1979. *Sociology and psychology: Essays*. Trans. B. Brewster. London: Routledge and Kegan Paul.

McKane, William. 1965. *Al-Ghazali's book of fear and hope*. Leiden: Brill.

McKeon, Richard. 1987. *Rhetoric: Essays in invention and discovery*. Ed. M. Backman. Woodbridge: Ox Bow Press.

Mehta, Uday. 1999. *Liberalism and empire: A study in nineteenth-century British liberal though*. Chicago: University of Chicago Press.

Mendel, Miloš. 1995. The concept of "ad-daʿwa al-islāmīya": Towards a discussion of the Islamic reformist religio-political terminology. *Archív Orientální* 63 (3): 286–304.

Messick, Brinkley. 1993. *The calligraphic state: Textual domination and history in a Muslim society*. Berkeley and Los Angeles: University of California Press.

———. 1996. Media muftis: Radio fatwas in Yemen. In *Islamic legal interpretation: Muftis and their fatwas*, ed. M. K. Masud, B. Messick, and D. Powers, 310–20. Cambridge, MA: Harvard University Press.

———. 1997. Genealogies of reading and the scholarly cultures of Islam. In *Cultures of scholarship*, ed. S. Humphreys, 387–412. Ann Arbor: University of Michigan Press.

Metcalf, Barbara. 1993. Living hadith in the Tablighi Jama'at. *Journal of Asian Studies* 52 (3): 584–608.

———. 1994. "Remaking ourselves": Islamic self-fashioning in a global movement of spiritual renewal. In *Accounting for fundamentalisms*, ed. M. Marty and S. Appleby, 706–25. Chicago: Chicago University Press.

———. 1998. Women and men in a contemporary pietist movement: The case of the Tablighi Jama'at. In *Appropriating gender: Women's activism and politicized religion in South Asia*, ed. P. Jeffery and A. Basu, 107–21. New York: Routledge.

Meyers, Diana. 1989. *Self, society, and personal choice*. New York: Columbia University Press.

Mill, John Stuart. 1991. *On liberty and other essays*. Ed. J. Gray. New York: Oxford University Press.

Minson, Jeffrey. 1993. *Questions of conduct: Sexual harassment, citizenship, government*. New York: St. Martin's Press.

Mir-Hosseini, Ziba. 1999. *Islam and gender: The religious debate in contemporary Iran*. Princeton, NJ: Princeton University Press.

Mitchell, Richard. 1993. *The Society of the Muslim Brothers*. New York: Oxford University Press.

Mitchell, Timothy. 1991. *Colonising Egypt*. Berkeley and Los Angeles: University of California Press.

Moench, Richard. 1988. Oil, ideology and state autonomy in Egypt. *Arab Studies Quarterly* 10 (2): 176–92.

Moghissi, Haideh. 1999. *Feminism and Islamic fundamentalism: The limits of postmodern analysis*. New York: Zed Books.

Mohanty, Chandra. 1991. Under Western eyes: Feminist scholarship and colonial discourses. In *Third world women and the politics of feminism*, ed. C. Mohanty, A. Russo, and L. Torres, 51–80. Bloomington: Indiana University Press.

Moore, Sally F., and Barbara Myerhoff, eds. 1977. *Secular ritual*. Assen: Van Gorcum.

Moore, Donald. 1999. The crucible of cultural politics: Reworking "development" in Zimbabwe's Eastern Highlands. *American Ethnologist* 26 (3): 654–89.

Morris, Rosalind. 2002. Theses on the questions of war: History, media, terror. *Social Text* 20 (3): 149–75.

Moruzzi, Norma Claire. 1994. A problem with headscarves: Contemporary complexities of political and social identity. *Political Theory* 22 (4): 653–72.

Moustafa, Tamir. 2000. Conflict and cooperation between the state and religious institutions in contemporary Egypt. *International Journal of Middle East Studies*, 32:3–22.

Mufti, Aamir. 2000. The aura of authenticity. *Social Text* 18 (3): 87–103.

Muhammed, Badr Zaki. 1996. Ḥuqūq al-mar'a baina al-thabāt al-naṣṣ al-islāmi wa harakiyyat al-maḍmūn. *al-Ḥayāt*, October 8.

al-Muslimūn. 1996. al-Masājid al-jāmiʿa khiṭṭatna lil-qaḍā' ʿala taṭṭaruf wa ḥarakāt al-ʿunf. November 6.

Myers, Fred. 1986. *Pintupi country, Pintupi self: Sentiment, place, and politics among Western desert aborigines*. Washington: Smithsonian Institution Press.

Najmabadi, Afsaneh. 1991. Hazards of modernity and morality: Women, state and ideology in contemporary Iran. In *Women, Islam and the state*, ed. D. Kandiyoti, 48–76. Philadelphia: Temple University Press.

———. 1998. Feminism in an Islamic republic: "Years of hardship, years of growth." In *Islam, gender and social change*, ed. Y. Haddad and J. Esposito, 59–84. New York: Oxford University Press.

Navaro-Yashin, Yael. 2002. *Faces of the state: Secularism and public life in Turkey*. Princeton, NJ: Princeton University Press.

al-Nawawi, Abu Zakariyya Yahya. 1990. *Sharḥ matn al-arbaʿūn al-Nawawiyya*. Cairo: Dār al-tauzīʿ wal-nashr al-islāmiyya.

———. n.d. *Riyāḍ al-ṣālihīn*. Cairo: Dār al-fatḥa lil-ʿālam al-ʿarabi.

Nedelsky, Jennifer. 1989. Reconceiving autonomy: Sources, thoughts and possibilities. *Yale Journal of Law and Feminism* 1 (1): 7–36.

Nederman, Cary. 1989–90. Nature, ethics, and the doctrine of "habitus": Aristotelian moral psychology in the twelfth century. *Traditio* XLV:87–110.

Nelson, Cynthia. 1984. Islamic tradition and women's education in Egypt. In *World yearbook of education 1984: Women and education*, ed. S. Acker, 211–26. London: Kogan Page Limited.

New York Times. 1998. Court further limits Turkey's Islamic schools. February 4.

al-Nūr. 1996. al-ra'īs al-ʿāmm lil-Jamʿiyya al-Sharʿiyya lil-Nūr. October 16.

———. 1997. Risāla widdiyya ʿila ra'īs al-jumhūriyya. February 6.

Nuttall, Geoffrey. 1992. *The Holy Spirit in Puritan faith and experience*. Chicago: University of Chicago Press.

Oakeshott, Michael. 1975. *On human conduct*. Oxford: Clarendon Press.

Obeyesekere, Gananath. 1981. *Medusa's hair: An essay on personal symbols and religious experience*. Chicago: Chicago University Press.

Ortner, Sherry. 1978. The virgin and the state. *Feminist Studies* 4 (3): 19–35.

Oxford English Dictionary (OED). 1999. 2nd ed. CD-ROM. Oxford University Press.

Pandolfo, Stefania. 1997. *Impasse of the angels: Scenes from a Moroccan space of memory*. Chicago: University of Chicago Press.

Peletz, Michael. 2002. *Islamic modern: Religious courts and cultural politics in Malaysia*. Princeton, NJ: Princeton University Press.

Peters, Rudolph. 1996. *Jihad in classical and modern Islam*. Princeton, NJ: Markus Wiener.

Pitt-Rivers, Julian. 1977. *The fate of Shechem or the politics of sex: Essays in the anthropology of the Mediterranean*. Cambridge: Cambridge University Press.

Pocock, J.G.A. 1985. *Virtue, commerce, and history: Essays on political thought and history, chiefly in the eighteenth century*. Cambridge: Cambridge University Press.

Povinelli, Elizabeth. 2002. *The cunning of recognition: Indigenous alterities and the making of Australian multiculturalism*. Durham, NC: Duke University Press.

al-Qaradawi, Yusuf. 1981. *al-Ṣaḥwa al-islāmiyya baina al-rafḍ wal-taṭṭaruf*. Beirut: Mu'assasāt al-risāla.

———. 1989. *al-Ṣabr fi al-Qur'ān*. Cairo: Maktabat wahba.

———. 1991. *Thaqafat al-dāʿiya*. Beirut: Mu'assasāt al-risāla.

———. 1992. *Awwaliyyāt al-ḥarika al-islāmiyya fi al-marḥala al-qādima*. Beirut: Mu'assasāt al-risāla.

———. 1993. *al-Ṣaḥwa al-islāmiyya*. Beirut: Mu'assasāt al-risāla.

———. 1996. *al-Niqāb lil-mar'a: Baina al-qaul bi bidʿiyyatihi wal-qaul bi wujūbihi*. Cairo: Maktabat wahba.

Rabinow, Paul. 1997. Introduction to *Ethics: Subjectivity and truth:* Vol. 1 of *Essential Works of Foucault, 1954–1984*, Vol. 1, by Michel Foucault, ed. P. Rabinow, trans. R. Hurley et al., XI–XLII. New York: New Press.

———. 2003. *Anthropos today: Reflections on modern equipment*. Princeton, NJ: Princeton University Press.

Radcliffe-Brown, A. R. 1964. *The Andaman Islanders*. New York: Free Press.

Radwan, Zeinab ʿAbdel Mejid. 1982. *Ẓāhirat al-ḥijāb baina al-jāmiʿāt*. Cairo: al-Markaz al-qaumi lil-buḥūth al-ijtimāʿiyya wal-jinā'iyya.

al-Rahman, Umar Abd. 1989. *Mīthāq al-ʿamal al-islāmi*. Cairo: Maktabat Ibn Kathīr.
Rancière, Jacques. 1994. *The names of history: On the poetics of knowledge*. Trans. H. Melehy. Minneapolis: University of Minnesota Press.
Rida, Rashid. 1970. *Tafsīr al-Qur'ān al-ḥakīm al-shahīr bi-tafsīr al-Manār*. 2nd ed. Vol. IV. Lebanon: Dār al-maʿrifa lil-ṭabʿa wal-nashr.
Robson, J. 1999a. Bidʿa. In *The Encyclopedia of Islam*. CD-ROM, version 1.0. Leiden: Brill.
———. 1999b. Ḥadīth. In *The Encyclopedia of Islam*. CD-ROM, version 1.0. Leiden: Brill.
Roest Crollius, Ary A. 1978. Mission and morality. *Studia Missionalia* 27:257–83.
Rorty, Amelie. 1987. Persons as rhetorical categories. *Social Research* 54 (1): 55–72.
Rosaldo, Michelle. 1980. *Knowledge and passion: Ilongot notions of self and social life*. Cambridge: Cambridge University Press.
———. 1982. The things we do with words: Ilongot speech acts and speech act theory in philosophy. *Language in Society* 11 (2): 203–37.
———. 1983. Moral/analytic dilemmas posed by the intersection of feminism and social science. In *Social science as moral inquiry*, ed. N. Haan, R. Bellah, P. Rabinow, and W. Sullivan, 76–95. New York: Columbia University Press.
Rose, Nikolas. 1998. *Inventing our selves: Psychology, power, and personhood*. Cambridge: Cambridge University Press.
———. 1999. *Powers of freedom: Reframing political thought*. Cambridge: Cambridge University Press.
Roy, Olivier. 1994. *The failure of political Islam*. Trans. C. Volk. Cambridge, MA: Harvard University Press.
Rubin, Gayle. 1984. Thinking sex: Notes for a radical theory of the politics of sexuality. In *Pleasure and danger: Exploring female sexuality*, ed. C. Vance, 267–319. Boston: Routledge and Kegan Paul.
Saad Eddin, Heba. 1997. Rajab wa shaʿbān wa ramadān. *al-Shaʿb*, January 3.
Sabiq, al-Sayyid. 1994. *Fiqh al-sunna*. 3 vols. Cairo: Maktabat al-Qāḥira.
Salim, Latifa Muhammed. 1984. *al-Mar'a al-miṣriyya wal-taghīr al-ijtimāʿi*. Cairo: al-Hai'a al-miṣriyya al-ʿāmma lil-kitāb.
Salvatore, Armando. 1997. *Islam and the political discourse of modernity*. Reading, UK: Ithaca Press.
———. 1998. Staging virtue: The disembodiment of self-correctness and the making of Islam as public norm. In *Islam, motor or challenge of modernity*, ed. G. Stauth, 87–120. Hamburg: Lit Verlag.
Samois Collective, eds. 1987. *Coming to power: Writings and graphics on lesbian S/M*. Boston: Alyson.
Sandel, Michael. 1998. *Liberalism and the limits of justice*. Cambridge: Cambridge University Press.
Scheff, Thomas. 1977. The distancing of emotion in ritual. *Current Anthropology* 18 (3): 483–505.
Schulze, Reinhard. 1987. Mass culture and Islamic cultural production in 19th century Middle East. In *Mass culture, popular culture, and social life in the Middle East*, ed. G. Stauth and S. Zubaida, 189–222. Boulder, CO: Westview Press.

Sciolino, Elaine. 2004. French assembly votes to ban religious symbols in schools. *New York Times*, February 11, 1.
Scott, David. 1999. *Refashioning futures: Criticism after postcoloniality*. Princeton, NJ: Princeton University Press.
Scott, James. 1985. *Weapons of the weak: Everyday forms of peasant resistance*. New Haven, CT: Yale University Press.
Scott, Joan. 1988. *Gender and the politics of history*. New York: Columbia University Press.
al-Sha'b. 1997. Li-man maṣlaḥat man tu'ammim wizārat al-auqāf al-daʿwa al-islāmiyya? February 6.
Shaikh, Nermeen. 2002. AsiaSource interview with Talal Asad. *AsiaSource*, December 16, 2002. http://www.asiasource.org/news/special_reports/asad.cfm.
Sherif, Mohamed Ahmed. 1975. *Ghazali's theory of virtue*. Albany: State University of New York Press.
Simhony, Avital. 1993. Beyond negative and positive freedom: T. H. Green's view of freedom. *Political Theory* 21 (1): 28–54.
Skinner, Quentin. 1998. *Liberty before liberalism*. Cambridge: Cambridge University Press.
Skovgaard-Petersen, Jakob. 1997. *Defining Islam for the Egyptian state muftis and fatwas of the Dār al-Iftā*. Leiden: Brill.
Smith, Wilfred Cantwell. 1962. *The meaning and end of religion: A new approach to the religious traditions of mankind*. New York: Macmillan.
Spivak, Gayatri. 1987. *In other worlds: Essays in cultural politics*. New York: Methuen.
———. 1988. Can the subaltern speak? In *Marxism and the interpretation of culture*, ed. C. Nelson and L. Grossberg, 271–313. Urbana: University of Illinois Press.
Stacey, Judith. 1991. *Brave new families: Stories of domestic upheaval in late twentieth-century America*. New York: Basic Books.
Starrett, Gregory. 1995a. The hexis of interpretation: Islam and the body in the Egyptian popular school. *American Ethnologist* 22 (4): 953–69.
———. 1995b. The political economy of religious commodities in Cairo. *American Anthropologist* 97 (1): 51–68.
———. 1996. The margins of print: Children's religious literature in Egypt. *Journal of the Royal Anthropological Institute* 2 (1): 117–39.
———. 1998. *Putting Islam to work: Education, politics and religious transformation in Egypt*. Berkeley and Los Angeles: University of California Press.
Strathern, Marilyn. 1987. An awkward relationship: The case of feminism and anthropology. *Signs* 12 (2): 276–92.
———. 1988. *The gender of the gift: Problems with women and problems with society in Melanesia*. Berkeley and Los Angeles: University of California Press.
———. 1992a. Future kinship and the study of culture. In *Reproducing the future: Essays on anthropology, kinship and the new reproductive technologies*, 44–61. New York: Routledge.
———. 1992b. *Reproducing the future: Essays on anthropology, kinship and the new reproductive technologies*. New York: Routledge.
Sultan, J. 1996. *Tajdīd al-ṣaḥwa al-islāmiyya*. Cairo: Dār al-risāla lil-nashr wal-tauzīʿ.

Tambiah, Stanley. 1985. A performative approach to ritual. In *Culture, thought and social action: An anthropological perspective*, 123–66. Cambridge, MA: Harvard University Press.

Tantawi, Muhammed Sayyid. 1994. Bal al-ḥijāb farīḍa islāmiyya. *Rūz al-Yūsuf*, June 27, 68.

Targoff, Ramie. 1997. The performance of prayer: Sincerity and theatricality in early modern England. *Representations* 60:49–69.

———. 2001. *Common prayer: The language of public devotion in early modern England*. Chicago: University of Chicago Press.

Taylor, Charles. 1985a. Atomism. In *Philosophy and the human sciences: Philosophical papers 2*, 187–210. Cambridge: Cambridge University Press.

———. 1985b. Kant's Theory of Freedom. In *Philosophy and the human sciences: Philosophical papers 2*, 318–37. Cambridge: Cambridge University Press.

———. 1985c. What's Wrong with Negative Liberty. In *Philosophy and the human sciences: Philosophical papers 2*, 211–29. Cambridge: Cambridge University Press.

———. 1989. *Sources of the self: The making of modern identity*. Cambridge, MA: Harvard University Press.

———. 1992. The politics of recognition. In *Multiculturalism and "The politics of recognition": An essay by Charles Taylor*, 25–73. Princeton, NJ: Princeton University Press.

———. 1995. Irreducibly social goods. In *Philosophical arguments*, 127–45. Cambridge, MA: Harvard University Press.

Torab, Azam. 1996. Piety as gendered agency: A study of *jalaseh* ritual discourse in an urban neighborhood in Iran. *Journal of the Royal Anthropological Institute* 2 (2): 235–52.

Turner, Victor. 1969. *The ritual process: Structure and anti-structure*. Chicago: Aldine.

———. 1976. Ritual, tribal and Catholic. *Worship* 50 (6): 504–25.

Umara, Muhammed. 1989. *al-Islām wa ḥuqūq al-insān*. Cairo: Dār al-shurūq.

van der Veer, Peter. 2001. *Imperial encounters: Religion and modernity in India and Britain*. Princeton, NJ: Princeton University Press.

al-Waʿi, Taufiq Yusuf. 1993. *al-Nisāʾ al-dāʿiyāt*. Cairo: Dār al-Wafāʾ.

al-Waʿi al-Islāmi. 2000. Wa raḥl faqīh al-ʿaṣr al-shaikh Sayyid Sābiq. March/April, 8.

Walker, Paul. 1993. The Ismaili daʿwa in the reign of the Fatimid Caliph al-Hakim. *Journal of the American Research Center in Egypt* XXX:161–82.

Warner, Michael. 2002. *Publics and counterpublics*. New York: Zone Books.

al-Wasaṭ. 1997. Daʿwa ḥisba li-waqf al-qānūn al-miṣri al-jadīd lil-masājid. January 20, 24.

Watt, W. Montgomery. 1985. *Islamic philosophy and theology: An extended survey*. Edinburgh: Edinburgh University Press.

West, David. 1993. Spinoza on positive freedom. *Political Studies* XLI (2): 284–96.

Wikan, Unni. 1991. *Behind the veil in Arabia: Women in Oman*. Chicago: University of Chicago Press.

Winter, T. J. 1989. Introduction to *The remembrance of death and the afterlife (kitāb dhikr al-mawt wa mā baʿdahu: Book XL of the revival of the religious sciences (iḥyāʾ ʿulūm al-*

dīn), by Abu Hamid al-Ghazali, trans. T. J. Winter, xiii–xxx. Cambridge, UK: Islamic Texts Society.

Yanagisako, Sylvia, and Jane Collier, eds. 1987. *Gender and kinship: Essays toward a unified analysis*. Stanford, CA: Stanford University Press.

York, Steve. 1992. *Remaking the world*. Production of the William Benton Broadcast Project and the University of Chicago in association with BBC TV and WETA TV. Alexandria, VA: PBS Video.

Young, Iris. 1990. *Justice and the politics of difference*. Princeton, NJ: Princeton University Press.

Zeghal, Malika. 1996. *Gardiens de l'Islam: Les oulémas d'Al Azhar dans l'Egypte contemporaine*. Paris: Presses de la Fondation Nationale des Sciences Politiques.

———. 1999. Religion and politics in Egypt: The ulema of al-Azhar, radical Islam, and the state (1952–94). *International Journal of Middle East Studies* 31 (3): 371–99.

Zubaida, Sami. 1993. *Islam, the people and the state: Essays on political ideas and movements in the Middle East*. London: I. B. Tauris.

Zuhur, Sherifa. 1992. *Revealing reveiling: Islamist gender ideology in contemporary Egypt*. Albany: State University of New York Press.

INDEX

Definitions of commonly used Arabic terms can be found in the Glossary on pages 201–3.

Abduh, Muhammed, 61
Abir (mosque participant), 176–80
absolute commands (*aḥkām ḥatmiyya*), 90–91
Abu Bakr, 146–48
Abu Shuqqah, Abd al-Halim, 66n.60, 103n.33, 110n.44, 111
Abu-Lughod, Lila, 8–10, 16n.25, 171n.14
Afghanistan, 197
agency
  and autonomy, 10–13, 20, 32
  Butler on, 19–21, 162
  and ethical formation, 29–32, 155–61
  and ethics, 34–35
  and fate, 173–74
  and feminist theory, 6–10, 13–14, 19–20
  and freedom, 10–12
  grammar of concepts, 16–17, 34, 180, 188
  multiple modalities of, 153–55, 167–68, 172–74, 188
  and norms, 21–25, 157, 179
  and power, 20
  reconceptualizing, 14–15, 29–34
  and resistance, 5–10, 24–25, 34–35, 175–80
Ahmed, Leila, 54n.26, 181
ʿalmana, *ʿalmāniyya*. *See* secularism/secularization
Amal (mosque participant), 156–57, 159
amr bil maʿrūf, 58–62
Amna (critic of the piety movement), 146–48
Aristotle
  on body/soul distinction, 134n.22
  on *habitus*, 135–39, 143, 157
  on potentiality, 147
  on theoretical and practical wisdom, 196n.4
  on virtues, 136
Aristotelian ethics, 25–26, 27–28
Aristotelian model of ethical formation, 135–39, 143, 157, 161
Asad, Talal, 34, 115–16, 127–28, 148
Ashmawi, Muhammad Said, 160–61
ʿaura, 106–107
Austin, J. L., 19, 145, 161–62
authoritative sources. *See* canonical sources
autonomy, 11–14, 148–52
  communitarian critiques of, 150–52
  feminist critiques of, 13–14
  and freedom, 11–14, 149–52
  within liberalism, 11–13, 148–52
  procedural versus substantive, 11–12, 148–49
Ayesha mosque, 41–42, 88n.19, 91–99
al-Azhar
  Islamist intellectuals trained at, 80n.2, 83n.10
  opposition to state policies, 75n.88, 76n.90

Society of Muslim Ladies' affiliation with, 67
state control of, 64, 77
and women's *daʿwa*, 66, 71, 84

Badran, Margot, 69
al-Banna, Hasan, 61n.43, 62–64, 80
Baron, Beth, 68–69
Benhabib, Seyla, 150–51
Benjamin, Walter, 113–14
bidʿa, 87
Boddy, Janice, 7–8
bodily form
and *habitus*, 136–40
of norms/virtues, 22–27, 29
and the pious self, 147–48, 160–61
and politics 119–20 , 122, 148–52
and pragmatic action, 126–28
Renaissance debates about, 134–35
in Romantic thought, 129n.18
and self-formation, 121–22
and spontaneity, 128–31
See also bodily practice; conventional behavior; interiority/exteriority; ritual
bodily practice
in acquisition of modesty, 156–58, 160–61
creating emotion through, 157
as developable means, 148, 166
in ethical formation, 29–31, 121–22
in feminist theory, 158–60
and performativity, 162–66
See also bodily form; conventional behavior; interiority/exteriority; ritual; self-formation
Bourdieu, Pierre, 26, 136, 138–39, 165n.10
Brown, Wendy, 39, 196
Butler, Judith
on agency, 19, 162–67
on Bourdieu, 26n.45, 165n.10
on Foucault, 17–20, 22
Hollywood on, 21n.38, 162n.2
on norms, 20–23
on performativity, 19–21, 162–67
on power, 17–18
reception of, 21
reworking arguments of, 22–23, 163–67
on sex/gender, 18–21
on subject formation, 18–19, 161–67

canonical sources
class differences in use of, 82, 83, 92–99, 109–10
and the concept of tradition, 116
in Islamic popular literature, 79–81
protocols of engagement with, 86–89, 100–111
See also *ḥadīth*; Quran
Chatterjee, Partha, 194
Christianity. *See* Protestant Christianity
Christman, John, 11–12, 149
classical Islamic texts. *See* canonical sources
Colebrook, Claire, 27
colonialism and Islam, 189–90
community obligations (*farḍ al-kifāya*), 62
Connolly, William, 33, 38, 165n.11
conventional behavior, 126–31, 146–52. *See also* bodily form; bodily practice; ritual; *ṣalāt*
Cook, Michael, 59
customary versus religious acts, 53–57

dāʿiyāt, 57
at Ayesha mosque, 42, 91–97, 99
controversial practices, 86–87, 93, 95–97
emergence of, 59, 63–64
Islamist press coverage of, 71
restrictions on practice, 65–66, 71–72, 89
measuring effectiveness of, 86, 92
at Nafisa mosque, 43, 44–45, 100–106, 140–44
as paradigmatic of Islamic Revival, 58, 63–64, 82
response to state licensing requirement, 76, 84
rhetorical styles, 41–43, 83–86, 91–97, 99, 100–106, 140–44
at Umar mosque, 40–41, 45–47, 83–91, 95, 107–10
Zaynab al-Ghazali's legacy, 67–72
See also *daʿwa*; names of *dāʿiyāt* (Hajja Asma; Hajja Faiza; Hajja Iman; Hajja Nur; Hajja Samira; Umm Faris)
dars. *See* mosque lessons
daʿwa
activities of Muslim Brothers, 63–64
and *amr bil maʿrūf*, 58–62
al-Banna on, 62–64
classical meaning of, 57

in contemporary Egypt, 57–58, 61–64
as individual versus societal obligation, 62, 64
and kinship demands, 175–84
knowledge necessary for, 61
and modes of sociability, 73–76
requirements for practice of, 65
Rida on, 61–62
as space for debate, 104–6
training programs in, 66–67, 71–72, 75, 84
women's participation in, 64–72
Zaynab al-Ghazali and, 67–72
See also *dāʿiyāt*; mosque movement; protocols of dissent and debate
daʿwa/piety movement, 3
critique of nationalist-identitarian position, 119
politics of, 24–25, 34–35, 76–78, 193–94
secular-liberal project and, 73–76, 78, 152, 191–92
state regulation of, 64n.55, 75–76
See also mosque movement
demographics of mosque participants, 41, 42, 43
Derrida, Jacques, 19
domestic relations. *See* kinship relations
durūs. *See* mosque lessons

education
effects on Islamic knowledge, 79–82
mosque participants' levels of, 41–43
state-run religious institutions, 64
women's *daʿwa* training, 66–67, 71–72, 75, 84, 92
educational system
challenges to piety, 101–3
modernization of, 55n.28
secularization of, 48
Egyptian state
and *amr bil maʿrūf*, 60
regulation of *daʿwa*/piety movement, 64n.55, 75–76
regulation of religion, 46–47, 64, 68, 74, 76–77
as secular, 76–78
Egyptian women's movement, 68–70, 73
embodied behavior. *See* bodily form, bodily practice, ritual
emotion, 123–31, 146–47
and moral action, 140–45
and ritual, 123, 128–31, 146–47
See also fear of God
ethical formation, 25–35
agency in, 29, 32–35, 155–61
Aristotelian model of, 161
bodily forms in, 23, 29, 160–61
of the mosque movement, 30–31
and politics, 32–35, 151–52
See also ethics; self-formation
ethical Islamic literature, 80–82
ethics
and agency, 34–35
Aristotelian, 25–26
and bodily form, 136–38, 147–48
distinguished from morals, 28
of feminist critique, 36–39, 195–99
Foucault's approach to, 27–31, 120, 122
Kantian, 25–26
and the mosque movement, 30–31
and norms, 23–27
and politics, 32–34, 119–22, 192–94
positive, 27–29
and secularism, 47–48, 192–94
exteriority. *See* bodily form; interiority/exteriority

Fatma (mosque participant), 49–51, 56
fear of God (*khashya*, *khauf*, *taqwa*)
and moral action, 140–45
relationship to piety, 145
as rhetorical strategy (*tarhīb*, *takhwīf*), 91, 140–41, 144–45
and ritual, 123, 129–31, 145
female circumcision (*khitān*), debate about, 85–86
female modesty. *See* modesty
female preachers. See *dāʿiyāt*
female sexuality
compared to male sexuality, 110–12
feminist anthropology on, 112
in the juristic tradition, 106–13
and male-female interactions (*ikhtilāṭ*), 100–113
and women leading prayer, 65–66 (See also *ṣalāt*)
and women's public appearance, 106–13

female sexuality (*cont.*)
  and social discord (*fitna*), 110–11
  See also *ʿaura*
feminism
  analytical and political projects, 10, 39, 195–97
  and autonomy, 11–14
  colonial and imperial projects, 189–90, 196–97
  and communitarian debates, 150–51
  ethics of critique within, 36–39
  and the mosque movement, 1–2, 4–5, 15, 36–38, 197–99
  and negative/positive freedom 10–12
  projects of social reform, 197–98
  and resurgence of the veil, 15–16
  rethinking politics of, 36–38, 197–98
feminist theory
  on agency, 5–10, 19–22
  ethical reflections on, 198–99
  poststructuralist, 17–22, 158–67
  social norms in, 21–25
  female body in, 158–60
Fiqh al-sunna, 80–81
fiqh, 80–82
fitna (social discord) and female sexuality, 110–11
folk and scriptural Islam, 95–99
Foucault, Michel
  Butler on, 18–19
  Colebrook on, 27
  on ethico-politics, 33–34, 120–22
  on ethics, 27–29
  four axes of ethics, 30–31
  on power and the subject, 17, 121n.3
freedom
  and autonomy, 11–13
  and historical/cultural projects, 14–15
  in liberal thought, 10–13, 148–49
  and mosque movement, 148–49
  as normative to feminism, 10
  positive and negative, 10–12
  rethinking individual, 149–50
  Taylor on, 150

gender inequality
  and demands of piety, 174–180
  feminist concerns about, 36–38, 195–99
  grammar of concepts, 16–17, 183–84, 179–80, 188
  and sexuality, 110–13, 197–99
  and single women, 167–74
  and social change, 36, 174, 197–99
  See also female sexuality; kinship relations
ghaḍḍ al-baṣar (lowering the gaze), 101–2. *See also* female sexuality; modesty
al-Ghazali, Abu Hamid, 62n.48, 137–38
al-Ghazali, Zaynab, 67–73, 180–84
  and women's equality, 70, 183–84
  domestic relations, 180–82
  early activism, 67–72
  and Egyptian women's movement, 68–70
  involvement with Muslim Brotherhood, 68
  and Society of Muslim Ladies, 67–70, 73
  on women's responsibility to kin and God, 180–84
  writings, 68
governance, 35, 75–77, 194
government. *See* Egyptian state
governmentality, 77n

habitus, 135–39
  Aristotelian notion of, 135–39, 143, 157
  in Christianity, 135n.26
  distinct from habits, 136
  Pierre Bourdieu on, 26, 136, 138–39
  related Arabic term *malaka*, 137–38
Hacking, Ian, 180n
ḥadīth (plural: *aḥādīth*), 41n.3
  and debate about militant action, 60nn. 40, 41
  as lived tradition, 98–99
  about male-female interactions, 102, 104–6
  protocols of engagement with, 97–99, 102–6
  scholarly and folk uses of, 97–99
  sound/authoritative (*ṣaḥīḥ*), 104–6
  weak (*daʿīf*), 85–86, 94, 97
  about women's appearance in public, 106–10
  See also canonical sources; Prophet and his Companions; Sunna
hajja, 40n.2
Hajja Asma, 185–87
Hajja Faiza
  on divorce, 89n.21

on female circumcision (*khitān*), 85–86
on male-female interactions, 107–10
on pious practice in daily life, 45–47
protocols of dissent and debate, 85, 88–91
rhetorical style, 40–41, 83, 84–86
on "trading" with God, 95
trajectory as *dāʿiya*, 83–84
on women leading prayer, 86–88
Hajja Iman, 102
Hajja Nur
on secularization, 44n
on the veil, 50–52, 54–56
Hajja Samira
on male-female interactions, 101–5
protocols of dissent and debate, 105–6
rhetorical style, 140–44
on secularization, 44–45
Hanafi school, 81n.4, 87, 88
Hanbali school, 81n.4, 87, 88, 171n.13
al-ḥayāʾ. *See* modesty
headscarf. *See* veil
ḥijāb, 50n. *See also* veil
Hirschkind, Charles, 56n.29, 117, 193
Hollywood, Amy, 21n, 162n.7
Hundert, E. J., 129n
Hussein, Adil, 51–52, 56

ʿibādāt. *See* religious obligations
identitarian politics and Islamic practices, 45, 48, 51–52, 118–19, 152, 166, 192–93
al-iḥtishām. *See* modesty
Iman (mosque participant), 168–69
individual obligation (*farḍ al-ʿain*) 62, 64
interiority/exteriority
and exemplary models, 147–48
pedagogical practices of, 134–39, 156–58
in Plato and Aristotle 134n.22
in Renaissance, 134
in Romantic thought, 129n.18
See also bodily form; self; self-formation; subject
Islamic law (*sharīʿa*), 81n.4
arguments for implementation of, 47n.14
modern transformation of, 98
as personal status law, 46n.11, 77
and social transactions (*muʿāmalāt*), 46
schools of (*madhāhib*), 87, 88
Islamic popular literature, 79–82, 97–98
Islamic nonprofit organizations, 58, 67–69, 72–73
Islamic Revival, 3, 58n34
dāʿiya as paradigmatic figure of, 58, 63–64, 82
differences of opinion within, 51–53, 118–19, 131–34, 146–48
different strands of, 3n.5
and identitarian politics, 45, 48, 51–52, 118–19, 152, 166, 192–93
intellectuals of, 51–53, 83n.10
and juristic tradition, 79–82
liberal reactions to, 37–38
and mass education, 53, 79–80
and mass media, 56n29, 79
and the promulgation of the *sharīʿa*, 46–47
social conservatism of, 37–39
sociopolitical effects of, 24–25, 34–35, 52–53, 118–19, 131–34, 146–48, 193–95
Islamist movement. *See* Islamic Revival

al-Jamʿiyya al-Sharʿiyya, 72–73
juristic tradition
on alcohol consumption, 90–91
differences of opinion within, 88–90, 103–4, 182–83
on female sexuality, 106–11
as foundation for debate, 85–91, 95–97, 109–11
on kinship relations, 100n.30, 182
and socioeconomic differences in reading of, 82–83, 95–99, 109–10
and *talfīq* (doctrinal flexibility), 81, 85–86, 88–91
widening use of, 99–100
on women's attire, 107n.40
on women leading prayer, 86–88
on women's obligation to kin, 182
on women's practice of *daʿwa*, 65, 178–79

Kant, Immanuel, 25–27
Khaldun, Ibn, 137
khashya. *See* fear of God
khauf. *See* fear of God
khushūʿ (humility), 123, 129–30
kinship relations
challenge of impious husbands, 184–88
close male kin, 100n.30, 105n.34, 110n.45
and God's calling, 180–84

kinship relations (*cont.*)
- opposition to *daʿwa* from husbands, 175–80
- women's responsibilities to God and kin, 181–83, 186–87
- *See also* gender inequality

lessons. *See* mosque lessons
liberalism
- and agency, 5–10, 20, 153–55
- autonomy in, 11–15, 148–52
- communitarian critiques of, 150–52
- Islamist movement's relationship to, 24–25, 63–66, 68–70, 85, 90, 191–92
- notions of freedom in, 10–13, 32–33, 148–49
- and social reform, 197–98
- *See also* secular liberalism

literacy
- effects on Islamic practice, 53, 79
- effects on women's *daʿwa*, 66
- *See also* education

literature, Islamic popular, 79–82, 97–98

malaka, 137–38
male-female interactions (*ikhtilāṭ*), 100–113
- debates about, 103–6
- female sexuality and, 106–13
- rules governing, 100–103
- *See also* kinship relations

Malinowski, Bronislaw, 127
maḥram (close male kin), 100n.30, 105n.34, 110n.45
Maliki school, 81n.4, 87n.14, 88, 171n.13
Maryam (mosque participant), 102–4
Messick, Brinkley, 81–82, 98
Minson, Jeffery, 25, 26
modern religiosity
- individualization of, 30–31, 62–64, 173n.19
- objectification of, 53–54, 56
- self-reflexivity within, 54–57
- *talfīq* (doctrinal flexibility), 81, 85–86, 88–91

modesty (*al-ḥayā'*), 23, 100–104, 155–61
Mona (mosque participant), 124–25
moral action
- and virtuous fear, 140–43
- emotions as modality of, 144–45
- morphology of, 25–27, 29, 119–22

mosque lessons (*durūs*; singular *dars*)
- attendees, 41, 42, 43
- at Ayesha mosque, 41–42, 91–97
- criticisms of, 86–88, 92, 140–41, 146–47
- at Nafisa mosque, 42–43, 44–45, 100–106, 140–44
- pedagogical materials used, 80–81, 83, 93–94, 100–101, 129–30
- rhetorical styles of preaching, 41–43, 83–86, 91–97, 100–106, 140–45
- as space for debate, 104–6
- state surveillance of, 75–76, 84
- at Umar mosque, 40–41, 83–91, 107–10
- *See also* protocols of dissent and debate

mosque movement
- challenges to secularism, 34–35, 47–48
- conditions of emergence, 2–4
- criticism of secularization, 43, 48–53
- and mass education, 66
- ethics and politics of, 4, 31–35, 152
- goals of, 44–48, 56–57
- and legacy of Muslim Brotherhood, 63–64
- and nonprofit Islamic organizations, 72
- socioeconomic differences within, 41–43, 83–85, 91–97, 107–10, 138n.30
- and Zaynab al-Ghazali's legacy, 70–72
- See also *daʿwa*; mosque lessons; protocols of dissent and debate

mosque participants, 41–43, 91–92. *See also* mosque lessons; *names of mosque participants* (Abir; Amal; Fatma; Iman; Maryam; Mona; Nadia; Nama; Rabia; Umm Amal)
mosques. *See* Ayesha mosque; Nafisa mosque; Umar mosque
muʿāmalāt (social transactions), 45, 46
Muhammed. *See* Prophet and his Companions
Muslim Brotherhood, 62–64, 68, 71

Nadia (mosque participant), 168–74
Nafisa mosque, 42–43, 44–45, 100–106, 140–44
Nama (mosque participant), 157–58, 159
Nasser, President Gamal Abdul, 62n.50, 68
niqāb. *See* veil
nonprofit religious organizations. *See* Islamic nonprofit organizations

outward behavior. *See* bodily form

patience. See *ṣabr*
pedagogical literature, 79–82, 97–98
performative behavior. *See* bodily form
performativity, 19, 161–67
personhood. *See* self; subject
piety/*daʿwa* movement. See *daʿwa*/piety movement
political and ethical agency of the piety movement, 24–25, 34–35, 73–75, 152
political effects of the Islamist movement, 52–53, 118–19, 131–34, 146–48, 192–94
politics
  and agency, 34–35, 174, 183–84
  and analytics of feminism, 10, 36–39, 158–60, 195–99
  concepts of the body, 26–27, 146–48, 166–67
  and ethics, 32–35, 152, 192–99
  of identity, 45, 51–52, 192–93 (*See also* identitarian politics and Islamic practices)
  and modes of sociability, 73–76
  normative subject of, 32–34
  social conventions/norms in the analysis of, 24, 148–52
poststructuralist feminist theory, 17–22, 158–67. *See also* feminist theory
pragmatic action, 126–28
prayer. See *ṣalāt*
preaching styles. *See* rhetorical styles of preaching
Prophet and his Companions, 31, 102, 104, 108–9. *See also* Sunna
proselytization. See *daʿwa*
Protestant Christianity
  debates about worship, 134–35
  parallels with Sunni Islam, 173n.19
  relationship between body and soul, 135
protocols of dissent and debate
  about canonical sources, 103–6
  class differences and, 95–99, 109–10
  regarding women's *daʿwa*, 64–66
  regarding female/male sexuality, 106–13
  regarding individual choice, 85, 90
  regarding kinship responsibilities, 174–84, 186–87
  talfīq (doctrinal flexibility), 81, 85–86, 88–91
  See also juristic tradition

al-Qaradawi, Yusuf, 83
Quran
  on *al-ḥayāʾ*, 156
  on *amr bil maʿrūf*, 59
  on *daʿwa*, 65
  exegesis of, 103–4
  on illicit sexual relations, 47n.12, 110
  on men as women's guardians, 65, 184n.26
  piety and fear (*taqwa*) in, 143, 145
  reciting, 93–94
  on veiling/modesty, 100
  See also canonical sources

Rabia (mosque participant), 104–5
Ramadan, 49–50
Raouf Ezzat, Heba. *See* Saad Eddin; Heba
religious obligations (*ʿibādāt*)
  and choice, 84–86
  ʿibādāt defined, 46
  and politics, 119–20, 122
  women's role in, 65–66, 86–91
  See also ritual; *ṣalāt*
resistance
  feminist literature on, 5–10
  and the piety/mosque movement, 24–25, 34–35, 175–80
  See also agency
rhetorical styles of preaching, 41–43, 83–86, 91–97, 100–106, 140–45
Rida, Rahid, 61–62
ritual
  and authentic emotions, 128–31, 145–48
  folklorization of, 48–53, 119
  and inward dispositions, 131, 134–35
  and politics, 119, 122, 148–52
  and spontaneity, 128–31
  See also bodily form; moral action; religious obligations; *ṣalāt*
ritual prayer. See *ṣalāt*
Riyāḍ al-ṣāliḥīn, 83

Saad Eddin, Heba, 52, 53, 56
Sabiq, Sayyid, 80n.2
ṣabr (patience/fortitude), 170–74, 186
sacred texts. *See* canonical sources
al-Ṣaḥwa al-Islāmiyya. *See* Islamic Revival
ṣalāt (ritual prayer), 122–26, 131–34
  and creation of dispositions, 135, 145
  different conceptions of, 124–26, 131–34

ṣalāt (ritual prayer) (*cont.*)
as means and end, 133
nationalist view of, 118–19, 131–34
parallels in Protestant Christianity, 134–35
women leading, 86–91
weeping in, 129–31, 145
See also religious obligations; ritual
Sana (critic of the piety movement), 171–74
secular-liberal governance, 35, 75–77, 194
secular liberalism
Islamism and, 34–35, 189–92
as life form, 191–92
and modes of sociability, 73–76
and the postcolonial state, 76–78
and regulation of the veil, 74–75
and religiosity, 74–75, 77–78
secularism/secularization (*ʿalmana* or *ʿalmāniyya*)
different meanings of, 47–48
and the Egyptian state, 76–78
piety movement's challenge to, 47–48
and proliferation of religious discourse, 79–83
mosque movement's interpretation of, 4, 44–45, 48–52
and the *sharīʿa*, 14n.47
as a sociability/lifestyle, 44–48, 73–75
and state regulation of religion, 74–78
self
anthropological approaches to, 120
communitarian discussions of, 150–51
politics and architecture of, 148–52
potentiality of, 31, 147, 148–49, 159, 166
in Romantic thought, 129n
self-formation
and bodily form, 120–21
emotions as means to, 140–48
exemplary models in, 146–48
norms/virtues in, 22–27
and performativity, 161–67
through ritual action, 134–39
See also bodily form; bodily practice; interiority/exteriority; self; subject
sex segregation. *See* male-female interactions
sexuality. *See* female sexuality
Shafiʿi school, 81n.4, 87, 88
sharīʿa. *See* Islamic law
shyness. *See* modesty
sociability, modes of, 73–76
societal obligations (*farḍ al-kifāya*), 62, 64
Society of Muslim Ladies (Jamāʿat al-Sayyidāt al-Muslimāt), 67–68, 73
socioeconomic composition of mosque movement, 41–43, 83–85, 91–97, 107–10, 138n.30
Starrett, Gregory, 139n
state. *See* Egyptian state
Strathern, Marilyn, 121n.5, 133–34, 190–91
subject
and agency, 32
Butler on, 18–19, 161–67
and ethics, 28–29
Foucault on, 17, 121n.3
humanist, 154–55
performativity in formation of, 19, 161–67
and politics, 14, 31–34, 166–67
and reflexivity, 32, 54–55, 146–48, 150–52
tradition and, 115–16
See also self; self-formation
subjectivation, 17, 20n, 28–31
subversion. *See* resistance
Sunna, 46, 57n.32

takhwīf. *See* fear of God
talfīq (doctrinal flexibility), 81, 85–86, 88–91
Tambiah, Stanley, 131n
taqwa (piety), 122–23, 145. *See also* fear of God
Targoff, Ramie, 134–35
tarhīb. *See* fear of God
Taylor, Charles, 150, 192
Taymiyya, Ibn, 61n.43
theatricality. *See* bodily form
tradition
common uses of, 113–14
as discursive formation, 114–16
literacy and the practice of, 95–98
Talal Asad on, 114–17
Turner, Victor, 128
ʿulamāʾ (religious scholars), 64
Umar mosque, 40–41, 45–47, 83–91, 95, 107–10
Umm Amal (mosque participant), 142–43
Umm Faris (*dāʿiya*)
protocols of dissent and debate, 97–99
rhetorical style, 92–95

on "trading" with God, 94–96
trajectory as *dāʿiya*, 92
use of canonical sources, 95–97

veil
bans on, 74–75
in colonial discourse, 54n.26
customary versus virtuous practice, 50–52
diverse forms of (*ḥijāb*, *khimār*, *niqāb*), 41–43
and female sexuality, 110–11
ḥijāb, 50n
Islamic debates about, 23–24, 50–53, 56, 101–3, 160–61
as means to piety, 23–24, 50–51, 157–58, 160–61
Quran on, 100–101, 107n.40
literature on resurgence of, 15–16
as symbol of identity, 52–53
as symbol of women's oppression, 195

virtue
Aristotle on, 27, 136, 139
Kant on, 25n.43
adverbial, 145. *See also* ethics

wāʿiẓāt, 65, 67. See also *dāʿiyāt*
weeping during prayer, 129–31
criticism of, 146–48
welfare organizations. *See* Islamic nonprofit organizations
Western perceptions of Islam, 4–5, 189–90, 195
westernization. *See* secularism/secularization
women's activism in Egypt, 68–69
women's agency. *See* agency
women's *daʿwa*. See *dāʿiyāt; daʿwa; daʿwa*/piety movement; mosque movement
women preachers. See *dāʿiyāt*
working women, challenges for, 99, 107, 155–56
worship. *See* religious obligations